Fishing Forays

Editors David Birley and Tom Lawrence

KENSINGTON WEST PRODUCTIONS LTD

HEXHAM ENGLAND

Acknowledgements

Fishing Forays owes its metamorphosis from a good idea into this, our third edition, to a number of extremely helpful individuals. Foremost, we would like to thank all those who kindly agreed to their names being published as contacts for fishing throughout the British Isles and Ireland. Some rely on visiting fishermen as a source of income but others kindly gave permission merely to further the enjoyment of others and for this we are very grateful.

The initial research for Fishing Forays took over two years to complete and as a result, we are able to feature over four hundred rivers, lakes, lochs, loughs and llyns. Throughout England and Wales we were generously assisted in our endeavour to provide up to date information by all manner of bodies, particularly the unswerving National Rivers Authority, the regional water boards and water companies. In Scotland, the sporting agencies played a significant role and were extremely forthcoming with their advice. From Ireland, we are indebted to the Central Fishery Board, in particular, Kevin Linnane and Chris Meehan on the Shannon Region; the Irish tourist Board; Foyle Fisheries Commission; Bann Systems Ltd and the Ministry of Agriculture (N.I.). We are also grateful to a number of sporting companies who specialise in game fishing holidays for their contributions.

None more so than Tarquin Millington of Frontiers for his advice.

Throughout our forays we received invaluable assistance from numerous fishing clubs, sporting agents, estate owners, managers and keepers, tackleists, hoteliers and publicans. As you can imagine, we have met some extraordinary people!

A special mention must also be made for Rosemary Coates whose wonderful hand drawn maps and illustrations grace this book. We would also like to thank all the other artists and photographers who kindly lent us their work for use as illustrations within Fishing Forays. Particularly Rosenstiel's of London for their excellent selection.

We are extremely grateful to Chris Poupard for contributing a marvellously scribed foreword. We are delighted to be involved with the Salmon and Trout Association and look forward to working closely with them in future years. I am particularly grateful to Pat Mackreth for his enthusiasm and advice. Finally, I should like to thank Ken Gregory for his advice and kindness— as expert publisher and fisherman his thoughts are particularly helpful.

Kensington West Productions Ltd
5 Cattle Market, Hexham, Northumberland NE46 1NJ
Tel: (0434) 609933 Fax: (0434) 600066

Editors
David Birley and Tom Lawrence

Consultant Editors
Simon Cooper, Simon Tilley, Jane Chambers, Liz Tennant, Tom Hawthorn, Mathew Rowlands

Cartography, Flies Photography
Rosemary Coates, Mike Sugg, M.D.Whittick

Origination
Trinity Graphics Ltd (Hong Kong)

Printing
Nordica International Ltd Hong Kong

Back Cover Artists: **George Cammidge FISHING IN CALM WATERS** *Courtesy of* **Rosenstiel's**
Wendy Reeves HIGHLAND RIVER *Courtesy of* **Rosenstiel's**
Don Vaughan PEACEFUL MOMENTS *Courtesy of* **Rosenstiel's**
Front Cover Artist: **Clive Madgwick TROUT FISHING, COUNTY MAYO** *Courtesy of* **Rosenstiel's**
Page One, Artist: **John King CAUGHT ON THE FINDHORN** *Courtesy of the Artist*

For someone who has been closely involved with fishing as I have and for so many years, I haven't actually caught that many fish—nor any impressively big ones, either.

There are a number of reasons for this but the principal one is that, for me, the old cliche holds good: 'There's more to fishing than catching fish'. In other words, it's not so much standing on the banks of my favourite loch, or river, for the express purpose of catching fish that really appeals to me. What hooks me on fishing is variety—new and exciting experiences.

The variety of fishing within these shores is extraordinary and I delight in the total experience of the environment and the wildlife around me; catching fish is always an unexpected bonus.

If you feel as I do about fishing, you tend not to do as much actual casting as the dedicated angler whose prime purpose is landing his pound of fish, if you'll pardon the mixed metaphor. If you adopt the *Fishing Forays* philosophy, you may not catch as many fish—but you will hear unfamiliar sounds, you will see unexpected sights and you will taste new and exciting flavours. These are the true pleasures of fishing for me.

When an opportunity arose to take up the Directorship of The Salmon & Trout Association, the proposition appealed to me strongly. I have a real chance to influence the welfare and protection not just of game fish species and the sport they provide but also of the environment in which they live.

Fishing Forays sums up perfectly the atmosphere and the opportunities that make fishing my favourite sport. And if the publishers can help to convey to others the breadth of pleasure that there is to be had from fishing and all that the sport encompasses then they, like me, are in the happy position of being able to bring some influence to bear on the future well being of a uniquely valuable resource.

By Chris Poupard, Director, The Salmon & Trout Association

Artist: Mick Causton Courtesy of Sally Mitchell Fine Arts

D.F.Dane

4

Crofter's Cottage – David Dane. Courtesy of Rosentiel's.

Introduction

The first two editions of *Fishing Forays* received wide praise and comment from many quarters. This third edition has been fully edited and revised, with prices brought up to date, wherever possible, and dozens of new fishing contacts added. Game fishing is supported by a plethora of books which describe in detail the attractions and infinite variety of views that surround the art of fishing. They cover tackle, techniques, particular rivers and even memoirs of great fishermen. Few, if any, actually give information on how to arrange a fishing break or indeed how to gain access to the rivers and water systems of Britain.

The book does not pretend to be a bible for the sport of game fishing in Britain and Ireland. What it does seek to do is to provide a range of up to date contacts which will enable you to gain access to the waters. As you can imagine, the fishing ranges dramatically in price, quality and variety. Prices have been included throughout the book to provide readers with a simple yardstick and all prices quoted were accurate at the time of going to print. There is, however, something here to meet everyone's budget whether you wish to fish the Tweed, a remote lough in Southern Ireland or the local lake.

Fishing and access differs enormously from region to region which is one of the more delightful facets of the sport. The differences will become apparent throughout *Fishing Forays*, whether they are geographical, historical, commercial or legislative. Compare Scotland's hundreds of natural highland lochs with the numerous commercial lakes of England. One created by nature, the other by market forces. You pay your money and take your choice and, in some cases, you will pay a lot of money!

We have endeavoured to give details for all areas covered in the book but as you would expect we are unable to comment fully on the existing state of some fisheries, as rainfall levels vary dramatically from month to month and season to season. Since 1993, nets have been bought off a number of rivers. Naturally this has benefitted the rod angler but drifting is still with us and consequently, runs of our migratory fish have continued to be badly affected. Last year, sea-trout fishing had declined badly in some areas. Since then there have been encouraging signs. Salmon fishing is clearly improving—we have endeavoured to point the way. As you can imagine, much of your success is in your own hands and, as ever, new waters should be investigated carefully before any excursion is planned. What we can say is that there are numerous good opportunities available with wonderful places to stay nearby.

The introduction of rod licences has not gone without it's critics. Yet the N.R.A. is a worthy organisation. They, along with various regional water companies, are by and large doing a good job in maintaining and improving waters.

It is equally satisfying to report the unequivocal welcome for the first two editions of *Fishing Forays* that we received from hoteliers. Some have their own waters which naturally differ in standard, others have local contacts and some have no fishing at all but are still thoroughly recommended and will delight non-fishing partners or friends! Once again, prices vary but there is something here for everyone. Luxurious manor houses contrast with cosy bed and breakfasts and friendly inns - all have a tremendous individual appeal. Whether you are planning the trip of a life time or a quiet weekend away from it all, we know you will find a number of good establishments from which to choose.

Our International Section has grown since last year, and together with some excellent tour operators, we have painted a brief, but hopefully stimulating, picture of some of the world's more remote but treasured waters.

If you have found the recommendations contained within the book useful, please tell us, but even more importantly, please tell your friends. Game fishing is one of life's most pleasurable pastimes and if this book can ensure that more people enjoy its appeal, one of its principal objectives will have been achieved.

Artist: Frank Wright TRANQUIL WATERS Courtesy of De Montfort Art

Contents

Funding Fishing

The question of funding in support of rod and line fishery protection has been a vexed issue. Most interested people—though not all—agree that fishing and the fishing environment depend for their future health and prosperity on monitoring and protection. At its most fundamental level, it is a job that needs policemen to react to problems and the policemen need the resources to fund their work.

The policemen, currently, are the NRA—The National Rivers Authority—and their job is a difficult one. They have to balance the leisure needs of the public at large with the demands of anglers; the rights of riparian ownership with the broader human rights of individuals; and the welfare of fish and their environment with the needs of all those who share the resource. One thing is certain, universal agreement on protectionist policy is a pipe dream.

However, the job remains to be done—and the NRA is certainly the best engine for action that we have at the moment. They merit our support.

The Government is withdrawing Grant in Aid support over the next three years and it is clear that the NRA needs, for its future survival, an alternative source of income. The first proposal that was put forward was a complex system of taxation on water resources. Those who owned water resources would be taxed since it was they, on the face of it, that would benefit materially from NRA policework and protection.

The water resource taxation plan depended for its fairness on an assessment of the worth of individual fisheries in terms of income or potential income. This meant that not only catch returns but potential catch returns had to be considered and among the factors that impacted on the latter was flow rate. The difficulty in making value assessments acceptable to individual owners using criteria like that—especially when flow rates are affected by general water usage over which riparian owners have no control—can be imagined.

Stillwaters were to be excluded from the plan, presumably because stillwater owners would implement their own protection measures, but river fishery owners saw this, not surprisingly, as unfair. And even the stillwater owners themselves were uneasy over whether or not, being isolated, they might expect to be taxed through local authority rating.

Also there existed the prospect that well-managed and therefore productive fisheries would be value assessed at higher levels than ill-managed and unproductive fisheries. The fact that, by implication, the former would financially support the latter would surely have provoked such a stream of appeals as would have terminally clogged the system.

To the credit of the NRA, who genuinely listened to all of the objections and opinions of those it consulted, they have now announced that the fishery taxation plan, Section 142 as it was dubbed, is officially scrapped and that a tiered system of rod licensing must be considered.

Proposed annual licence duties (at the time of writing) are:

• Coarse fish: £15.00

• Trout (including coarse fish): £22.00

• Migratory salmonid: £75.00

Concessionary rates will be available to juniors and to senior citizens; in 92/93, concessionary licence sales represented thirty per cent of the total.

The general reaction to the rod licensing proposals are split into two main camps. One agrees in broad terms with tiered licensing but will not accept a figure of £75 for migratory fish, which most salmon and sea trout anglers regard as unjustly predatory and also divisive within the sport. The other favours a one-price system covering all species but seeks legislation to prevent access to fishing without a valid licence—much in the same way as shotgun cartridges may not be purchased without a valid shotgun permit.

A short term licence would also enable 'occasional anglers' to legitimately fish. While this would detract from overall income potential from annual licences, it would also inhibit default by the holiday angler unwilling to invest in an annual licence for a couple of days here or there while on vacation.

The three-tier licence plan as presented will raise an estimated £13m annually assuming no change in the numbers of licences sold. Therein lies the rub: by the NRA's own admission, only 876,000 licences were sold in the 1992/93 season to an estimated target of two million active anglers. Clearly, if the NRA is to fulfil a watchdog role and also support itself adequately at the same time, it must first look to the fundamental policing problem that exists on its own doorstep.

Anglers are the best day-to-day monitors of the fishing environment because it is they who are most closely in touch with it; the ability to react is the province of the NRA. An equitable solution to the funding problem needs to be found because fish and fishing need that level of attention and protection.

Pat Mackreth, Press Officer, The Salmon & Trout Association

There are certain subjects that drivers stuck in interminable traffic jams in the south of England are given to dreaming of and one of them, curiously enough, is a Scottish fishing trip. As the motorway cones grow nearer and some wretched truck sprays you with dirt and grit, thoughts can all too easily stray to the Scottish Highlands where the only traffic problems are likely to be caused by sheep straying carelessly into the road to check your speed. Unlike motorways which supposedly run in man-made straightened lines, the country margins of Scotland are fashioned by nature and should be treated with consequent respect. Thus, you will be ushered around the mazes of gracious lochs or follow the path of a bubbling stream rather than be constrained by central reservations and white lines.

As you struggle to navigate the one lane of motorway that is open consider the single track that often constitutes your passage through the Highlands. Passing spots are provided but there is so little traffic they seem quite superfluous. Here time is not of the essence, as you inspect the rustic lanes for sheep or deer. Stuck in your traffic jam, such an idyllic scene can seem but a passing dream, far removed from urban reality.

Several 'greats' number among Scotland's rivers and for those not lucky enough to fish one of the big name rivers there are plenty of alternatives. A small spate river fished in the right conditions will afford much better sport than a poor beat on a famous river. The fish may not run so big but it is better to catch an eight pounder than return from a big sluggish pool empty handed.

Not to be forgotten are the lochs, which come in all sizes: from the positively enormous, like Loch Shin to the thousands of smaller hill lochs or lochans that can be found only on the largest scale maps, lying behind crags in hidden glens waiting for your casts. Remember your traffic jam once more with its mass of discontented humanity and reflect that back in Scotland you may be the only person for miles - whisked away into a wonderfully private universe. Many hotels can arrange a day's fishing on these lochs, so if conditions on the river are against you there is no need to leave your rod in the tackle room while waiting for a change in the water. The smaller lochs will often be off the beaten track and require quite a walk but the scenery and surroundings will more than compensate for the effort. The trout are not big but a fish weighing over a pound is often one to remember. They are invariably beautifully marked, wild and make wonderful eating.

The rivers of legend are here to behold; they are not impossible to fish and a holiday spent in such surroundings will be one to remember. Whether you are fighting a salmon on the Findhorn or a brown trout on an uncharted loch we wish you good cheer and good health. This is a land of fishing lore; let the game commence.

Ulbster Arms Hotel

Anglers are beginning to rediscover the delights of brown trout fishing on the remote hill lochs of the northern Highlands. Apart from the natural beauty of their setting and the peace which surrounds them, they provide both fish and fishing of a quality far higher than most people today realise. Examples of the best of them are the hill lochs managed by Thurso Fisheries Limited for the Ulbster Arms Hotel, which has boats on these lochs and can arrange permits for others in the area.

The Hotel is the centre for fishing the River Thurso, one of Scotland's finest fly only salmon rivers, having both a spring and autumn run.

As well as fishing, many other outdoor pursuits can be undertaken using the hotel as a base; birdwatching, photography, rambling, painting and geology, to name but a few, can all provide the visitor with the relaxation or stimulus that is desired.

The Hotel also arranges shooting and stalking over a wide variety of moors.

Caithness is renowned for its resident and visiting sea birds and waders, and fully equipped boats can be chartered for sea angling in the Pentland Firth. There are also many sites of archaeological interest in the area and exploring the castles, cairns, standing stones and old buildings can fill fascinating hours.

Ulbster Arms Hotel
Halkirk
Caithness
KW12 6XY
Tel/Fax: (084783) 206/641

Scotland

Artist: **John Trickett** *FISHING THE LOCH* Courtesy of Sally Mitchell Fine Arts

Scotland

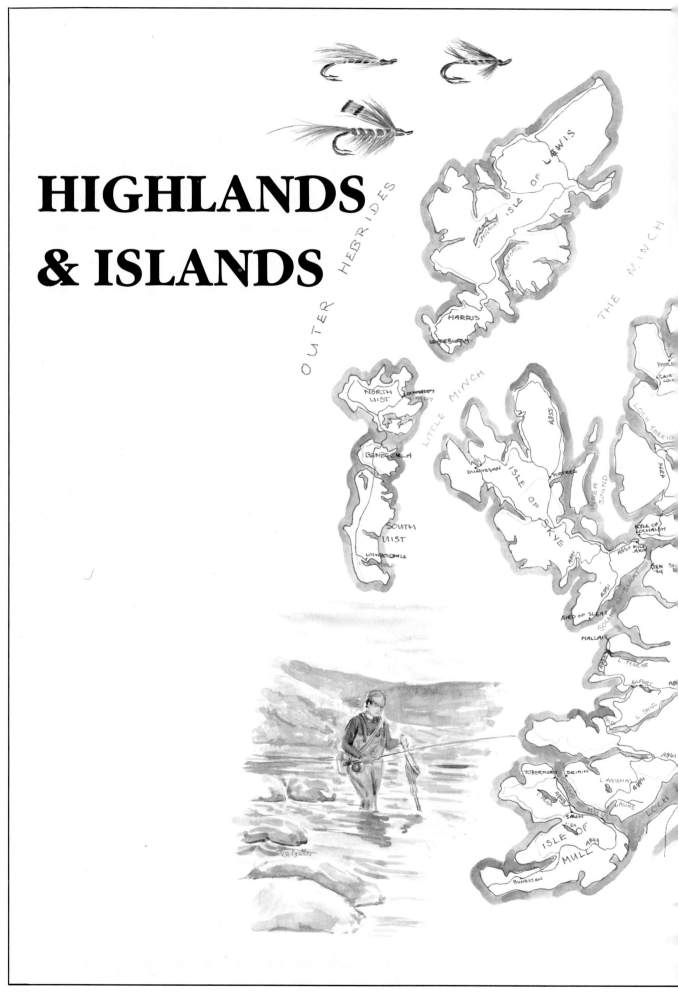

HIGHLANDS
& ISLANDS

Caithness is the most northerly county in Britain. These days, the much-improved A9 makes getting there much less of a tortuous route march than it once was. Further time can be saved by using the new bridge over Dornoch Firth, where previously one had to journey via Bonar Bridge. It should be pointed out that the longer route allowed the opportunity of making a small detour to the Shin Falls, a sight which cannot fail to gladden an angler's heart, and for those of you with time on your hands this route should still be considered. Travelling on main roads is undoubtedly quicker but turning off at Helmsdale on to the Melvich road will afford a fisherman's treat, for the road follows the Helmsdale. After Forsinard, into Strath Halladale. Already the office seems a distant memory and the heart pounds—not from pressure of work, but from sheer exhilaration.

The Halladale

For those who aspire to discover the undiscovered, the Halladale falls into the 'hidden gem' category. The water is now under the auspices of the the Bulmer family—they of cider fame—who are keen fishermen, and run the river through the Halladale Partnership. Although some twenty miles in length, there are no lochs in the system and it is very much a spate river. As a result, Halladale rods look for rain and the sport which almost inevitably follows. At Forsinard it is a tumbling stream but for much of its journey it can appear unpromising and sluggish. This, however, is the deceptive face of the river and there is fishing of the finest quality to be found for a persevering angler. It is a fly-only river and the season runs from January 12th to September 30th. The best time has traditionally been from June to September, although a good spring run has been had of late. Weekly rates vary from £132 to £660 plus VAT, and day permits are restricted to locals (to discourage poaching!). The river is let through an agent, Mrs J. Atkinson, 8 Sinclair Street, Thurso (0847) 63291. The Forsinard Hotel (0641) 7221 has one of the upper beats and a popular fishing lodge which sleeps fourteen.

As the Halladale flows through peat country it is heavily stained when in spate and virtually unfishable. But rest assured, for the very next day it will as often as not fall and begin to clear. In such conditions patterns such as the Garry Dog and Yellow and Orange are as good a bet as any. The pools are of a size that can be easily covered and favourites include Bridge, Macbeth, Munroes, Run Out and Ashill. Being generally slow-moving and a fly-only river it is sometimes necessary to gently handline to give your fly a touch of life. The average size is about 7lb, though fish of 14lb and 15lb are caught, the best fish in the 1990 season being 16lb. Assuming the rain gods are kind, the numbers can be excellent. Sea-trout may be caught in the estuary but there is not much of a run up into the river. Apart from the all-important hip flask, insect repellent is a must to combat the midges! The Melvich Hotel (06413) 206 is a good place to stay and has delightful views out onto the estuary. The proprietors can arrange salmon fishing for you, if given enough advance warning, and also provide trout fishing on their three lochs, with arrangements possible on several others.

As in every other fishing 'mecca' there are no shortage of keen fishermen here only too pleased to pass on learned local opinion, and the newcomer to the area should always endeavour to pick the brains of seasoned locals. It might cost a dram or two but it may well be worth it. There's an old racing saying that advises the cautious punter never to back an Irish tip at Cheltenham. The reason is simple: if it's going to trot up, you'll be the last to be told! Fishing folk have a different attitude and it is often based on the theory that if you have nothing to say it is because you have nothing to tell and if you've nothing to tell you're not worth talking to! A little severe, maybe, but worth bearing in mind.

The Forss

The Forss takes its name from an old Norse word meaning waterfall, but despite its fairly extensive headwaters and tributaries, the area of the Forss of greatest interest to the serious fishermen is the fairly short section flowing out of Loch Shurrery. Favoured flies include the Munro Killer and fish average at around the 8lb mark. The river is fly-only and it fishes best in the spring and from July to September. This is a time share river but it is sometimes possible to get on it through Salar Management Services Ltd (0667) 55355. The cost varies between £150 and £350 per week and £20 to £50 a day depending on the time of season. If you do get a day's fishing, Falls Pool is likely to be the most productive even in low water, or so I am reliably informed by local luminaries!

The Thurso

Arguably the most prolific river in the area, the Thurso used to be regarded as one of the best spring rivers producing bright silver ingots of fresh-run fish. In common with many other rivers, however, (with not even the mighty Spey excluded), spring runs are nothing like they used to be and the best sport is often autumnal. Although netting still takes place, the nets and estuary are owned by Thurso Fisheries. The boats are manned by ghillies, with the result that the rod fisherman's sport is born very much in mind. The dam and sluice gates at Loch More allow reasonable water levels to further the fisherman's enjoyment.

Although there may be salmon in the Thurso in January and February the season doesn't really get under way until March when, surprisingly, the upper beats near Loch More can prove most productive. At this time of the year two-inch tubes in patterns such as the Munro Killer or Yellow and Black can prove effective; worthwhile alternatives include long-winged flies such as the Tadpole or Collie Dog. June can be a difficult month on the river if the weather is hot, but you can always try your luck on Loch More which fishes surprisingly well in such conditions. Late July, August and September are the best time (assuming a decent rainfall!) and old favourites like the Stoats Tail, Hairy Mary and Garry can all work well. In all its twenty-five mile journey from Loch More to the sea the river only falls some three hundred feet, and consequently there are quite a few slow-moving pools. In such conditions it is worth trying *backing-up*. This involves starting at the bottom of a pool, rather than the top, and casting a long line straight out. Allow a few seconds for the fly to sink to the required depth then draw in a few yards of line to set the fly on its way. Taking a few paces upstream will keep the fly on the move and you can work your way up the pool like this. It sounds illogical and is against all tradition, I know. But it works. The locals promised it would and our experience did little to disprove the theory!

The whole river is owned by Thurso Fisheries Ltd, which belongs to Lord Thurso, and prices vary between £560 and £860 a week, including accommodation, according to the time of the season. Bookings are taken through the company secretary's office (0847) 63134. The fish average about 9lb but there is a chance of a 20lb fish. This is a most agreeable river to fish and is divided into fourteen rotating beats. As the whole river is under the control of one riparian owner, it is probably the only river in the British Isles that can be fished in its entirety within the space of a fortnight! This, moreover, is an area where the wild brown trout are truly wild. A dam on the river is used to catch the native fish which are then transferred to the lochs. The Ulbster Arms (0847) 83206 is the place to stay here. This comfortable, well appointed hotel offers excellent trout fishing. It has ten hill lochs (seven with boats) and can also arrange fishing on Lochs Watten, St John's and Calder. It is particularly suitable for a family holiday not only because of the scenery and solitude but also because their lochs have difficult fishing for the experienced rod and easier water for novices and children.

The Wick

Fishing on the River Wick, lying to the east of the Thurso, is managed by the Wick Angling Association. This river offers reasonably priced salmon fishing at either £50 a week or £12 a day. Permits can be obtained from the Hugo Ross tackle shop in Wick (0955) 4200 which can also offer boat fishing on Loch Watten and Loch Hempriggs if required. The average catch on the river is 250-300 salmon a season with the average being 9lb, though a fish of over 22lb was caught in 1979. It is a spate river and somewhat sluggish in character. Some nine miles long, it can all but disappear in times of drought.

The Wester System

There is little sea-trout fishing in the rivers we have discussed thus far but a few miles north of Wick there is the classic water of the Wester Sysytem (a loch and a river). The river is only half a mile long so sea-trout have easy access to the loch and can provide tremendous sport in the autumn. As we know, these wonderfully shy, hard-fighting fish give a very good account of themselves, especially here where the average is 1lb 8oz and most seasons produce at least one memorable fish of over 5lb. One chap in 1991 had eleven sea-trout to his name at the end of the day, all over a pound—due no doubt to the salmon and sea-trout restocking programme. Daily permits are available from Auchorn Farm, Lyth (0955) 83208, for £5 per day (boats available).

Artist: John Oldfield HIGHLAND WATERS

Caithness is renowned for its lochs and the genuinely wild brown trout they produce. The angler who is accustomed to fishing the stillwater stocked lakes in the south, where anglers moan if the stocking size is under one and a half pounds and fish of five to ten pounds are regularly caught, may wonder why people rave about loch fishing for wild brownies when a fish of one pound is often considered a good fish. To such cynics, I would simply advise them to try it in the confidence that they will quickly be converted! These trout come greedily to the fly and having taken it, set off at a furious pace giving the fisherman a memorable tussle.

Loch Watten

Scotland is blessed with some fine brown trout fisheries but few are as bounteous as Loch Watten, where £7 buys you a day ticket with a boat and there is no bag limit. The fish average a pound but run to over two. Some three miles long by up to three quarters of a mile wide, the loch can often be windy, so an outboard motor is essential unless you are either a fitness freak or a rowing blue. The fish are of excellent quality, a challenge to catch and a delight to hook. Both boat and bank permits are available, and for further information contact Mrs Wilson on (095582) 370. The best fishing is in May, June and September.

Loch St John's

Another renowned Caithness loch is St John's near Dunnet Head. Much work has recently been done to improve the quality of fishing here. A full day with a boat will cost £10 (£5 for an evening) and there are significant mayfly and cranefly hatches. Please contact the Northern Sands Hotel (0847) 85270 if you require more details.

The Dunnet Head Lochs

These are the most northerly lochs in Britain. In fact Dunnet Head is the most northerly point of Britain and not John O'Groats as popularly thought—look at a map before dissenting. You can win many a pint at a bar armed with this little known fact! The lochs are stocked on a regular basis and the fish average around the 2lb mark. These lochs are also an ornothologist's delight, for there are several pairs of red-throated divers and fishermen are expressly asked not to disturb them. Permits are available from The Dunnet Head Tearoom between 12.00 noon and 9.00 am (0847) 85774. Packed lunches (including vegetarian) are also available.

Loch Heilen

The most fickle loch in the area. On these 170 acres of windswept, shallow water one may never see a fish all day, but of course they are there and run up to 8lb. Anything less than 2lb should be returned. It is the type of water that can either reduce one to tears or provide a real red letter day. Please contact H. Pottinger Esq. (0847) 82210 for further details.

Loch Calder

Unusual for two reasons. Firstly Calder is the only loch in the area which is fishable on a Sunday. Secondly it is the only Caithness loch not restricted to fly-only. However, one or two of the riparian owners are looking to make changes so check with Harpers Fly Fishing Services (0847) 63179 before arriving with spinners on a Sunday! Other lochs in the area worth noting are Stemster, Airig, Lethaigd, Garbh, Caol and Ruathair and of course there are the hundreds of hill lochs which can often provide a memorable day.

Green Highlander (fully dressed) Mike Sugg

Living off the land has never been easy in the Highlands, and a crofter's life is notoriously tough. But existing here is certainly easier than it used to be. If you fish Loch Naver spare a thought for the two thousand crofters exiled in the nineteenth century—evicted by the Duchess of Sutherland to make way for sheep-farming. The statue local people erected to her husband overlooks the sea, not his estates. The countryside is still sparsely populated and roads are few and far between. It is an area of great natural beauty and of course there is fishing—some of the finest in the kingdom!

The Naver

Probably the best salmon stream in the far north, and privately owned by four estates making up the River Naver District Salmon Fishery Board. Only as a guest of one of the owners can one cast a fly on this fine water. Those lucky enough to do so will find the six beats have fifty named pools divided between them. However, all is far from lost as the Bettyhill Angling Club has the right to fish for salmon and sea-trout for a mile or so above Naver bridge. There are three main pools and three permits a day are available at a cost of £14 each from the Tourist Information Centre at Bettyhill (06416) 342. Below the bridge the fishing is free. June to August is a good time for the grilse run.

The Borgie

Journey west of the Naver and you will quickly reach the River Borgie. This beautiful and well-managed river covers some seven miles in its journey from Loch Slaim to the sea. A hatchery means that each year the river is stocked with salmon fry and this augurs well for future anglers. Like so many in the area it is essentially a spate river, but the sluice gates at the loch help to maintain reasonable water levels. Four beats with two rods per beat are available from Mather Jamie (0509) 233433 at a cost of between £200 and £400 per rod a week. There are also one and a half miles of permit water on which tickets are obtainable from David Crichton (0641) 2231, the Water Bailiff. Good management has improved the fishing over the past few years and the salmon are in great condition in May, when Waddingtons are particularly effective. For the grilse run in June and August it is on to doubles and in September it's the faithful Waddingtons again.

The Dionard

Travelling further west we come to Strath Dionard and Cape Wrath, or the Parth as it is known locally. A quick glance at the road atlas will show you why this area is so special. The A838 is the only road in the area—you are alone! Those prepared to explore the remote hill lochs will be particularly well rewarded and are liable to return with a heavy basket of breakfast-sized trout. Fishing may well also have been accompanied by the piping of greenshanks. This is an area for the true fisherman but ghillies are available to help the newcomer.

A distance of twelve miles separates the Dionard from its source in the loch of the same name, to the sea at the Kyle of Durness. Fishing on the lower water is held jointly by E.G. Fishings (0387) 54424 and The Cape Wrath Hotel (0971) 511212, while the fishing above Rhigolter Bridge is owned by the Gaulin Estate (0971) 521282. E.G. Fishings allow four rods on their water and a week will cost £285. Cape Wrath Hotel has four beats with two rods per beat at £345 a week. Gaulin Estate can offer five beats and fishing on the loch on a rotation basis at a cost of £60 a day for two rods. Recent years have seen several improvements including a stocking programme. Like many rivers, fishing on the Dionard has been variable with 280 fish caught in 1989 and 80 in 1990, though 7 fish have been caught in a day. The average weight is around 7lb, but each season produces a fair amount of heavier fish with the odd one over 20lb. Falls Pool is probably the best and also one of the prettiest pools in the North.

The Durness Lochs

If conditions on the river are against you, do try the limestone lochs at Durness. These waters are famous for their land-locked sea-trout. The fish feed off freshwater shrimp, are pink-fleshed and make superb eating. They can also be rather large! Loch Larlish which is the smallest, produced a whopper of fourteen and a half pounds in 1990. Local opinion is divided on whether the fish are brownies or sea-trout but if you are lucky enough to catch a fish like that, terminology matters little! Loch Borralie, which is the deepest, also holds Arctic char. The fish in these lochs average just under three pounds and anything under a pound should be returned. It is important to remember that being limestone, the waters are crystal clear and so casting errors must be avoided. The Cape Wrath Hotel will be able to assist you in fishing these lochs.

Loch Hope

Loch Hope is probably the best sea-trout fishery in the far North. It lies close to the Borgie and its six miles are divided into five beats. The Altnaharra Hotel (0549) 81222, a renowned fishing hotel, is the place to stay here. It can also offer fishing on eight other lochs and the River Mudale. Permits for this loch are available from Mr I. MacDonald at the Keeper's House (0847) 56272. Outboard motors are not allowed on Loch Hope which has a reputation for being windy, so it is advisable to have a ghillie, both for his expert advice and to avoid having aching shoulders at the end of the day! The sea-trout run to 7lb and there are some huge brownies, one of 7lb 13oz being recorded recently.

A favourite and very successful method on this loch is *dapping*. Some people frown at dapping, but it is not as easy as it may appear, especially if the wind is up. For the uninitiated, dapping is a method which entails eliciting the help of the wind to blow your fly around. For this method you will require a floss-silk dapping line. Experts have it that the more blustery and dull the day, the more the fish are likely to take. If they spot the fly above them they will race towards it and come leaping out of the water often to three or more feet and will perhaps take it while the fly floats in the air or when it touches the surface. To see the fish rocketing from the depths is a memorable sight which will cheer many a fireside memory. One further point. If having tempted your prey you lift the dap at the last moment there's a good chance he may take the traditional wet flies being used by your fellow rod.

Lochs Stack, Loyal & More

In 1874 Francis Francis wrote, 'The Laxford is by no means a large or heavy river and Loch Stack is quite a small sheet of water compared with many of its neighbours and the stream is a short one, but the crowds of sea-trout and salmon that constantly swarm up it are prodigious.' Fishing is not what it was, but that applies to every water and Loch Stack is the best in the area. As recently as the 1970s two rods accounted for 50lb of fish in a day. It is well stocked every year and the best fish in 1990 was a six-pounder. Five boats are available and there is no bag limit though fish under a pound should be returned. Most fish are taken close to the shore for the loch has many bays and corners where the fish lie. You might care to try Wilson's Bay, North Bay or the bays where the feeder streams enter. July and August are the best times for sea-trout and because of the fame of this loch, advance booking is a must. The cost for two rods including a boat at this time of year is £40, falling to £30 in September. A ghillie will charge you £30 for the day.

Just the other side of Ben Screavie is the more modest water of Loch More. Here a boat for two rods will cost you £30 if you fish at the Kinloch end or £20 for the Smiddy end. After mid-August prices fall to £25 and £15

respectively. Like Stack this is a fly only water and is stocked every year. Similarly there is no bag limit and fish under a pound should be returned. Sea-trout average 1¾lb and August is the best time for them.

Both Loch Stack and More are owned by Reay Forest Estates and permits are available from the Scourie Hotel (0971) 502396. This comfortable and well appointed hotel was originally built as a coaching inn by the second Duke of Sutherland. Guests can enjoy fishing in the many hill lochs, 250 of which abound in the hotel's 25,000 acres. The hotel can also offer salmon and sea-trout fishing on waters such as the Lower and Upper Duart and Badna Bay. Travellers of the turf may be interested to note that here you can see the peaks of the original Foinaven and Arkle! The legendary chaser was owned by the Duchess of Westminster. As you look around you do remember that Arkle as a racehorse was never bettered. Name and place are singularly appropriate.

Artist: S R Percy AFTER THE STORM Courtesy of Rosenstiel's

Another good water in the area is Loch Loyal, managed by Tongue & District A.C. This loch is famous for its wild brownies and there are also sea-trout and some salmon to be found. This is a fly only and no bag limit water but fish under ten inches should be returned. The season runs from 15th March to 6th October. The cost is £3 a day or £12 a week for bank fishing and boats with outboard motors are available at £15 a day. Permits are available from the Ben Loyal Hotel at Tongue (084755) 216 which also has fishing on thirteen hill lochs and the Kyle of Tongue where a 3¾ lb sea-trout was caught in 1993.

Sutherland has been described as 'the half-pound county' for the lochs and lochans abound with fish of this size. While it is only natural to want to catch a good fish these trout offer memorable tussles especially if you use very light tackle. Other lochs especially worth trying in the area include Meadie, Mor, Caol and Modsarie.

Cape Wrath Hotel

Situated in one of the last truly unspoiled counties of Scotland, the Cape Wrath Hotel stands on a peninsula of the beautiful Kyle of Durness. You will marvel at the sheer beauty of the scenery surrounding the hotel, heather clad moorland alive with wild life, picturesque lochs and rivers teeming with fish, and the rugged grandeur of the mountains rising from the glens originally gouged out by the ice-age and little changed since.

The Cape Wrath Hotel offers full facilities to all guests, including two well stocked bars, and two comfortable lounges.

The hotel prides itself on the high standard of cuisine in the fine restaurant. There is also a better than average cellar from which to choose the most appropriate wines to complement the delicious food.

For the game fisherman this region is a dream come true. Salmon fishing is available on three rivers, the Grudie, the Dall and a two mile stretch on one of Scotland's finest salmon rivers, the Dionard. Last year an average of 50 salmon per month, weighing 8lb-10lb, were caught and landed on these rivers.

Brown trout, renowned for their size and fighting characteristics, are found in any of the four well stocked limestone lochs, just fifteen minute's walk from the hotel. The record brown trout caught some years ago weighed in at an amazing 14½lb. This may be difficult to beat, but trout weighing 4lb-5lb are regularly caught on these waters and some thirty other lochs on the estate. Sea-trout fishing is also available on the Kyle of Durness. Throughout the year 'walk up' shooting is available to hotel guests over some 40,000 acres of mountains and moorland, the natural habitat of Highland game including the famous red grouse.

For those interested in antiquities and archaeology there are many fine examples of ancient civilisations and early churches to explore. For those tired of hunting, shooting, fishing and walking, miles of sandy beaches, nestling between outcrops of harsh unyielding rocks, provide a restful haven.

Cape Wrath Hotel
Durness
Sutherland IV27 4SW
Tel: (0971) 511212
Fax: (0971) 511313

This is yet another Scottish example of unspoiled moorland, mountain and shoreline. All manner of rivers thread their way through this remote area and the fishing, needless to say, is wild and wonderful. It is also fairly tricky to get on to the region's principal water, the Helmsdale. However, there are possibilities and there are also numerous hill lochs which produce some excellent game fishing, with brown trout that fight with a vigour that belies their size.

The Helmsdale

There are fewer more famous or productive salmon rivers in Scotland than the Helmsdale. The reasons are largely self evident, for here is some of the best fishing in Sutherland and, for that matter, the whole of the north of Scotland. Furthermore, there can be few more idyllic settings than the Strath of Kildonan. Although we all know of its reputation, facts are more difficult to ascertain. This is primarily due to the secrecy of those who fish this river and it has been said that your best chances of a spot on this river are through divine relationship (or intervention!). The question begs itself—what is all the fuss about? Although catch figures are seldom reported, a few years ago Beat 4 produced 31 fish in a day with a best week of 94 and a season's total of 599.

The river is owned by six estates which jointly make up the Helmsdale River Board. It is divided into twelve beats, the dividing point being the Kildonan Falls. The beats rotate on a daily basis and there are two rods per beat. The season runs from January 11th to September 30th but fish are unlikely to mount the falls until the water rises to an acceptable level, usually around the end of March. However, the overall quality of the Helmsdale is outstanding and there is a good chance of landing a salmon on the opening day. At the start of the season the pools may be frozen over and you and your ghillie may have to break the ice to clear a pool. This may well stir up the fish which could mean using a big tube fly such as a Willie Gunn, Garry Dog or Black and Yellow on a sinking line. April and May are traditionally the best months and a Stoats Tail may prove effective during this period. The grilse run is from June to August. A popular technique for fishing the broken headstreams of pools in low water conditions is *dibbling*. This involves fishing with a dropper which should be longer than normal—say about seven inches and tied about six feet above the point fly. The dropper dibbles across the surface cutting a wake in its path. Favoured flies for dibbling are such patterns as the Garry, Shrimp Fly and Elver Fly.

Those lucky enough to fish this first class river will always want to return, but because it is so good it is among the most difficult river to get on. However, do not despair, for the Garvault Hotel (0431) 3224 can sometimes get you a rod on one of the private beats and the Roxton Sporting Agency Ltd (0488) 683222 in Hungerford lets beats. Much more generally accessible is the Association water which comprises the lower mile of the Helmsdale. Prices range from £14.10 to £17.63 a day according to the time of year. Day tickets are from 9.00 am to 9.00 am the following day—so you can fish all night for sea-trout—and these can be obtained from A.

Sangster Esq. (0431) 2343. It is worth mentioning that in the summer time there is almost constant daylight while in the winter months the evenings come correspondingly early.

The Berriedale

Travelling north from Helmsdale we come to the Berriedale Water. Owned by the Langwell Estate, this wild, natural river produces over fifty fish a year with an average weight around the 8lb mark. The Berriadale is divided into three beats which rotate on a daily basis and whose two rods can fish thirty-eight named pools. Access to some parts, particularly the middle beat, can be awkward—so elderly gentlemen (not to mention your exhausted editors!) should tread carefully. In fact there is one somewhat gruelling story that tells of a sprightly octogenarian breaking a somewhat spindly leg whilst endeavouring to fish the water. He was not rescued for twenty-four hours but the resourceful chap managed to land a 6lb fish shortly before dawn and his eventual rescue. There may be an element of exaggeration here but the moral (or one of them at least!) is to exercise caution at all times. The cost for this water is £110 per rod per week and permits are available from the Estate Office (0593) 5237. A good place to stay is the Navidale House Hotel (0431) 2258 in Helmsdale which can also arrange trout fishing on at least five lochs.

The Brora

South of the Helmsdale lies the Brora. This fine river has good early runs and February, which is when the season starts, can produce upwards of a hundred fish. The river is of two parts, the Upper and the Lower, which are divided by Loch Brora. The Blackwater, which joins the Upper Brora at Balnacoil, can also provide good sport and the average over the last five years is thirty-two salmon. As a spring river the best time is February to May, though providing there is enough rain to provide reasonable water levels, salmon and grilse fishing in June and July can be rewarding. It is also fine sea-trout water.

Conservation is a topic which is discussed at length by fishermen and other interested parties up and down the country—concrete results are somewhat more difficult to find. How refreshing it is, therefore, to find a river whose management are proving that actions speak louder than words. As a result, the fishing is improving. This will surely be to the longer term benefit of all. The season on the Blackwater closes early on September 1st to allow the fish a chance to get to the upper reaches for spawning. On the Brora all sea-trout caught before May should be returned and no hen fish may be killed on any beat after September 15th. On most waters spring fishing calls for fishing deep with a sinking line, but on the Brora the fish will often take a big fly such as a Collie Dog or Tadpole fished close to the surface on a floating line. This defies tradition and convention but it can work extremely well. The traditional methods, however, should also prove effective. If you are after sea-trout on Loch Brora you will find that Kenny's Killer more than justifies its name. A team of wet flies of such tried and trusted favourites as Black Pennell, Dunkeld and Peter Ross will stand you in good stead.

The Brora is certainly accessible to visitors and anyone booking well in advance should be able to get on this water. Ownership of the river is held by Sutherland Estates (0408) 633268, Gordon Bush Estates and Cadogan Estates. Gordon Bush Estates let the Upper Brora through the Roxton Sporting Agency (0488) 683222. They also let Balnacoil Lodge which sleeps up to twelve and overlooks the river. Cadogan Estates bought the north bank of the Lower Brora in 1990 and their letting is handled by Finlayson Hughes of Perth (0738) 30926. Sutherland Estates (which includes the Blackwater) let their fishing with their three sporting lodges, which can take parties of up to fourteen. Prices range from £550 to around £800 for four rods for six days and beats alternate with the Cadogan Estate water to provide variety. Sutherland Estates can also arrange stalking and grouse shooting, so there is always a chance of a McNab! Day tickets on the tidal water are available from Rob Wilson's tackle shop (0408) 621373.

The Fleet

The Fleet runs close by but is understandably overshadowed somewhat by its famous neighbour. The nine miles of this lesser known river which flows into the tidal waters of Loch Fleet, can fish well, depending on the water levels. However, if the river is low and good water is hard to find, the best bet is to head for the loch. This too is good sea-trout water and small flies of traditional patterns such as the Dunkeld and Zulu are effec-

tive. The river is privately owned, but fishing can occasionally be obtained through Bell Ingram in Bonar Bridge (0863) 2683. Rogart Angling Club also have a long term agreement with the Morvich Estate to fish a small section of the Lower Fleet which includes Polsons Pool and Davoch Beat. From May to October every Monday, Wednesday and Thursday is split into three eight hour sessions which cost £8 each. Permits are obtainable from the Post Office Stores at Rogart (0408) 641200.

Helmsdale Lochs

Lochs in the area include Badanloch, Rimsdale and Nan Clar to name but three. The Garvault Hotel near Kinbrace (0431) 3224, which is on the road from Helmsdale to Melvich, has fishing on ten lochs and can arrange fishing on over twenty others. The best fish from the hotel's lochs was an 8½ pounder three years ago and 1991 yielded a 5-pounder. A short distance away at Forsinard one finds the Forsinard Hotel (0641) 7221 which has exclusive fishing on six lochs and can arrange fishing on a further fourteen These lochs are full of wild brownies weighing in generally around the 3¼lb mark. Anything over 2lb is a good fish. Because they are little known and off the beaten track these lochs offer unexpectedly tremendous sport as well as that elusive quality in these busy times, solitude. Now that there are so many trout waters in the south fewer people go to Scotland for a trout fishing holiday. However, when was the last time (if ever!) you caught over sixty fish in a day? As Tony Henderson of the Garvault Hotel will tell you, it is perfectly possible on the lochs in this beautiful and unspoilt area.

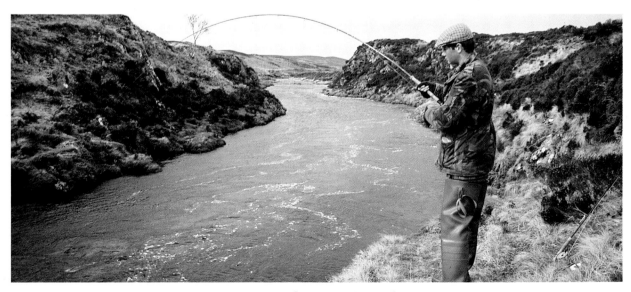

Success (Forsinard Hotel)

Before the advent of the new bridge over the Dornoch Firth anyone fishing the Helmsdale or more northerly rivers had to make the long detour via Bonar Bridge. However, this afforded the chance to see the Carron, Shin, Oykel and Cassley. There must be few places where one can see four such notable rivers within such a small area. Sadly, these rivers have all been affected by hydro-electric dams. No fisherman can but shake his head in sorrow at the ugly dam at the east end of Loch Shin which has reduced the river to a mere shadow of its former self.

The Carron

Driving to Bonar Bridge the River Carron is the first river one sees. Its character has been somewhat changed by the hydro-electric dam at its source, but this has had one beneficial effect, for the water level falls very quickly during a spate. This is a first class salmon river with about ten miles of fishing belonging to nine owners. Three falls make natural divisions of this river. The lower part is from the Firth to Gledfield Falls. The best time to fish here is considered to be March and April, for fish will stay below the falls until the water temperature rises above 38°F. The middle section is up to Morell Falls which fishes well in April and May. When the water temperature is above 42°F the upper reaches up to Glencarvie Falls will provide good sport from May to September. Prices vary according to beat and season and range from £150 for two rods to £4500 for four rods, including a comfortable lodge which sleeps eleven. Some beats do become available but the best ones are very hard to get on. Finlayson Hughes of Perth (0738) 30926 may be able to help you. As on so many rivers, September sees some fine runs. Spring, however is more likely to produce big fish and the best fish for 1990 was a 24lb beauty taken in April from the Cornhill beat.

The Shin

When Andrew Young had the fishing of the River Shin in the nineteenth century the cost was £12 a month and in 1849 Major Cumming caught twenty-two salmon in ten hours. His fellow rod, Mr Fitzgibbon, the fishing correspondent of Bell's Life, took fifty-two fish in fifty-five hours! It is worth remembering that these prodigious feats were done with the heavy tackle then in use. Anyone who has spent a day casting with a big split cane salmon rod can imagine how their shoulders must have ached at the end of the day—but oh, how pleasurably! Paradise Pool is justly famous for producing big fish. Sadly, this pool was washed away in the torrential rains of 1988 but the damage was quickly repaired. Just north of Invershin are the Shin Falls. This is one of the few falls which are easily accessible to man and motor and as a result they are a popular tourist attraction complete with roadside cafe. The sight of a salmon leaping is one of the wonders of nature and when they are running here you will see hundreds of them. One can but

watch in awe at the strength and bravery of the fish as they try to leap the falls. Often they will hit a rock and fall into the pool below, but driven by some primeval instinct they will keep on trying until at last they lie spent and exhausted in the pool above.

A few miles further on the A836 is the town of Lairg. Here is the Aultnagar Lodge Hotel (054) 982245 and the Sutherland Arms Hotel (0549) 2291 which will provide a comfortable pillow and has fishing books going back to 1861—and what fascinating reading they make. This hotel has a lease on the River Shin and can also arrange fishing on Loch Shin and Loch Craggie. Loch Shin is the largest loch in Sutherland and being some twenty miles long, it is possible to get marked weather differences at either end. Due to the hydro-electric power sluices there are few salmon but it is good trouting water and there are Arctic char at the western end. There can be a very large mayfly hatch which will naturally produce superb fishing. Permits may be obtained from R. Ross in Lairg (0549) 2239, the only tackle shop for miles around. A day's bank fishing costs £3 and a boat with an outboard motor £20. The Overscaig Hotel (0549) 83203 on the north side of the loch offers guests free fishing on this and other lochs, including Loch Merkland.

Loch Craggie

There are three lochs in Sutherland called Craggie, meaning big stones or rocky. The one we are referring to here is situated three miles north-east of Lairg and factored by the Sutherland Arms Hotel. Here you will find some of the best trout water in Scotland. The average weight is just under the pound and the best fish for 1991 was 4½, but there are some very big fish. Fishermen should note that there is no bank fishing whatsoever and a day for two rods, including a boat, costs £24 with a bag limit of ten fish per boat. If your fellow rod gets more than his fair share then one feels justified in feeling a trifle peeved ... but such is life!

The Oykel

From its source in Loch Ailsh to Dornoch Firth, the course of the River Oykel covers some thirty-five miles and varies in character from tumbling rapids to gentle pools. It has long been famous as a prolific salmon water and is, as a result, hard to get on. George Ross (0549) 84259 is the fishing manager of the Lower Oykel fishings and people in their forties write to him hoping to get on when they retire! His wife, Irene, ties superb flies which are sold all over the world and if you have the opportunity of casting them on the river you are indeed a fortunate fellow.

The Lower Oykel runs from Oykel Falls to the Kyle of Sutherland. These seven miles are divided into four beats and here you will find such famous pools as George, Blue, Junction and Langwell. The Upper Oykel is from Oykel Falls to Eileag Burn and is also very difficult to get on. There is a long waiting list and the expression 'dead man's shoes' comes speedily to mind. The splendid Oykel Bridge Hotel (0549) 84218 handles the lets and may be able to help you. These four miles are divided into three beats which rotate at 6am. There are three rods per beat. Salmon run, on average, at about the 9lb mark and it is also good sea-trout water. Slightly more accessible is the stretch from Eileag Burn to Loch Ailsh. This water is let through the Inver Lodge Hotel (05714) 496 and is kept exclusively for hotel guests. These three miles are divided into two beats with two rods per beat and the costs vary between £25 and £50 a day. The best time is from July to September when it is not uncommon for two rods to account for a dozen salmon in a day. The average weight is 6lb and the best fish recorded in the last two years tipped the scales at 18½. Among the notable pools are Lornas Corner, Edmund's Pool, Keeper's Pool and the Laird's Run. Advance booking is essential. The hotel also has three beats on the River Kirkaig available at between £18 to £50 per day per rod. Furthermore, guests can take advantage of free fishing on Loch Ailsh and trout fishing on several other lochs. Trout fishing for non-residents is available at £17.63 a day including a boat.

Upper Cassley fishings, which are let through Bell Ingram of Bonar Bridge (08632) 683 per rod per week, at a cost varying from £55 in May to £200 in September. The Upper Cassley beats comprise some seven miles with thirty-seven pools, while rods on the Glencassley beats enjoy five miles and thirty-three pools. From March Cottage to the Achness Falls is the Glenrossal beat and below these falls is the Rosehall beat. The cost of a rod on the Glenrossal beat varies between £70 and £125 a week and on the Rosehall beat from £550 to £1050 per week, but that is for three rods and also includes the services of a ghillie. The Achness Hotel at Rosehall (0549) 84239 can arrange the fishing for you, but there is a waiting list.

Just north of Invershin is the turning for the A837. The road follows the course of the Oykel and is the nearest that many will get to this famous river! Continuing on this road will lead to Inchnadamph and Loch Assynt. The loch is some seven miles long and is good trout water. The average weight may be around half a pound, but eight and nine-pounders are not uncommon. Here you will often find Willie Morrison who, with seven years experience behind him, knows the moods of the loch well. The Inchnadamph Hotel (0571) 2202, of which Willie is proprietor, has five boats for the use of the guests and a day's fishing with an outboard motor costs £16. The Assynt Angling Club has fishing on some thirty-two lochs and further details can be obtained from the Tourist Information Office (0571) 4330. The Inver Lodge Hotel also has a single boat on Loch Assynt.

The Cassley

Also flowing into the Kyle of Sutherland is the Cassley. This is a superb spate river which, given good water levels, provides excellent salmon fishing. June often sees a great grilse run. The upper reaches of this river down to Duchally are owned by the Balnagowan Estate (0862) 842243 which belongs to Mr Fayed of Harrods fame. This water can fish well from July onwards and is often fished by stalkers staying at the estate lodges when they want a break from the hills. From Duchally to within a stone's throw of March Cottage, the north bank becomes the Glencassley fishings, while the south bank is the

The Inver

The Inver is a short river and its six miles separate Loch Assynt from Inver Bay. It is here that in 1870, Dr. Almond caught a monster 27lb 4oz brown trout: the largest fish taken from this river. It is divided into three beats with the top and bottom beat being owned by the Ben More Estate, while the middle beat belongs to the Bradford family. The top beat is let through the Inver Lodge Hotel (05714) 496 at a cost of between £18 and £45 per rod per day according to season. The beat is roughly a mile long and in a good season can produce upwards of a hundred salmon as there are several good pools, including the noted Black Pool.

The Kircaig

The Inver Lodge Hotel may also be able to arrange fishing for you on the Kircaig which lies just south of the Inver and is on the boundary between Sutherland and Ross-shire. The salmon, as the Romans knew when they christened him, is a great leaper, but no fish could ascend the fifty foot Falls of Kirkaig so, although the catchment area of the river may be eighty square miles, it is only the two miles down from the falls that hold fish. The river is divided into three beats and only the lower beat will suit those of advanced years. The middle beat requires some agility, and on the upper beat, where the river becomes a raging torrent as it flows through the gorge, it is more advisable to wear climbing boots than waders!

White Shrimp, Ally's Shrimp (Mike Sugg)

Lochs Sionascaig & Oscaig

The A837 ends just south of Lochinver, but those with a sense of adventure will follow the secondary road to Inverpolly and Lochs Sionascaig and Oscaig (try saying these after a few wee ones!). This is the heart of the Inverpolly Nature Reserve and the unspoilt landscape of Wester Ross is some of the finest imaginable. Loch Sionascaig is some three and a half miles in width and set against the backdrop of Cul Mor, Cul Beag and Stac Polly which all rise above 2000 feet. The loch has many bays with half-pounders lying in wait. It also boasts scattered islands which are forbidden territory to anglers: teeming with wildlife they are a further attraction to a marvellous setting.

This is one of the few places left where, if you are lucky, you may see the majestic osprey. Rival he may be but there are no finer anglers than these magnificent birds. The loch is as deep as two hundred feet in places and these murky depths are the haunt of large ferox trout; one of 16lb 14oz was caught in 1989. Permits for this water and other lochs may be purchased from the Inverpolly Estate Office (0854) 82452. A day's boat fishing will cost £12, and an outboard motor can be hired for £8. Bank fishing is fly only and costs £3. The Garvie, which has a heritage as a sea-trout water, flows out of Loch Oscaig. The Summer Isles Hotel (085482) 282 can arrange permits for you to fish the loch, which offers good grilse fishing in high summer. A glance at the map will show you that this area is peppered with lochs and lochans nearly all of which will provide a good day's sport.

The Polly

The River Polly flows from Loch Scionascaig through the Polly Lochs to the sea at Polly Bay. There is a good run of grisle in the Polly from mid June onwards and in September 1991 the first ever salmon was taken on Loch Sionascaig. The fishing on the Polly is let on a weekly basis together with accommodation in Inverpolly Lodge (085482) 452. Prices range from £650 to £1210 per week.

The Ullapool & Loch Achall

A journey around the shore of Loch Lurgainn, which lies in the shadow of Cul Beag, will bring you back on to the A835 and a short distance south lies Ullapool. Apart from being able to take the ferry to the fishing delights of Lewis and Harris from here, there is also the River Ullapool and Loch Achall. The river is short and exciting and is divided into three beats. A day on the lower beat costs £5 while the cost for the upper beat is £15. Salmon on this river average around the 6lb mark and sea-trout, which can also be taken on Loch Achall and in the estuary, almost 2lb. Ullapool Angling Club issue permits through Ullasport (0854) 612621 on Argyll Street. All proceeds go towards stocking and Tom McDougall, the club secetary, has written a beginners guide to fishing in the area. Permits may also be obtained from the Highland Coastal Trading Company (0854) 612373. The main beat of the river, in addition to unique and remote salmon fishing on the Rappach River (a tributary of the Oykel River), is let through Rhidorroch House. The House, overlooking Loch Achall, sleeps thirteen. Fishing on the loch and numerous other hill lochs can be let with the House, details from (0854) 612548.

The majestic Loch Achall is abundant in brown trout and has some salmon and sea-trout fishing. There are three boats for hire and bank fishing is also allowed—all bookings through Ullasport (0854) 612621.

Flies by Mike Sugg

A precis of the joys of fishing in Scotland would not be complete without a word about the ghillie. A good ghillie is worth his weight in gold for no matter how often you may have fished a piece of water, there is always something new to learn. If you haven't fished the water before, the ghillie is an essential advisor and companion. They know if there are fish in a pool, where the lies are and what fly is likely to do the trick. As if that wasn't enough, they will also row for you. You can read all you like in books but there is nothing to beat the experience of the man on the spot who knows every mood of the water. They are men of many talents for they are often first class naturalists and can, if you are lucky, tie exactly the right fly for the particular state of the water. They are a fund of local lore and knowledge. Some people may be too proud to ask for their advice but they will really be poorer without it.

The Guinard & the Little Guinard

Coming south from Ullapool, the road follows the shore of Loch Broom. If you take the A382 coastal road you pass through the Dundonnell Forest. After skirting Little Loch Broom this road will bring you to Gruinard Bay, where the Gruinard and Little Gruinard end their journeys. These rivers are certainly more accessible today than they were in Victorian times. An old fishing guide suggests taking the train to Achnasheen, which is only fifty miles or so away and from there a coach service often runs for most of the rest of the way. There is no mention of the frequency of the service or how fishermen were to finally reach their destination! However, in those halcyon days there wasn't the pressure of modern office life and if one's holiday overran by a week or two it didn't matter. These are both spate rivers and while the salmon runs may not be what they were, there has been very good sea-trout fishing from July to September. The rivers are owned by Letter Erwe Estates (044584). Fishing is let with a cottage for around £800 plus VAT but there is a long waiting list here and no day permits are available.

The Gruinard drains Loch na Sealga which is famous for the fighting qualities of its brownies. There are salmon here too, and that tug on your line could be the start of a memorable fight as anyone who has caught a salmon on a trout rod will know! The Boat Pool is a favourite on the Little Gruinard where salmon average around 6lb and like its big sister, has good sea-trout water as does Loch Fionn. Trout here average half a pound although there are some bigger ferox. This loch is surrounded by mountains which funnel the wind down so rowing can be fairly strenuous, especially at the end of the day when a long pull may be required.

Loch Maree

Leaving Gruinard, the road meanders alongside Loch Ewe and then on to Poolewe. Do take a minute to stop and take deep breaths of the fresh Atlantic air—it's marvellously bracing and you also have the pleasure of a glorious Hebridean view if the weather's fair. The River Ewe drains Loch Maree and is one of the most celebrated examples of the long loch and short river systems. At just over a mile long the river is one of the shortest in Scotland. Fairly sluggish to begin with, the Ewe narrows. Many fine holding pools such as Hen, Manse and Tee Pools are produced, separated by white-water rapids. This river was first made famous by Sir Humphrey Davy who thought nothing of catching twenty or more salmon a day. However, times have changed, as they also have on Loch Maree. This is one of the most famous sea-trout fisheries in the world which in 1935 produced a record fish of 21lb. Up to the late 1960s double figure fish were not unusual but then came U.D.N. which pretty well wiped out these big sea-trout and catches declined. In recent years it has had other problems: escapee farm salmon are a threat to the native stocks, the netting of sand eels, which are the staple diet of sea-trout, not to mention seals. Indeed grey seals have often been sighted in the river and even at the head of the loch.

However, things are looking up for this famous water. In 1988 Frank Buckley took over as Fisheries Consultant and his tireless efforts have brought about many improvements. By involving the Duke of Edinburgh Award Scheme and other volunteers a hatchery has been built and the spawning grounds in the feeder burns, which had been choked, are now cleared. Dedicated work like this brings results and the last couple of years have seen a best salmon of 22lb, a sea-trout of 6½lb and a brownie of 4½lbs, with fifteen fish being caught in a day by one boat. Given another couple of good seasons, the loch may even be restored to its former glory as the best salmon and sea-trout loch in the country. Dapping is the favoured technique on these fourteen miles of water which are over 300 feet deep in places, though trolling is permitted up to the end of June. The Loch Maree Hotel (044584) 288 has the fishing rights on about two thirds of the loch and its water is divided into ten beats. Boats are available and the cost for a day's fishing for two rods including a boat is £15 from April until the end of June, rising to £25 for July and August and £20 from then until the close of the season in October. From July to the end of October fly fishing only is allowed. Trolling and spinning, however, are permitted in April, May and June.

Between Loch Maree and Loch Carron is an area of unspoilt countryside which has many good lochs such as Loch Damph, Lundie and Bad an Sgalaig. Roads are few and far between but those prepared to walk for their sport will have a memorable day. There are also some very good small spate rivers such as the Balgy, Torridon and Badachro. Fishing these rivers is a real delight and emphasises the overall high standard and availability of fishing in Scotland.

Loch Glascarnoch

Taking the A835 across country from the Braemore Forest will bring you to Loch Glascarnoch where the fishing is free! This three and a half mile long water is owned by the Hydro-Electricity Board. If you are thinking that any fishing which is free must be of poor quality, then reconsider. Members of the Inverness Angling Club, who fish the water regularly, will change your mind. South of here and below Fannich Forest is the fine water of Loch Fannich which is part of the River Conon system.

The Conon

For many years, not only the River Conon but also its tributaries and lochs have been dammed for hydro-electricity and this has naturally, or should I say unnaturally, affected water levels. Two of the dams have salmon counters which show a consistently good average number of fish. The system is also a notable brown trout water, for it was from Loch Garve, at the top of the Blackwater, that a monster of 26lb was caught in 1892. Frasers Newsagents at Strathpeffer (0997) 21346 issue permits for the four beats on the Upper Conon which is owned by Loch Achonachie Angling Club, at a cost of between £5 and £15 per day, according to season, and spinning is allowed when the water is up. Permits for fishing this part of the river are also available from the East Lodge Hotel at Strathconon (0997) 7222. This hotel can also issue permits for the Blackwater and sometimes arrange for guests to fish the Brora, Glass and Beauly.

Most Conon salmon are originally from the Blackwater. The hens are netted and stripped at the top of the upper beat and the eggs are hatched in the Contin hatchery. Fishing on the Blackwater can be arranged through Lady Elisa Leslie-Melville (09974) 242 or Mr R. Smith (090855) 586, alteratively contact the Craigdarroch Lodge Hotel (0997) 421265 which is conveniently situated about four hundred yards from the middle beat. The Fairburn Estate own part of the Middle Conon and lets are available from the Estate Office (0997) 3273. Some of this section is timeshared during the summer and autumn (although not the south bank owned by the above) but from January to the end of June lets can be obtained from either Savills in Brechin (0356) 22187 or the Coul House Hotel, Contin (0997) 21487 at a cost of between £50 and £400 (excluding VAT) per rod per week according to season. If this is too expensive, Seaforth Highland Estate (0349) 61150 can offer you trout fishing at £3.50 a day or £12 a week and also lets out several holiday cottages.

The Lower Conon may not be the same quality of fishing but it is more affordable. It is managed by Dingwall Angling Club and the cost is £15 a day. Permits may be obtained from the Sports and Model shop in Tulloch Street, Dingwall (0349) 62346. These permits also cover Lochs Achanalt, Chuillin and Luichart.

The Glass

Between Dingwall and Alness is the River Glass. This river is not to be confused with the water of the same name which is part of the Beauly system. It is totally different in character, quality of fishing and price. The river rises in several hill lochs under the shadow of Ben Wyvis before flowing into Loch Glass. This part of the river and downstream to the gorge is privately owned by the Wyvis Estate. Black Rock Gorge is over a mile long and is an awesome spectacle, for there is a sheer drop of up to two hundred feet and in some places it is only six feet wide. If standing on one of the footbridges looking at the raging torrent far below doesn't make your head spin, the smell of the wild garlic will! This grows so profusely that it is harvested twice a year by the cheese factory in Tain. From the gorge to Cromarty Firth the river is known as the Allt Graad and this three quarter mile stretch is divided into three beats. Permits may be had for £7 a day or £25 a season from Alcocks Newsagents in Evanton High Street (0349) 830672. The river is stocked on an annual basis and is the type of water that offers the chance of an occasional salmon or sea-trout at a very modest cost.

The Alness, the Blackwater & Loch Maree

A few miles north of the Glass lies the well known Alness (or Averon, as it is sometimes known). This used to be prolific sea-trout water but, like so many rivers, it has seen a decline in recent years, but the salmon fishing has improved and now averages four to six hundred fish a year. The best year in recent times was 1985 when over eight hundred fish were caught. Conifer plantations have encroached on the banks of this river and its main tributary, the Blackwater, and have led to flash floods which have done some damage to the spawning grounds. However, improvements are in hand and the river is stocked every year. Sea-trout average 1½lbs and salmon 6½lbs, though September usually sees some better fish of up to 20lb. The river, which is largely owned by Novar Estates (0349) 830208, drains Loch Morie. This is good brown trout water and also offers the chance of char and ferox which run well into double figures; the best for 1991 being 15lb 4oz. A day's fishing costs £15 for two rods including a boat. Water from the loch to Strath Rusdale is also owned by Novar Estates. Alness Angling Club (secretary Brian Poe (0349) 883963) lease one beat. Permits cost £16 a day between July and September and can be obtained from Pattersons Ironmongers in Alness High Street, (0349) 88286. The Castle Water, which extends to Dalreoch Burn, is private and retained for family and friends. So, if you're a friend of the family—good fishing. If not either get acquainted or find pastures new! Below the burn, Novar Estates have four beats. The cost of the Novar Estates water ranges from £12 to £35 per day per rod, weekly lets are sometimes available and trout fishing on their three top beats below the loch cost £3 per day. The Coul House Hotel at Contin (0997) 21487 can also arrange for guests to fish the Novar Estates water. Needless to say the advice is, as usual, to book as far in advance as possible.

The three watchwords for a fishing trip to the Highlands are undoubtedly Preparation, Preparation and Preparation! Hotels and river owners want their guests to catch fish and are only too pleased to give advice on flies. However, it never ceases to surprise them how many guests either never ask or wait until they have arrived to find out which are the favoured flies. A phone call before you go could transform an enjoyable holiday into a successful holiday. It is well worth checking all your tackle and making sure you have plenty of spare casts before leaving home, so be prepared and check before you go. If this sounds somewhat patronising—please forgive me. I am only reciting a lesson learnt from personal and bitter experience!

The Beauly

The Beauly is a superb salmon river and as a result it is very, very hard to get on! It is easy to assume that the desire to own salmon fishing stems from recent times but the Beauly has always been a prized water. After the estate had been forfeited following the Jacobite uprising of 1715, Lord Lovat asked his friend the Duke of Gordon to present a petition to the King. The request was that one *lea rig* behind the castle might be given to him and his heirs in perpetuity. Amused by such eccentricity, King George I granted the request only to find that lea rig in fact meant the river! A century and a half later the Master of Lovat proved just what a bargain had been extracted by taking 156 fish in five days. That is an average of thirty-one fish a day and was achieved using a twenty-five rod!

The Beauly is still a prolific salmon river and an average of 7000 fish a year are counted at the two dams. Catches of forty fish in a day are not uncommon, so it is not surprising that when Lovat Estates put seven beats on the market in 1990 the asking price was over £10m. The pur-

chaser, Landmatch PLC, formed The River Beauly Fishing Company (0763) 241181 to manage the now syndicated river. All the management are keen fishermen and the managing director is William Midwood, whose family used to own the Naver. The company is undertaking a variety of conservation measures and its stocking policy gives us great hope for future years; it also has a first class consultant in William Shearer, the leading salmon biologist. In 1990 the Falls, Home and Downie beats twice produced over a hundred fish in a week. Favoured pools on these beats include Glide, Castle, Charlies and Greenbank. As with most time-shared fishing, it is possible for outsiders to get the odd week and further details may be had from the company. In spite of the river's prestige, you don't have to be a millionaire to gain coveted access to it. A day's permit from Morrisons (0463) 782213 in Beauly's West End will enable you to fish the tidal water from below Lovat Bridge to Wester Lovat Farm at a cost of £8 a day (except Thursdays and Saturdays). Alternatively, for £3.50 a day you can also fish the North and South Estuary, where spinning is allowed.

The catchment area of the Beauly extends to beyond the Great Glen in the North West Highlands and the whole system has been harnessed for hydro-electric power, resulting in many dams and power stations. I am not sure if there is a collective noun for dams but there are many fishermen who have seen the character of rivers changed beyond recognition and would term the situation a damnation of dams! In the interests of fairness it must be pointed out that dams do have their uses and can help to maintain reasonable water levels, thus making a river fishable for longer periods.

This appears to be a river of many components. From the new dam at Loch Mullardoch a tunnel carries the

The River Beauly (River Beauly Fishing Company)

water through Loch Beinn a' Mheadhoin and thence to the River Affric which goes on to join up with the River Glass. Water from Mullardoch also forms the River Invercannick, which itself later joins the River Glass. The Glass is joined by the Farrar below Struy and, at the confluence of these two streams, the Beauly is born.

All these tributaries are outstanding salmon streams. Fishing of this quality is understandably hard to come by but Lovat Estates (0463) 782205 have six beats on the right bank of the River Glass. A week's permit will cost you in the region of £40 plus VAT per rod. Season tickets per rod vary from £1000 plus VAT for May up to August 24th, after which the cost is £1500 up to the end of the season on October 15th. L.A.H.Mure Esq., (0456) 5251 has two miles of the left bank of the Glass which are divided into three two-rod beats. Understandably these beats are quickly snapped up. F. Spencer-Nairn Esq., (0463) 76285 may be able to help with fishing on the Farrar and also let cottages.

Lochs Monar & Mullardoch

The Glen Affric Hotel (0456) 415214 issues permits for the fine trout waters of Lochs Monar and Mullardoch, where good bags of 20lb fish or more are possible in the right conditions. The cost of £25 a day includes a boat with a maximum of four rods. The hotel also has a fly casting school—this could be the chance to brush up your technique. It always surprises me that many first class shots will go to a shooting school before the start of the season to get their eye in again, yet once a fisherman thinks (and I repeat thinks!) he has mastered the art of casting he rarely bothers to seek expert guidance again. I know that at the start of every season my casting is pretty rough and it always requires a few days practice before the fly is landing where I want it to. Time at a casting school is never wasted, for one can always improve one's technique and learn new tactics.

The Torridon

The River Torridon is owned by the Loch Torridon Hotel (0445) 791242. A day on this river is available to guests at a cost of £13.50 a day. This is a flash spate river and can be quite reasonable fishing.

Grouse and Claret, Garry Peg, Munroe Killer, Greenwells Glory, March Brown, Blue Zulu (Rosemary

The question that every honest fisherman dreads having to ask, usually after a blank week, or even day, is where is the next salmon going to come from? The problem is that, like most other things, salmon fishing is a very inexact art. Trout, by way of contrast, are somewhat easier to assess. If a fish is rising and you can match the hatch there is a fair chance of catching him. As we know, salmon do not feed when they swim up a river, and as a result it is extremely difficult to predict taking times. It would appear nevertheless that early morning, around lunchtime and evening are the optimum times. This is the same pattern as trout and we all look forward to the evening rise and will often stay out until the light goes. So why is it a different story with salmon? Part of the problem is that, understandably, ghillies go home for their tea at around 5.30 pm! After a day on the river the thought of a bath, a dram and some good eating is a very appealing prospect—after all, this is meant to be a holiday! But if you want to catch a fish, I strongly urge you to fish on. It is surely no coincidence that many big fish—including Miss Ballantine's—were taken late on in the day.

The Ness System

The Ness System is the largest catchment area in the Highlands and at twenty-five miles long the loch is monster sized! However, the river is only about six miles long. It used to be regarded as the queen of Scottish rivers due to very productive yields and its great width. A fish that inhabits wide open waters will give a much better fight than his cousin in a small river, who has less water to manoeuvre in. Steam navigation and the Caledonian Canal were thought to be the culprits, for the decrease in salmon and the value of the fishing fell from £1100 p.a.—a considerable sum in Victorian times, to a quarter of that amount. This queen may have lost her crown, but the Ness is still a respectable salmon river.

As with so many other rivers, the spring runs are a mere shade of times gone by but this has been more than compensated for by the increase in the summer runs of salmon and grilse. The Ness is a wide river and early season spinners will use a ten-foot rod and when the fly comes into its own from June onwards, you will need a carbon rod of fifteen feet or more. At the end of a day's fishing with such a rod you will be more than ready for a bath and a large dram or two! Inverness Angling Club has three miles of both banks where fly, worm and spinning are allowed. The cost of a day's fishing is £12 and permits can be obtained from J. Graham & Co., the tackle dealer (0463) 233178. Above the club water is Ness-side where lets are handled by Angus Mackenzie & Co., (0463) 235353. These beats have produced some good fish, with a lady taking a twenty-four pounder in 1990 and in 1989 a gentleman of the cloth had a twenty-five pounder. Next is the mile or so of Ness Castle water where the agent is Mr R. M. Robertson (0542) 22411. Beyond this is the time-shared Laggan water which is factored by Mr G.S. Dawson (031) 449 3973. Weekly lets

may sometimes be available. Finally, there is the Dochfour Estate beats and further details may be had from the Estate Office (0463) 86218.

Due to its size, fishing from a boat on Loch Ness can prove hazardous if there is a wind whipping up white horses. The golden rule is, if in doubt, don't go out. While the fly works well for sea-trout, trolling with two spinning rods is the favoured method for salmon which can run up to 30lb. The fishing is privately owned but hotels such as Inchnacardoch Lodge Hotel (0320) 6258 and Whitebridge Hotel (0456) 3226 may be able to help. The Glenmoriston Lodge Estate, whose Head Keeper is Mr Alastair Mackintosh, also has two boats on the loch; including outboards they cost £30 a day per rod. In 1990 these boats accounted for sixty-nine salmon.

The Moriston

Glenmoriston Lodge Estate (0320) 51219 can also offer good trout fishing on twenty one hill lochs and eight miles of salmon fishing on the River Moriston. The cost of a day's fishing varies between £20 and £40 according to season. Mr Macintosh's own pattern, the Wee Tosh is particularly successful, but old favourites like the Hairy Mary and Stoats Tail work well. Seven miles of the headwaters of this river are owned by the Cluanie Inn (0320) 40238 and offer the occasional salmon at a cost of only a few pounds a day. One should not expect top class fishing but for a modest sum you are at least in the running for a catch. No permit is needed for fishing on Loch Cluanie. A boat for two rods and a day's fishing on the delightful Loch Ruthven can be had for £10 from R.Humfrey Esq., (0808) 3283. These 375 acres produce good fighting brownies averaging around the pound mark, which are often taken on the local favourite fly—the Badger.

The Enrick

The River Enrick rises in Loch nan Eun and flows alongside the A831 on its course through Loch Meiklie to enter Loch Ness at Urquhart Bay. The fishing is generally unexceptional but the scenery is gorgeous. Permission for the Enrick can be obtained from Mr R. Sorenson at Kilmartin Hall (0456) 476269. Mrs Elizabeth Taylor (0456) 476275, Kilmartin House, may not have any Oscars on her mantlepiece but she does issue permits to fish Loch Meiklie at £6 a day (9.00 am—3.30 pm) including a boat. This super little fly-only loch has beautifully marked pink-fleshed trout which average one pound and any under twelve inches should be returned.

Loch Quoich & the Garry

Loch Quoich covers some four thousand acres and is the kind of water where an outboard is essential. As with any water of this size, weather conditions are an important factor, but on the right day, the fishing can be excellent and may be had for £22 a day for a boat with an outboard and fuel. The Gearr Garry drains this loch and flows through Lochs Poulay, Inchlaggan and Garry. Tomdoun Hotel (0809) 2218 can arrange for you to fish all the waters and also has three and a half miles of salmon fishing on the north bank of the River Garry, which is free to hotel guests. Fishing the south bank is through Garry Gualach Ltd (0809) 2230, who run sporting holidays and can arrange shooting and stalking for you, should you wish to swap rod for rifle. A nymph fished on a sinking tip may well prove to be the downfall of a big 4lb plus Arctic char on Loch Garry which is also excellent trout water. Mr J.Morgan at Ardochy Lodge (0809) 2232 has rights for salmon and trout fishing but as he says, the loch is large and the salmon are few. R.B.Scott Esq., at the Invergarry Post Office (0809) 3201 can arrange for you to fish the Garry between Loch Garry and Loch Oich at a cost of £25 a day. The price also includes salmon fishing on Loch Oich, where trout fishing may be had from Glengarry Castle Hotel (0809) 3254 for free, although a boat will cost £5 for a half, or £9 for a full day.

Inexpensive salmon fishing can also be had on the River Shiel. £10 is the price for a day; contact Mrs Campbell (0599) 81282. A few miles west is Glenelg, which is just across the water from Skye. Here you will find the lovely Glenelg Inn, which arranges marvellous ceilidhs and a very original form of pub crawl, using inflatable dinghies! Before anyone writes to say that the Shiel cannot be so cheap, I would point out that this is the one that flows into Loch Duich.

The Shiel

The other River Shiel (forty miles south) that drains the Loch of the same name is a totally different kettle of fish! This is another example of the long loch and short river system. These rivers can produce those great days we all dream of. The river is only three miles long. By comparison, the loch is some eighteen miles in length and for its size it is one of the narrowest in Scotland. Although there can be excellent summer runs of salmon and grilse, the river is probably best known for its sea-trout fishing. Unless there is a breeze to stir the water, which is fairly slow, night fishing is likely to prove the most productive method. Catches may not be what they were thirty years ago, yet the loch still ranks among the best sea-trout waters. An old advertisement for the Shiel Hotel offers fishing for five shillings a day! Alas, today it is one of those rivers that is almost impossible to get on unless you are prepared to wait fifteen or twenty years before fishing such pools as Garrison, Grassy Point and Parapet. Still, if you are looking for a long term plan then this is a tremendous water. Write to: R.S.—L.S.D.F.B., c/o C. Kennedy Esq, Robertson Neilson & Co., 95 Bothwell Street, Glasgow G2 7JH.

Artist: Wendy Reeves Fisherman's Paradise Courtesy of Rosenstiel's

Loch Shiel

Loch Shiel is much more accessible and what is more, it must also be one of the prettiest in Scotland. The Jacobite uprising of 1745 began here, for it was on the shores of Loch Shiel that Bonnie Prince Charlie raised his flag. This used to be very good sea-trout water but like so many others, has seen a decline in numbers caught in recent years. Because this is such a large loch, salmon are usually trolled for. Make sure you tackle up, as twenty-pounders are not uncommon and the best fish in recent years was a forty-two pounder. There are many sand and gravel bays which provide excellent spawning grounds and a good spot for a picnic lunch while admiring the soaring mountains that surround you. It is also good trout water with an average of three quarters of a pound, and two-pounders are not uncommon here. The Stage House Inn (0397) 83246 and the Glenfinnan House Hotel (0397) 83235 at the eastern end and Loch Shiel Hotel (0967) 85224 and Clanranald Hotel (0967) 85662 at the western end all have boats and can offer a day's fishing at around £15. Guests of E.Macaulay of Dalilea Farm (0967) 85253 will find the price of their accommodation includes fishing and boats with outboards. The Road to the Isles, (A830) can be found at the northern end of Loch Shiel and, if you travel west on this road, you will find two jewels, the River Ailort and Loch Eilt. A week's fishing, which includes both the river and the loch, costs £250 from Salar Management Services Ltd (0667) 55355.

Loch Morar

As we continue westwards we come to Loch Morar, which lies a few miles south of Mallaig. There is also a railway service to Mallaig, which must be one of the prettiest train journeys one could wish for. Not terribly practical for fishermen, but a marvellous journey—should the motor fail you. The loch is twelve and a half miles long and while there are salmon and sea-trout, it is mainly a trout water. A permit for bank fishing is available at £2.50 a day per person per rod and a boat with an outboard can be hired for £16.00. Permits may be had from Morar Motors or Loch Morar Adventure Centre (0687) 2164. The Morar Hotel (0687) 2346 has three boats for guests and can also arrange fishing on several hill lochs.

The Nevis

Returning eastwards one finds Fort William, where you can fish in the shadow of Ben Nevis—Britain's highest mountain. There is no better way to appreciate the grandeur of the mighty Ben than by fishing the River Nevis which skirts round it. Snow from the peaks above the glen help to maintain reasonable water levels for most of the season, although it can run low. It is essentially a spate river and thus all depends on getting the right conditions. On its day it can produce terrific fishing, especially for sea-trout which average about a pound, while salmon are about the 6lb mark. A day's permit costs £5 from the Rod and Gun Shop (0397) 702656 in Fort William.

The Lochy

The Nevis joins the River Lochy just before it flows into Loch Linnhe. The Lochy is the largest and best salmon river in the area and so very hard to get on. It is largely owned by the River Lochy Association, a group of private owners, and the waiting list is long. Wading can be particularly dangerous as there is a power station at the western end of Loch Lochy. If it starts to generate, the water level can rise very quickly, so it is safest to fish the larger pools from a boat. Beat 7, which stretches from the tidal waters to a mile above Fort William, is available from the Rod and Gun Shop (0397) 702656 at a cost of between £17 and £22 a day. This is good water which produces about 450 salmon a year, some of which exceed 28lb.

The Spean

Heading north from Fort William on the A82 will bring you to Spean Bridge with its famous war memorial. It was in this area that the brave Commandos did much of their training during the Second World War. In the days before fishing conservation was treated seriously, the headwaters and the feeder lochs of the River Spean were harnessed to provide power for the British Aluminium plant, which would have wiped it out as a salmon river were it not for its main tributary the river Roy. As a result, the best fishing is from Roybridge down to the Lochy. The Spean Bridge Hotel (0397) 712250 can offer guests fishing on the stretch between the old viaduct and Wade Bridge at a cost of £10 a day. The Rod and Gun shop may be able to help you get on other beats of this river and many other waters in the area. This is a good river where sea-trout average 1½lb and salmon 8lb; but it has a deserved reputation for producing big fish—a 37 pounder was caught in 1976

The Roy

Is there a river that has not had its character changed and harmed by man? Well, yes! There are thankfully a few and one is the Roy, which rises close to Loch Spey, the source of that great river from which it takes its name. How refreshing it is to find such a river that has been left to its own devices. The fish like it too—for nearly all salmon and sea-trout which run the Spean are heading for the Roy. It is very much a spate river and as there is no loch for it to drain it can make for a very frustrating time with weather against you. Permits may be had from the Roy Bridge Hotel (0397) 712236 and Stronlossit Hotel (0397) 712253 for £15 a day. Mrs Irene Pryke (0449) 741481 lets three beats which rotate and can also offer self-catering accommodation. There are two rods on each beat and currently the cost is £12 per day per rod.

Lochs Lochy & Arkaig

Fishing is free on Loch Lochy, which is the most western loch in the Caledonian Canal system. It is almost solely a trout water but there are five-pounders for those prepared to work at fishing this deep water. Boat moorings are controlled by the West Highland Estate Office (0397) 702433 who also issue permits for Loch Arkaig at £2 per day. Before the Caledonian Canal was built this loch abounded in salmon. An old game book records the following: 67 fish in a week, 289 fish in a month, 19 fish in a morning and one week only produced 37 fish, beside which is written 'disappointing'—all these fish were to two rods. If only all fishing was similarly disappointing!

For the intrepid wanderers among our brethren (and who of us doesn't have a certain degree of wanderlust?) there are the Islands, each of which has its own unique delights and pleasures for the visiting fisherman. With ferries and air flights, communications are much easier than they used to be. In the early nineteenth century Colonel Jameson was invited to stay with a friend on Lewis to enjoy some fishing and stalking. At Ullapool the weather was against him and it was eight days before he could get across. The sport began in earnest and every day's entry for a period of five weeks records a good day with salmon, sea-trout, trout and stalking. The least successful day records two sea-trout of 1½lb and 2lb and a fight with a hefty salmon who broke him; whereas the best day produced eleven salmon, four sea-trout and some good trout. Getting back to the mainland was a problem and he had to wait three days for the weather to improve. On his way back to Lancashire the axle of the coach broke. However, the local laird invited him to stay and so much did he enjoy the trout fishing, that it was two weeks before he made his departure. Those were the days!

Just across the Firth of Lorne is Mull, one of the most beautiful islands of the Inner Hebrides. Here you will find pine forests, wild moorlands, deserted beaches, mountains and the famous fossil tree preserved in the lava of Ben More millions of years ago. You are unlikely to find gold, but it is certainly there! A Spanish ship carrying a large quantity of gold to pay troops sank off Tobermory during the time of the Armada. But despite many attempts no-one has yet found the wreck. From a fishing point of view there are good spate rivers for salmon and trout and several noted trout lochs.

The Aros

The Aros is perhaps the best known river for it was here that in 1911 a 45lb salmon was taken on Ash Tree Pool after a six hour fight—the main run on this river, which is just under five miles long, is in July but this may be later if there is a hot dry summer. Salmon average 7lb and it is also noted for its sea-trout which usually tip the scales at around 1½lb but run up to 3lb.

Loch Frisa

Nearby is Loch Frisa where salmon and sea-trout are often seen but seldom caught. It is, however, an excellent trout water and being quite dangerous by island standards, is best fished from a boat. Do be careful if the wind is up for the loch can be quite bold. Permits are available from the Forestry Commission (0680) 300346 at £2 per day for bank fishing or £15 to include a boat. The Forestry Commission also issue permits for the River Lussa with its famous Pedlars Pool. This is very much a spate river and fish may take some time to ascend the waterfall at Tor Ness. Most of the bigger fish, including a thirty-four pounder, have been taken below the falls.

Salmon and sea-trout are about the same size as in Aros and it is widely regarded as one of the best rivers on the island.

The Forsa, the Ba & the Coladoir

Arguably the best fishing is to be had on the River Forsa. At ten miles long it is the longest river and has some forty pools—double figure fish of up to 18lb are caught, though the average is around 8lb. Like so many of these island spate rivers it rises and falls very quickly and is best fished when in spate. Another fine river is the two and a half mile long Ba which is privately owned. There is a big pool near its mouth at Killiechronan where you can often see salmon and sea-trout waiting to run—an invigorating sight. The River Coladoir has four miles of pools broken by gentle falls and offers good sea-trout fishing and the occasional salmon. Another fine sea-trout water is the River Bellart on which it is possible to catch a dozen in a day. But those will often be finnock (small sea-trout) and once you have caught enough for supper, you are urged to return any further catches so as to conserve stocks for the future.

Lochs Torr, Ba & Assapoll

At the northern end of the island is Loch Torr which was purpose-built for fishing in 1899. This is a fly-only water which is stocked with rainbows and brownies and produces the occasional salmon and sea-trout. If trouting is more your thing then do try the three Mishnish lochs which lie between Dervaig and Tobermory or lochs Pellach, Meadhoin and Carnain an Amis.

Loch Ba, like the river of the same name, is let by Killiechronan Estates (0680) 300438. This loch fishes very well for salmon and especially sea-trout—double figure fish are not uncommon! Sguabain is Gaelic for windswept and the loch certainly lives up to its name. Weed is a problem here so take care when playing your fish. At the southern end of the island on Ross of Mull is Loch Assapoll where salmon average 8lb and sea-trout 2lb. This is superb fishing and the loch is also famous for its brownies which run up to 7lb.

Tackle and Books in Tobermory (0688) 2336 can arrange for you to fish most waters as can many hotels like the lovely Western Isles Hotel (0688) 2012) which is also in Tobermory.

The Laggan & the lochs of Islay

Just south of Mull are the islands of Islay and Jura, names to conjure with for any lover of malt whisky. Most salmon fishing on Islay is privately owned, but not impossible to attain. The cost for a rod per week is in the region of £240 and fishing begins on the 1st of July with the salmon running to a reasonable average of 7¼lb. This great little spate river does not really require wading as you can fish from the both banks. The Islay Estate has various four rod packages for the Rivers Sorn, Grey and the Laggan. In addition, fishing on many lochs, including Loch Gorm can be had, the latter is very shallow so watch out for rocks when boating. Salmon fishing averages at about £400 per four rods per week from Mr B.Wiles at the Headkeeper's House, Bridgend (049681) 293. The Machrie Hotel (0496) 2310 in Port Ellen has great brown trout fishing on the Machrie Burn and is also a good centre for any holiday. The Port Askaig Hotel (049684) 245 organises bookings for the Dunlossit Estate. As well as three beats on the river Laggan they have six very good trout lochs with Ballygrant, Lossit and Allan providing the best fishing. Wet and dry flies both do well and bank fishing costs £4 for an evening, £8 for a half and £12 for a full day. Incidentally, you will not need your hiking boots, as these three gems are accessible from the road.

The Lussa

Walking boots of some description are something of a must for Jura. This wild and wonderful island has only one road, which finishes at the cottage where George Orwell completed *1984*. Fishing on this island, famed for its stalking (*jura* is gaelic for island of deer) is predominantly for brown trout. However, the River Lussa when in spate can produce interesting salmon and sea-trout fishing. Contact Mr C.Fletcher at the Ardlussa Estate in Ardlussa (0496) 82323.

The Machrie

Across from Kintyre we come upon the delightful isle of Arra, more renowned for breathtaking scenery than its game fishing and dominated by the 2868 foot high Goat Fell. However, the Machrie river can produce good sport, especially from dusk onwards and the salmon tend to average around the 6lb mark. Contact Mr J.T. Boscawen at the Strathtay Estate Office, Boltachan, By Aberfeldy, Perthshire (0887) 820496. Prices vary between £90 and £145 per rod per week. For the River Iorsa and its loch contact the Dougarie Estate Office (0770) 84259.

Skye Waters

Separated from Mull by the Ardnamurchan Peninsular—the most westerly point of the mainland—is Skye and its romantic associations with Bonnie Prince Charlie and Flora Macdonald. Being relatively easy to get to, it is popular with tourists and likely to get much busier with the proposed new road bridge. Ullinish Lodge Hotel (0470) 72214 has the rights for the River Ose and the upper four miles of the River Snizort and fishing is available to guests at between £10 and £15 a day depending on condi-

tions. Fishing on the lower eight miles of the Snizort is available to guests of the Skeabost House Hotel (0470) 32202 at a cost of £10 per day. Both hotels can also arrange trout fishing on lochs as can the Misty Isle Hotel (0470) 22208 on the shore of Loch Dunvegan. This is run by experienced fishermen who can also arrange sea fishing. Permits for the Uig Angling Association water on the River Hinnisdale are available from the bar of the Ferry Inn (0470) 42242 at £15 a day. As one would expect, these are spate streams and rain is the all important factor. Portree Angling Association can offer visitors a wide choice of loch and some river fishing and permits may be had from Jansport in Portree (0478) 612559 at a cost of between £3 and £5 a day.

Scots and fishermen consider that Lewis, Harris, North Uist, Benbecula and South Uist make up the Western Isles. If you have the opportunity to visit, do go. They are a fisherman's paradise. There is outstanding salmon and sea-trout fishing and literally hundreds of trout lochs. The Islands' remoteness ensures that you can enjoy your fishing in perfect tranquillity, disturbed only by the sight of red deer on the hills or rare birds like the red-necked phalarope. I strongly advise you to make sure your fly box is suitably filled before coming here as tackle shops are few and far between. The Stoats Tail is a popular choice for salmon, while for sea-trout I would take traditional patterns such as the Peter Ross, the Mallard and Claret, Silver Invicta, some Zulus, a Wickham's Fancy, a Goat's Toe and my old favourite, the Muddler Minnow.

The Grimersta & the lochs of Lewis

Lewis has several hundred lochs full of hard fighting wild brownies which can go up to 6lb. The Grimersta is a great river by national as well as island standards, and one of the most prolific waters you could wish for—fifty-seven fish taken on the fly in one day is a record that will take some beating. The fishing is owned by a syndicate which was formed by Lord Leverhulme in 1922 and is managed by Grimersta Estates Office (0851) 72358. The river itself is only some two miles long, above which is a chain of lochs culminating in Loch Langavat which, at seven miles long, is the longest on the islands. It is fly-only water except for Langavat where spinning is also permitted. A favoured technique is to fish a very small fly on the point and something much larger like a Muddler Minnow tied on a size 6 as a dropper. There are four beats, and such famous pools as Bridge, Battery, Captains and Sea Pool. While Autumn may be the best time, May and June can produce catches of up to fifty fish a week but are not so predictable.

The Laxay

There are three miles of the River Laxay above Loch Valtos and one mile below it. River fishing is mainly on the three pools of the lower section which are appropriately named Top, Middle and Lower: the loch is divided into beats each with a boat and a ghillie. Sea-trout average 1½lb and salmon 7lb though a 33lb fish was caught back in 1933. The Creed is another good river. Its five miles are divided into four single rod beats which rotate on a daily basis while its loch is fished by two boats. The river flows through Lady Levers park with its magnificent rhododendrons and noted pools include Fall, Bond and Junction. A day's bank fishing permit costs £10 from the Stornoway Trust Estate Office (0851) 702002, and £16 will pay for a boat and one rod. The Blackwater fishes well especially on the lower section which has some good holding pools. It is aptly named for the river is rather peaty and you will probably find that a fly with some orange or yellow will work best. The Uig is very much a spate river but if you hit it in the right conditions it can be very good. It was near here that the famous 12th century Lewis chessmen were found. Scaliscro Estates (085175) 325 can offer salmon and sea-trout fishing on the Rivers Creed and Blackwater and six lochs including Langavat. It also offers trout fishing on nine other lochs. The trout fishing is superb. Take for example Loch Fhreunadail where the trout average half a pound and the best day's log was fifty-five. The premier loch in my opinion is Loch Bruiche Breivat where they average ³/₄lb and run to 4lb plus. The most successful day record here was one hundred brownies and two Arctic char! Trout fishing on Lewis is superb but do be prepared to walk or hire an argocat to get you across country.

Harris Waters

Harris is world famous for its tweeds and no visit would be complete without a visit to see how they are made. Guests of the North Harris Estate (085986) 200 can stay at Amhuinnsuidhe Castle which is the most westerly castle in the country and enjoy fishing on eight large lochs where salmon range from 5-8lb and sea-trout 1-5lb, though there are bigger fish as the records are 18³/₄lb and 11 lb. Other good fishing on Harris includes the Scarista and Horsacleit which is very much a spate stream. The Rodel Hotel at Leverburgh (08598) 2210 offers guests good salmon, sea-trout and brown trout fishing on a number of lochs. Ardvourlie Castle (0859) 2307 is a great place to stay if you are fishing in the area. Here on the shores of Loch Seaforth you can see otters and if you are lucky golden eagles. The lunches are both sumptuous and scenic. It is not unknown for an eagle to time his fly-past as you are seated—a marvellous diversion, wouldn't you agree?! Fishing for guests can be arranged on the nearby Aline Estate which boasts some first class water.

Loch Nan Geireann

Lochmaddy Hotel (0876) 3331 is the place to stay for fishing North Uist and Benbecula or if you wish to be independent from the hotel, the North Uist Estate Office (0876) 3329 will be able to help you. There are many first class trout lochs and the Skelter System offers salmon and sea-trout fishing. At the northern end of the island is Loch Nan Geireann. Here, at low tide, there is a tidal pool where you can see salmon and sea-trout leaping and splashing in the clear shallow water, a sight that will delight any fisherman.

Lochs of South Uist

The Lochboisdale Hotel (0878) 4332 manages most of the fishing on South Uist, which has some of the best Hebridean fishing. Two-pound trout are the norm rather than the exception when fishing Grogarry Loch which fishes well from the bank as well as from a boat. Other good lochs include Bornish, Kildonan and Stilligarry. Lochs Howmore, Ollay, Fada and Roag are known for their salmon and superb sea-trout, which run up to 8lb and are often over 4lb. It is also worth emphasising once more the scenic beauty of these islands, field glasses are almost as important as your hip flask.

Although Orkney is only six miles across the Pentland Firth from Caithness, it was part of the Viking Kingdom of Norway and Denmark until 1468. The islands are rich in history, something the locals are proud of. Here you can see the standing stones of Stenness, a small circle dating from the third millenium BC. Close by is Maes Howe, the finest chambered tomb in Western Europe built before 2700 BC. It houses the largest collection of runic inscriptions to be found in any one place in the world! Beneath the waters of Scapa Flow are the remains of the seventy-two German Naval vessels scuttled in 1919. It is also the only place where you will see a round hazard sign for otters crossing the road.

Loch Harray

From a fishing point of view there is some of the best trout water in the world. At 2528 acres Loch Harray is the largest Orkney water. With an average depth of eight feet and rarely exceeding fourteen feet it is perfect trout water. There are good hatches of midges, olives, sedges and later on daddy-longlegs while an abundant supply of freshwater shrimp helps to give the flesh a lovely pink colour. Although a seventeen-pounder was caught thirty years ago they average about three quarters of a pound. However, these fish will fight like nothing you have met before and many an experienced angler has been convinced that he must be into at least a two pounder from the way it has fought and has been surprised to find that when brought to the net it is only a one pound fish. These fish are very surface active and fast risers so quick reactions are needed. The Merkister Hotel (0856) 77366 is an ideal place to stay as the manager, Angus MacDonald, is a local expert.

Lochs of Orkney

Loch Swannay may be only a quarter of the size of Harray but it is a favourite with the locals and produces fish of 2lb and more with amazing regularity. Good baskets in recent years have been ten fish for 17½lb, four for 8¼lb and three for 12½lb—need we say more?! Loch Stennes is famous for the record 29lb fish taken at the turn of the century and today fish of 5-7lb are caught quite often. This is the one loch where it is worth casting a fly over the weed beds as these make good cover for trout avoiding the attention of the seals present throughout the year. It also serves as a larder, for these trout are piscivorous—one fish's bulging stomach revealed a twelve-inch eel, fifteen spined stickleback, lugworm and coalfish, as well as more normal samples of diet like midge, snails and daddy-longlegs. Two other good lochs are Boardhouse and Hundland, which often fishes well in bright conditions. There are also several other smaller waters. Good Orkney flies include Black Pennell, Zulu, Invicta, Soldier Palmer, Dunkeld, Alexandra and local favourites like the Loch Ordie. There are no rivers and the only lochs for sea-trout are Stennes and Kirbister, but sea-trout can be caught in the bays and shorelines of the coastline. Further details may be had from the Orkney Tourist Board (0856) 872856. The Orkney Trout Fishing Association have a beat on Loch of Skaill. The trout here average at around 2lbs. Muddlers and Whickams Fancy are recommended flies and all you have to do to enjoy this fishing is join the association! As a visiting angler you can expect to pay £10, unless you are a pensioner, in which case £6 will cover the cost. Further details may be had from the Secretary, M. Russell Esq. (0856) 76586

Lochs of Shetland

The Shetland Islands are closer to Norway than Scotland and for hundreds of years were allowed to run their own affairs without interference from the mainland. Then oil was discovered in the North Sea and the islands were developed. However the trout are still there and there are hundreds of lochs with good fighting brownies of up to 8lb and more; an added bonus for fishermen is that there are no midges here. Favourite lochs include Tingwall, which is regularly stocked with native-bred fish, Benston where the average is 1½lb and Girlsta which produced the 12½lb record for Shetland.

The outer islands have good fishing too. Whalsay has three first class lochs including Huxter. Unst has Lochs Cliff and Snarravoe and good sea-trout fishing at Burra Firth and Dales Voe. Yell has sea-trout and brownies in Loch Papil. Even tiny Fetlar has three lochs and you may see a snowy owl.

As on Orkney, salt water spinning in the Voes is the thing for sea-trout and a strip of mackerel belly on the treble may help. The same flies as suggested for Orkney should do the trick though you might care to add a Ke-He. All this fishing is available for £10 for a season, £7 a week or just £2 a day by joining the Shetland Anglers' Association whose secretary is Mr A. Miller (0595) 3729. The Association publishes a particularly useful booklet which includes maps, hints on technique and specific information on over one hundred lochs. Alternatively, the Shetland Isles Tourist Board (0595) 3434 will be able to help and advise you.

Artist: John Oldfield TIGHT LINES

The Highlands of Scotland are some of the most remote and delightfully unspoilt regions of Britain. The accommodation to be found ranges from the matter of fact to the grandiose but the fishing is invariably outstanding. The Melvich Hotel (06413) 206 is a comfortable country hotel which is situated at the mouth of the river Halladale. It enjoys magnificent sea views over the Pentland Firth to the Orkneys and makes a good centre for all manner of country pursuits, with salmon and trout fishing predictably taking pride of place. The Melvich also boasts a range of over 100 malt whiskies and some splendid Highland cooking.

The Forsinard (0641) 7221 is another great favourite for those fishing the Halladale. The lodge here is particularly good for parties. The hotel's loch fishing is first class and the variety of waters that the visitor has available adds to the appeal. The hotel is set up as a sporting establishment and succeeds bountifully in its objective. It is also a friendly, hospitable place to pass away the time before your next foray onto waters new.

Halkirk is home to the Ulbster Arms (0847) 83206, a celebrated sporting hotel which strives to maintain consistently high standards. Good food and abundant friendliness makes this a great fishing favourite. The hotel itself stands on the banks of the Thurso which will captivate the hearts of all fine fishermen. Imagine yourself—glass in hand, the memories of the day sift through your mind and the promise of more fine fishing tomorrow—marvellous!

Loch Watten, a superb fishing loch is extremely convenient for the Mount Pleasant House (0955) 82372. There are numerous other lochs in the area and this small modern hotel is a good base from which to tackle them. The hotel is also convenient for Wick airport which is a useful communication point for those fisherman who are seeking to reduce the journey time, which can be long and tortuous by car.

Scotland's hotels are often close to water and many of them are riparian owners or have access to lochs or rivers that run nearby. Failing this, the hotelier, as a community figure, will often know someone who knows someone else, or will be able to help! Those hotels that do not have their own water often enjoy spectacular settings or boast first class facilities or restaurants. Fishing hotels may sometimes be more modestly equipped, but as long as the beds are comfy and the bar full, many of us will be more than happy. There are a growing number of self-catering lodges to be found in Scotland and many fishermen will have been travelling to more established dwellings for years! They will not need advice on their own patch but will hopefully find other points of interest to enjoy while journeying, or as a diversion, to try a new water. There will be hotels that are modestly priced, there will be some that are somewhat expensive, but all should serve you well on your excursions through Scotland.

Halladale to Wick

The Altnaharra Hotel (054981) 222 is a renowned fishing venue which has recently seen some excellent improvements in its facilities, done without jeopardizing the charm of this former coaching inn. There are numerous outdoor pursuits that can be arranged from the hotel but the memorabilia on the walls leave the fisherman in little doubt that this is a real home from home. The whole atmosphere is one of peace, tranquillity and the great outoors. Two annexed cottages are well equipped for slightly larger groups or families and add to the twenty or so comfortable bedrooms.

There are numerous opportunities for enjoying some of the wildest and most beautiful landscapes in Britain and should you be venturing to the rugged delights of Cape Wrath then we suggest you visit Kinlochbervie en route. Here the Kinlochbervie Hotel (0971) 82275 is a companionably remote place at which to take stock. The hotel stands on an isolated hillside overlooking the sea and the bustling lounge bar is an excellent place to consider plans for the rest of your trip. The hotel does not proclaim to be a fishing hotel but it is worth a visit just the same, not least for its excellent restaurant where the smoked salmon from the hotel smokery is an absolute must. Lobster and game are also excellent and if you fancy a break from the fishing this is certainly one for the shortlist.

Even further north we come upon Cape Wrath—a wild, remote but captivating part of Britain. Here the Cape Wrath Hotel (0971) 511212 offers some super fishing and provides a splendid welcome to all fishermen and many others beside. It is easy to understand why so many people in high pressure business love to fish. The reasons are simple. Firstly, fishing like golf is a great leveller, you might be able to buy the water but that does not guarantee you the fish. Secondly, fishing provides a thorough and undivided escape, a visit to the welcoming Cape Wrath Hotel will allow thorough relaxation far removed from the seemingly nonsensical pace of the twentieth century.

Somewhat further round this marvellous coast we arrive at Tongue. Here the Ben Loyal (084755) 216 is a small but extremely friendly hotel. Good value lunches can be found here and some thirteen bedrooms are similarly kind to the pocket, the fishing that the hotel is able to arrange is of course a welcome bonus. There is superb Loch fishing in this area and this is accompanied with all the delights that such wild and unspoilt scenery bring with it. The weather, however, is sometimes cruel and as you trek wearily via Loch Loyal, Loch More and Loch Stack some warm respite is most definitely in order. Fear not, for Scourie has two obvious options in which to escape the storms. The Scourie Hotel (0971) 502396 is our first consideration. Some 25,000 acres of land are at the disposal of guests and this includes some splendid game fishing. The hotel itself is a welcome, unpretentious establishment with cosy bars, tartan carpets and comfortable bedrooms—the ideal place to stay when fishing in the region, a splendid bar is perhaps worth noting! Eddrachilles Hotel (0971) 2080, an eleventh-century house set in its own 300 acre estate is also one for the notebook. It enjoys wonderous views across Badcall Bay and its islands and is also a paradise for naturalists as opposed to naturists! Seals and dolphins and a multitude of birds are a delight to behold. The bedrooms are fairly small but cosy enough and the restaurant is good, the views, however, are breathtaking and are really worth a trip, fishing or nae!

This is a marvellous place to enjoy the very best of Britain's landscape. Yes, it's remote—but that's half its charm. The other half is its wildlife and fishing. Fishing records which run back over a century can be seen at Altnaharra and this sets the scene for the unspoilt fascination of the area. It is without question a paradise for the fisherman and the hoteliers know this. As a result they are thoroughly looked after and a visit is to be highly recommended for those who have not yet discovered its beauties.

Helmsdale Country
Helmsdale is yet another Scottish example of unspoiled moorland, mountain and shoreline. All manner of rivers thread their way through this remote area and the fishing, needless to say, is wild and wonderful. It is also fairly tricky to get on the region's principal water, the Helmsdale. However, there are possibilities and there are also numerous hill lochs which produce some excellent game fishing, with brown trout that fight with a vigour that belies their size. After all this you will no doubt wish nothing more demanding than the comfort of a relaxing chair, a pleasant bar and accommodation. I hope the following ideas are of interest.

In Helmsdale itself we find a former shooting lodge which is set amidst woodlands and colourful gardens, the Navidale House (0431) 2258. The hotel is not a renowned fishing hotel but its open fires, tremendous views over the Moray Firth and pleasant bedrooms make it a good base from which to explore the numerous lochs in the area. The hotel is delighted to help you arrange any such fishing jaunts.

The Garvault Hotel (0431) 3224 is wonderfully placed to organise magnificent loch fishing and the hotel also boasts an idyllic setting, which should appeal to the nomadic angler. The Forsinard Hotel (0641) 7221 is another hotel which champions the cause of the fisherman and the hotel is a wonderful place from which to enjoy loch fishing. A number of the sporting agencies have lodges for rental for parties but the Forsinard is a splendid alternative. The bedrooms and bar are both comfortable which is just as well as many fishermen may only seek the solace of these chambers. This is a completely unspoilt hotel and if you are seeking good value and good hospitality you won't go far wrong here.

A quick word now for the visiting angler who may well have the old golf bag in the boot of the car—definitely a wise move in these parts. Brora, Golspie and the celebrated Dornoch links make a handsome trio. A fine hotel to stay in Golspie is the Sutherland Arms (0408) 633234, while in Brora The Royal Marine (0408) 21252 and The Links (0408) 21225 are well worth a visit. The former boasts particularly wide ranging leisure facilities. In Dornoch itself, The Royal Golf (0862) 810283 and the delightful Dornoch Castle (0862) 810216 should also be shortlisted.

The thought of combining a golfing tour with a fishing trip positively lifts the heart. It is surely time to crank up the motor, pack the bags—and family if necessary—and make haste. When you arrive you will love it and when you depart you will crave more of that precious commodity, time.

The Shins to the Ullapool
Loch Shin points northwards like an accusing finger and leaves a tear on the map for all to witness. There are many smaller abrasions and these waters offer celebrated game fishing on river, loch and stream.

Bonar Bridge is the southernmost point of our area and here there are two hotels which merit consideration. The Caledonian Hotel (08632) 214 has much to offer the visitor. Its most marvellous asset is perhaps its location, enjoying breathtaking views over the Kyle of Sutherland and the distant Ross-shire Hills. A pleasant atmosphere pervades this hotel which can also arrange fishing. The aptly named Bridge Hotel (08632) 204 is an old fashioned hotel which is a delightful port of call to those heading north on the A9. Bar and restaurant meals are wholesome and varied and there is some good accommodation, should you wish to break your journey at this most pleasing spot.

Due north of Bonar Bridge, through marvellous scenery, we come to Lairg which nestles alongside Loch Shin. There are relatively few hotels to be found in this glorious vicinity but do not be put off for The Sutherland Arms (0549) 2291 is a fine exception to this rule, splendidly situated in the centre of the village, proudly overlooking Loch Shin. This is a renowned fishing hotel and thoroughly recommended. Its facilities are good, and lunches and dinner are worth a detour should you only be passing through the area.

The Altnaharra Hotel (0549) 81222, also in Lairg, can also be recommended. If you are merely travelling by, then perchance you are visiting Inchnadamph and the Inchnadamph Hotel (05712) 202 which is something of an angler's retreat. Make no mistake, this is not a luxurious hotel but its reputation amongst fishermen is celebrated. It stands at the head of Loch Assynt in the midst of some of Scotland's most joyous scenery, surrounded by rugged mountainside. This is another haven for lovers of wildlife, with the bird reserve at Handa and nearby seal colonies,two particularly splendid examples. The fishing for salmon and brown trout is renowned and good lunches and dinners can also be enjoyed. Imagine the fishermen's tales that have been exchanged here. This is not only a traditional, unspoiled and welcoming hotel for fishermen, it is something of a paradise.

Heading relentlessly westwards through magnificent landscapes one arrives at Lochinver and the Inver Lodge Hotel (05714) 496 which can also arrange salmon and trout fishing. The hotel is a modern edifice standing proudly amidst heather gardens and lawns. Many rooms enjoy splendid views over Lochinver Bay to the distant Hebrides. There is no question that this is a very comfortable hotel and the residents lounge is particularly relaxing. The bedrooms are extremely well equipped and the restaurant is also highly thought of. This is a hotel in which to pamper yourself in a sauna or solarium after fishing—after some days this will be an exhilarating thought!

Someway south of Lochinver one finds one of those delightful out of the way hotels, in this case, at Achiltibuie, the Summer Isles Hotel (085482) 282. There are country walks, good fishing and bird watching available but if you really want to escape and do nothing, well that's just fine. The restaurant is noted for two reasons: firstly its celebrated dinner meals and secondly the view. On a clear day, they are simply breathtaking. There can be very few finer places to end a day having enjoyed some first class fishing.

Scotland's delights include the variety of the scenery, the hotel accommodation and the overall feeling of peace. One highly individual place to pass a few hours in is the Ceilidh Place, Ullapool (0854) 612103. There are many reasons for visiting, not least, but not solely, the fishing. A coffee shop combines with a book shop which in turn revolves around something of a thespian's paradise. There are also tremendous views of loch and hill and bedrooms are cheery. This is a marvellous place to stay.

If perchance you enjoy good cooking we have a directive for you; venture to the Altnaharrie Inn (085483) 230. A boat crossing is required to reach the inn and this cocktail of sea breezes will prepare you for some of the most distinguished cooking in Scotland. The no-choice five course dinners are legendary; game, seafood, and superb cheese and puddings will leave you somewhat lighter of pocket but immensely satisfied. For those wishing to stay over, seven charming bedrooms are at your disposal. As with so many of the best hotels and restaurants it is essential to book well in advance.

Having been on an impressive diversion it is now necessary to concentrate the mind on the job in hand, game fishing. The Oykel Bridge Hotel (0549) 84218 is a legendary angling hotel. It is booked years in advance and boasts celebrated fishing. Due to its popularity it is well versed in the needs of the fisherman and your stay here will be memorable, especially if you enjoy a tight line or two.

A less celebrated but a worthy fishing hotel can be located at Rosehall. The Achness (054984) 239 is a popular haunt amongst the fishing fraternity and its bedrooms are comfortable. The food is reputed now to be excellent, although the fishing remains of prime importance and that's no bad thing, surely.

Loch Maree to Cromarty Firth

South of Ullapool we can find some rare loch and river fishing. As we venture further south hotels tend to be thicker on the ground but the countryside remains unspoilt and the fisherman can still find peace. The coast here is amongst the most striking and beautiful in Britain and from sea lochs and coves flow some excellent rivers. A few discoveries are definitely in order.

Those of you travelling this far should consider the Dundonnel Hotel (085483) 234 which enjoys splendid views down Little Loch Broom. The hotel is shielded by the An Teallach mountains and has an impressive location and also offers attractive accommodation. In Aultbea the Aultbea Hotel (044582) is another which boasts a splendid view, on this occasion, over Loch Ewe. This water is also cross examined by the Pool House (044586) 272 which sits at the head of the water—once again this is an ideal hotel for fishermen touring this delightful spot and especially good for those with an eye towards Gruinard Bay. One of the most intrusive waterways into this area of the Scottish Highlands is that carved by Loch Maree. It is hoped that this Loch is on the way back and one of the first people who will know are the proprietors of the Loch Maree Hotel (044584) 288, which is certainly a must for those of you wishing to fish once celebrated waters. The hotel itself is a purpose built fishing hotel situated on the bank of the loch. It dates from pre-Victorian times but recent refurbishment has kept the hotel's standard high while retaining character—a fine place to stay. At Kinlochewe we find another unspoilt hotel, The Kinlochewe (044584) 253, which offers a cheery welcome, tasty, homely cooking and good accommodation.

Gairloch is perhaps better known as part of the Prince of Wales poetry but it has other claims to fame, one of which is the Old Inn (0445) 2006 which has a splendid situation overlooking the harbour. This is a fine place to escape and another point from which to plan a fishing foray or two! Another equally splendid hotel is the Creag Mor Hotel, Charles Town (0445) 2068. The hotel is happy to organise fishing for guests and the restaurant specialises in seafood, salmon, trout, Highland beef and venison—lesser nourishment is available throughout the day.

Torridon sits proudly betwixt the river and Loch of that name. The Loch Torridon Hotel (044587) 242 is a former hunting lodge which stands at the head of the Loch. As the word lodge implies this is a house of log fires, cosy lounges and splendid malts in stock—a fisherman's paradise. The hotel offers Loch and river fishing for salmon and trout and is a fine place to go if you love good fishing and a good time. Another beautifully situated hotel is found in Shieldaig, The Tiegh An Eilean (05205) 251 a small family run hotel, it is delightfully peaceful and ideal for a relaxing visit.

Loch Carron is yet another of the celebrated sea lochs of Western Scotland. The Loch Carron (05202) 226 is a beautifully situated hotel which lies on the shores of the Loch. This may not be a fisherman's paradise but its remote setting makes it an ideal point from which to explore the coastal highlands.

From west coast to east our journey now takes a turn to the fishes of Scotland's North Sea coast. The Conon is a first rate water and it is well served by hotels. In Contin, the excellent Coul House Hotel (0997) 21487 is justly proud of its water which include celebrated beats on the Conon and some Loch fishing. The country mansion enjoys a wonderful setting with fine views toward mountain and over forest. The accommodation is first class, the food follows in a similar vein and, for fine fishing in style, this hotel is a fine catch. Of equal quality is the Contin House Hotel (0997) 21920, centrally placed for the West coast and Loch Ness. A hotel which boasts a first class Highland welcome is the East Lodge Hotel, Strathconon (0997) 7222, yet another to consider before making your plans. A similar commendation can be made of the remotely placed Inchbae Lodge (09975) 269 which is a comfortable place to stay. Bedrooms are finished in pine and the hotel can arrange fishing trips, should you so wish.

There are all manner of less celebrated hotels, bed and breakfast and inns that you might wish to consider and the same can be said of the fishing in this area of Scotland. Aside from the noted rivers and lochs there is an abundance of small rivers, hill lochs and streams. It should be emphasised, however, that many of the favoured hotels are booked up many years in advance and planning for the complete angling tour should be made months and in some cases, years in advance. They say half the fun of a holiday is in the planning—we hope that the above information assists you in your quest for salmon, trout and sea-trout.

Beauly to Torridon

There are all manner of good reasons for going fishing, some less obvious than to catch a fish! If you happen to be heading for Scotland then the chances are that, given sufficient planning and luck, a fish will be landed. It might not be a very big one but, after all, what does size matter between friends?! It is certainly true to say that good salmon fishing is fairly pricey but it is not fair to say that all fishing is over expensive. Hotel waters are often the answer and a number of hotels warrant closer inspection in this slice of Scotland that has huge appeal.

Our first suggested port of call is the Cozac Lodge (04565) 263, formerly an Edwardian Shooting Lodge which has since been transformed into a delightfully secluded hotel. The location is breathtaking. It is situated beside Loch Sealbhanach, halfway up Glen Cannich, where wildlife is abundant. This is a really wonderful place to stay if you are someone who delights in the natural beauty of the British Isles. The hotel is run in a particularly friendly, informal manner and fine food and wines add further good reason for passing through this way.

Someway north of here we find Struy where the Cnoc House (046376) 264 is also to be recommended. The food is fresh and wholesome and the bedrooms are extremely comfortable—another for the shortlist when fishing in the area.

The Kyle of Lochalsh is an important port of call for the fisherman, not least because it houses the ferry terminal to Skye. Those of you seeking to venture Skyewards

should certainly consider the Lochalsh Hotel (0599) 4202. Bedrooms and bathrooms are all of a high standard and a 24 hour lounge service is an obvious benefit for people who are unable to time their journey to the second. The hotel can arrange fishing and the restaurant is growing in stature, with seafood a particular speciality. The marvellously named, but distinctly un-Scottish sounding, Plockton is another that needs consideration. Here the Haven Hotel (059984) 223 is good value and thoroughly welcoming. Local produce is used to good advantage and the restaurant is very popular. This good value hotel is a real favourite.

Someway south of the Kyle of Lochalsh one finds another friendly and comfortable hotel, the Glenelg Inn (059982) 273 which overlooks the Sound of Sleat to the Isle of Skye. The dinner menu here is extremely well thought of and fresh produce, particularly the abundant seafood, can be enjoyed. Bedrooms are comfortable and, make no mistake, this is a hotel to consider when travelling through or staying in the area. They can also organise some particularly good brown trout fishing on a number of hill lochs.

It matters little whether you are passing through Sgurr Na Lapaich or heading forth on the Road to the Isles, this is an area of infinite beauty, some first class fishing and a number of fine hotels. Those of you lucky enough to know it well will recognise your good fortune in staying in its countryside and enjoying its fishing.

The Great Glen

The coast of Western Scotland, which runs from Knoydart through Moidart to Loch Linnhe, continues the trend of the Highlands in that it offers remote, rugged scenery that is largely quite unspoilt. The Ness System dominates much of the landscape as it moves from the North southwards. Given the attraction of a certain beastie in Loch Ness, and many other more visible historic sights, the area is popular with tourists and a number of good hotels can be found. We have listed a small number of them.

Some two miles east of Inverness we came across a prestigious house that was Bonnie Prince Charlie's during the fateful battle of Culloden, Culloden House (0467) 790461. Today the scene is somewhat more settled and the hotel boasts excellent standards of accommodation. Furthermore, exceptional dining can also be found here. Three miles west of the town we come upon Bunchrew House (0463) 234917, which is also steeped in history. The hotel dates from the seventeenth century and features some fine furnishings, open log fires and bedrooms which are extremely comfortable. Once again,the restaurant is to be noted for lovers of fine cuisine. Dunain Park (0463) 230512 is another delightful country house near to Loch Ness which offers a great deal. The Glen Mhor (0463) 234308 occupies a prime position opposite the River Ness. The hoteliers are happy to give advice on game and fishing opportunities, and provide a good standard of food and accommodation, particularly in the 11 bedroom annexe on the river. Given the number of time-share and association waters in the area, I hope these hotels will be able to cater for you. There are, however, many more options in and around Inverness.

South of Inverness and some nine miles from Fort Augustus the traveller will find Whitebridge. Here the Whitebridge Hotel (04563) 226 is a fine place to stay. The hoteliers are often able to arrange fishing for guests and the hotel is particularly good value. A more pricey but nevertheless outstanding hotel is Knockie Lodge (04563) 276. This former hunting lodge proudly surveys Loch Nan Lann and boasts a delightful air of peace and calm. The drawing room offers peat and log fires and has superb views. Bedrooms are cosy and the set dinner is generally excellent. Some fishing can be organised from the hotel and this is definitely one for the short cut.

Fort Augustus is a settlement at the southern tip of Loch Ness and a number of hotels are situated here. The Inchnacardoch Lodge (0320) 6258 is one such establishment. It is actually a converted hunting lodge which has the additional benefit of overlooking the huge and mysterious Loch Ness. Food is good here and standards of accommodation are also to be commended. The hotel is not an out and out fishing hotel but contacts through the hotel may allow you some good sport. A similar comment can be made of another extremely welcoming Highland hotel, the Glenmoriston Arms (0320) 51206 in Invermoriston. One should always make a quick phone call to check the state of play, particularly at this popular hotel where the proprietors are generally keen to advise on the fishing, stalking and shooting opportunities that are available locally.

If a mansion should suit your fancy more than a lodge then pencil in the Glengarry Castle, Invergarry (08093) 254, a Victorian house which offers good value accommodation. The ruins of Invergarry Castle lie within the grounds and the food and hospitality are well above average. The Tomdoun Hotel (0809) 2218 should also be contacted when planning your fishing trip to this area. Good free fishing is available to guests in addition to some fine hospitality.

Those fishing the Roy should consult the Roy Bridge Hotel (0397) 81236, a nineteenth-century coaching inn, the Stronlossit Hotel (0397) 81253, for permits and residential details, and the Glenspean Lodge (0397) 81224, which has a lofty position some two miles east of Roy Bridge. The hoteliers are eager to please and will endeavour to help in the management of your sporting activities. Letterfinlay Lodge (039781) 622 is another relaxing hotel to consult. Situated on the banks of Loch Lochy, it exudes Scottish charm. The scenery is gorgeous and the well-packed bar particularly cosy. Game fishing is available and for a fishing break this hotel has much to commend it. In Spean Bridge itself, The Spean Bridge (039781) 250, which offers fishing on the Roy, is a more modern abode but also one to note.

Finally we arrive at Fort William. There are all manner of hotels in this busy town which overlooks Loch Linnhe. Our two recommended hotels are situated north of the town in the shadow of Ben Nevis. The first thought is for those of you who can think of nothing better than spoiling yourself. Inverlochy Castle (0397) 702177 is a formidable establishment which positively exudes excellence. The grounds, gardens and views are wonderful

and the interior offers all manner of style and excellence. Service is outstanding and the elegant restaurant is also first class. All manner of country pursuits can be enjoyed from this hotel—once a favourite haunt of Queen Victoria—including some game fishing. This is a hotel of excellence and for some, fishing can take a backseat. The other place of style is more a restaurant than a hotel, though seven stylish bedrooms are available; the Factor's House (0397) 705767. Game and fish are outstanding and once again we have a house of real quality—clearly an area to spoil yourself—on and off the water!

One final thought for those of you who seek to journey further westwards, perhaps to the remote hills of Moidart and its fine game fishing, is Arisaig. Arisaig House (06875) 622 should be your port of call. It has an enchanting setting and peace and relaxation are very much the order of the day. This is a hotel to escape to, perhaps for a day away from the fishing, to spoil a loved one who is less keen on our marvellously captivating sport!

Loch Shiel is a wild and lovely place which attracts many fishermen. There are numerous hotels that we have mentioned that can organise your fishing and they all have their own merits. Please have brochures sent so you can pick the most appropriate for your own wishes, whatever your travel and budget preferences. This is always the best plan of attack. One thing is certain, however, you will be warmly received and find some good salmon and brown trout fishing—a splendid place to get away from it all. Further adventures can be had in the gorgeously unspoilt countryside here, such as in the delightful areas of Knoydart and Loch Morar. Here, the Morar Hotel (0687) 2346 is a really super place to stay, far from the madding crowd.

The Islands
If you really want a get away from it all type of holiday, you could not wish for anything more enjoyable than a fishing foray to the Islands. While some fishing is as expensive and hard to come by as on the mainland, there is a great variety of loch and river fishing at very affordable prices.

The mainland of Scotland may have some celebrated salmon rivers, but if you are seeking brown trout fishing, then the Islands are the big brother of the mainland. Perhaps this is because they are remote, perhaps there is another reason, but as you ponder away, one thing is certain, you will not regret a trip to the distant Islands of the Highlands of Scotland.

Mull is a beautiful isle and the principal port of call is Tobermory. The Linndhu House Hotel (0688) 2425 has fishing all over the island including a beat on the Aros. Tobermory is the busiest part of the island and the Tobermory Hotel (0688) 2091 is a delightful place to stay. Lovers of wildlife will also wish to consider Ulva House (0688) 2044. The proprietor here is an authority on the island's wildlife and organises expeditions to take in the charming wilderness of the countryside and the animals that seek shelter within it.

To the south of the island, the fisherman who wishes to spoil himself will visit Tiroran House (06815) 232. This is a delightfully remote hotel surrounded by the most stunning scenery. The house is extremely comfortable and there is a deliberate homeliness in the welcome. Dinner here is something of a treat and a special excursion is thoroughly recommended.

Although Arran may not be the best island in terms of fishing it boasts some majestic scenery and for people wanting to really relax and enjoy a number of pursuits, golf, walking, riding, fishing etc it is a splendid place to head for. The Auchrannie Country House Hotel (0770) 2234, in Brodick and the Lagg Hotel, Kilmory (0770) 87255 are two hotels to consider.

The Isle of Skye beckons and many visit. The Ullinish Lodge Hotel (0470) 72214 is a distinguished fishing hotel and is an extremely welcoming place to stay as is the Skeabost House (0470) 32202. The latter has a splendid woodland setting with fine views over Loch Snizort. There are a number of fine leisure facilities including a nine hole golf course as well as some fine river fishing— as a result it is a great favourite with anglers. Another great favourite with visitors to the isle is the Three Chimneys (047081) 258; here we find Scottish cooking at its best. A visit is thoroughly recommended to this fine restaurant in Colbost, near Dunvegan.

Lewis is home to some remarkable fishing. It is wonderfully remote and accommodation is somewhat difficult to come by. In Stornaway, the island's major hotel can be found, the Cabarfeidh (0851) 702604. It's a fine hotel and a good base for exploring the islands and the many fishing opportunities available. North Uist is another treat for those of us who have to get away from it all. Lochmaddy Hotel (0876) 3331 is the place to escape to

and the fishing from here can be excellent. South Uist also beckons the angler. The hotel which gives perhaps the finest welcome is the Lochboisdale Hotel, Lochboisdale (08784) 332. Fishing prints adorn the walls and while the hotel has no pretensions to luxury it is welcoming and a delight for the fisherman.

Orkney is a wonderful island to visit and if you have been stuck in a rut, fishing the same water for years or worse still only fished in a reservoir a few miles from home consider a trip to Orkney, its waters are celebrated throughout the world. Loch Harray is the major attraction and the place to visit is the Merkister Hotel (085677) 366. The proprietor knows his fishing and when you set eyes on the bar you will know your trip has been a 'goodun' when you commence fishing. There will be serious questions asked as to when you will return. Sadly, it may not be possible to make that second trip but not to make that first pilgrimage is a tragic omission for anyone who enjoys the thrill of trout fishing.

Shetland, Orkney and the islands are generally well served by their tourist boards and all manner of ideas for self catering and small guest house accommodation can be found by contacting their offices. In the north of the island, in Brae, is the scenic Busta House Hotel (080622) 506. It is a delightful little hotel in an eighteenth-century country manor house and useful if you are journeying to the waters of this area or heading towards Yell or Unst. In Kerwick itself The Shetland Hotel (0595) 5515 is purpose built, but comfortable, for those of you who are seeking a port of call after your ferry journey.

There are all manner of out of the way, sometimes undiscovered, waters in the Islands of Scotland. They are remote, hotels are often matter of fact and self catering lodges are often the favoured form of accommodation. What is for sure, they provide a wonderful escape from the pace of the 1990s.

Modern and traditional Salmon Flies (by Mike Sugg)

HEARTLANDS

The Seafield Lodge Hotel

Now under the personal management of experienced hoteliers Alasdair and Kathleen Buchanan, assisted by Chef Alastair Garrow, the 'Lodge' has now been restored to it's former glory.

Our guests, many of whom return year after year to enjoy the sporting delights of the river Spey and surrounding countryside, enjoy the informality of a sporting lodge combined with the facilities and personal service expected of a first class hotel.

Open for visitors since 1881, recent major improvements to the public areas and bedrooms provide discriminating guests with every modern comfort in elegant surroundings.

All bedrooms are en suite with direct dial telephone, television, hairdryer and hospitality tray. Our Trout and Salmon Suites provide more spacious accommodation with separate sitting rooms and bathrooms with spa bath.

Residents lounges and the Lodge Bar, with its fine array of malt whiskies, welcome you with open log fires and our barbecue and garden area is a popular venue in the summer months.

Chef Alastair Garrow uses all his culinary skills in creating an ever changing menu using the finest of local produce for which Speyside is famous. Game, fresh Spey salmon in season, prime Aberdeen Angus beef, Moray lamb and west coast scallops all feature prominently on our tempting menus.

The Seafield Lodge is synonymous with Spey fishing and is the home of Britain's longest running angling courses under the personal supervision of renowned Chief Instructor Arthur Oglesby. Residential Courses are held in April, May and August. Private fishing arranged on the Avon and Spey including such famous beats as Castle Grant, Kinchurdy and Tulchan. Good loch fishing for trout is also available. Our resident ghillie who is a qualified A.P.G.A.I. instructor, is available to give advice on equipment, fishing and private tuition.

However, other sports and activities are well catered for including golf on one of our many challenging courses, hill walking, stalking, pony trekking, bird watching and in winter, skiing on nearby Cairngorm and the Lecht. Grantown is at the start of the world famous Whisky Trail and no visit to Speyside would be complete without a Distillery Tour and a dram or two.

The Buchanan family look forward to your visit to Grantown on Spey and their very special Seafield Lodge where discriminating travellers and sportsmen can be assured of a warm welcome and traditional Highland hospitality.

Seafield Lodge
Grantown-On-Spey
Moray
PH26 3JN
Tel: (0479) 2152,
Fax: (0479) 2340

Speyside is an intoxicating area not only by virtue of its glorious river but also as a result of the number of distilleries in the area. Driving down Strathspey you will happen across the source of many a famous whisky. High street brands mix with lesser known labels, making for a veritable treat. The local tourist board have coined the area the Whisky Trail and according to a local gossip it is impossible to lose one's way even though the route is badly sign posted. 'Follow the bodies!' he said. Perhaps the answer is to take an extended holiday so you can do justice to at least some of the unique malts of this area.

The Spey

From source to mouth some hundred miles long, the Spey begins in the small Loch Spey near the River Roy, not far from Loch Lochy. From the loch it is joined by small burns from Corrieyairack Forest. These burns present a problem, for as they tumble down the steep slopes they wash away the soil from the forestry plantations and, as a result, the spates are much more pronounced. When in spate the water is very coloured, in fact almost black. The Upper Spey has been harnessed for hydro power but at Blargie it is joined by the River Mashie and from here begins to take on its true character.

This is Jacobite country. As you look at Cluny Castle, which was rebuilt in the nineteenth century, spare a thought for Cluny Macpherson. Following the failure of the 1745 rebellion, this clan chief hid for eight years in the hills above and had to suffer the ignominy of watching 'Butcher' Cumberland's troops razing his ancestral home to the ground. Also in the area are the ruins of Ruthven Barracks, scene of one of the few Jacobite successes. It was here that the interestingly named Gordon of Glenbucket defeated the government troops. How different history might have been had Bonnie Prince Charlie not turned back at Derby and retreated north. Harried all the way, the retreat became a rout until the desperate last stand at Culloden. Alas, claymores were no match for muskets nor was the fierce but poorly organised clan loyalty very effective against the regimented discipline of the government army.

For over fifty years, the Scots and English sympathisers had lived in hope of seeing a restoration of the Stuarts. Their hopes had been raised when Dutch William— William of Orange—died after a fall from his horse, which stumbled on a mole hill and gave rise to the Jacobite toast 'To the little gentleman in black velvet'. After the failure of the 1715 rebellion they continued to drink to the health of the King across the water out of the beautifully engraved Jacobean glasses with their secret Stuart motifs. All these hopes died at Culloden: this was one of the bloodiest battles fought on British soil and the rapacity with which survivors were hounded down, and the clan system destroyed, put paid to the last aspirations of those who espoused the Stuart cause.

But enough of history, what of the fishing? Some of the estuary nets have been bought off, and hence the fishing has improved. That's all very well—you might say—but how do I get to fish? Surprisingly, despite the Spey's reputation, fishing is possible if you know where to go. The best beats are expensive and are impossible to get on. However, various hotels, fishing clubs and estates offer days or weeks that can be taken up if you book early enough. The clubs often have various restrictions. For example, Aberlour Angling Club requires that visitors fishing their one mile stretch stay the night(s) prior to fishing in one of the village's three hotels. They also have a bag limit of two fish per day—one above the bridge and the other below. Any further fish caught have to be handed over to Munro's Tackle Shop to be sold 'for the good of the club and the village'. This does not happen very often! The following is a list of contacts that will be able to help you to fish this majestic river:

(For Badenoch A.A.) A. & L. Donald, Main Street, Newtonmore (0540) 3242; Speyside Sports, Grampian Road, Aviemore (0479) 810656 (new Abernathy A.A. stretch, £15 per day, £45 per week excluding Sunday); Alvie Estate, Kincraig (0540) 651255 or Dalraddy Caravan Park (0479) 810330 (three beats, £20 per day and £96 for a weekly salmon ticket, £10 a day for trout); Lynwilg Hotel, Aviemore (0479) 810209 (three miles and four lochs); The Paper Shop, Kinguissie (0540) 661207 and Ashdowns (0540) 673242 (a stretch of the Spey from Kinguissie to the dam, full day £3.00), Rothiemurchus Estate, by Aviemore (0479) 810703 (three beats, £15, £20 and £25 per day, plus two stocked and two wild lochs); Craigard Hotel, Boat of Garten (0479) 83206 (Abernathy A.A. six and a quarter miles both banks at £15 per day); The Boat Hotel, Boat of Garten, (0479) 83258; Allens, Boat of Garten (0479) 83372 (also Abernathy A.A.); Caledonian Angling do personalised packages from the simple to the luxurious (0479) 82363.

Strathspey A.A. have a seven mile stretch with several permit issuers in Grantown; Mr and Mrs Hayward at Mortimers (0479) 2684 (£100 for seven days), Spey Valley Hotel (0479) 2942, Seafield Lodge Hotel (0479) 2152; Strathspey Estate, Grantown (0479) 2529 retain three beats available for weekly hire by parties; Nethybridge Hotel, Nethybridge (0479) 82203; Blairfindy Lodge Hotel, Glenlivet (0807) 590376 let the Carron/Laggan Beat for one week each year at £2500 plus VAT for five rods (can also arrange rods on the Avon); R.& R. Urquhart (0309) 72216; Aberlour A.C. have outlets in the town, for example: J.A.J. Munro in the High Street, Aberlour Hotel (0340) 871287; Lour Hotel (0340) 871224, Dowans Hotel (0340) 871488; the favourite, Craigellachie Lodge (0340) 881224; Linc Holdings Ltd (0205) 79444; Orton Estate (0343) 88240.

Loch Insh

The next feeder stream of any consequence is the Truim and then, at Newtonmore, the Spey is joined by the Calder, while below Kingussie we find the junction with the Tromie. Sadly, both the Calder and Tromie have been dammed for hydro power. Just above Kincraig it flows through Loch Insh whose shallow waters contain large quantities of trout and salmon, along with more than adequate supplies of pike and arctic char. The loch also contains a watersports centre with canoeing, windsurfing and sailing but this hasn't prevented some forty salmon being caught from approximately one hundred and twenty boat lettings. The largest of these, weighing in at an impressive 23½lb was taken by the Director of Loch Insh Watersports and Skiing Centre, Clive Freshwater (05404) 272, who will prove a fount of information and assistance for prospective visitors.

In the church at nearby Kincraig is St Eunan's bell. This masterpiece of celtic bronze work was carried in front of funeral processions fourteen hundred years ago. Below the loch are the junctions with the Feshie, another victim of afforestation, and the Druie. After passing through old villages it is quite a surprise to come to Aviemore with its clusters of chalets and modern hotels. Most incongruous. On our way to Fochabers we have often watched skiers coming down the runs and thought that skiing and salmon fishing would make an unusual biathlon event! A couple of miles further the A9 is the fork for the A95 and the quaintly named village Boat of Garten, so called because a ferry was the only means of crossing the river until the bridge was built.

The Nethy & the Dulnain

The next tributaries to join the Spey are the Nethy and Dulnain. Strathspey Angling Association has twelve miles of the River Dulnain. This is first class salmon fishing and also offers sea-trout, grilse and brown trout. As one would expect, it is fly-only except when the water is high, when spinning is allowed. Permits at a cost of £100 a week may be had from Mortimers in Grantown (0479) 2684 but you have to be staying locally.

After this we journey on to Grantown-on-Spey. This is the seat of Clan Grant and the capital of Strathspey. Although a popular tourist resort it is also well known to fishermen for it is here that Arthur Oglesby (who has probably forgotten more about salmon fishing than most of us will ever learn!) runs his excellent fishing courses. From Grantown to the estuary is the best fishing on the Spey with a succession of big deep holding pools broken by stretches of white water rapids. These pools can be deceptively dangerous and the greatest possible care should be taken when wading. Due to the fact that the river is so fast, the slightest slip can produce tragic results. There are far too many fishing accidents and while it may be tempting to wade a little further so that one can cover more water it is just not worth the risk.

The Avon

At Ballindalloch the Spey is joined by the Avon, known as the Aan by locals. To whisky drinkers the Avon is famous for its tributary the Livet, source of that lovely malt, Glenlivet. Because the Avon's source is in the granite and quartz slopes of the Cairngorms it is crystal clear and so demands a careful approach to avoid alerting the fish. The Ballindalloch beats are prime salmon fishing, especially Junction Pool which has also produced a notable 8lb brown trout. There are many famous names hereabouts, Upper Pitchroy, Lower Pitchroy, Phonas Water, Knockando, Laggan and Carron, Wester Elchies Kinermony, Aberlour, Easter Elchies and Craigellachie. All are superb fishing but are expensive as well. In 1989 a mile of north bank fishing on Faster Elchies which had six named pools, was put on the market at an asking price of £900,000!

At Craigellachie, you can watch salmon and sea-trout running the rapids to Bridge Pool by standing on Telford's bridge. A mile or so downstream the Spey is joined by another stream whose name is well known to whisky drinkers, for the Fiddich is the home of Glenfiddich. It was the steep wooded sides of this valley, combined with the need to be able to cover the big pools, that led to the development of Spey casting. This method keeps the line in front of you at all times and is worth learning as it can come in useful on many other rivers.

The Gordon Arms Hotel at Tomintoul (0807) 580206 can offer guests two miles of fishing on the Avon at £17.50 a day, £90 for six days. Also there is the Richmond Arms Hotel (0807) 580209 which can offer guests fishing on over six miles of this gin-clear water at a cost of £135 a week. R.G.Heape Esq. at the Ballindalloch Estate Office (0807) 500205 can offer fishing on six miles of the Avon. This water averages 166 salmon and 226 sea-trout a season. Both the Gordon Arms and the Richmond Arms can offer fishing on the Livet. If you're under fourteen, permits to fish the long stretch of the Fiddich leased by Mortlach Angling Club may be had for £4 a day from TV Services in Dufftown (0340) 20527. Any older than that and you can expect to pay £7.

The Lossie

A few miles west, along the coast, we find Lossiemouth and the River Lossie. This river is overshadowed by its famous sisters the Spey and the Findhon but is the type of water that offers the occasional salmon at a modest cost. It is also a good sea-trout water for, while salmon average around 150 per season, sea-trout catches in recent years have varied between 1179 and 3166. Summer is the time for sea-trout and autumn for salmon. As it flows through arable land the bed of the river is muddy and pools tend to be small and deep. The course of this river from its source in Seven Sisters Spring to the Moray Firth is some thirty-four miles. On its journey it skirts the town of Elgin. Here you can see the ruins of the cathedral known as the Lantern of the North. This term does not derive from evangelical fame but the fact that it was repeatedly burnt to the ground! Permits to fish the upper waters may be had for £10 a season from Mr W. Macdonald, President of the Dallas Angling Association (0343) 89367 provided you are staying in the parish. Incidentally, salmon do get up this far if there has been enough water for them to ascend the rocks at Kellas. A little way south of Elgin is Glen Latterach Reservoir (0343) 86234, where a full day's bank fishing (with no bag limit) will cost only £2.60.

The Findhorn

Continuing west along the A96 brings you to Forres and the River Findhorn. This is top quality salmon fishing in beautiful surroundings. Many years ago the then Earl of Moray netted Sluie Pool and took over 1300 salmon in one night—an early demonstration of the detrimental effect of netting. The course of the river was much changed by the tremendous floods of 1829 when the river rose by over fifty feet in places causing widespread loss of life and livestock. It still rises very quickly when in spate and can rise by as much as two feet in ten minutes, so do be careful. The river's source in the Monadhliath Mountains is some sixty miles from the Moray Firth. Apart from the occasional conifer plantation, the river is very open down to Dulsie Bridge. Below here, the river thunders for some twenty miles through a gorge with sheer sides over two hundred feet high in places. The river relies on snow melt to maintain its level and this cold water usually stops fish running beyond the gorge before May. However spring fishing in the gorge can produce twenty and even thirty-pound fish. July is the time for grilse and as one would expect September is the best time for the upper river. It is a hard river to get on and you may find yourself on a long waiting list. The following may, however, be able to help you. J.Mitchell, Tackle Shop at Forres (0309) 672936 has access to private beats on one and a half miles at a cost varying from £200 to £300 per week per rod. Cawdor Estates (0667) 7666 let some of their beats. Mr D.McConnell of Moray Estates Office (0309) 672269 has a waiting list but serious enquiries for the future will be considered. Logie Estates (0309) 611208 lets beats at a cost of £935 per week for four rods, though there is a waiting list. R.& R. Urquhart (0309) 672216 let the Coulmony Beat at a cost of £50 per rod per day. Muckrach Lodge Hotel (0479) 85257 at Dulnain Bridge has two miles on one bank. This water holds four rods and the cost of a day's fishing is £30 a day and a ghillie is available.

The Nairn

A few miles to the west lies the River Nairn. This is an area rich in history. Here you will find Clava with its Druidical remains, Jacobite ghosts on Culloden Moor, and Cawdor Castle—immortalised in Shakespeare's *Macbeth*. The source of the river is high in the mountains, south of Loch Ness. Parts of the upper river suffer from salting but downstream there are many good deep holding pools, although the bankside bushes and trees can cause a few casting problems. However, being a narrow river it is not too difficult to cover the water. May and June are the best months for sea-trout fishing which can be superb, while August and September are best for salmon. It is a productive river, and though spring runs are not what they were, salmon are caught in March and April. S.Newbould Esq., of the Nairn District Salmon Fishery Board (0667) 53495 may be able to help you get a day on one of the private beats. Nairn Angling Association has

***Artist: Clive Madgwick THAT ELUSIVE TROUT
Courtesy of Rosenstiel's***

eight miles of fishing upstream from the harbour. Permits for this water cost £10 a day or £35 a week and may be had from Pat Fraser, Radio, TV & Sports Shop, Nairn (0667) 53038. Clava Lodge Holiday Homes (0463) 790228 have a mile and a quarter of the south bank, costing £4 per rod per day.

Lochindorb

Should you not be lucky enough to get on one of these rivers, you might care to have a day's trouting on Lochindorb. Bank fishing is free but is only permitted on the north eastern quarter of the shoreline where the public road runs immediately adjacent to the loch. There are six boats for hire, available for a morning, afternoon or evening for £5. Hire of a boat from 8.00am to 5.00pm costs £9 and a full day—8.00am to 10.00pm—costs £10. Contact Mrs Young (0309) 651270 for details. *Lochindorb* means 'lake of the small fish', and the wild brownies here average between a half and three quarters of a pound. The loch is self-stocking but has relatively poor feeding with the result that there are large numbers of

small trout present. For this reason there is no restriction on size of trout killed. With a breeze from the south or west rippling the surface you will do well to fish a team of dark pattern flies—good baskets may result.

Loch Morlich

Slightly better fish averaging around the one pound mark can be caught on Loch Morlich. This is near Aviemore so don't expect good catches until the snow melts and the water warms up. May is the recommended month. At three quarters of a mile long, it fishes particularly well from the bank but don't discount hiring a boat as trout up to two and a half pounds are regularly caught. The loch is shallow, with fish covering the entire area and the loch also has a watersports facility. Permits cost £3.10 a day or £11.50 a week (£1.50 and £6 junior prices) and can be had from the Forestry Commission Warden (0479) 861271 and the Loch Morlich Watersports Centre (0479) 861221. The manager of the watersports centre is a keen fisherman himself and will gladly point you in the direction of other lochs he fishes.

The Dowans Hotel

Set high above the village of Aberlour, overlooking the most famous of all salmon rivers, the Spey, sits the Dowans Hotel, the sporting hotel of Speyside.

Under recent new ownership, the Dowans has been extensively refurbished andnow offers all seventeen comfortable bedrooms en suite. With versatile meal times to suit all sportsmen and women, the dining room offers the best of the local game, salmon and seafood; the bar a large selection of malt whiskies. Other facilities like a drying-room, rod-racks, gun-safe, and a deep freeze are on hand for the convenience of sportsmen.

If you enjoy fishing, shooting, stalking or just walking in the countryside, then this is a hotel you will enjoy. If you play golf, there are fifteen golf courses within half an hour's drive.

For further details, or to arrange fishing, shooting or stalking please contact Penny Millington-Jeffries, or Peter Neep.

The Dowans Hotel
Aberlour
Banffshire
Scotland
AB38 9LS
Tel: (0340) 871488
Fax: (0340) 871038

Knockomie lies well off the road with views over the Royal Burgh of Forres and on towards Findhorn and is a rare Scottish example of the Arts and Crafts house. The hotel stands amid twenty-five acres of grounds. Part of the house dates back 150 years.

As you enter by the front door you are immediately welcomed by the panelled hallway with its beamed ceiling. To your right is our Cocktail Bar where you can relax in the warm friendly atmosphere. Our well stocked bar offers a wide selection of Liquors and Spirits and we pride ourselves on an enviable collection of Malt Whiskies. Superb Bar Lunches are available at reasonable prices.

In the Fully Licensed Restaurant, which caters for up to thirty-five people, the hotel endeavours to produce culinary art with flair and imagination, whilst utilising the very best of Scottish produce. Set and A La Carte Menus are offered. The Wine Cellar boasts an extensive Selection of wines from various countries.

The Flower Room is a small area within the main restaurant. It is ideal for parties of ten—creating an atmosphere of privacy and intimacy. The walls feature fine watercolours and silks of flowers.

Fourteen tastefully decorated bedrooms are individually named after local Distilleries. All offer en suite shower/bathroom, tea and coffee making facilities, direct dialling telephones, 24hr laundry service, television and room service menus. Hairdryer, trouser press and ironing facilities are also available.

The hotel has just completed an extension, with another panelled Lounge area with fire place, overlooking the garden towards Forres. There are a further seven en suite bedrooms and one suite with four rooms on the ground floor, one with additional facilities for the disabled. Some rooms feature half tester beds, some rooms four-posters. Two rooms have patio doors opening on to the gardens.

The hotel has books, magazines and games to help you relax. Enjoy a stroll around the gardens. Practice on our Croquet Lawn or learn to play Boules.

Grantown Road,
Forres
Moray
IV36 0SG
Tel: (0709) 673146
Fax: (0309) 673290

One of the obvious but nevertheless perilous hazards of spring fishing is that grand old British institution, the weather! Ocean racing has been compared to standing under a freezing cold shower while tearing £50 notes and the same could be said of spring fishing—hopefully the notes would be of a smaller denomination. While March can produce times when shirt sleeves are the order of the day it can be and often is, bitterly cold and naturally January and February are less hospitable. Yet being British we think nothing of it and are prepared to pay large sums of money for the pleasure of being frozen to the marrow! There is often a howling gale either blowing straight into one's face or down one's neck just to make casting that bit more challenging. To add to the pleasure there may be rain or sleet coming down the valley in almost horizontal sheets. But of course there is always the chance of a fish, providing one's hands are not too numb to play him.

The Ythan

The river Ythan (pronounced eye-than) is truly a peach of a river for it used to be famous for its pear-mussels and it is believed that the large pearl in the crown of Scotland came from the river. It is also one of the best known sea-trout fisheries and catch figures more than justify its reputation. Added to this, it is one of the few rivers where salmon are on the increase. From its source in a spring-fed well in a schoolmaster's garden at Strabocie to the estuary at Newburgh the Ythan flows through about thirty-one miles of rich agricultural land. Newburgh is less than fifteen miles north of Aberdeen which with its airport makes fishing in this area very accessible for us and European fishermen. The airport has daily services from Paris and Amsterdam so don't be surprised if some of your fellow rods are French or German or Swiss as they know this is the finest sea-trout fishing in Europe and you can't keep quiet about something as good as the Ythan.

Such is the fame of the estuary fishing that the river itself tends to be overloaded, but those in the know are aware that there is good fishing to be had here at a reasonable cost. Fyvie Angling Association has three miles of the upper river where a day's fishing up until 31st August costs £5. Permits are available from the Vale Hotel, Fyvie (0651) 891376. The Buchan Hotel at Ellon (0358) 20208 has a mile at £10 a day and the Aberdeen Angling Association also has some water. All netting has been stopped for over ten years now, and if the salmon runs continue increasing the prospects for the future are excellent.

For most the Ythan means estuary fishing. This of course is tidal water and so not so dependent on rainfall as further upstream. At high tide it is rather like a lake and then at low tide it changes into a small river. Here you will see sea-trout splashing and crashing about all over the water; a sight which is sure to get the pulse racing! The water is fished from both bank and boat depending on the state of the tide. On an incoming tide, especially when it is half way up, most rods will prefer to fish from a boat while bank fishing is at its best from when the tide begins to ebb. There are seventeen pools and fishing is by fly or spinner. Fly is the most popular method but it will often be presented on a spinning rod because of the need to cast a fairly long line. Also there is quite a lot of weed which is much easier to remove when using spinning tackle. Popular flies for traditional fly fishing include Peter Ross, Dunkeld, Zulu, Golden Butcher and the special Ythan fly of Eddie Forbes, the fishery manager who has done so much to improve things. Most spinners will use an Ythan Terror which is an imitation minnow of blue and silver with some feathers on the end. This water is owned by the Udny and Dudwick Estate and has recently been leased for a twenty-one year period on a time share basis which can if required include a cottage. Ythan Valley Fisheries (0358) 689052 will be able to give you further information on this scheme and let you know if there is a spare day or week. Day permits for the eleven-acre fishery, three miles north west of Ellon, cost £12 per day, with reductions for OAPs, juniors and larger parties. Some may say statistics are boring, but this water has a record of 17lb and 10lb plus fish are regularly taken. There was of course the day in 1953 when two rods had sixty-three fish for 169lb in two and a half hours! The average is two pounds, but these silver tornados will feel three times that weight and they fight like demons. Just to complete this fishing paradise the area is a nature reserve and bird sanctuary with large colonies of eider duck.

The Deveron

While quite a lot of the Spey is difficult to get on, the Deveron which is twenty miles or so east is much more accessible to the visiting fisherman. The river is some sixty miles from its source at the foot of Hill of Three Stanes to the coast at Banff and Macduff. Unusually for a river of this size there are no lochs in the system and, so being a spate river, rain can play an important part in the fisherman's luck. However it is not that chancy for in an average year it will produce at least 1000 salmon and a similar figure for sea-trout, while a good year will yield 2500 salmon and 3000 sea-trout. It is also a big fish water which produced a fifty-six-pounder in 1920, but even this was eclipsed by Mrs Morrison's magnificent sixty-one pounder in 1924. The fish in recent years may be of more modest proportions but within the last five years there has been a thirty-four-pounder and quite a few over twenty pounds, while the average is around ten pounds.

From its source the Deveron flows to Carbrach village after which it rushes through the gorge formed by the steep banks of Meikle Firbriggs and Daugh of Corinacy. It is then joined by Black Water and flows through Glenfiddich Lodge Beat, Lesmurdie and Beldorney (which averages sixty salmon per season). The latter is let by Bell Ingram of Aberdeen (0224) 644272 at £110-£130 per rod per week. Next come the Edinglassie and Invermarkie beats and the Huntly Angling Association water. Salmon fishing on these upper beats is fairly dependent on water levels but there is very good trouting to be had. Brown trout of 3lb and more are often caught and there are a few rainbows which have escaped from the fish farms. Best bets fly-wise include Gold and Dunkeld.

At Huntly (the start of superb salmon fishing on the lower beats) the Deveron is joined by the Bogie. This tributary which rises near Rhymie village offers good fishing for the salmon and sea-trout on their way to the spawning grounds in the headwaters. Then there are the Huntly Lodge, Castle Hotel, Corniehaugh (with its famous Still Pool) and Avochie beats which regularly produce salmon of the 15-20lb class. The Castle Hotel at Huntly (0466) 792696 has one and a half miles of double-bank fishing on which hotel guests have priority. The cost varies between £10 and £15 per day, and £40 and £150 a week, depending on the time of year. The Huntly Angling Association (0466) 792291 can offer fishing on six miles of both the Deveron and the Bogie at £30 a week, £40 a month or £50 a season—a day permit costs £15 but must be bought and used on the same day. At Inverisla the river is joined by the Isla which attracts few spawning fish as upriver access is difficult. The next

beats downstream are Woodsie, Conieclugh, Rothiemay Castle, Upper Mayen, Mayen House, Redhill and Carronhaugh. The weir at Connieclugh halts the passage of fish when water temperatures are low and several large fish have been taken here. Rothiemay has the well known Sunnybrue pool and both this beat and Mayed can be fished by guests of the Forbes Arms Hotel (0466) 81248 at a cost of between £5 and £25 a day according to season.

Continuing our piscatorial voyage downstream we come to the Glennie, Turtory Ardmeallie, Church, Boat of Tortory, Marnoch Lodge and Euchrie beats. Noted pools here include Falconers, Bridge and Islands. Then it is on to beats such as Netherale, Carnousie, Forglen, Mountblairy, and the excellent Montcrofter. In 1987 Netherale produced a superb sea-trout of 14lb and Mountblairy as well as yielding The Fish (61lb), has also produced the best fish in recent years. Below Turriff the flow of the river is reduced due to abstraction for drinking water and some of the lower pools can silt up. However, the District Fishing Board is doing its best to clear them.

Finally the river flows into the sea between the towns of Banff and Macduff. Recently fishing has been fairly poor here, especially in summer, when water is low and an over abundance of weed growth prevails. As one would expect with a river of this size there are a number of owners and the following may also be able to help you. Jay-Tee Sports of Banff (0261) 815821 issues permits at a cost of £5 per day and £10 per week (Monday to Friday) for the Banff and Macduff Angling Association Water. Sea-trout here average at 1½-3lb, and there is a bag limit

The Castle Hotel

The Castle Hotel is a magnificent eighteenth-century stone building, standing in its own grounds above the ruins of Huntly Castle, on the banks of the River Deveron. Sandston, as it was originally known, was built as a famly home for the Dukes of Gordon.

The hotel was purchased in March 1990 by a very keen fishing and hotel family. The Castle beat is the hotels own double-banked salmon and sea-trout fishing which has recently undergone an extensive improvement scheme and now offers a variety of attactive pools which are a delight to fish especially with a fly. The beat is let regularly to guests of the hotel. We can also arrange fishing on other private beats of the river Deveron.

Folowing a recent refurbishment programme all bedrooms now have en suite facilities. The newly decorated dining room and bar, with their open log fires, lend themselves to the country house hotel atmosphere. We have improved our facilities for fieldsportsmen and women - a new rod room, drying room, strong room for guns, fly tying desk, an impressive list of sporting videos, availablility of late night and early morning snacks and a delicious picnic menu.

As well as fishing we can also arrange roe deer and red deer stalking, grouse and pheasant shooting, walked up and mixed shooting.

Our aim is to ensure that all visiting sportsmen and women have both enjoyable and successful visits.

Situated on the main A96 betwen Aberdeen (45 minutes away) and Inverness the hotel is easily reached by road, rail and air.

The Castle Hotel
Huntly
Aberdeenshire AB54 4SH
Tel: (0466) 792696
Fax: (0446) 792641

of twenty per day. Tickets for the Turriff Angling Association (fly-only) are available from Ian Masson Fishing Tackle (0888) 62428 at a weekly cost of £50. In the spring the Association has five private beats where a day will cost between £6 and £10. The Drummuir Estates (0542) 81225 water is usually booked well ahead but some spring lets are available and it may be possible to get a day later on in the season; the cost of a week here for four rods varies between £215 and £345. Salar Management Services (0667) 55355 let the Avochie Beat and Scotia Sporting Services may be able to help with other beats. The County Hotel in Banff (0261) 25353 can arrange fishing for guests. If you prefer to take a cottage Mr G. Manson of Huntly (0466) 792482 may be able to help and also looks after eight beats of the middle stretch where the cost varies between £5 and £27 a day. A limited number of weekly tickets occasionally become available due to post-Easter cancellations. The Montcrofter Fishings are handled by Savills in Edinburgh (031) 226 6961. Good trout flies are March Brown, Black Pennell, Grouse and Claret and Greenwells Glory, while favourite salmon flies include the Black Doctor, Stouts Tail, Garry Peg and Munro Killer.

The Don

The Don flows into the North Sea at Bridge of Don which is just north of Aberdeen and the Dee. Despite their proximity the two rivers are very different in character for while the Dee is one of the great Highland spate streams, the Don wends its way at a leisurely pace through water meadows and good farmland rather like a southern chalk stream. It used to be said that 'a mile o' Don's worth two of Dee unless it be for fish or tree'—a reference to the plantations on the upper Dee. It is perhaps unfair to compare the fishing, for few rivers can compete with the Dee and the Don is certainly among the finest salmon and trout streams of Europe, particularly now that the nets have been bought off. It is also one of the few rivers which still has a good spray run. Trout fishing begins in April, with a heavy run of fish in September and October.

This is another area that is rich in history and you will tread the same roads as that pioneer of Highland roads, General Wade, the brilliant but ill-fated supporter of Charles I. Monymusk House used to have a relic of St Columba that was carried in front of the Scottish Army at the Battle of Banockburn in 1314. The spectacular ruins of Kildrummy Castle, a victim of the 1715 Jacobite rising, bear mute witness to the capture of Robert the Bruce's brother in 1306, while Pictish cairns are evidence of an even older civilisation.

There are some sixty-three beats on this river whose source is Well of Don on Little Geal Charn in the far off Grampian Mountains. Its head-waters are fast flowing but below Inchmore its progress starts to become more sedate. In this beautiful moorland setting you can hear the cry of the golden plover and watch pied wagtails. At Cock Bridge it crosses the A939 which can often be blocked by snow in winter and here it sheds the Highland burn character of its infancy and becomes a more mature river. The Colquhonnie Hotel at Strathdow (0975) 651210 has seven beats on which a days salmon fishing can be had for £15 and a day's trouting costs £7. An added attraction of the Don is that it is one of the best trout streams anyone could wish for. Trees may test our casting abilities but in the water beneath their leafy shade lie brown trout—frequently over 2lb. There is also a hatchery at Stathdon which releases 750,000 fly a year into the headwaters to ensure good fishing for the future. Near Candacraig House is the Pot of Poldullie, which is the favourite pool for trout fishermen and can produce lovely 3lb plus brownies. Then it is on to Deskry and Glenbucket Castle. At Glenkindie are the ruins of Towie Castle and the Glenkindie Arms (0975) 641288 whose beat costs £10 a day for salmon fishing or £6 for trout. Downstream are the Kildrummy Fishings; managed by Mr T. Hillary (0975) 571208, this is one of the best upper Don salmon beats and costs £10 for a daily permit. Tickets are also available form the Kildrummy Castle Hotel (0975) 571288.

At Bridge of Alford the river opens out and becomes a lady of more majestic proportions. Permits for here may be had for £8 or £4 a day (depending on whether salmon or trout is the quarry) from the Wardens office of the Grampian District Council (0975) 562107. Retaining the municipal theme, Gordon District Council (0467) 20981 control the Haughton Fishings at Alford, with a daily salmon permit costing £11 for an adult between May and September, £5.50 for a child. For the rest of the season daily tickets cost £13 and £6.50 respectively. W. R. Murray of 27 Main Street (0975) 562366 also handle booking for the Moonhaugh House beat which holds three rods—advance booking is recommended. Just below are the Castle Forbes and Monymusk waters. It is no coincidence that Castle Forbes was once known as *Putachie* (gaelic for trout), as many consider these waters with the famous Dam Pool to be the best trout fishing in Scotland. Forbes Estate Office (09755) 62524 has five beats where trout fishing may be had for £7.50 a day or £45 a week. A week's salmon fishing costs between £90 and £120 plus VAT, depending on the time of season. Locals and visitors staying in the area can get a £5 reduction on the price of a daily permit, which otherwise costs £25. Forbes Estate Office do not offer a season ticket. The Grant Arms Hotel at Monymusk (0467) 7226 offers over ten miles of salmon and trout fishing on the Monymusk Estate water at £22 a day or £95 per rod per week. All red salmon must be returned to the river, as must trout under eight inches. The hotel is run by Colin Hart, a great fisherman, and its water includes the well known Paradise Wood.

It's downstream again to Kenmay where Messrs J.J. Watson (0467) 20321 issue permits for Inverurie Burgh Water at £10-£12 a day (£6 Trout only)—they can also arrange for you to fish the Manar beat for between £10 and £12 per day, and the Ardmurdo Beat at £8 per day for two visitor rods. Sunday fishing is allowed on the River Ury. On the Kintore, J. Copland (0467) 32201 can arrange salmon and trout fishing by the day at around £11 or £32 for a week with children, OAPs and disabled people paying half price. In Aberdeen, J. Somers & Son of The Tackle Shop issue permits for the town's Angling Association's ten miles of water at £15 a day for salmon and £4 a day for trout.

Among others who may be able to help you is Mr McIntosh (0975) 651302 who lets the Tornashean Water. The Banchory office of Strutt & Parker (0330) 24888 lets the Tillypronie Estate water and cottages are available. Mrs Petrie (0975) 571342 issues daily permits at £10 a day for salmon, £6 for trout. The gamekeeper Mr Steven Sharpe can arrange for you to fish a good hill loch for £12 a day including a boat. Kemnay Fishings can be contacted through Mrs Milton (0467) 42220 and offer daily salmon permits for £12 and trout for £6. The sporting agencies may also be able to help. Macsport in Kildrummy (0975) 571377 have two miles where a day costs £20 plus VAT. Ian Black of Meadowland Sporting (0224) 724286 can also arrange fishing on the Dee and mixed sporting holidays. Scotia Sporting Agency (0339) 886891 have access to Don and Deveron beats where the cost ranges from £20 to £50 a day.

The lower river tends to suffer from pollution and poaching, but the latter wouldn't happen if the fish weren't there so don't ignore it! Popular salmon flies for the Don are Munro Killer, Stoats Tail, Harry Mary, Shrimp Fly, General Practitioner and Garry Dog, while one of those big brownies may be tempted by a March Brown or Greenwells Glory.

Grampian Waters

There are not many lochs in the area and the only one of any size is Loch Strathbeg. There is no bank fishing on the loch, but a day with a boat can be had for £6 for one person, £7 for two people, or £8 for three from the Post Office in Crimond (0346) 32229. Sadly, the quality of fishing here has deteriorated in recent years and fishermen who are more concerned with the day's catch are turning to some of the excellent stocked waters in the area. Crimongate Fishery (0346) 32203 is five miles south of Fraserburgh off the B9033 and has a six-acre lake well stocked with brownies and rainbows in a lovely rural setting. A full day's fishing, with a five fish limit, will cost £15. A short journey west, meanwhile, will bring you to Fedderate Reservoir. This is a 250 acre loch which is amply stocked with rainbow and brown trout. If you are not lucky enough to fish the estuary water at Newburgh you can console yourself with a day on Ythan Valley Fisheries' eleven-acre lake, which is also stocked with rainbows and brownies and is only a few miles upstream at Ellon.

Artist: Roger Desoutter **SEPTEMBER EVENING** *Courtesy of Rosenstiel's*

In the earlier part of the nineteenth century few people visited Scotland and before the age of the railway or reasonable road surfaces, large areas were inaccessible. However, Queen Victoria's purchase of the Balmoral Estate was largely responsible for changing public attitudes and the novels of Sir Walter Scott, with their talk of daring deeds and descriptions of magnificent scenery that awaited the visitor, added the romantic flavour that the Victorians enjoyed so much. Osborne on the Isle of Wight may have been a popular holiday resort for the Royal Family but it was Balmoral that held the special place in Victoria's heart. 'It seems like a dream', wrote the Queen, 'to be here in our dear highland home again. Every year my heart becomes more fixed in this Paradise.'

The Dee

From the wells of Dee, some four thousand feet above sea level in the Cairngorms, to the sea at Aberdeen the course of the Dee is some eighty-five miles long. As with the Spey, snow melting at its source helps to give and maintain good spring and early summer water levels. This is one river that does not suffer from being hydroised and there are no natural or artificial obstructions until we reach the Linns above Braemar. The fishing is even better now that the Atlantic Salmon Conservancy Trust has bought out the netting stations at the mouth. As a result several beats have broken all past records and the sea-trout catch has trebled in three years. There are over fifty miles of first class salmon fishing on this exceptionally clear water which still has a good spring run. This, of course, is excellent news for fish and fishermen but what of the more distant predators? Today, catches in all our waters are vastly affected by deep sea netting. This is particularly commonplace in the migratory routes near the Faroes, Greenland and the like. It is a desperate situation and little seems to be being done. Life goes on however and in our simple way, rod in hand, let us return for a morning's fishing.

The Dee tumbles down from its lofty birthplace through Glen Dee. Here we find Chest of Dee where the river crashes down a steep staircase of broken rocks and pools. After a heavy rain or snow melt you can hear the river's angry roar for some distance. Next on to White Bridge where salmon rest after their fight through the Linn of Dee. There is a path from the road to the Linn and you can watch salmon as they leap or lie in the pools gathering strength for their continuing journey. Below the Linn, the Dee widens into a broad crystal fed stream with Scots pine adorning its banks. Nearby is Mar Lodge, built by Queen Victoria for her eldest daughter, Princess Louise and her husband the Duke of Fife. Braemar Castle is another interesting edifice. It was burnt to the ground twice in under thirty years; firstly, in 1689 as a result of the Earl of Mar's failure to support the Jacobite cause and then in 1716 by the Duke of Argyll's

forces because the Earl had led the Jacobite troops at the battle of Sheriffmuir. The Earl was known as 'Bobbing Johnnie' for his habit of changing sides, but he always seemed to end up on the losing one. At Invercauld Robert Louis Stevenson wrote most of _Treasure Island_, a book which, despite the passage of time, still delights each successive generation. Nearby, Queen Victoria leased Gordon House until she bought it in 1848 and employed the services of the local architect in Aberdeen. After some rebuilding and enlarging, the house was renamed Balmoral.

Ballater is a favourite place for visiting fishermen for nearby are such famous beats as Birkhall, Monaltrie, Glenmuick and Abergeldie. At Countrywear in Bridge Street (03397) 55453 you can see the cast of the famous 42lb fish caught by Arthur Wood in 1926. As well as inventing the greased line method of fishing, this great sportsman grassed 3490 salmon from the Cairnton Fishings beat between 1913 and 1934. Countrywear also issue permits for the Mar Estate Water. This beat which is some six and a half miles long holds four rods and costs £20 per rod per day. They can also arrange for you to fish the Glebe Pool beat for £15 a day. Between Ballater and Aboyne the Dee is joined by three tributaries—The Gairn, the Muick and the Water of Tanar. The banks and surrounding hills are thick with Scots pine, birch, alder, willow and oak. Timber used to be a major Deeside industry with logs being floated down river to the Aberdeen mills. This must have played havoc with the fishing. Below Aboyne the river loses the impetuosity of its highland youth and flows gently through fertile farmland. Around Banchory, where the Dee is joined by the Feugh are such well known beats as Cairnton, Woodend, Commonty, Blackhall, Crathie, Invery, Park and Drum. Banchory is the centre for fishing the lower Dee and here you will find the Invery House Hotel (0330) 24782 which can arrange for guests to fish the Commonty beat at a cost of between £350 and £520 plus VAT per week, including a ghillie. In 1991 an Austrian doctor staying at the hotel had two twenty-pounders, and one of twenty-six pounds. The hotel also has sea-trout fishing on the Feugh which flows through its grounds. The Banchory Lodge Hotel (0330) 22625 has three quarters of a mile of double-bank fishing for guests at the same price as Invery House, also including the services of a ghillie.

Between 8000 and 13,000 salmon are caught every season on this superb river where the average fish weighs 8lb. An unusual feature is that all but six of the forty-five beats are single-bank and it is one of the very few rivers where spring fishing is still the best. Although spinning may be permitted most rods will prefer the fly and a Blue Charm, Logie, General Practitioner or Jeannie may do the trick. As one would expect with fishing of this quality, it is not an easy river to get on. However the sporting agencies may be able to help you. Graham Scott at Highland Trophy (0339) 886465 has access to various beats where the cost ranges between £250 and £1000 per week. Meadowhead Sporting (0224) 724286 and Macsport of Kildrummy (0975) 571377 may also be able to help. Glen Tanar Sport and Leisure (03398) 86451 normally let their water on a weekly or fortnightly basis but day permits are available in August and they also have a well stocked ten-acre loch. If your ambition is to have your own fishing then time shares on the Ardoe and Myrtle beats are for sale through Savills' Edinburgh office (031) 226 6961.

The North Esk

Some forty miles South of Aberdeen on the A92 we find the town of Montrose and the North and South Esk. The North Esk is a fine river which now that some netting has been suspended is likely to improve. Actually, so far only two netting stations have been discontinued and those only temporarily, however, it is hoped that this will become permanent and that other nets will follow. The sources of the river are the waters Mark and Lee, two streams which come tumbling down the Grampian Mountains to join forces at Invermark and form the North Esk. It then flows through the beautiful heather and rowan landscape of Glen Esk and here you will find beats such as Invermark and Millden. The Dalhousie Estate Office (0356) 624566 lets the Millden Fisheries beat where the weekly cost for three rods ranges from £75 to £660 and day tickets are sometimes available. The estate also lets well-appointed cottages which can sleep up to six.

Downstream lies Craigoshina and then it is on to Burn Loups and the Gannochy Estate (0356) 47331 water. This is usually let by the week but days are sometimes available. The Estate also has a number of cottages available. After Loups the river flows through fine farmland in the succession of long holding pools. The North Esk District Fishery Board has done a great deal to improve the river and Burn Loups is now the only obstacle fish face in the course of their run. The entrance to Glen Esk is guarded by Edzell Castle with its beautiful gardens of rambling roses and orderly box hedges. West Water—which with its good spawning grounds is an important feeder—joins the Esk at the famous Junction Pool which has produced many fine catches of salmon and sea-trout.

There are many well known beats such as Arnhall, Strachthro, Pert, Gallery, Morphie and Craigo to name but a few. However, this productive river which can often produce a fish on opening day is very popular and you may have to join the queue before casting a Blue Charm or Thunder and Lightning on this water. However, Mr G. Luke (0674) 73535 the secretary of the Montrose Angling Association may be able to sell you a permit at a cost of between £8 to fish their eleven and a half miles on a Thursday, Friday or Saturday as a guest of a member providing you can prove you are a whisky drinker and not a lager lout! Scotia Sporting Agency may be able to help with several beats while Joseph Johnston and Sons (0674) 72666 issue both daily permits and weekly lets. The Morphie Fishings have recently been time shared and a few units are still available from Savills (031) 226 6961. The North Esk is very much a spate river and as one would expect spring and autumn tend to be the best times. However, the summer months can see good runs of grilse and sea-trout depending on the water level. Sea-trout average around 2lb and salmon 9lb though twenty-pounders are caught every season.

The South Esk

The South Esk is also a spate river and as there are no feeder lochs in the system, the headwaters are of little interest to the fisherman. But it is a totally different matter after the White Water joins the river at the head of Glen Clova where some fine sport can be enjoyed. The Clova hotel (0575) 5222 has three miles of double-bank fishing which holds eight rods. Spinning and bait as well as fly are permitted on this water which costs £13 a day. Downstream from the glen there are some good holding pools and the river broadens out when it meets the Prosen Water just beyond Cortachy Castle. From here down to the Montrose basin is very good fishing, particularly for sea-trout which average two and a half pounds, but most seasons produce at least one six-pounder. Famous beats include Careston, Finavon, Kinnaird and House of Dun. One of the best stretches is the Finavon Castle Water. There are two miles of double-bank fishing and two and a half miles of single-bank divided into three beats, Castle, Indies and Balgarrock Meadows which share more than thirty pools and lies between them. The manager is Miss Dawn Darling (0307) 85344 and prices for these outstanding beats may be had on application. Mr H. Burness (0575) 73456 is the secretary of Kirriemuir Angling Club which has seven miles of double-bank fishing where a Dunkeld or Blue Charm may produce the magic tug. Spinning is also permitted and locals use a Toby, Devon or Mepps. The cost here is £50 a week or £10 a day but no day tickets are issued on a Saturday.

Invicta, Dunkeld, Soldier Palmer: Rosemary Coates

Lochs Nan Eun & Bainnie

These are two fine hill lochs, on which a day's fishing will be rewarded by a bag of up to a dozen hard fighting wild browns. Good flies for these lochs are Black Pennell, Soldier Palmer and Peter Ross tied on a size 12 or 14. Bainnie is a fairly level two and a half mile walk from the A93 just south of Braemar. The walk to Nan Eun is also fairly level, but it is nine miles! So it could be an idea to hire a four-wheel drive vehicle even though the last two miles are still on foot. The effort is well.worthwhile for the trout are genuinely wild and there are majestic Grampian peaks all round. Permits may be had from either the Invercauld Estate Office (0339) 741224 or the game keeper, Mr R. Hepburn (0250) 885206. The season for this fly only water is March 12th to August 11th and the cost is £5 a day or £25 for the season.

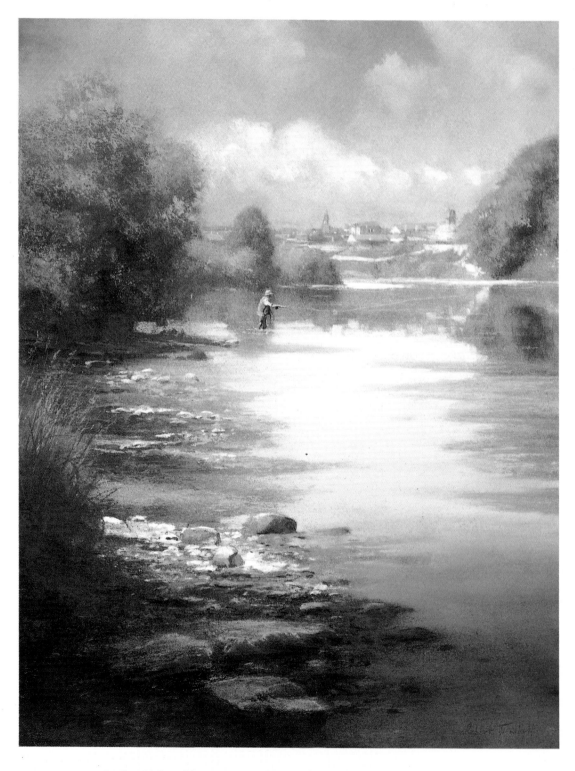

Artist: Robert Turnbull A PERFECT DAY Courtesy of The Artist

Despite the huge amount of research, all too little is known about the sea habits of the salmon. It is a commonly known fact that they return to the rivers of their birth to spawn, and this is where netting becomes an important factor. Stake nets are bad enough and it is encouraging to see how many of these are now being bought off, but it is difficult to avoid the feeling that the drift-net industry must shoulder a fair degree of responsibility. Huge nets six hundred yards long trap the fish on their return to spawning grounds. The north east coast drift net fishery employs just under five hundred people, while fishing in Scotland supports five thousand jobs and is valued at £50 million a year. So with up to £320,000 being asked for a week's time share on the Tay, isn't the fisherman entitled to expect a reasonable level of fish in the river? Something has got to be done and I urge you to support the associations which are trying to change this disturbing state of affairs.

The Tay

To see what the Tay can produce you only have to walk to Hardys in Pall Mall, for there in a case is a cast of THE fish. At 6.15pm on October 7th 1922 Miss G.W.Ballantine, spinning bait– a dace–was taken in Boat Pool on the Glendevine Water. Nearly two hours later (8.05pm to be exact) it was landed. In 1820 the Earl of Howe is said to have landed a fish of 69lb on the Tweed, but this is somewhat legendary and at 64lb Miss Ballantine's fish holds the official record. In April of the same year Major Baker Carr took seventeen fish in a day which varied in weight from 9lb to 30lb. Back in Victorian times the Duke of Atholl regularly used to take six or seven salmon before breakfast. But perhaps this is not surprising considering the catch records of the time. Take 1843 for example, when returns show that 35,126 salmon and 43,617 grilse were killed, and the river wasn't fished anything like as hard as it is nowadays. What a river!

Perth was formerly the capital of Scotland and was fortified by the Romans, who were so awestruck by the mighty Tay that they compared it to the Tiber. But, as Sir Walter Scott wrote in 'The Fair Maid of Perth':

'Behold the Tiber,' the vain Roman cried,
Viewing the ample Tay from Baiglies side;
'But where's the Scot that would the vaunt repay,
And hail the puny Tiber as the Tay?'

The Tay drains more than 2200 square miles of country and carries the largest volume of fresh water in the British Isles. It begins its 114 miles in the hills near Tyndrum on the west coast. Two feeder streams, the Dochart and Lochay, merge to become Fillan Water. This then tumbles past Crianlarich and on into Loch Dochart where, perched on an island, the ruins of Dochart Castle still keep watch over the narrow pass into the glen. It is joined by the wild waters of Benmore Burn as it threads its way though boggy ground and on to Loch Iubhair.

Then it is on to the falls of Dochart at Killin which is on the western shore of Loch Tay. Salmon rarely ascend the falls until the temperature is right, which is not usually before May. Loch Tay is some fourteen miles long by three quarters of a mile wide and is over four hundred and fifty feet deep in places. Trout average three quarters of a pound but three and four-pounders are taken regularly, while big ferox lurk in its murky depths. The shallow areas of the east and west ends are probably the best fishing and, as on all big lochs, a ghillie is an indispensable asset. Trolling is likely to be the most successful method, especially in the spring when the average fish is a hefty 17lb. Above the western shore are the ruins of Finlarig Castle, seat of Black Duncan, the Earl of Orchy. The well preserved dungeons and beheading pit are ample evidence that the Earl lived up to his nickname. Overlooking the northern shore is the 3984 feet lofty eminence of Ben Lawers. From the summit of this mountain on a clear day you can see both east and west coasts. Its slopes are covered with rare mosses and lichens such as mossy cyphel, Alpine forget-me-not and campion.

The Ardeonaig Hotel (0567) 2400 is the only hotel on the south side of the loch and is halfway along the shoreline, yards from the ancient ruins of Mains Castle. It is the ideal place for a fishing holiday, as with one of the hotel's five four-rod boats you can cover both the east and west ends of the loch. Moreover, if you feel like a break from fishing you can always try the hotel's nine-hole golf course. Other fishing hotels are Clachgaig Hotel (0567) 2270 which has three boats and Croft-na-Caber (0887) 830236 which also has a water sports centre. Permits for a day's trouting can be had for £3 from the Kenmore Post Office (0887) 830200. The Kenmore Hotel (0887) 830205 has three boats for loch fishing and two miles of river fishing which is available to guests at £11 a day and non-residents at £16.25 a day. On January the 15th, which is the first day of the season, fishermen are piped down to the water and a bottle of whisky is cracked over the bows of one of the hotel's boats. Most rods will troll using Rapallas, Kynochs or Tobies. This method may not suit the purist, but on the other hand it does catch fish! Now that many of the downstream nets have been bought off and the Lochay has been improved, catches on the loch should improve in a few years time.

The Lyon

A short distance downstream from Kenmore is the junction with the River Lyon, one of the Tay's biggest tributaries. Like the Lochay this river has been hydro-ised and the dam at the eastern end of Loch Lyon prevents fish from reaching the loch and spawning the headwaters. The hydro scheme has, however, created some good deep holding pools and fish now spawn in the river's tributaries and its lower reaches, with the best fishing on the lower seven miles down to the junction with the Tay. Much work has been done to improve the Lyon in recent years. Spawning grounds have been improved and it is being stocked with fry. It is a superb river to fish with large deep holding pools, cascading falls, and white

Set on a hillside overlooking the Vale of Strathmore to the Sidlaw Hills beyond, are 10 acres of tiered and rambling gardens, at the heart of which lies the 'Lands of Loyal'.

This impressive Victorian Mansion was built in the 1830s, commissioned by Sir William Ogilvy, who, on his return from Waterloo, chose Loyal Hill as the site for this magnificent home.

The Lands of Loyal was subsequently owned by a succession of families until being converted into a Hotel in 1945.

It has since been very prominent in the area, holding fond memories for the oldest generations. It is also highly regarded as a second home to country sportsmen who have remained loyal for many years. More recently, an extensive refurbishment programme, carried out in the public rooms, has further enhanced the unique atmosphere of this much respected country house hotel.

A highly acclaimed restaurant in its own right, our style of cuisine is traditional and imaginative, making full use of local fish and game.

An extensive wine list, featuring several wines and madeiras,

some over 150 years old, is available to complement your meal.

The Lands of Loyal makes an ideal base for the ambitious golfer. Perthshire has 30 golf courses in total with remarkable variety. All courses are within an hour's drive of the hotel with some of the most famous and desirable spots only a few minutes away.

As fundamentally a sportsman's hotel, The Lands of Loyal appreciates the needs of the golfer. Very early breakfasts and unusually flexible dining arrangements, quality packed lunches etc., are offered courteously. Private rooms for parties can be requested in advance.

The Hotel management are delighted to arrange a complete itinerary for the golfer, whether an individual or a group. Tee times can be arranged and green fees paid. Any correspondence with golf clubs will gladly be undertaken by us.

The Lands of Loyal provides a complete and competitive golfing package. A full colour brochure and tariff is available on request.

Alyth
Perthshire
Scotland
PH11 8JQ
Tel: (08283) 3151
Fax: (08283) 3313

water runs. There are some particularly attractive pools on the Fortinglass water and here in the churchyard you can see the oldest tree in Europe, a 3000 year old yew. Although the back end of the season is likely to be best, the Lyon also produces good springers. The Coshieville Hotel (0887) 830319 has the first one and a half miles of water above the junction. This water has six pools, taking four rods and a boat is available for fishing Castle Pool. A day's trouting costs £5 while salmon fishing varies between £10 and £15. Two and a half pound trout are not uncommon here. The Post Office House (0887) 866221 at Bridge of Balgie issues daily permits for fishing some of the upstream beats.

Between the junction with the Lyon and Aberfeldy are the Tay's Farleyer and Bolfracks beats. It was from here that the Black Watch began its road to fame and glory in 1740. Until that date it had primarily been used to keep the peace between feuding Highlanders. However, war with Spain had broken out and troops were needed. It was decided that the regiment should be force marched to London and rumour spread that they were destined for the West Indies. Travelling south of the border was a big enough wrench for men who had never left their homeland before, but the West Indies with their lethal fevers was the worst of possible fates (my how things change!). Some of the men deserted but those that were captured were shot in the Tower of London. However, the regiment was sent to Europe and at Fontenoy opposing officers dropped handkerchiefs to signal that fighting could commence.

At Aberfeldy, where the Urlar Burn joins the Tay, is the Farleyer House Hotel (0887) 20332 which can usually arrange fishing for guests, although it can be expensive. The Weem Hotel at Weem (0887) 20381 has privileged access to one and a half miles of good water for guests. If you think that all fishing on the Tay is expensive Mr and Mrs J. Garbutt of Grandtully (0796) 482207 have a pleasant surprise for you. They have a mile of single bank fishing above the Kinnaird beat where the cost of a day is £7. Now you may think that at this price the fishing must be mediocre at best and that a £40 a day stretch is likely to make more productive use of your landing net. If you do, you are missing a great opportunity, for a twenty-five pounder was recently caught on this water and the average weight is around ten pounds.

The Tummel

As one might expect with such a big river as the Tay, many of its tributaries are fine salmon rivers in their own right and one such is the Tummel, which joins the Tay at Logierait. Although its character has been effected by the hydro dam at Faskally, this is good fly water and April sees some fantastic rises of trout to hatching olives. To whet your appetite there is a fish pass with a viewing gallery at Pitlochry. The Angling Club here has the fishing of the right bank and those hoping to fish are asked to write to the Secretary. Alternatively, you could try the Atholl Estate Office (0796) 81355 which has fishing on the Tummel, Garry and Tilt, or stay at the impressive East Haugh House Hotel (0796) 473121 which has leasing arrangements on various beats of the same three rivers and also the Shee. Salmon prices vary between £35 and £100 per day and trout between £2 and £5.

Artist: Andrew Benfield EARLY MORNING RISE Courtesy of De Montfort Art

Much of the Tay has wooded banks and, added to its considerable width, it is often much more practicable to fish it from a boat. While it may be tempting for the bank fisherman to wade so as to cover that little bit extra water (which is sure to hold a fish), wading can be extremely dangerous as this is a fast flowing river and the pools can be very deep. The conifers surrounding Dunkeld House are thought to be more than two hundred years old and are particularly striking. The town in medieval times was the religious centre of Scotland and you can see the tomb of Robert II in the cathedral. To most fishermen, Dunkeld is synonymous with the fly of the same name. This brightly coloured little temptress has proved the undoing of many a fat trout, and one that has personally brought a degree of luck. The river is joined here by the Braan whose Black Linn falls are impassable to salmon. Just below the town are the Birnam Woods of *Macbeth* fame, while downstream is Glendelvine where Miss Ballantine caught her fish. Now that some of the nets have been bought off, Dunkeld is seeing much better runs of sea-trout. Dunkeld & Birnam Angling Association have two combined beats and day permits are available for £2 from Kettles of Dunkeld (0350) 727556. A good place to stay is the Stakis Dunkeld House Hotel (0350) 727771 which has two miles of double-bank fishing. The hotel is in the middle of its four beats, which hold twelve rods and the services of two ghillies are available. Hotel guests understandably have priority but bookings from non-residents are welcome. Mr M.C. Smith (0350) 727593 lets the Dalguise Salmon Fishings, which are one and a half miles of double-bank at between £20 and £35 a day according to season. Not far downstream is the Kinloch House Hotel (0250) 884 237 which can arrange spring and summer fishing for guests on two beats, where the cost ranges from £60 to £200 a day.

The Isla & the Ericht

Below Glendelvine are Kercock and Meikleour, after which the Tay is joined by the Isla at Islamouth. This is superb fishing but very expensive! The Tower of Lethendy fishings at Meikleour have recently been time-shared on ninety-nine year leases with a top price of £350,000, and that's just for one week. Both the Isla and its tributary the Ericht, which has good spawning beds have a justly deserved reputation for producing excellent fishing. Richmond & Co. (0382) 201964 manage the Gauldry beat on the Isla where a week for four rods costs £400. Also on the Isla, Mrs Henderson (0828) 7226 can arrange for you to fish about one and a half miles of single bank, which has four named pools at between £15 and £25 per rod per day. Spinning tends to be best on the slack water here, but there are some nice runs which take the fly well.

On the Ericht, the Bridge of Cally Hotel (0250) 886231 water costs between £20 and £25 a day; Ian Stewart (0250) 872968 is the ghillie and can give you further details. Or you can try Finlayson Hughes (0738) 30926 who let the Craighall Rattray beat where you can enjoy such pools as Witches, Cauldron and Pipers Cave. There is a tradition of spinning on the Tay, partly because of its size and also because it is an early spring river and spun baits allow you to get down better and fish the Tay water. But where streams and pools can be covered by fly it is well worth a try. Beats such as Islamouth and Benchil have excellent fly water. However, you will need a big rod, for although a fifteen-footer may cover some of the upper beats, an eighteen or twenty-footer will be needed for the bigger pools. On the big pools another alternative to spinning is *harling*. This involves trailing three lures on set lengths of line from a boat. With this method the boatman does all the work and the fisherman just has to wait until the rod bends and the reel plays its merry tune. This may seem boring but Miss Ballantine, to name but one, found it rather effective!

The lower beats are superb and very difficult to get on especially at prime times, unless you are lucky enough to be invited as a guest or happen to be a millionaire. The Tayside Hotel at Stanley (0738) 828249 has access to time shared beats from May to July, where a day can be had for £20. Perth District Council (0738) 439911 owns some fishing and, if you can prove you are a resident of this fair city you can purchase a permit at £5 for five years. If you can prove you live within fifteen miles of the city you are eligible to join the Perth and District Angling Club. Applications for membership can be had from the local tackle shops and the fishing on the club's water can be excellent and is great value compared to the expensive adjoining beats.

If conditions are favourable, just west of Pitlochry there is excellent loch fishing to be had on lochs Tummel, Rannoch and Dunalastaire Water, where you will find the Dunalastaire Hotel (0882) 2303. The eastern end of Rannoch is guarded by Schiehallion, 'The Fairy Hill of the Caledonians'. However, it is fat trout and not fairies that you will find here where the murky depths, more than 300 feet in places, hold quantities of large ferox—seven pounders are not uncommon. Much of the loch's banks are crowded with conifers and the shallower margins of the western shore are the best fishing areas. A day here with such flies as Greenwells Glory, March Brown or Blue Zulu should produce a good basket of three quarter pound brownies, while for the big ferox, trolling is the best method. The loch is fed by the outflow from Loch Laidon, which lies some six miles to the west and where a day spent fishing its attractive bays can produce twenty or more large bags of lively trout of between a half and three quarters of a pound. Loch Rannoch Hotel (0882) 2201 is a good place to stay for fishing these lochs or exploring Rannoch Moor, whose waterlogged peat with tufts of cotton grass and coarse sedges is alive with the calls of snipe, curlew and grouse. Permits for Loch Tummel are obtained from the Pitlochry Tourist Information Centre (0796) 472215 at £3 per day and £10 per week (trout, pike and perch only).

The Tay is a colossus among the waters of the world. It may have reported decreasing catches, and this is a worrying sign, but it is still a symbol of strength, power and beauty. Scotland is a land rich in scenic wonders and there are few more compelling sights than the waters of the Tay and her tributaries. There may be finer waters in Canada, Scandinavia or even Scotland but few, if any, have the stature of the Tay—a symbol of salmon and of Scotland.

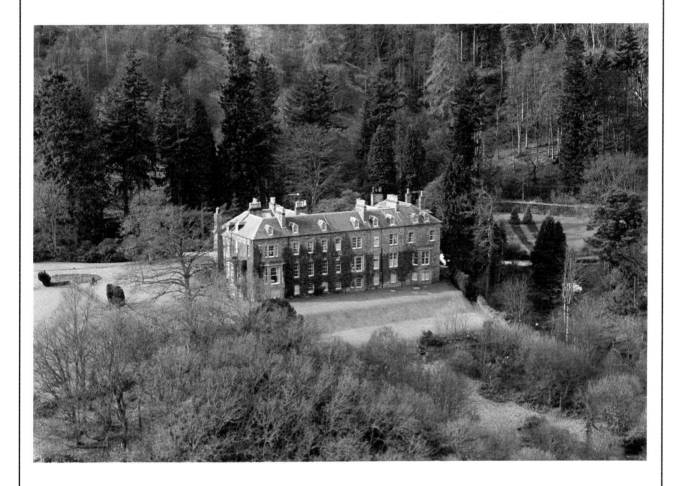

Mrs Constance Ward invites you to Kinnaird, a splendid country house dating in part from 1770, set in its own estate with lovely views over the Tay valley. With glorious gardens, open fires, a genuinely warm welcome and bedrooms of great charm and comfort, Kinnaird is a delightful spot for a relaxing break and is ideally situated for visiting the many beauty spots and places of interest in Perthshire.

Kinnaird owns over 2.5 miles of high quality fishing on the Tay and employs two full time ghillies. The Lower Kinnaird Beat is renowned for its fishing in September and October and consists of seven attractive pools, while the Upper Kinnaird Beat is a spring beat with an increasing annual catch. The three hill lochs provide fishing for brown trout and pike amongst some of Perthshire's most scenic surroundings.

In addition the estate offers a variety of other sporting including superb pheasant shooting for groups of eight guns, duck flighting and roe stalking.

Less taxing perhaps are the lovely walks that are available from a gentle stroll round the garden to longer walks on the hill and

moor. The outdoor tennis court and a croquet lawn provide entertainment for summer afternoons, although should the weather prove inclement, the cedar panelled sitting room provides a selection of amusements including bridge, backgammon, billiards or simply good conversation.

The award-winning restaurant, directed by Chef John Webber, offers modern cuisine of the highest standard; There is an extensive and detailed wine list partnered with a comprehensive selection of Malt Whisky. Both dining rooms enjoy magnificent views, while the former drawing room features exquisite painted panels of figures and landscapes. These superb surroundings provide a stunning setting for a menu of carefully chosen dishes, imaginatively prepared and beautifully presented. In addition to table reservations, private luncheons, dinners and meetings may be reserved. Lunch and dinner are always available for both resident and non-resident guests and booking is appreciated.

On the Kinnaird Estate as well as the hotel there are at present 5 Country Cottages available for let, for more information on fishing and reservations please telephone (0796) 482440.

Kinnaird
Kinnaird Estate
By Dunkeld
Perthshire PH8 0LB
Tel: (0796) 482440
Fax: (0796) 482289

A breathtaking location on the banks of the River Tay, 280 acres of grounds and a superb hotel offering a warm welcome to experienced anglers and novices alike.

Two miles of salmon fishing water offering the opportunity to fish from the bank or boat. Spinning and fly fishing available. Experienced ghillies who specialise in giving help and advice, not to mention catching fish!

Excellent trout fishing also available on our fishing beat or on a local loch. Make a day of it!

For an opportunity to catch a truly magnificent fish take advantage of our special 'Fishing Forays Package'.

A 3 day break to include 2 day's salmon fishing on the River Tay dinner, bed and breakfast and all the fun that a 'Fishing foray' promises!

For more information or to make a booking please contact us on the number below:-

Dunkeld House Hotel
Dunkeld
Perthshire PH8 0HX
Tel: (0350) 727771
Fax: (0350) 728924

Many scribes have pondered long and hard over the special appeal of loch fishing. One of the things I enjoy about fishing is getting away from the hustle and bustle of town life and being able to enjoy the solitude of the countryside. Standing in a line of fellow anglers fishing some supposed 'hot spot' is not my idea of fun. Don't misunderstand me, I have had many happy days on stocked water and enjoyed some good tussles with rainbows. However loch fishing is a totally different phenomenon. The fish may be small but they are wild and I would rather face a hard fighting half pounder than a number of one pound 'stockies' which often have little or no flavour to their flesh.

Loch Lomond

Having described one of the joys of loch fishing as being able to enjoy the quiet and solitude of the country you may think it inappropriate to discuss Loch Lomond. After all it is only a short distance from Glasgow and there is a main road along the whole of the western shoreline. It is also a major tourist attraction. However, Lomond is a big water covering some twenty-seven square miles and this, combined with its many small wooded islands, ensures that there is ample room for both tourist and fisherman. One of the fascinating aspects about Lomond is the difference in character between its north and south ends. This is principally because it is a product of the Ice Age. There is a geographical fault line running from Arden to Balmaha and the loch differs dramatically below the village of Luss. Above this point it is narrow, steep-banked and as deep as 450 feet in parts. South of Luss the loch broadens out and gets progressively shallower as you near Balloch at the southern end. This is important from a fishing point of view for, while twenty feet of water may suit sea-trout, salmon prefer much shallower water, a depth of between five and eight feet. The great banks of silt and sand such as Pilot Bank above Ross are the product of glacial deposits from the Ice Age.

As it is such a vast expanse of water, bank fishing is pretty unproductive and the only really practical method of fishing is from a boat, drifting gently between the islands. In medieval times mainlanders used the islands as a sanctuary for themselves and their livestock. This however, was no guarantee of safety from the marauding Norsemen. In 1263 King Haakon sailed his galleys up Loch Long and then carried them overland to Lomond— no mean feat! Here they were relaunched and the islands were systematically plundered. Several centuries later the islands were used to house drunkards and lunatics, but all is quiet now except for the piping of birds.

The most likely way of catching a salmon is to _troll_. This involves using three rods with two carrying lures some twenty-five yards behind the boat and a short stiff rod, usually called a poker, fishing some ten yards nearer in. The start of the season will see natural baits such as the golden Sprat and at the beginning of June, artificials like Rapallas and the Kynoch Killer are favoured. This method calls for some smart action when you get a take. The first thing to do is to head for deeper water, then to wind in the spare lures and start playing the fish, as rapidly as possible.

May sees the beginning of the fly season when a team of traditional flies such as Black Pennell, Peter Ross and Dunkeld will be used, for this is also good sea-trout water. Among the local favourites are the Turkey and Gold and the Burton. Dapping is also a popular technique but because Lomond is so big and regularly fished by the locals, you will find that everyone has their own method and their own favourite fly. Among the islands, Inch Moan and Inch Fad are popular but the best advice on a likely place will come from those who hire out the boats as they will know what's been happening. Macfarlane & Sons of Balmaha (0360) 87214 hire out boats at £12 a day for two people or £20 to include an outboard. More than two people will pay £14 or £25. April 13th 1991 was a lucky day for one of these boats which took a lovely twenty-seven pounder from the 'Stables', near Ross Priory. Permits and advice can also be obtained from The Balloch Hotel (0389) 52579, Ardlui Hotel (03014) 243 and The Tarbet Hotel (03012) 346. R.A. Clement & Co of Glasgow (041) 221 0068 issue permits on behalf of the Loch Lomond Angling Improvement Association. The cost of a day's ticket is £9 while a week is £27.

The Fruin and the Endrick

The Loch Lomond Angling Association is also responsible for fishing on the rivers Fruin and Endrick. Public access, however, is restricted to full members of the Association. A subscription ticket costs £115, together with a £25.54 joining fee. These permits cover salmon and trout; eight to twelve ounces is the average for trout which will be found all along the shores, though the northern end is likely to be more productive.

The source of the River Endrick is in West Stirlingshire and flows into the loch near Balmaha. The upper part of the river is not worth fishing for, although the salmon is a mighty leaper, no fish can ascend the ninety-foot Loup O'Fintry falls. Below the falls there are some good pools but downstream there are more falls, the Pot of Gartness, and salmon need the right level of water to ascend them. Below the Pot is the meeting with the Blane, which is the main tributary and the junction pool known as the Meetings of Lynn is a favourite spot. Below Drymen the river flows through rich pasture and woodland and can be a bit sluggish. It really requires a good spate to provide exciting fishing; but then pools such as Oak Tree and Coolies Linn can produce salmon of around 10lb and sea-trout which average around 2lb. It takes the right conditions to get fish into the river and many find that trolling on the loch by the mouth of the river can produce excellent results.

The Leven

Despite the mass of water in the loch, the Leven which connects it to the Clyde is relatively slow moving due to the barrage at Balloch. As is to be expected from being so near a big city, the river is heavily fished. This is also because it can be very good as Mr S.Burgoyne will tell you, for in July 1989 he caught a magnificent sea-trout of 22lb 8oz. This river is also controlled by the Loch Lomond Angling Improvement Association and day tickets can be had for £12.50 while £57.50 is the cost of a season's ticket.

Loch Leven

Heading north over the Forth brings you to the start of the M90 and in a short while you are alongside Loch Leven. This water is world famous and many international fishing competitions are held here. Its reputation derives from the superb hard fighting qualities of its brownies which have been used to stock waters all over the world. It is fair to say that in recent years catches have fallen and also that the trout seem to feed off the bottom. This is a perplexing change and one which will surely keep the experts busy for some time. As a result of these developments many rods are now using sinking lines, but as most of the loch is shallow you don't have to go down too far. Despite such problems this is still one of the great trout waters and you will find that traditional small double-hook flies such as March Brown, Dunkeld, Invicta, Black Pennel and Soldier Palmer can be effective. One of the attractions of the loch is the size of the trout, for they average around one and a quarter pounds and three pounders are taken regularly. The best fish in recent years has been 6lb 6oz. It should also be noted that boats are essential on this water. Permits can be had from Loch Leven Fisheries at The Pier (0577) 863407, where you can also hire boats and it is a good idea to book in advance. The day is divided into two sessions; 10.00am to 6.00pm, which costs £21 and 6.30pm to 11.30pm for £28. There is an afternoon session (2.00pm to 6.00pm) for £14, and at weekends dawn (which can be 2.30am!) to 9.00am costs £24. The Loch is not only a tremendous water, it is also a most beautiful one. Imagine the scene as the sun comes up—you have fished hard and had good results, the occasional joke has rudely disrupted the lapping of the water on your boat. This is what life is about; a holiday with your head buried in the sand in Southern Spain is unlikely to evoke such gratifying memories. Make no mistake—to enjoy a dawn on Loch Leven is a memory you will treasure.

Continuing still further north on the M90 towards Perth brings you to Bridge of Earn. It is a mistake to regard the River Earn as a tributary of the Tay for it flows into the Firth below the tide. This is, however, not a bad salmon river and some say better than the Tay for sea-trout which average 2lb and can be over 7lb. The Earn flows out of Loch Earn which is a good water-sports centre. There is trout fishing on the loch and permits may be had from St Fillans and Loch Earn Head Post Office (0764) 685309 who can also hire you a boat. The cost of a day's fishing on the loch is only £3 but that reflects the quality of the fishing. The lower river tends to be slow and sluggish but upstream from Kinkell Bridge at Strathallan it is a pleasing streamy river with some good pools. The Earn Angling Improvement Association has been doing sterling work to improve fishing here. The river is now being stocked with native fish and all but two of the nets have been bought off. The fact that two miles were recently sold for £570,000 will give you some idea of the quality of the fishing. A day on the Lawers Estate Co. Ltd. (0764) 670050 water costs £50 and season tickets are available. This beat is a little awkward to reach but well worth the effort. Rather more affordable is the Crieff Angling Clubs water which costs £8 a day for salmon or £3 for trout (which can be excellent). Permits from Mr J.Boyd's newsagent shop in Crieff (0764) 653871 and it is advisable to book ahead for weekends as Sunday fishing is allowed.

The Forth & its Tributaries

Fly fishing on the River Forth? Incredulity would be the natural reaction of many a southerner brought up on images of factories discharging waste into the river. The ill-informed might argue that there was no point in going and that you might just as well try a day's salmon fishing on the Thames, as the result would be the same. How wrong can you be! In 1988 over 1000 salmon and grilse were taken from the Town Water at Stirling alone. The Scots really care about their fishing and a tremendous amount of work has gone into improving the rivers. The Forth is one of the great success stories and the river and its tributaries, the Teith, Allan and Devon, also have good runs of sea-trout. The good news story continues for the spring run is actually increasing. Opening day, February 1st 1991, produced a twenty-five pounder at Callander and April has seen several fish of around thirty pounds. A day's permit for the Forth costs £23.25 and a seasons ticket is £85 which strikes me as being good value for money. They may be had from Country Pursuits (0786) 834495.

Mr D.Crockart (0786) 473443 can also arrange a day for you on the Blue Bank Fishings on the Teith where the cost varies between £11 and £32 a day. James Bayne of Callander (0877) 30218 also issues permits for the Teith and the Town Water at a cost of £15 a day.

The Devon still suffers from some pollution, but this is reflected in the cost of £3 a day or £12 for a season and it can fish well in the Autumn—contact Devon Angling Association (0259) 215185.

The Allan, where a day costs between £10 and £25, is beginning to be very good for sea-trout and are increasing. Tickets may be obtained from McLaren Tackle (0786) 833530. In Bridge of Allan, meanwhile, Bridge of Allan Reservoir (0786) 834495 offers boat fishing for trout at £12 (boat hire covers two people).

Central Region Waters

There are a number of stocked fisheries in the area. Examples of enjoyable fishing available are Carron Valley Reservoir (0786) 442000 where a week day ticket costs £19.30 (£5.80 for the hire of a boat), Lake of Menteith (08775) 664 (the comfortable Lake Hotel), near Aberfoyle, where a full session's boat fishing costs £22 per boat, and Loch Dochart at the northern tip of Loch Lomond. Fishing here is either bank or boat and details can be obtained from either Muirlaggan Farm (0877) 4219 or Portnellau Lodge House (08383).

If you fancy a change from rainbows what about American book trout? Unless you have fished in the States, which has some great trouting areas like Montana, you may not have come across these fish before, but of all the stocked varieties they are the ones most likely to put up a memorable fight. There are two fisheries in the area which are stocked with them: Mill Dam and Loch Monzievaird and permits can be had for them from Kettles in Dunkeld (0350) 2556 and Mr Groot of Crieff (0764) 3963.

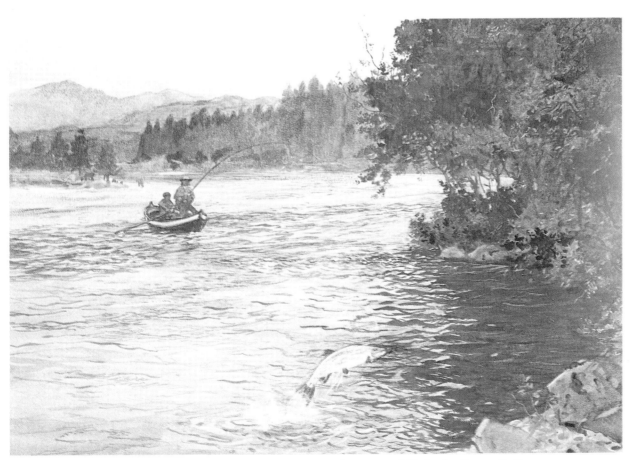

Artist: Ernest Briggs   TROUT FISHING   Courtesy of Malcolm Innes Gallery

Despite its undoubted beauty, this is a region that has suffered from the demands of twentieth-century man. Over fifty per cent of Argyll has been ravaged by forestry—why, oh why, did we ever let it happen? Of course it is understandable that any landowner wishes to maximise the return from his holdings, but surely afforestation on this scale here and also in many other parts of Scotland is ill-conceived. Tax concessions have played a great part in these schemes but what is their purpose? No doubt the mandarins of Whitehall looked at the balance of trade in timber and decided we should try and become more self-sufficient. A glance at the map indicated sparsely populated areas of Scotland and the decision was made.

The Awe

The River Awe is one of those rivers affected in recent times by the dubious benefits of man's intervention—in this case by a sixty-foot dam. Before this development, the river truly justified its name with its roaring torrent of fast flowing pools and deep rocky runs. It was renowned for producing fish of awesome proportions; in 1921 Major Huntington had a fifty-seven pounder while four years later, his wife had one of fifty-one pounds. There are a number of other fifty-pounds plus fish recorded, while twenty-pounders were a weekly, if not daily, occurrence..While it may no longer be a glass case river it is still very, very good and a day or, if you are lucky, a week on one of its seven beats will be a treasured memory. As it drains, Loch Awe is half- river half-estuary, after which it tumbles down the Pass of Brander before assuming a more gentle pace, with banks decked with silver birch and oak, flowing through rich meadows to join the salt water of Loch Etive. Over three thousand fish a year are counted through the barrage and further good news is that UDN, which has plagued the river for more than twenty years, is on the decline. Bell Ingram (0738) 21121 can arrange for you to fish the Barrage Beat at a cost of approximately £210 although availability is unsurprisingly limited. Mr Campbell-Preston of Inverawe Fisheries (08662) 446 may also be able to help you cast a fly on the illustrious river. The cost per rod is £30 a day or £140 a week and three charming cottages are available for letting. As one would expect with a river of this quality, it is a fly-only water where the early season will see large tues fished on a sinking line. As the water warms up rods will change to an intermediate floating or sink tip depending on their preference. Flies tend to be fairly small, and black is the favourite colour, so a size 10 Stoats Tail, for example, would be a popular choice.

Loch Awe

Loch Awe is a long thin ribbon of a loch which has become very popular as, in addition to salmon, sea-trout and brown trout, its waters also hold ferox of monster proportions, perch, char, pike and escapee rainbows from a fish farm. I cannot help thinking that in some cases not enough thought has been given to the operation of fish farms. Escapees can cause havoc with stocks of fly and, small as they have been here, this can result in some big fish. One rod took nineteen rainbows in a day with five of them over 7lb. Nineteen eighty-eight saw several double figure fish with a best of 14lb, while two years earlier a massive rainbow of 21lb 4oz was taken by Mr Graham. The ferox are rather more elusive but they are huge. One was washed up on the shore with a partially eaten belly which still weighed in at over 21lb. Then there is the monster 37lb 8oz fish of Mr W. Muir which was caught in 1866. Trout fishing is good and at present free, though the riparian owners have applied for a protection order so that it can be properly managed and stocks conserved. Sea-trout fishing is not what it used to be, but this is a common tale of woe on west coast waters. Most salmon are taken from the northern end and fishing round the islands is likely to be most profitable. Because trouting is free, it is sad to say that there are quite a few who don't bother to obtain a salmon permit. This is not fair on those who do or the riparian owners. Needless to say, anyone fishing with a suspicious looking trout rod should be reported.

A day's ticket only costs £2 and for £20 you can hire a boat with an outboard. Tickets can be obtained from the Ardbrecknish House at Dalmally (08663) 223. The loch can be dangerous water for it is nearly three hundred feet deep in places and the wind can whip down it, so always wear a life-jacket. Although it is very popular it is still easy to find a quiet, secluded spot as the loch is some twenty-five miles long. It is an attractive setting with wooded shores and islands such as Fraoch Eilean, where you can see the ruined castle of Lorne, a delightful sight. Fishing in its compass is an exhilarating experience.

The Orchy

The reason why most salmon are taken from the northern end is that they are bound for the spawning grounds of the River Orchy. This river drains Loch Tulla and its ten mile journey takes it through Glen Orchy which, with its famous Iron Bridge Falls, must be one of the prettiest glens you could wish to find. The barrage on the Awe has affected this river, as salmon which used to enter the river in March and April will not be seen in any number until the beginning of June and July through to September. As a result, these are now the best months. Salmon tend to be held back by the falls until the June spates and pools below the falls such as Pulpit and Gut can be particularly rewarding. Those wishing to fish the upper river may care to stay at the Bridge of Orchy Hotel (08384) 208 which has a beat reserved for hotel guests. Some of the best fishing is the Craig Beat which has recently been time shared. There are twenty-one named pools on these two miles and the five yearaverage is ninety fish. The owner of the Upper Craig Beat is Mr L. Campbell (08383) 282 and day tickets are available at a cost of between £12 and £22. Croggan Crafts (08382) 201, the tackle and country clothing shop in Dalmally, has daily permits for five privately owned beats and others where the cost ranges between £14 and £25 a day. Carraig Thura Hotel (0838) 2210 can offer guests fishing on its own water. The Dalmally Beat is managed by West Highland Estates of Oban (0631) 63617. Their chalets, which sleep 4, cost between £160 and £200 a week and the fishing costs

between £70 and £125 per rod a week according to season. Incidentally, the hotels are also available for non-fishing holidays. Spinning is probably the best method of fishing the rocky gorges near the falls, but much of the river deserves to be fly-only water, especially as the fly works so well.

Loch Fyne Waters

South east of Loch Awe are the salt waters of Loch Fyne and its spate rivers. Argyll Estates (0499) 2203 can arrange fishing for you on the Rivers Shira, Aray and Dubh Loch at a cost of between £600 and £1000 per week, which includes self-catering accommodation in a lodge and fishing for four rods.

Artist: Clive Madgwick LOCH TUMMEL Courtesy of Rosenstiel's

In 1110 AD, Meckau, son of Magnus Barefoot, King of Norway, met the Scots on the banks of the river that flows through this glen. The fighting Scots won the ensuing battle and the bodies of their slaughtered enemies were thrown into the water, turning it red with blood. The river passed into history as Ruail and the Glen as Glen-da-ruail, the Glen of red blood. Over the years the name became anglicised to the modern Glendaruel.

Despite its violent beginnings, the river now provides a somewhat more pleasing pastime - fishing. The hotel offers private salmon and trout fishing to its guests on the Ruel, which flows directly behind it. In addition there are arrangements with local angling clubs to fish many other waters including the hiring of boats to fish larger lochs and sea.

The hotel itself is small, friendly and family-run. It offers the best in Scottish hospitality with delicious home-cooking. Naturally the private rooms offer the usual range of modern facilities, including colour TV, and most have ensuite bathrooms.

For a fascinating break from fishing, the surrounding area offers a wealth of open opportunities. Deer stalking and rough shooting are available, as is golf on three courses. Hillwaiking provides a rare opportunity to experience first-hand the splendour of the Highland countryside and the possibility of seeing some of the roaming wildlife, including red and roe deer, buzzards and golden eagles. All of this, and not to mention the wealth of history that surrounds the local area.

The Glendaruel Hotel
Clachan of Glendaruel
Argyll PA22 3AA
Tel: (036982) 274
Fax: (036982) 317

The Aray is a good salmon and sea-trout water and provides an attractive setting on its lower reaches where it flows through the park surrounding Inverarary Castle. The ornamental gardens and ornate bridges here are in marked contrast to the heavily wooded upper beats. The afforestation causes rapid changes in water levels and the ability to spey cast will ensure that you don't lose too many flies in the trees.

Both the Shira and the Fyne are victims of hydro schemes but offer good sport. Fishing on the Fyne was owned by Lord Glenkinglas but has now been divided between his sons. The four beats are owned by Ardinglas Estate (0499) 6261 and Cairndew Estate (0499) 6255. The season starts at the end of June and extends until the first week in October. A week's fishing for two rods costs in the region of £800 and though it is a popular river those who investigate well in advance may be lucky. Loch Shira is really a bay of Loch Fyne, while just above it is Dubh Loch in whose tidal waters you may also find grey mullet. Salmon usually rest in Dubh in July and August before running the river in September. On the western shore of Loch Fyne is Douglas Water. This little river is twelve miles long but impassable falls three miles upstream from the Loch confine fishing to the lower river. There you will find ten good pools with Roman Bridge Pool probably being the best. Day permits can be had for £6 from Argyll Caravan Park (0499) 2285.

Loch Eck & the Eachaig
On the opposite shore is Strachur and taking the A815 south brings you to Loch Eck and its river the Eachaig which connects it to Holy Loch and its naval bases. The Eachaig may be under five miles long but there are forty pools divided between three beats. Although famous for both the number and size of its sea-trout—1989 saw a 15lb 8oz fish taken on Ashtree Pool—it is also good salmon water. Further details may be had from Salar Management Services Ltd. (0667) 55355. The Loch is a narrow water some six miles long and up to a hundred and forty feet deep, and largely surrounded by forestry. As well as salmon, sea-trout and brown trout, its waters hold some powan, a rare relation of the grayling, and I am sure some ferox must stalk its depths. Permits can be had from the Whistlefield Inn (0369 86) 440 where a day including the use of one of the hotel's three boats with an outboard, which can hold up to six rods, costs £20. Fly works well at the northern end where the Cur flows in but trolling will produce good results, in all parts. Talking of good results the best salmon and sea-trout for the 1990 season were 19lb 6oz and 8lb 1oz respectively. It is also very good trout water as the average weight of 2lb proves.

Purdies, the tackle shop in Dunoon (0369) 3232, issue permits for the Dunoon and District Angling Club who have fishing rights on several small rivers and lochs in the area. In the way of clubs, the Oban and Lorn Angling Club have twenty-three lochs, most of which are easy to get to though a few involve a cross country hike. Anglers Corner (0631) 66374 will issue you a permit if you pretend you live within twenty five miles of Oban (southerners will have to brush up on their accent!)—the first year including joining fees costs £22. A further £5 will get you a boat permit. Lochgilphead and District Angling Club has the fishing of several lochs and rivers and permits for these are available from The Sports Shop (0546) 2390

Kintyre Waters
The A83 runs south of Lochgilphead into Kintyre. There may be an airport at Campbeltown but the long detour, which involves driving round the head of Loch Fyne, ensures that the visitor will be able to enjoy the peninsular's lochs and little rivers in perfect peace. Having said that, because of its remoteness, there is a certain free and easy approach to fishing on some rivers. This especially applies the further south you go and it has been suggested that those wishing to fish the Breackerie or Connie Glen Water, which lie at the southern tip, could be well advised to ask the local poachers in case they interfere with their poaching operations! A similar spirit exists on Machrihanish Water. The Lussa flows from its Loch through a pretty glen to enter the sea at Peninver. Even here there is no escape from hydro schemes and the erection of a dam, with no compensating flow on the Loch has severely altered the character of the river, where the best fishing is on the bottom beats. The river still manages to produce around 400 salmon a season and it is also good sea-trout water. At £8 a day or £80 a season it must be some of the least expensive salmon fishing available. Permits for the Lussa, which produced a best fish of 14lb in 1991 may be had from Inland Fisheries of Peninver (0586) 552774.

The Add
Perhaps the best river in the Kintyre district is the Add. Several tumbling burns continue to form this river and in the upper reaches there are steep rocky pools. The river becomes more sedate as it nears the Crinan Canal and the flow fades away; in fact the last two miles of the river are tidal. This is another river which has suffered from both a hydro scheme and afforestation which give it a Jekyll and Hyde character as one day there will be a flash spate while another day it may be almost dead for there is little compensatory flow. The upper reaches are owned by David Bracey of Kirnan Hotel (0546) 605217 while the lower river is owned by Robert Malcolm Esq., of Dunhrune Castle (05465) 283. The river is divided into three beats, Minard, Kirnan and Poltalloch. Both Kirnan and especially Poltalloch fish well and, although Mr Malcolm does not let his water on a regular basis, a day's fishing can be had for about £10.

Culcreuch Castle, the home of the Barons of Culcreuch since 1699 and before this the ancestral fortalice of the Galbraiths and indeed Clan Castle of the Galbraith chiefs for over three centuries (1320 to 1630), has now been restored and converted by its present owners into a most comfortable family-run country house hotel, intimately blending the elegance of bygone days with modern comforts and personal service in an atmosphere of friendly informal hospitality. The eight individually decorated and furnished bedrooms all have en suite facilities, colour television and tea and coffee making facilities. Most command uninterrupted and quite unsurpassed views over the 1600 acre parkland grounds, described by the National Trust for Scotland as a 'gem of outstanding beauty', and beyond a kaleidoscope of spectacular scenery of hills, moorlands, lochs, burns and woods comprising the Endrick valley and the Campsie Fells above.

All the public rooms are decorated in period style and furnished with antiques giving the aura and grace of a bygone age. Log fires create warmth and intimacy and the candlelit evening meals in the panelled dining room make for most romantic occasions, well complemented by freshly prepared local produce and a carefully selected wine cellar.

The Loch Lomond, Stirling & Trossachs area offers the visitor a wide and varied range of country activities, including golf, fishing, shooting, water sports, nature study and bird watching, historical research, or simply walking and exploring in stunningly beautiful countryside.

With over 40 golf courses within a 25 mile radius of the Castle, Culcreuch is a golfer's paradise. A special Golfing Brochure is available on request which gives details of the packages available at a large number of these venues.

Culcreuch is best known, however, for its extensive fishing packages, covering a wide area of the Loch Lomond area including fishing on Loch Lomond itself. The angling season is as follows: Salmon and Sea Trout: 11th February to 31st October, Brown Trout: 15th March to 6th October (Sunday Fishing is strictly prohibited)

Packages are available on the following waters. Salmon and Sea Trout - Loch Lomond, River Leven, River Fruin, Luss Water (except Arden Estate Water), The Gareloch (part) and the River Endrick (major part, - The River Endrick flows through the Culcreuch Estate). Full details, including maps of each water showing pools and other important information, are available in our Fishing Brochure available on request.

Whether for either business or pleasure, Culcreuch is a most convenient, centrally positioned base for visiting Edinburgh (55 minutes by motorway), Glasgow (35 minutes) and Stirling (25 minutes). For business clients there is no comparable venue for entertaining and the Castle specialises in offering its unique facilities for small meetings.

From Autumn to Spring, reduced terms for off-season breaks are offered, together with House Parties over the Christmas and New Year Holidays; and during these cooler months the log fires offer a cheerful welcome on your return from a day out in the Trossachs.

The location of Culcreuch is rural but not isolated, and with the fresh air of the countryside, the space, grace, comfort, good wholesome food and that unique warmth of friendship and hospitality offered from a family run home from home, a stay here is most conducive to shedding the cares and pressures of modern day life and utterly relaxing. We look forward to your company. — The Haslam Family

Culcreuch Castle
Fintry
Stirlingshire G63 0LW
Tel: (036 086) 288
Fax: (036 086) 555

Speyside

In order to benefit the whole community and not just the fishing, many waters are only available to people who actually stay in the area. There is no major problem here because there are some fine places to stay covering most requirements and budgets. The local tourist office is always a good source of accommodation and many now operate a room booking service which is worth remembering if you happen to want to change plans at the last minute.

The Spey however demands long term planning—it is, after all, one of the principal jewels in the crown of Scottish rivers. Having said that, occasional beats do become available at the last minute, so it is worth phoning around prior to going off if you are looking for some new adventure.

This is an area of great beauty. The hills of Cromdale and the Cairngorms, which so often crowd the horizon, are sights to behold and there are a number of hotels which are equally pleasant. In Kingussie, The Columba house (0540) 661402 is a fine place in which to stay as is The Osprey (0540) 661510, idyllically situated in the heart of the Spey valley. People who enjoy fine food should make a special expedition to the unpretentious but extremely fine restaurant, The Cross (0540) 661166. The fixed price menu features delightful game and local produce and there are three bedrooms should you wish to stay after dinner—a marvellous idea.

Venturing forth through the Monadhliath Mountains, we find further relief for those who have fought long and hard on the banks of the Spey. An enjoyable place to stay is The Boat, at Boat Of Garten (0479) 83258, a charmingly friendly establishment. A little north of here, we find Carrbridge. The Dalrachney Lodge (0479) 84252 is now a splendid country house hotel with a delightful lounge and dining room. The lodge is convenient for the River Dulnain and lies a short distance east of the village. A similar type of establishment which is also close to the River Dulnain is the Muckrach Lodge (0479) 85257. It is quiet and peaceful and the bar and lounge are particular focal points. One final Lodge to consider is the Auchendean Lodge (0479) 85347 which lies in the shadows of the Cairngorms. This is a stylish but extremely welcoming hotel where the restaurant is excellent and well worth a detour, whether or not you choose to stay here.

Grantown-On-Spey is something of a landmark and is a busy spot with much to commend it. The Garth Hotel (0479) 2836, which stands close to the town centre in its own grounds, is well worth considering, firstly, because it is a congenial place to stay with fine facilities and secondly, because fishing can be arranged on the Spey.

The Seafield Lodge Hotel (0479) 2152 is another hotel which fishermen should frequent. It hosts the Arthur Oglesby Fly Fishing Courses and the proprietor himself is a keen fisherman. The hotel is extremely welcoming and the bar a wonderfully comfortable place to enjoy a drink or two. Bedrooms are also comfortable and this is a first rate place to stay for those who wish to fish hard, play hard and sleep well. A more humble dwelling, but one which welcomes fishermen is the Cran-Tara Guest House (0479) 2197 which offers good value food and accommodation and makes for a fine staging post for any assault

on the Spey and the many lochs that surround Grantown. Finally, take a note of the Tyree House Hotel (0479) 2615 which welcomes fishermen and is a well run and welcoming establishment.

There are two further establishments to consider which lie a short distance from Grantown-On-Spey. Tulchan Lodge (0807) 5200 is one of the best fishing hotels in Scotland but it is expensive. It is supremely well cared for and was originally built as a hunting and fishing lodge, a role it continues to play. The lodge itself is delightful and the bar, bedrooms and dining room are all first class. If you happen to have a healthy bank account this is the place for you to part with some of your hard earned loot.

If you are seeking to fish the Avon then there are a number of hotels to consider. The Gordon Arms at Tomintoul (0807) 580206 is a fine choice, as is The Richmond Arms (0807) 580209. Both are friendly and welcome fishermen. Lovers of whisky will no doubt head for Glenlivet, famous for its distillery. The Blairfindy Lodge (0807) 590376 is a friendly place to stay. Blazing log fires in the hall and bars will help to lift any chill, and once again, the hotel can arrange fishing on a number of rivers, including the Avon. The Delnashaugh Inn (0807) is another fine place to stay.

Craigellachie (0340) 881204, situated twelve miles south of Elgin is a Victorian fishing hotel which has recently been impressively refurbished. This is a great favourite with fishermen so do book well in advance. The hotel has excellent connections and all manner of first class fishing can be arranged. In short, this is a tremendous hotel! A similarly popular fisherman's haunt is the Gordon Arms Fochabers (0343) 820508. The hotel does not organise fishing itself but will put you in touch with Mr Connelly (0343) 820327, who can organise fishing for you. As a result, many people fishing in this region stay at the former coaching inn. The bar here is a particularly popular haunt of the fishing fraternity. Dowans Hotel (0340) 871488 is also well worth a visit.

Little Elgin is further off the beaten track but there is an hotel here which should not be overlooked—the Mansion House (0343) 548811. It has a garden setting beside the River Lossie. It is an impressive house which dates from the mid 19th century and has much to commend it—a fine wine list, distinguished cooking and some extremely comfortable bedrooms, not to mention the fishing that can be organised locally, or on the Spey.

If you are fortunate enough to be fishing the River Findhorn, then the unpretentious Ramnee in Forres (0309) 72410 should be considered. as should the Knockomie Hotel (0309) 673290. In Nairn, there are a number of hotels to consider and an excellent course for lovers of the fairways. The Clifton Hotel (0667) 53119 is a splendid and refined place to stay, while the Golf View Hotel (0667) 52301 has obvious merits for the links man. The leisure facilities here are particularly good.

The Spey is a splendid old man of a river. It is most definitely fishable and there are many who will help you organise your trip. There are several other fine waters and, all in all, this is an area which has much to commend it. Before we move on, one final thought. You have fished well and fought hard; you may have stayed at a number of hotels, you may on the other hand have been coming here for years and frequented only your favourite haunts. Whatever the case, visit Drybridge and the Old Monastery Restaurant (0542) 32660. This delightful eating place has breathtaking views across Spey Bay and the food is quite outstanding.

As you stop and stare, imagine the activities of years gone by and the wonders of the salmon that will return to the bay and the legendary river. One may have your name on—unlikely, but give him a wave just the same!

The Deveron to the Don

The burns, streams and rivers north of the Grampian Hills provide a positive feast of fishing opportunities. The scene north of the Dee is remote, generally unspoilt and peaceful. There are a fair number of good fishing hotels and so without further ado let us plan our assault on these splendid waters.

Aberdeen airport may conceivably be your first port of call and on the off chance you wish to have a quick kip then the Skean Dhu Hotel (0224) 725252 is your best bet. There are numerous other good hotels in the city, but more of that when we come to the glories of the Dee.

Kildrummy is a tremendous place to start or conclude any fishing foray. Kildrummy Castle (0975) 571288 is a striking castellated mansion which is surrounded by superbly kept grounds. The picture is made still more complete when we consider the ruins of the 13th century castle which the hotel overlooks. There is an excellent blend of tradition with modern comforts, the striking fireplaces and impressive tapestries are a joy to behold. The bedrooms are also well equipped and the restaurant is extremely well thought of. The hotel can arrange fly fishing for salmon and trout on the Don, for residents and this really provides the icing on an extremely impressive gateau. Lovers of heritage might also wish to sample Pittodrie House (0467) 6444 which dates from 1675. It's a fine all round hotel and a delight in which to stay.

Should you wish to enjoy another extremely welcoming hotel then make a note of the Castle at Huntly (0466) 792696, formerly the family home of the Gordons. It's a great favourite with fishermen and is a charming traditional hotel in which to escape the traumas of the twentieth century. The fishing that can be arranged by the hotel is particularly impressive. The Forbes Arms (0466) 81248 also offers some good fishing and is a fine place in which to stay. The Calquhonnie Hotel (0975) 651210 serves the angler who searches for waters on the Don. The Grant Arms (0467) 7226 in Monymusk is another welcoming fishing place.

Somewhere East of Huntly we find the River Ythan; a spot to head for here is Newburgh and The Udny Arms Hotel (0358) 689444. The bedrooms are characterful and it's a pleasant location from which to explore neighbouring scenery. The same can be said of Meldrum House, Old Meldrum (0651) 22294 which provides a delightful country house atmosphere in a marvellous setting, the restaurant here is also good.

As you would imagine, there are all manner of activities available aside from fishing—golfing and walking are two obvious examples. The Deveron is a fine river and if you should be visiting Banff then The County (0261) 25353 is a charming Georgian house in which to stay. It has fine views up the Bay and can also arrange fishing for guests.

There are a fabulous array of fishing opportunities available in the Grampian region of Scotland and while certain beats await the shoes of deadmen, others are positively alive with opportunity. We wish you good sport, whether you are treading in the steps of phantoms or wading in the waters of the fit and well!

Royal Deeside

The Queen Mother's love of the Dee is celebrated and it is fitting that this lady should grace these royal waters. Of course, the river and the salmon care not a jot for pomp or ceremony, but it is surely fair to say that the Dee is a queen amongst rivers. As a result of this lofty position in the realm of river fishing, the Dee is often difficult—sometimes impossible and at other times and in other places, a little tricky—to get on. Let us hope that the following lines reflect some of the opportunities available in this marvellous part of Scotland.

I must say that if Balmoral ever went under the hammer, God forbid, then the lucky purchaser would be really tempted to turn this castle into the sporting hotel of Scotland. Given that this eventuality is unlikely, let us suggest more appropriate accommodation. The Maryculter House (0224) 732124 enjoys the most marvellous setting on the south bank of the River Dee. The hotel does not have its own fishing but can arrange fishing for about £20 a day. The hotel itself is fascinating and parts of the original building remain. In the bar an exposed stone wall towers up three storeys to reveal a splendid vaulted ceiling. The bedrooms are extremely well equipped and the principal restaurant here is well thought of.

Moving westwards down the A93 we come to the home of the celebrated fishing waters of the Dee, but we should not stop here, for there are some of the most wonderful fishing hotels imaginable in a very small radius. You have to persevere, however, because the fishing is extremely popular and people book year after year. Let us consider a few hotels which are particularly excellent. Banchory Lodge (0330) 22625 is a charming Georgian house on the banks of the River Dee. The hotel owns both banks and can, naturally enough, arrange fishing. People, however, book year after year and it is extremely difficult to get in but it isn't impossible, so do try. The proprietors are wonderfully welcoming and the hotel is inundated with antiques, paintings and flowers. The dining room is also first class and if you are lucky enough to stay there and fish, then you will be an extremely happy chappie—and the very best of luck to you.

Raemoir House (0330) 24884 is another delightful hotel. It is run by Kit Sabin and family and they are a charming team. The hotel is magnificently set in 3500 acres but does not actually front the river. The house itself is delightfully preserved and you cannot fail to be charmed by its many delights. The bar is particularly inviting and the counter is made from a Tudor four-poster bed. The bedrooms are also splendid. If you love your fishing, fine hotels and, perhaps more than anything else genuine service and welcome, then contact Raemoir House.

Invery House (0330) 24782 at Bridge of Feugh is another glorious hotel in which to stay. In order to reach the house you must drive through a half mile canopy of silver birch and beech trees alongside the River Feugh. The hotel is delightfully peaceful and also has rights on the River Dee. Sir Walter Scott was a frequent visitor to the house and marvellous bedrooms are named in his memory. This is a first class hotel and the restaurant is similarly distinguished. It is expensive but if you do have a love of fishing and the good life, then there are few finer places to visit.

Aboyne is another place to note and here we come upon Birse Lodge (03398) 86253 another friendly and well run hotel. The former dower house which is set in its own gardens is close to the River Dee. The hotel does not have its own water but the management have a number of contacts in the village who can often help in arranging fishing. A similar situation occurs at Craigendarroch (0339) 755858 who use the services of a local expert. Fishing can be arranged on a number of rivers including the Dee and the approximate charge is £40 for a half day. This is a fine hotel to take non-fishing friends to, as it has an excellent Country Club—it is also part of a substantial time share complex. The hotel is particularly plush and the restaurant has an extremely good reputation.

Arranged fishing can also be made through Tullich Lodge (0339) 755406 who work closely with Cliff Jeffries at Countrywear, Ballater. The hotel enjoys splendid views of the Dee valley and is set amidst acres of pleasant woodland and garden. This is a very smart but informal country house hotel which offers some first class accommodation. It also provides outstanding dinners in the contrastingly formal dining room. Other fine accommodation can be found at Darroch Learg (0339) 755443 which also offers inspired views over the River Dee. Monaltrie (0339) 735417 is another fine hotel and several of the bedrooms overlook the Dee, an inspired view for the angler to look out onto as dawn comes. Fishing can be arranged on local waters although the hotel does not have its own beat.

The Delnashaugh Inn

In the heart of the Highlands, the Delnashaugh Inn is beautifully situated. Formerly the Drovers Inn, it has been refurbished by the proprietors David and Marion Ogden and yet it has lost none of its original charm.

The hotel provides nine bedrooms, all en suite with colour television and tea and coffee making facilities.

The restaurant boasts a different dinner menu every night and all meals are created using local fresh produce. The bar also stocks many local malts, as here the visitor is in the heart of one of Scotland's oldest industries. The Whisky Trail is open between April and October for those wanting to learn more about the making of whisky and the opportunity is there to take a 'dram'.

As the Delnashaugh is part of the Ballindalloch estate there are plenty of opportunities for sportsmen in the area. The estate provides sea trout and salmon fishing on the Avon and shooting for eight guns can be arranged, as can roe buck stalking. For the winter visitor, Aviemore and Tominton are within easy reach for skiing.

Grantown-on-Spey, Elgin and Boat-of-Garten all have golf courses and so, with the beautiful walks around the area there really is something for everyone.

The area itself is peaceful and yet Inverness and Nairn are not too far away and access to the hotel is reasonably easy. This is a beautiful part of Scotland where visitors are guaranteed the peace and quiet that many of us are so eager for.

The Delnashaugh Inn
Ballindalloch
Banffshire AB37 9AS
Tel: (0807) 500255

Braemar, home of the highland gathering, has a hotel of some distinction which also, by virtue of local contacts can arrange fishing on the Dee. The Braemar Lodge (0339) 741627 has been well converted and apart from the fishing contacts the expertise in the catering department is also worthy of note. This granite built lodge is a fine place to stay and a visit is positively encouraged.

Moving away from the Dee we journey to other celebrated waters, those of the princely South Esk. The Clova Hotel (0575) 5222 is a splendid fishing hotel and is thoroughly welcoming. The situation is delightful and while the fish can not be guaranteed a really good trip can be!

It has to be said that finding fishing on the South Esk is difficult but there are possibilities. The Panmure Arms (0356) 4420 has no water of its own but if you were to book a year or so in advance you may find a week or two could be arranged. Whatever the case, make sure you visit for dinner—it is justly popular for miles around and the watering hole of many a fisherman. Naturally, many of the estates have lodges which can be let and many of these are taken by syndicates or time share owners. Many of these visitors come back year after year and many people will stay with friends or more often than not stay in self-catering accommodation. The local tourist boards are a wealth of knowledge on this type of accommodation and they are also able to provide lists of Bed and Breakfasts. As a result, a quick telephone call should always be made before you finalise your plans if you seek this type of establishment.

The Tay and its Tributaries

Perthshire is a delightful part of Britain and boasts a large number of really outstanding hotels, self-catering accommodation and all manner of places in which to stay. A particularly peaceful place and a fine fishing hotel can be found on the south shore of Loch Tay at Ardeonaig. The Ardeonaig (0567) 2400 is extremely relaxing and an ideal choice for peace, quiet and fishing.

Kenmore is a charming village at the foot of Loch Tay. The Kenmore Hotel (0887) 830205 is an idyllic 16th century hotel which has a beautiful position beside the River Tay. There are some fine bedrooms here and a pleasant dining room and bar. The hotel organises fishing for its guests and makes for a delightful place in which to stay. Splendid loch fishing can also be organised on Loch Tay through the Croft-na-Caber Hotel (0887) 830236. This is a really friendly hotel which offers good bar meals and a selection of self-catering accommodation if preferred. The Fortingall Hotel (0887) 830367 is another popular haunt where fishing is a plus. Good value

accommodation is an additional reason for including it in your Tayward plans. Loch and river fishing can also be arranged through a number of hotels centred in Aberfeldy.

The first is the Weem hotel (0887) 820381, a comfortable hotel which offers good value accommodation. Those of you who have a somewhat less restricted budget should consider Farleyer House (0887) 820332, located just outside Aberfeldy. The hotel is extremely elegant and its bedrooms are of an excellent quality. The restaurant here is outstanding and one to note if you are passing through the area or staying in self-catering premises. The Coshieville Hotel (0887) 830319 is located at the entrance to Glen Lyon which many feel is one of the most beautiful glens in Scotland. The hotel has two beats on the Lyon and is extremely keen to welcome lovers of the sport. Another unpretentious hotel which offers fine cooking is located at Killiecrankie. The Killiecrankie Hotel (0796) 473220, which stands close to the celebrated pass, is a friendly place to stay and worth a detour. All around is majestic scenery with forest, loch, hills and river forever in our focus. The fishing is grand but merely being in Perthshire has much to commend it.

Midway between Dunkeld and Kenmore one finds the Grandtully Hotel (0887) 840207. The hotel has some impressive fishing and this really is a first class hotel for the person who is keen to fish the Tay. Good food and fishing facilities are further plus points. A hotel with outstanding sporting facilities can be found at Dunkeld. The Stakis Dunkeld House (0350) 2771 is a first class hotel in which to stay. The house dates from the turn of the century when it was built by the 7th Duke of Atholl. The leisure complex is a more recent addition but will surely please anglers who have had a hard day on the Tay. Bedrooms are comfortable and the bars are well stocked. What more could one ask for?

Well, one can ask, but it is often difficult to actually find fishing on the River Tay. The Ballathie House Hotel (0250) 83268 is a splendid Baronial-style mansion in a near perfect situation overlooking the Tay. The standard of the hotel is excellent with a fine restaurant and elegant bedrooms. Fishing is also available and if you give plenty of notice you might be lucky enough to get on. It is a relief therefore to be able to add to the list of possibilities an absolute pearl of a hotel and restaurant. Kinnaird House (0796) 482440 is situated on the Kinnaird Estate and is surely one of the most appealing hotels in Britain for the fisherman. It is pure paradise. Here, he can go back in time and reminisce about the great house parties of former years. The fishing is first class, the food is marvellous and the hotel is splendid. If you only had one more fishing weekend this would have to be on that sacred shortlist.

A little way south in Stanley itself, we come upon The Tayside Hotel (0738) 828249, which is another popular centre for fishing parties. The hotel provides a warm welcome and practical, rather than plush, accommodation. The hotel is excellent value and should certainly be on the itinerary when heading towards the Tay. Lovers of fine food should also try and visit Murrayshall Country House Hotel (0738) 51171– a superb restaurant can be found here together with a championship golf course and really outstanding hotel.

Returning northwards in search of more fine fishing and fodder, we might chance upon Alyth, and more fortuitously still, the Lands of Loyal Hotel (0828) 33151, a Victorian mansion which will not fail to impress. The Bridge of Cally Hotel (0250) 86231 is a friendly hotel which offers comfortable bedrooms and a pleasant restaurant which merits consideration.

There are an abundance of trout lochs and small streams that will appeal to the less demanding fisherman and a hotel which is somewhat different to the more traditional Scottish hotel is the Log Cabin Hotel (0250) 881288, which is made wholly of Norwegian Pine. The restaurant here is extremely good and offers the best of Scottish fayre. All manner of country pursuits can be enjoyed from the hotel, not least trout fishing in the hotel's own loch. Elsewhere the fisherman might wish to visit Aldchlappie (0250) 881224, which resides beside the River Ardle and is thoroughly welcoming. The Malt Room bar has a fascinating range of malt whiskies to sample after a day or two on the river. Fishing can be arranged on the Dulmunzie House Estate, Spittal of Glenshee. The hotel (0250) 885224 is tremendously welcoming and all manner of leisure pursuits can be enjoyed to the full. It is a grand but delightfully informal hotel in which to stay and one which merits a detour.

There are a number of good hotels in Blairgowrie, but one of the most appealing while on a fishing tour is lovely Kinloch House (0250) 84237. Splendid furniture graces the impressive interior of this former Scottish country house and a number of Scottish dishes which are prepared here are excellent. The hotel can arrange a number of leisure pursuits including fishing. The Tummel is one of the Tay's most splendid tributaries and a brace of hotels should be mentioned for those who are going to fish the waters. The Green Park Hotel, Pitlochry (0796) 473248 is the only hotel on Loch Faskally. The gardens reach down to the water and make for a splendid view. Fishing can be arranged from the hotel and, once again, Scottish dishes are the source of some fine cooking.

Loch Lomond to Loch Leven

Aside from the celebrated lochs of Lomond and Leven, there are a number of excellent rivers which run through this region. Hotels in the Kingdom of Fife are a touch thin on the ground (golf courses hold centre stage here), but south Perthshire has a whole multitude of self-catering and hotel accommodation to whet the appetite.

Dunblane should be our first port of call as it sits happily midway between Loch Leven and Loch Lomond and is therefore a fine place from which to take in the entire scene. It is also home to Cromlix House (0786) 822125, where a charming mix of Edwardian and Victorian architecture make up one of Britain's most celebrated country house hotels. The library, conservatory, chapel and an abundance of fine paintings and antiques are delightful. The house sits in a 5000 acre estate and, needless to say, fishing can be organized through the hotel. The restaurant is also first class and if you are celebrating your first salmon (or 100th for that matter), or even if you've caught nothing for years, do make a point of dining here, it's positively exquisite.

Another hotel which merits considerable attention and a fairly huge bank balance is the delightful Gleneagles Hotel (0764) 62231 whose leisure facilities are simply unrivalled. This is the place at which to spoil yourself to the extreme. Leisure centres, three championship golf-courses, riding, tennis, shooting and just about everything else you care to think of. But what of the fishing? The hotel has two boats on the Tay and fishing ranges radically in price with the season. Rods can be reserved but the boats do get very booked up. The hotel offers two day salmon fishing packages and these should be considered if you are one who loves to stay in the very best hotel accommodation. Gleneagles is first class in every way—to stay there is a magnificent experience.

Comrie lies close to the River Earn and the Royal Comrie (0764) 670200 is a superb traditional hotel with comfortable bedrooms and fishing can be arranged. Lochearnhead (0567) 3229 is another small hotel which is pleasantly situated on the shores of Loch Earn. Fishing is not organised through the hotel but arrangements are relatively easy to make.

Loch Leven is a superb trout loch and those seeking to fish its waters will often stay at the Green Hotel (0577) 63467, an old coaching inn which now boasts a number of more contemporary facilities. The hotel has private fishing on the loch and also arranges trout fishing on other lochs nearby. The hotel is also able to arrange salmon and sea-trout fishing on the Rivers Tay and Earn.

Returning from loch to river we come to Lavander and

the River Teith. The Roman Camp Hotel (0877) 30003 is a delightful establishment. It dates from 1625 and offers excellent accommodation, a first class restaurant, and twenty acres of grounds. The River Teith runs through the property and guests are free to fish in these good trout waters. Salmon fishing is not so hot here, but the hotel can arrange other waters should guests so require. Loch Lomond is a majestic piece of water and also has much to attract the visitor. There are, however, surprisingly few good hotels in the region, and it is therefore a case of either remaining east of the Loch or staying in some of the many self-catering establishments that are available. However, people should know the Inverbeg Inn, Luss (0436) 86678, an attractive inn which stands close to the banks of the Loch. It has no illusions of grandeur but is comfortable and well located. Culcreuch Castle (036086) 228 at Fintry has fishing over a wide area of the region, and is highly recommended.

From Gleneagles to a small tent in a wooded valley, Scotland caters to all sorts. You don't have to be a millionaire to fish in this majestic country. Loch and small river fishing are both easy to find and good value sport. If, on the other hand, you are staying at Gleneagles you are thoroughly fortunate, probably American and will have a splendid time—which will be made even finer if you take a fish from the Tay.

Oban to Kintyre

Now this, dear reader, is a splendid part of the British Isles. Lochs mix with expanses of mountains and hurry through hillsides. A number of gracious Scottish country houses have been converted to hotels and they provide some first class facilities for people travelling through this area. Yes, awesome dams and forests have not made fishing any easier but the scenery is still superb and the fishing can often be outstanding.

There are a number of staggeringly beautiful country house hotels south of Fort William and many proudly overlook Loch Linnhe. These are not by and large great fishing hotels but it is worth mentioning a brace, just in case the waters are poor or you feel like a change of scenery. Certainly one thing these houses boast is some majestic locations. In Port Appin, Airds (063173) 236, is a delightful hotel in which to stay. The interior is wonderfully stylish but cosy and welcoming and the restaurant here is absolutely excellent. If you enjoy fine cuisine make a diversion—you will not be disappointed. Another hotel which offers first class cooking and a friendly house party atmosphere is Ardsheal House, Kentallen (063174) 227. Before you even arrive you will be in love with the place; as you approach you will pass countryside of outstanding beauty. This is an inspiring location in which to stay, even so far as to put the fishing on hold for a short time!

Some six miles south of Oban, halfway along the shore of Loch Feochan, we find another distinguished country

house hotel with more splendid views and another popular restaurant. The hotel offers an excellent array of malts and can organise all manner of sports including trout, salmon and sea fishing. Returning inland we come to the River Orchy. It is a wonderful sight which will delight all who love to fish and many who don't. The nearby hotels may not be smart country house hotels but they are welcoming and, for the majority of fishermen, will be just what's required. The Bridge of Orchy (08384) 208 and the Carraig Thura (08382) 210 are two for consideration.

The Awe is a huge water and in places its depth is witnessed by dark, almost fearsome, waters. There are numerous opportunities for fishing and a fine place to stay is Portsonachan Hotel (08663) 224 which can arrange fishing. Carraig Thura (08382) 210 offers free salmon fishing to guests and is another fine place to stay. The hotel exudes tranquillity and the dining room, where game is strongly featured, overlooks the majestic loch.

Another superb scene is that which greets you at Loch Fyne. There are several good hotels in this area and two to note are the Creggow Inn (036986) 279 and the Kilfinan Hotel (070082) 201; both are able to arrange game fishing for their guests and both offer good value accommodation. The restaurant at Kilfinan is particularly good. There are two fine hotels for people heading towards Dunoon. The Enmore Hotel (0369) 2230 is luxurious and delightful and Ardfillayne (0369) 2267 has a super setting and can arrange fishing on Loch Eck. The Glendaruel Hotel (036982) 274 is also well worth making a detour for. Those intrepid explorers who are seeking the delights of Kintyre should shortlist The Stonefield Castle Hotel, Tarbert (0880) 820836 which enjoys a marvellous setting and leisure facilities for the more active. For those heading further south, a number of hotels are well placed—The Royal (0586) 52017, which overlooks the harbour and the Seafield (0586) 54385 are two which will not disappoint.

Finally, for those seeking to escape to the islands or Argyll, a number of waters and hotels should be considered on Islay. The Bridgend (04961) 212 is a long established fishing hotel while in Port Askaig, the Port Askaig Hotel (049684) 245 is welcoming, and well equipped—a fine recommendation for those visiting and fishing this super part of Scotland.

The Roman Camp Hotel sits on the North Bank of the River Tieth amongst twenty acres of mature and secluded gardens, which nestle by the picturesque village of Callandar, the Gateway to the Trossachs and the Highlands of Scotland.

The House was originally built as a Hunting Lodge for the Dukes of Perth in 1625 and was given its name from the conspicuous earth mounds, believed to be the site of a Roman Fort, which are visible across the meadow to the east of the walled garden.

The building has grown over many years as each consecutive family has added their own embellishments to this lovely home. The most obvious of these are the towers, one of which contains a tiny Chapel.

Today under the guidance of Eric and Marion Brown the traditional country house atmosphere still evokes its alluring charm. As you enter you will notice the abundance of freshly cut flowers, their scent lingering in the air, and be greeted to this peaceful retreat by great log fires.

Our Library and Drawing Room are of grand proportions, with an atmosphere of warmth and relaxation and are places to enjoy and reflect on the days sport, especially after dinner in the company of friends and a fine malt.

The tapestry hung Dining Room is crowned by a richly painted 16th century style ceiling. Here dinner is served at candle lit tables, laid with fine silver and crystal, while you choose from menus of local game and fish, prepared by our chef and accompanied by vegetables and herbs from our own gardens.

Each of our bedrooms has its own distinctive style and character, and is equipped with all the little thoughtful extras to make your stay as comfortable as possible.

At the Roman Camp Country House you are within easy reach of many Championship and picturesque Golf Courses, and we are able to arrange and book tee times at the local course, only two minutes walk from the hotel.

We have three-quarters of a mile of river running through our gardens, enablng guests to fish complementary for Wild Brown Trout and Salmon on our private beat. There is also the opportunity for the hotel to arrange fishing on the many lochs and other private beats surrounding Callander.

We hope that you will be able to make the Roman Camp your favourite country retreat.

Callander
FK17 8BG
Tel: (0877) 30003
Fax: (0877) 31533

SOUTHERN UPLANDS

R easons why people choose fishing as their preferred pastime are almost as diverse as the places in which they practice their sport, but high on the list must rank the chance of escape from the rigours of the daily grind into some of the most beautiful countryside imaginable. You may think this an odd remark with which to preface this section, which takes in Glasgow and its industrial heartland, but in Scotland you are never far away from the countryside. Despite the geographical size of this area there is little fishing of note. There are few lochs, but none that can compete with the fame of their more northerly sisters. However, as one would expect in such an industrial area, there are a great many reservoirs. There are some good trout fisheries and Drew Jamieson of the Lothian Regional Council in Edinburgh (031) 229 9292 (ext. 3849) is the best person to advise you on them.

The Clyde

There is of course the Clyde—to most sassenachs the Clyde conjures up images of shipyards and heavy industry. Or it did before the economic climate changed. So what do we expect now—a deserted and polluted wasteland? Wrong, wrong and thrice wrong! There is excellent fishing to be had here. There is some first class trout water and salmon and sea-trout are being re-introduced. This is clearly a river of the future and, though the pre-industrial revolution glory days which saw salmon of over 40lb and sea-trout of 14lb may not return, it seems likely that good salmon and sea-trout fishing will be restored. The reasons? Well, purely and simply, something has been done about the situation. The Clyde River Purification Board has done much hard work, as have the various clubs, such as the United Clyde Angling Protective Association. The work has included cleaning, restocking, creating and improving pools as well as buying out estuary nets. Conservation is not new here, for the UCAPA was founded in 1887 and has always been at the forefront of fishing improvements. Many people associate the Clyde with Glasgow alone but the river is some eighty miles long. Its source is in the Lowther Hills, not far from the Wells of Tweed, and its upper reaches abound with half and three-quarter pound trout. On its way the river broadens out and so do the trout! Two-pounders are regularly caught on some of the lower reaches such as Crawford, Hazelbank and Crossford. Permits for the Lamington and District Association water may be had from Brydens Newsagents (and tackle shop) at Biggar (0899) 20069 for £4 a day (half-price for OAPs). The average weight here is one pound and, just to whet your appetite, May 1991 produced an eleven-pounder! Permits for the UCAPA water may be obtained from tackle shops or the secretary, J. Quigley Esq. of Wishaw (0698) 382479.

Perhaps the reason that the Clyde is not better known is that the Scots are a canny race and understandably believe in keeping a good thing to themselves! But take a tip, the Clyde offers very good trouting at present and, judging by what's happening, I am sure it will be a good salmon and sea-trout water given a few more years.

The Garnock & the Irvine

South East of Glasgow on the A736 is the Ayrshire coastal town of Irvine and it is here that the rivers Garnock and Irvine share a common estuary. A further attraction is that if you fancy a change from fishing, the renowned golf courses of Prestwick and Troon are both a few miles away. Mind you, there are many others, and playing these Open courses is sometimes more difficult than finding good autumn fishing! The source of the Garnock is east of Largs and its course is some fifteen miles long, making it one of the country's smallest salmon rivers. Despite much excellent work, the river still suffers from pollution and there have been some tragic occurrences. That there are still a reasonable number of salmon says much for the resilience of this river's stock. All the same, it can produce a memorable day and hopefully things will improve. A day on the Eglinton Angling Club water can be had for £10 a day from Jameson's Ironmongers at Kilwinning.

The Irvine has a varied life in its twenty-five mile journey to the sea. It flows through agricultural, industrial and urban areas. Hopefully pollution is a problem of the past. Much work has been done by a local improvement association and the river now shows consistent good sport, especially since the nets have been bought out. The lower reaches of the river were damaged in the eighteenth and nineteenth centuries by the erection of dams to provide power to drive a variety of mills. The mills are now disused but the dams are still intact and impale migrating fish at low water. The river is also well stocked with trout and a day's permit for the Dreghorn Angling Club's three miles of water costs £5 and is obtainable from Alysons's Flower Shop in Irvine (0294) 76716. This club also has fishing in the Annick Water. This is a delightful little trout stream where spider patterns such as a size 12 or 14 Black and Peacock or Black Spider do consistently well.

Loch Thom

Those who like their loch fishing might care to try Loch Thom. The Loch lies north of the Garnock at the head of the Naddsdale Water and is a short distance south of Greenock. At just under 500 acres, this is not a big water, nor does it hold particularly large trout, for the average weight is around the half pound mark. However, it does offer good fishing at a modest cost. A day costs £2 and a week £6, permits are available from Brian Peterson at The Fishing Shop in Greenock (0475) 888085. It is one of the waters that should be fished with very light tackle and skimming a moth imitation across the surface around dusk can make for some exciting moments.

One of the greatest of many mythical enigmas surrounding the art of fishing is the incredible success achieved by the fairer sex. Miss Ballantine represents perhaps the most celebrated example, but through the years there has been no doubt that ladies have a consistent knack of catching salmon and often big ones at that. To rub salt in the wound, they will often succeed in the exact places where men have failed. I have heard many stories of men who have returned disconsolate to the hut after trying a good pool without a sign of a fish. They have duly passed the rod to the wife, only to see it bent over within a few minutes and the inevitable excited cry of 'fish'!

The Ayr

The Ayr is the largest river in the county and has a wide catchment area. As a result its spates are less flashy and, like the Nith, take longer to get started and last longer. It is, however, another river that has been a victim of the Industrial Revolution. A great deal of the pollution problem here comes from disused coal mines. On top of this, there are several sewage and other discharges in the area. There are dams and weirs that used to power the now redundant mills and there is a fair amount of poaching—this is one factor that cannot be blamed on the Industrial Revolution! Despite such problems it is still a good river and when the difficulties are resolved, it could be extremely good. On top of the problems created by man, the fish have had to contend with UDN, which so devastated the spring stock that the early run has never really recovered. At present August, September and October are likely to be the best months and most locals will choose to spin or worm. A Yellow Belly Minnow or Zebra Toby can often prove successful for the spinner. There are parts of the river which take the fly well and favourites include the Brown Turkey, Blue Charm and Stinchar Stout.

The river is some thirty-nine miles long from its source on Wardlaw Hill to the popular seaside resort of Ayr. A wide and shallow river, it can be prone to flooding in its lower reaches. The best salmon and sea-trout fishing is from the weir at Catrine down to the estuary. Perhaps the most attractive stretch is from Failford to Stair. Salmon average around 6lb and sea-trout 1½lb. All the river fishes well for trout and it is stocked every year. The Sorn Inn at Sorn (0290) 51305 which is just up from Catrine has a small stretch. Linwood & Johnstone, the newsagents (0290) 50219 in Mauchline, issue permits. The Failford Inn at Failford (0292) 541674 has two and a half miles and the cost here on a weekday is £5.

The Doon

Just south of Ayr is the River Doon. This river drains Loch Doon and the A713 follows much of its course from Glen Ness to the sea. It is a difficult river to get on as much of it is either privately owned or syndicated. However, the Skeldon Estate sometimes issue day tickets for their water, which has twelve named pools and it can be worth contacting the Estate Manager (0292) 56656.

The Stinchar

Continuing our coastal drive south on the A77 will bring us to Ballantrae which some people will associate with Robert Louis Stevenson's famous novel of Jacobite times. To fishermen, however, it is famous for being at the mouth of the Stinchar. In recent years the Doon has fished well but the Stinchar is the most productive river in Ayrshire. Unlike other rivers in the county, the river has not suffered from pollution for it lies well away from industrial areas and towns. As a result the water is remarkably clear and this well-managed river with its fine holding pools is one of the best fly waters in southwest Scotland. Many would argue, indeed, that it is a crime to fish it using any other method.

The source of the river is Loch Linfern in the Carrick Forest and in its twenty mile journey to the sea it is joined by its tributaries, the Duisk, Muck and Water of Tig. Loch Linfern is fairly small and as there are no reservoirs the river has spate characteristics. Afforestation, which covers much of its catchment area, has made the situation worse. Heavy rain in late Autumn can bring the river into flood but it does not take long to fine down to a good fishing level. Although there is no stocking programme and still some netting, salmon and sea-trout spawn throughout the length of the river and its tributaries. Very few salmon enter the river in the early months of the season and July, with its good grilse run, is really the start of the season. Summer sport is highly dependent on rain, but can produce some great days and this is also the time for sea-trout. As rain becomes more predictable with the approach of autumn the tempo increases. September and October are often the finest months.

Some of the best fishing is on the Duke of Wellington's Knockdolian Estate which can produce up to 700 fish a season. A popular fly here is the appropriately named Duke's Killer. On the first occasion that the Duke tried it he hooked four fish! As one might expect this is a difficult beat to get on, but if you are prepared to take a summer week while waiting for a back-end one, it may be worth contacting the Estate Office (0465) 88237. Some water round Colmonell is owned by the Church of Scotland and forms part of the Rev. Jones glebe. The fishing here is handled by Mrs G. B. Shankland of Barnfoot Farm (0465) 88220. The upper stretch is fly-only and a day's fishing will cost £12 per person per rod. Spinning is allowed further down where the price of a day permit is £10. The Dalreoch Estate has one and three quarter miles of mainly double-bank fishing where a daily permit costs between £35; it is available until the end of August, after which it is let on a weekly basis at a cost of approximately £190 per rod per week. A self-catering lodge is sometimes available. Permits can be obtained from the head keeper Mr D. Overend (0465) 88214. Bob Anderson of the Bardrochat Estate (0465) 88202 may also be able to help.

Stinchar salmon average around 8lb and sea-trout 1½lb. There are also some rainbows which have escaped from fish farms that run up to 3lb. It is not a large river and a single-handed ten- foot carbon should prove adequate for summer fishing and can also be used for sea-trout. A double handed fourteen-footer will be required when the river swells with late autumn rain. The most popular and effective fly is the Stinchar Stoat, which is much the same as a standard Stoat's Tail except that the hackle is orange rather than black. Another popular fly here and on many other waters is the General Practitioner which was first tried by the late Colonel Esmond Drury.

The Nith

Dumfries and Nithsdale is an area of much historical interest. Much of Robert Burns' work was written while he was working as an exciseman at a time when smuggling was a major local industry. His farm at Ellisland and house in Dumfries are now museums. Other buildings of note are the ruins of Sweetheart Abbey and Caerlaverock Castle with its nature reserve. At Sanquhar you can see Britain's oldest post office. Robert the Bruce murdered his rival John Comgh during the struggle for Scottish independence at Dumfries, and Arbigland is a popular spot with American tourists. It was here that John Paul Jones, the founder of the American navy, was born.

It is also an area of much piscatorial interest for here is the River Nith, Solway's crowning glory and one of the finest salmon and sea-trout rivers in Scotland. Sea-trout catches have averaged 3400 in recent years, and in 1989 the rod catch for salmon and grilse was 3641. These figures would have been better still were it not for the activities of poachers. The average salmon was around 9lb, grilse about 5lb and sea-trout 2lb. The best months are September, October and November and the Burgh Water in Dumfries produces about twenty fish a day. This is also the time for big fish which can be up to 30lb, although no fish today is likely to compete with the reputed sixty-seven pounder caught by Jock Wallace, the poacher, on the Barjarg water in 1812!

The Nith is born in Ayrshire, but its life at its source near Dalmellington is short lived as it enters Dumfriesshire at Kirkconnel and then flows on past the main centres of Sanquhar, Thornhill and Dumfries to join the Solway Firth. Above Sanquhar there are long stretches of sluggish canal-like water. The only white water to be found is in Drumlanrig Gorge but there are many excellent holding pools. Above Thornhill are seven miles of double-bank fishing divided into four beats, all owned by the Duke of Buccleuch whose seat, Drumlanrig Castle, is nearby—quite a lot of fishing around Thornhill is controlled by the Mid-Nithsdale Angling Association. Lower beats include such famous names as Closeburn Castle, Friars Carse, Portrack and Barjarg.

The river has many feeders and tributaries but the principal one is Cairn Water which joins the Nith below Lincluden College. The Cairn has some great fishing, especially in the small pools between Moniavie and Dunscore. The pool below Cluden Rock acts as a temperature barrier to fish and, unfortunately, as a magnet to poachers. The Cairn has other attractions besides salmon, for the Dumfries and Galloway Angling Association planted out 10,000 sea-trout fry in 1987. The same year saw the introduction of 3500 brown trout some of whom are now up to 2lb. This is a water which needs the autumn rains as in a hot dry summer it can be very weedy and shrink to a mere trickle.

The outbreak of UDN in 1967 did tremendous damage to the spring stock and so spring runs are really a thing of the past, but fishing below the caul in Dumfries at this time of the year can be productive. Flies that are well worth trying are Colonel's Wood, Castledykes and Slae Bushes.

The Nith is a spate river and, with no feeder lochs in the system, results are heavily dependent on rainfall. But rain is a mixed blessing since Upper Nithsdale is the victim of large scale afforestation. After heavy rain the river can be very coloured and it can be two or three days before serious fishing can begin again. Initially, worm will be the most productive method, while the next day will be suitable for spinners and then you should revert to fly. Because of its character most rods equip themselves with fly, spinning and worming tackle. It is a medium sized river and thigh waders will enable you to cover most waters.

Popular flies include the Hairy Mary, Blue Charm, Shrimp Fly, Stoats Tail and of course that local favourite, the Brown Turkey. In high water a two-inch Yellow Dog tube fly can prove deadly, but many will be spinning with a similar size or slightly larger Devon Minnow, in colours such as black and red, blue and pearl, green and yellow and brown and gold. In high water, sea-trout are also taken on a worm or a spinner such as a Mepps or small Toby, but in reasonable water levels fly is the most popular method. Two flies are normally fished on the leader as Nith sea-trout are often tempted by a bushy dropper such as a Black Pennell. Good patterns here are Blue and Silver, Wickham's Fancy, Greenwells Glory and Peter Ross. Later on in the evening and before dawn a team of spider patterns often works particularly well.

The Nith is an exceptional river and well worth a lot of effort to get on. Amongst those who may be able to help you are the Mid-Nithsdale Angling Club, where the cost is between £15 to £25 a day or £70 to £125 a week. Permits can be had from S. & I. Milligan of Thornhill (0848) 330555. Ian Milligan is a fount of local information and can be contacted for further details. The Killylong Estate (0387) 720415 has three-quarters of a mile of double-bank fishing: autumn fishing here is well booked with a waiting list, but summer sport is available. Nithsdale District Council (0387) 53166 charge £30 a day—visitors are only allowed to fish Monday to Friday. The Dumfries Office of Smiths Gore (0387) 63066 are the agents for the Blackwood beat. A week on the Buccleuch Estates (08486) 283 water costs between £100 to £800 plus VAT, but that is for two rods. They also offer day permits for the Linns beat for between £12 and £40 plus VAT. Further details from the Estate Office. Mr E. Tagg of The Blackaddie House Hotel at Sanquhar (0659) 50270 handles fishing on the Ryehill beat where the cost is between £15 and £35 a day and he can also arrange for you to fish the Upper Nithsdale Angling Club's water, two pools of which are right outside the hotel. There are no lochs which really stand out in this area but there are many good small lochs and stocked fisheries. Enquire locally for what would suit you best.

Many novices consider the wild Highlands of Scotland to be the exclusive terrain of game fishing. How wrong can they be! The Nith is a marvellous river and although the autumn beats are both expensive and popular they are well worth trying for.

Warmanbie, a Georgian Country House Hotel and Restaurant, set in 40 acres of secluded woodland grounds overlooking the River Annan, has been owned by the Duncan family since 1953. It has many interesting architectural and decorative features and is tastefully furnished with a combination of the Duncan family's antiques and more contemporary furniture. Rod Duncan, who converted it into a hotel in 1983, still runs Warmanbie for the family. He looks on Warmanbie as the family home and won't do anything that will spoil it.

Fishing for salmon, sea-trout and brown trout is free on the hotel's private stretch of the River Annan In addition the hotel has access to numerous other stretches of water on the Annan and to fishing on both the River Eden, near Carlisle, and the River Nith, near Dumfries. They can arrange for a ghillie to help and advise you or give you tuition, and the hotel has a supply of rods/tackle for sale/hire, a large freezer and drying facilities. Meal times are of course completely flexible to suit your fishing.

All the bedrooms have a private bathroom, colour television, tea / coffee making facilities and direct-dial telephone to ensure your complete comfort, as well as many thoughtful extra little touches such as fresh flowers, iced water and sweets. The Master bedroom is delightfully furnished with a solid mahogany four-poster bed and

deep Victorian tub bath. The hotel is awarded four crowns, commended by the Scottish Tourist Board, and is recommended by Egon Ronay and the Cadogan Guide.

Here is somewhere where you can relax and unwind from the pressures of everyday life and enjoy service which, although relaxed and friendly, is still of the highest standard.

Dinners are a mixture of the creative and traditional. You'll enjoy the large steaks (using local beef) and fresh mussels, or you can try one of the hotel's more creative dishes such as pork fillet in pastry with a mushroom, cointreau and orange stuffing, or avocado and smoked salmon salad. The Scottish breakfast which the hotel serves can only be described as huge. How about porridge with Drambuie, or a champagne breakfast with smoked salmon and scrambled eggs. The cosy bar has an excellent selection of malt whiskies for you to savour while discussing the day's catch.

You'll find wildfowling, golf, tennis, squash, curling and various water sports all nearby. Clay pigeon shooting can be arranged with prior notice. Warmanbie is also an ideal base for beachcombing on the Solway Coast and exploring the picturesque countryside of South West Scotland, the Borders and Lake District.

Warmanbie Hotel
Annan, F / F
Dumfriesshire, DG12 5LLL
Tel: (0461) 204015

One of the most disturbing yet most neglected aspects of fishing is the increasing number of accidents related to the sport. I suppose this is not really surprising as fishing is becoming increasingly popular. However, I cannot help thinking that a number could be prevented by common sense and a little forethought. Wading can be dangerous, especially on some spate rivers where the water level can rise very quickly in a short space of time. Personally, I carry a wading stick and will always ask local advice, as even shallow river beds can be deceptively dangerous. I cannot understand those who don't wear a life jacket while boat fishing on big lochs. They always restrict one's movement a little but big lochs, especially those where the wind is funnelled between mountain sides, can rapidly change character and become dangerous places.

The Annan

A few miles east of the Nith is the Annan which is a good salmon river and even better for sea-trout. Its source is on the slopes of the delightfully named Devil's Beef Tub from whence it flows to Moffat. This attractive little town is just off the main road that connects Carlisle and Glasgow and was one of only two spa towns in Scotland. However, the only waters we are interested in are those that take the fly and the Beattock House Hotel (06833) 402) at Beattock, which is just below Moffat, issues permits for the Upper-Annandale Angling Association Water. Downstream from Moffat the river is joined by Evan Water and Moffat Water. The tributaries are far bigger than the Annan at this stage of its journey. Some would argue that the true source of the river is Loch Skeen, at the top of the Moffat Water, just above the beautiful Grey Mare's Tail waterfall, which you can see from the A708. This is a river that has many picturesque names and among its tributaries is the Water of Milk. Others join it on its way to Annan and the Solway Firth: Kinnel Water, Dryfe Water and Mein Water.

Beats on the Annan include the Annandale Estate, Halleaths with its deep slow-moving pools, Royal Four Towns, Hoddom with its famous Goats and Kirkyard Pools and Newbie which is now time-shared. Permits for the Castlemilk Water, which includes the Royal Four Towns beat, may be had from the Estate Office in Lockerbie (05765) 203. The cost of a day ranges between £17.72 and £28 plus VAT. Regular permit holders are given priority over visitors and no visitor permits are issued for Saturdays in October. Rather less expensive is the Hoddom and Kinmount Estates Water, whose Water Bailiff is Miss Marsh of Hoddom (05763) 488. The Warmanbie Hotel at Annan (0461) 204015 has a small stretch for hotel guests. Those wishing to fish the time shared Newbie beat are advised to contact the water-bailiff Mr Mick Aprile (0461) 202608.

The Annan is a spate river and forestry drainage from its catchment area naturally leads to fast run-offs and coloured water. In normal conditions it can be on the sluggish side and gentle hand-lining is the way to make the fly swim. Due to its colour in spate, worming and spinning are popular methods but it is good to know that a number of beats have a fly-only rule. The Annan used to have a good spring run but this has declined and springers are now usually taken below Milnbie. A wet summer can make for some exciting days, especially for sea-trout which average around 2lb, although most seasons will produce better fish of over 6lb. For salmon, autumn is the best time, when several 20lb plus fish will be recorded and the average is a high 12lb.

The Border Esk

The Border Esk is aptly named—not only does it cross the border but part of it and its main tributary the Liddle actually form the border between England and Scotland. Although its mouth and lower reaches are in England, the middle and upper reaches and principal tributaries

Bladnoch Fishing (Richmond Leisure)

are all in Scotland. The river is formed by the junction of the Black Esk and White Esk just below Castle Oer. After this it is joined by a number of tributaries, the main ones being Meggat Water, Ewes Water and the Wauchope, before reaching the town of Langholm. From this point south the A7 runs alongside the river as it collects the Tarras Water and below Canonbie it is joined by the Liddle, which has its source in Kielder Forest. This is a noted salmon and sea-trout water in its own right. At Longtown, road and river part company as the Esk heads for the Solway Firth and just north of Metalbridge it receives its final tributary the Lyne, before spilling over the mud-flats of Rockcliff marsh.

There are some wild brown trout in the river's upper reaches and tributaries, but these parts can take some getting to, so be prepared for a little rock climbing. For people who love a little extra adventure this is, however, a marvellous way to start the day and when you are finally fishing you feel alone, satisfied and totally at ease.

Autumn is the best time for salmon. Though they average ten pounds, a superb twenty-two pounder was caught in 1993 Popular flies are the Blue Charm and a Silver Doctor. The Garry Dog is the local favourite.

Afforestation on the upper reaches of the river and its tributaries can make for variable water levels with occasional flash floods. Much of the river between Langholm and Canonbie is tree-lined so the ability to spey cast will be a useful asset. Do be careful when wading for although some pools are easy to wade, others are deceptively deep, so do make a thorough reconnaissance before going out at night.

Night fishing of course means sea-trout and this is the Esk's main claim to fame, indeed it is one of the great sea-trout waters. In most seasons over 5000 of these shy warriors are taken with some topping the 8lb mark. Locals tend to use a double handed twelve-foot rod, but a single handed ten-foot carbon will enable you to cover the water and, being more sensitive, will give you a better feel when the action begins. A floating line is the best for the dusk rise, after which it may be advisable to change to a sink tip or intermediate. Popular flies are the Mark Brown and the Black Spider.

There is something magical about night fishing. First there is the dusk rise with sea-trout plopping all over the pool. As night approaches things become quieter and the flat surface of the water is only rarely broken by the rings of the rising fish. After this there is the fun of stalking fish or casting over the likely lie you noticed earlier in the day. When day breaks it is time to head for home and proudly display the results of your night's work. That at least is the theory! I would add that rods are particularly asked not to take too many herling—young sea-trout—so as to conserve stocks for the future.

The river is largely owned by Buccleuch Estates and most of it is controlled by the Esk and Liddle Fishery Association. Day permits cost between £6 and £30 and further information may be had from the Factor, G.L.Lewis (03873) 80202 or Mr George Graham, the Head River Watcher (03873) 71416. The Cross Keys Hotel at Canonbie (03873) 71205 also issues weekly permits.

The Tweed

The Wells of Tweed are a few miles north of Moffat and the Annan and it is here that the Tweed commences its illustrious journey to the sea at Berwick-Upon-Tweed. Its prominence is perhaps best summed up by the fact that it is the only river I know that has its own telephone line! In fact the aptly named Tweedline has three numbers, (0898) 666410 for fishing reports and prospects, (0898) 666411 for river levels which are updated daily and, most importantly from our point of view, (0898) 666412 which is the number for last minute rod vacancies.

Sparkling burns like Carr Water and Tweedhope Burn join the Tweed as it flows north to Tweedsmuir, which was the childhood home of John Buchan. There is very good trouting here and the Crook Inn at Tweedsmuir (08997) 272 has its own stretch which is free to residents. This hotel also issues permits for the Peebles Trout Fishing Association water which costs £6 a day. Talla and Fruid, which once used to swell the infant river, have now been dammed to provide water for Edinburgh.

After being joined by Biggar and Holms water, the rough moorland banks give way to a more noble setting of pastures and parklands. By Peebles the river is joined by the swirling peaty Manor Water and the Lyne, another reservoir victim. Just west of Peebles is Neidpath Castle, whose walls bear the scars of Cromwell's artillery.

Peebles, with its famous fifteenth-century bridge, is where salmon fishing really begins. Blackwood & Smith (0721) 20131 handle lets for the Peebleshire Salmon Fishing Association, which is an association of fishing proprietors who allow fishing by permit. Day permits cost between £25 and £35 a day or £115 for the season. Fish average around nine pounds.

Below the town the river skirts Kailzie Gardens and the dense conifers of Cardrona Forest and here you will find such beats as Haystoun, Horsburgh Castle and Traquair. Traquair House, the home of Maxwell Stuart, is Scotland's oldest occupied home and legend says that The Bear Gates will never be opened until a Stuart sits on the English throne again. Innerleithen is famous for its textile manufacturing and just downstream at Walkerburn is the Scottish Textile Museum.

The Traquair Arms Hotel (0896) 830229 can offer good autumn fishing on four beats for £4 a day. The Tweed Valley Hotel at Walkerburn (0896) 87636 has some private beats in beautiful surroundings, where the cost of a day's fishing varies between £25 and £40. Many of their guests are regulars, but the proprietor, Charles Miller, can sometimes arrange for his guests to fish other beats. The best fish taken in 1992 by guests was an 18¾lb salmon. This hotel also has two miles of private trout fishing on the Tweed and two lochs, one with wild brownies and the other with stocked rainbows, which can be fished for £7.50 a day.

The Ettrick

Below Innerleithen the banks are again victims of conifer plantations. Here are beats such as Caddonfoot, Sunderland, Thornilee, Elbibank and Peel, as just north of Selkirk it is joined by the Ettrick which marks the beginning of the Middle Tweed. The Ettrick is a good salmon river in its own right and, like its tributary the Yarrow, is noted for its trout which go up to 3lb. Buccleuch Estates at Bowhill (0750) 20753 issue day tickets for their water on the Ettrick, Yarrow and Teviot at a cost of between £15 and £30 a day.

Ettrickshaws Hotel at Ettrick (0750) 52229 has two miles of single-bank fishing on the Ettrick, which is available free to guests or to anyone else at between £15 and £20 a day. The water here is a spate river and fishes well late in the season. At Selkirk there is a statue to that intrepid Victorian explorer, Mungo Park, who discovered the source of the River Niger in Africa.

Gala and Allan Water join the Tweed above Melrose, where the heart of Robert the Bruce is reputed to be buried in the ruins of the Cistercian Abbey. A Roman fort stands guard over the town and river and from its lofty position on Eildon Hills, would also have given a clear view of Dere Street, the main England to Scotland road in those days. On this stretch will be found such famous beats as Drygrange, Maxton, Merton, Rutherford, Gledswood, Bemersyde and Ravenswood.

From where the Leader Water joins the Tweed at Leaderfoot is what is widely regarded as the best salmon fishing in the world. In 1730 the Earl of Home caught a 69lb 12oz salmon and 1866 produced one of 57lb 8oz. Fish of such majestic proportions, or anything like them, have not been seen for many a year, a fact which may well be connected with the drift net industry. Nowadays most Tweed salmon are around ten pounds or slightly better, with the odd thirty-pounder occasionally falling to some lucky rod. Nearby is the small town of St Boswells where Sir Walter Scott and Earl Haig of First World War and Poppy Day fame are buried. As one might expect, water of this quality is extremely difficult and expensive to get on. However, if you are lucky enough to be able to afford it you might care to buy one of the weeks on the Lower Floors beat which the Duke of Roxburghe is selling on a thirty-year lease through Savills' Edinburgh office (031) 226 6961.

The Teviot

At Kelso we find the most famous pool on the river—Junction. This is where the Teviot joins the Tweed and, despite the fact that a week here for five rods is over £17,000, it is booked for years in advance. The Teviot is another tributary that is a fine salmon river in its own right—it has such good pools as Ferry Stream, Lower and Quarry which have all produced fish of over 20lb. Mr Bill Wright of Hawick (0450) 85252 has his own beat for two rods on the Teviot and may be able to organise other fishing, including the Tweed when available. Tweedside Tackle of Kelso (0573) 25306 can arrange days on various private beats subject to availability, and also issue permits for the Kelso Angling Association Water.

There are some famous beats between Junction Pool and below Coldstream, where the Tweed receives the Till. Among names to conjure with are Sprouston, Birgham, Carham, Wark, Cornhill and Lennel. From the junction with Eden Water the Tweed forms the boundary between England and Scotland. The Till is also a fine salmon and sea-trout water. Its headwaters are sparkling burns which tumble down the Cheviot Hills and it is only at Chillingham Castle, with its famous wild white cattle, that it becomes the Till. Many rods fortunate enough to fish the beats in this area stay at either the Ednam House Hotel (0573) 24168 or the Crown Hotel at Coldstream (0890) 2558. Coldstream has military connections other than the famous regiment of Guards which bears its name, for just south of here is the site of Flodden Field.

From Till junction the Tweed progresses at a stately pace with deep pools, wide rapids and streaming round the many islands. It is here that you will find the famous Lady Kirk and Norham beats. Norham Castle was painted by Turner and Sir Walter Scott termed it the most dangerous place to be in England.

Whiteadder & Blackadder

A mile east of Paxton the border crosses the river which is now wholly in England and, shortly after this, it receives its last tributary, the Whiteadder. The upper reaches of this river have been dammed and flooded, forming a reservoir to provide water for Edinburgh. It is, however, good trout water. The Allanton Inn at Allanton (0890) 818260 issue permits for the Whiteadder Angling Club Waters, at a cost of between £10 and £20 a season. Its tributary, the Blackadder, offers good sporting trouting and a season ticket may be had from the Cross Keys Hotel at Greenlaw (03616) 247 for £5. Below Whiteadder junction the Tweed is affected by tides which ebb and flow, shifting sands and mud, until the river enters the North Sea at Tweedmouth.

Trying to book fishing yourself on the Tweed can be a headache to say the least. There are many beats and good tributaries but there is also a lot of competition for them and, as you can imagine, many people return year after year. You could spend several days on the telephone and get nowhere Alternatively you could save a lot of time by ringing the sporting agents.

Ted Hunter of Anglers Choice in Melrose (0896) 823070 has access to some private beats. James Leeming of Kelso (0573) 470280 was a land agent in the early eighties but soon moved towards becoming a fishing agent. He had access to eleven private beats in 1993, where the cost varied between £25 and £500 a day. E. MacDonald Sports of Peebles (0721) 20979 (formerly I Fraser Sports) is an excellent tackle shop and issues trout permits. However, Mrs Lena Fraser carries on her late husband's salmon fishing as Fraser's Salmon Fishing and Hire Ltd (0721) 722960. They have two beats which are let from £30 a day.

As on so many rivers, the spring run is not what it used to be. Most springers are taken below Kelso, because fish will stay below the caul until the water temperature has risen. Summer fishing can, as one would expect, be rather chancy. However, a wet autumn and its attendant spates will see thousands upon thousands of fish running the river. Autumn fish average around ten pounds but twenty and thirty pounders are not too rare. This is a big river and you need to have as long a rod as you can comfortably handle and I would suggest either a fourteen or fifteen footer. Although some pools are very deep, most fish are taken in fairly shallow water and a medium or intermediate sinking line should suffice. Popular flies include the Garry, Willie, Gun, Comet or patterns such as the Munro Killer, Hairy Mary and Stoats Tail for summer fishing. The best advice is to go to one of the tackle shops like Anglers Choice in Melrose and find out the latest thoughts on flies, times and locations of recent catches.

Megget Reservoir & St Mary's Loch

For those who like their stillwater fishing, taking the A707 south from Selkirk will bring you to Megget Reservoir and St Mary's Loch. Megget covers some six hundred and forty acres, is two hundred feet deep in places and—for the statistician—holds on average thirteen and a half thousand million gallons of drinking water! Tibby Shiels Inn (0750) 42231 issue permits which cost £2.90 a day for bank fishing and boats are available. There is a modest stocking programme every year and Arctic char are being introduced on a small scale as an experiment. This brown trout water is fly-only and traditional wet flies work well as do nymphs. Dapping is becoming increasingly popular. As this is over 1000 feet above sea level it can be very cold so do not forget to take an extra sweater. Anglers Choice of Melrose (0869) 823070 issue permits for St Marys Loch costing £3 a day for fly fishers or £5 a day for spinners and those using bait. This price differential probably says quite a lot about the availability of this water. The large loch also holds perch and pike and there is a watersports centre. I understand spinning is popular and the trout average a good pound, but I must confess that the idea of trolling for trout with a spinner does not appeal to me. Perhaps that is because I am still dreaming of getting a week on the Tweed! Incidentally, two other contacts for visiting anglers are W.S. Renton (Berwick) 3060268, who controls Watch Water Reservoir, and Mr T Hardie (Galashiels) 2345, of Galashiels Angling Club.

Cringletie House Hotel

Cringletie is a distinguished mansion which has retained the warm atmosphere of a private country house. It is set well back from the Peebles/Edinburgh road (A703) in twenty-eight acres of garden and woodland, in peaceful surroundings. Only twenty miles from Edinburgh, it is an excellent centre.

All rooms are tastefully decorated and furnished to a high standard of comfort, with colour televisions, direct dial telephones and en-suite facilities. There are magnificent views from all rooms. The restaurant has been consistently recommended since 1971.

Recommended by Johansen; Egon Ronay; The AA; The RAC; Signpost; Ashley Courtenay and other guide books.

Cringletie House Hotel
Peebles EH45 8PL
Tel: (0721) 730 233
Fax: (0721) 730 244

Corsemalzie House Hotel, a secluded country mansion is set in the heart of the picturesque countryside of the Machars (moors) of Wigtownshire, away from the rigours of city life. Relax in a setting which is hard to beat, the only noise to upset the tranquillity are the cries of the whaup (curlew) and the babbling burn. The seasonal changes create a different backdrop for the hotel, making Corsemalzie a delight to stay at whatever time of year is your preference.

The gastronome will find Corsemalzie has a great deal to offer, with dishes created using only the finest ingredients carefully and enthusiastically supervised by the proprietor Mr Peter McDougall. Fresh and local produce is used whenever possible.

This attention to detail is carried throughout the hotel with Mr and Mrs McDougall ensuring that your stay will not only be memorable for the cuisine but also for the little things that make the difference between a good hotel and a great hotel.

If you can drag yourself away from this comfort, the surrounding area has much to offer, with riding pony trekking and walking, some superb golf on your doorstep, a whole host of 9 hole courses, with 18 hole courses at Portpatrick, Glenluce where the hotel pays half your green fees, Stranraer and a little further afield at the famous Turnberry Links course.

For the game sportsmen, shooting and fishing are here in an abundance, Mr McDougall will personally organise and assist you shooting for pheasant, grouse, partridge, duck geese, snipe woodcock, rabbits and hares in the hotel grounds and neighbouring estates amounting to some 8,000 acres. The hotel has exclusive salmon and trout fishing rights on four and a half miles of the River Bladnoch and five miles on the River Tarff. Fishing can also be organised in the Mazie Burn. A gillie is available for most of the season to advise and assist wherever needed.

Corsemalzie House Hotel
Port William
Newton Stewart
Wigtownshire
Scotland DG8 9RL
Tel: (098 886) 254
Fax: (098 886) 213

Sunlaws House stands in the heart of Scotland's beautiful Border country, in 200 acres of gardens and mature parkland along the banks of the Teviot, three miles from the historic town of Kelso. There has been a house on the same site at Sunlaws for nearly 500 years and from its beginnings it has always been a Scottish family house – and that, to all intents and purposes, is how it will stay!

Sunlaws has a place in history, from the faint echoes of ancient strife when English armies of the 15th and 16th centuries came marauding through Roxburghshire and the Borders, to the Jacobite rebellion of 1745. Indeed Prince Charles Edward Stuart is reputed to have stayed on November 5th 1745 and to have planted a white rose bush in the grounds.

Sunlaws hope that their guests will find that in the intervening year there have been some welcome changes. Its owner, the Duke of Roxburghe, has carefully converted Sunlaws into the small, welcoming but unpretentious hotel of comfort and character that it is.

There are 22 bedrooms, which include the splendid Bowmont Suite and six delightful rooms in the stable courtyard, all furnished with care to His Graces' own taste and all with private bathroom or shower, colour television, radio and direct-dial telephone. Disabled guests too are provided with the amenities they need.

The spacious public rooms are furnished with the same care and elegance, which adds to the overall atmosphere of warmth and welcome with log fires burning in the main and inner hall, drawing room, library bar and dining room, throughout the winter and on cold summer evenings.

Flowers and plants, from the gardens and the conservatory, will be found all over the house; herbs too are grown for the kitchen and will be found in many of the traditional dishes that are prepared for the dining room. Not only is Sunlaws right in the heart of Scotland's beautiful Border Country, it is also the perfect centre for a host of holiday activities. Sporting and cultural interests are well served, too.

Salmon and trout fishing, and a complete range of shooting are available at the Hotel, with golf, horse-riding, racing and fox hunting all nearby.

Sunlaws is the perfect location for touring the Borders, with great country houses including Abbotsford, the home of Sir Walter Scott, and a number of abbeys and museums all within easy reach.

Sunlaws House
Kelso
Roxburghshire
Tel: (05735) 331
Fax: (05735) 611

Irvine & Clyde

The Kirkhouse Inn in Strathblane (0360) 70621 is a pleasant house for a break from the wheel. It's popular locally and is more elegant than many of the towering city centre establishments in Glasgow. Gleddoch House (047554) 711, Langbank is another well appointed hotel, overlooking the countryside north west of the city. Bedrooms are comfortable and leisure facilities including golf and riding are welcome additions to the hotel's virtues. So, up to the city, where there are a number of hotels from which to choose. Montgreenan Mansion (0294) 57733 is an impressive edifice of Georgian style, convenient for the Irvine. A similar description can be made of Chapeltoun House (0560) 82696, two miles out of Stewarton. It is small but extremely luxurious and ideal for those who enjoy country house style hotels. The Hospitality Inn at Irvine (0294) 7427 may lack a little of the charm of such houses but is comfortable and has some good facilities, including a fine restaurant. In Troon, the Marine Highland (0292) 314444 is more popular with golfers than fishermen but it is a good hotel for those visiting the area. West of Edinburgh one finds another hotel favoured by golfers, Dalmahoy Hotel, Golf and Country Club (031) 333 1845. It's a tremendously well equipped hotel and a superb place to break your journey, as is Houstoun House (0506) 853831, a baronial house with splendid bedrooms and a fine restaurant and popular bar—a fine place to complete our expedition into Scotland's northern climes and the fishing offered there.

The Ayr to the Nith

Much of the water in Ayrshire and Dumfries and Galloway is club or estate water but hotels are often well-connected and able to introduce their guests to some good fishing.

In Alloway, the Burns Monument (0292) 42466 is a first class place to stay. The hotel is set at the very heart of Burns country. A thoroughly appealing hotel, its Alloway Lounge and landscaped gardens offer wonderful views over the river Doon on which fishing can be organised. Its splendid setting make this a good place to stay when in Ayrshire.

Turnberry is a landmark better known to golfers than anglers. Its two celebrated championship courses are most impressive and the hotel itself is marvellously comfortable and well equipped. Additional leisure facilities have been completed recently, reinforcing the hotel's international pedigree. A less grand but nevertheless thoroughly welcoming hotel can be found in Girvan, the King's Arms (0465) 3322—a clear cut golfing hotel which also acts as a fine base for those who represent the fishing fraternity.

There are numerous lochs and rivers in the area, many of which merit the attentions of serious fishermen. It does not take too long to reach the Borders of Scotland and it's a mere hour or so from there to Ayrshire. The journey time to get here is dramatically less than it is to more northerly outposts, but the scenery is still superb and a visit should be made whenever possible! Kildonan (077082) 207, in Barrhill is a splendid example of a wonderful hotel that is beautifully hidden away and delightfully peaceful. The house, designed by Sir Edwin Lutyens, is charming and the leisure facilities here are excellent. This is definitely one to consider if you are travelling to the area. Furthermore, the hotel can arrange game fishing.

Some distance to the west, we come to the superb hotel, Knockinaam Lodge (077681) 471. There are few hotels which will give you such a friendly welcome and this Victorian Lodge, in a charming glen, is one of the most pleasurable places to have dinner in Britain. A trip is therefore thoroughly recommended.

Travelling around the coast we come to Port William. Here we find another wonderful hotel in which to stay, which also organises fishing. Corsemalzie House (098886) 254 is an absolute delight and its splendid scenery will surely inspire you to great things on river and loch. If not, well fear not—the bar is a welcoming place to forget the one that got away. In fact, later in the evening you'll have probably landed him three or four times! There are a number of fine hotels in and around Newton Stewart. Creebridge House (0671) 2121 is a popular haunt and, formerly a shooting lodge for the Earls of Galloway, is one for the notebook. It's well-equipped, offers enjoyable food and is an ideal port of call. Torwood House Hotel (0581) is no less agreeable and welcomes many anglers year after year. Returning southwards to Gatehouse of Fleet, we find Cally Palace (0557) 814341, another pleasing place in which to stay.

There are all manner of unspoilt nooks and crannies in Southern Scotland and Culgruff House (055667) 230 is one such delight. The hotel proudly overlooks the village of Crossmichael and the Ken Valley. There are log fires which give a homely feel and the welcome is equally warm. Woodlea in Moniaive (08482) 209 is a superb hotel in which to unwind; there are good leisure facilities here and, once again, the focus is on relaxing. Our final thought for the day can be found at Sanquhar—here the Mennockfoot Lodge (0659) 50382 has a wonderfully serene location beside the Mennock water where it joins the River Nith. The hotel is not luxurious but is good value and has a pleasant atmosphere. When you are on holiday, what could be a better formula for success?

The Annan to the Tweed

The Border country makes for a perfect fishing expedition for many fishermen who live south of the border. The Borderers are a friendly bunch (unless, of course, the Calcutta Cup has drifted south) and they also know a dram when they see one. Be warned however, to get into a drinking session with one of those fine British beasties is a fate akin to death. In fact, the only cure to what can be the most ridiculous hangover is to get up early and embark upon a spot of fishing.

Beattock is a splendid place to start or end your tour. Rivers converge on the town from all sides and fishing is available through a number of fishing hotels. The Auchen Castle (06833) 407, situated about a mile north of the village, has a lovely situation surrounded by woodland. The hotel is not a fishing hotel as such, but if you are seeking to fish the Annan it is a fine place to stay.

Another hotel which welcomes visitors and has some fishing of its own is the Beattock House (06833) 403. This is not a grand hotel but it's good value and friendly. In Moffat, the Moffat House Hotel (0683) 20039 is a well run hotel with good bar meals. In Lockerbie, meanwhile, Lockerbie Manor (05762) 2610 is quite superb.

In Annan itself we find a hotel which is particularly popular with the fishing fraternity. The Warmanbie hotel (0461) 204015 is informally run and makes for an ideal base for your fishing foray. The Eskdale Hotel, (03873) 80357, in Langholm is another unpretentious but thoroughly worthy and well equipped hotel for your sporting break. Fishing permits are available from the hotel and, once again, this is a good base from which to explore the Borders. Eskdalemuir is somewhat more hit and miss when it comes to fishing the Esk and when the water is low things will be tough, but when its high the fishing can be extremely good. The place to stay if you are in these parts is Hart Manor (03873) 73217 which enjoys a delightful setting and also boasts some excellent dining.

An inn which has no pretence of trying to organise fishing but should still be considered for your visit is the marvellous Riverside Inn (03873) 71295 in Canonbie. The river to which it borders is the Esk and the cuisine here is outstanding. There are also a small number of attractive bedrooms, should you require overnight accommodation.

The Tweed is an illustrious water and, as a result, it is difficult to get on, but a number of hotels are able to help you in this respect. Other hotels are merely for your reference should you have secured water through friends or estate owners. The Cringletie House (0721) 30233 in Peebles is a splendid place to unpack the old suitcase. Its turreted architecture adds to its beauty and the restaurant is also to be recommended. Tweedsmuir is another point to mark and an establishment of great character is the Crook Inn (08997) 272. The hotel is to be found in the upper reaches of the Tweed Valley and dates from the early seventeenth-century. The hotel is thoroughly welcoming and a delightful location from which to enjoy an informal fishing holiday.

The Traquair Arms Hotel (0896) 830229 is a friendly fishing hotel which has much to commend it, not least four beats on the Tweed. The Tweed Valley Hotel (089687) 636 in Walkerburn is another fine hotel in which to stay and has great appeal to the sportsman. The sauna might appeal after a wet day's fishing before a fine dinner. Those people who are fishing the Ettrick will surely visit the splendid Ettrickshaws, Ettrickbridge (0750) 52229. This is a superb place in which to stay with fireplaces,

oak panelling and some very comfortable accommodation. The fishing here, assuming spate conditions, is first class, and as you can imagine, October does become extremely busy. The Woodburn House Hotel (0750) 20815, in Selkirk, is another establishment that will certainly not disappoint.

There are a number of super hotels in this delightful Border country and hopefully these ideas will whet the appetite. The Woodlands Country House Hotel (0869) 4722 in Galashiels is an impressive country house and the restaurant is well worth a visit. In Melrose, Burts Hotel (089682) 2285 is a splendid place for the game fisherman to stay. The hotel advises guests to consult Anglers Choice in Melrose for their fishing information. Indeed, it is fair to say that a number of hotels who do not actually have rods themselves are eager to provide information on people who can help. Another friendly establishment which is in a similar position is the Buccleuch Arms (0835) 22243, St Boswells. Trout fishing on the Tweed can be organised fairly readily but when it comes to salmon fishing there is little available. But the hotel does have contacts, so do call and you might be fortunate. Whatever the circumstances the hotel is an extremely friendly and comfortable place to stay.

We now come to a superb recommendation together with somewhat of a cautionary tale. Sunlaws House Hotel (05735) 331 is situated just outside Kelso and is one of the most delightful hotels in which to stay. The bar exudes character, the bedrooms are cosy and the restaurant is outstanding. People staying here are able to fish the Teviot and the hotel has its own pond which is beautifully laid out and great fun to fish.

Now for the cautionary tale. Do not listen to people who say fishing is impossible to find. It is difficult but not impossible. Indeed, as I was researching into this area I came across two prime beats which had become available on the Tweed. The cost was high, but good quality in any sphere does not come cheaply. The point is that some fishing is available and, for around £2500, I could have arranged for four rods on the Tweed. Yes, I would have had to stay at Sunlaws House but that is an added bonus. The moral here is, if you don't ask, you can't possibly find out!

Another fine place to stay is the Cross Keys (0573) 23303, which has a delightful situation overlooking Kelso's cobbled square. This is a delightful old inn in which to stay. Our final thought of Kelso is the renowned fishing hotel, Ednam House (0573) 24168. It has a wonderfully welcoming atmosphere and has a marvellous situation overlooking the River Tweed. The hotel has its own excellent fishing, which is an added bonus.

Another welcoming establishment can be found four miles south east of Greenlaw. Purves Hall (089084) 558 has a delightfully rural and unspoilt setting and welcomes fishermen to it doors. A stay here is also to be recommended. Make no mistake, this is a splendid area in which to fish—the Highland and Islands will have to wait for next year!

Lockerbie Manor
COUNTRY HOTEL

Set amidst 78 acres of tranquil park and woodland, Lockerbie Country Manor is a haven of peace and relaxation, yet it is situated only one mile off the A74. Built in 1814 for Sir William Douglas and Dame Grace Johnstone, whose great-grandson, the Marquis of Queensbury, formulated the present day boxing rules, it became the smart country hotel it is today in 1920.

Guests can enjoy the traditions of a bygone era at Lockerbie Manor. The long, tree-lined driveway gives a taste of the luxury that lies ahead. Both of the public lounges are furnished in authentic period style with an Adam fireplace amidst period furniture and walls lined with oil paintings. The atmosphere exudes warmth and hospitality; a home away from home for the traveller. All 30 bedrooms are individually decorated with private bathrooms, colour television and every comfort. There are five four poster bedded suites, with front-facing views over the fields and surrounding countryside. The Queensbury Dining Room with its wood panelled wall ornate chandeliers and magnificent views, is the ideal setting for a delectable meal. The cuisine is of an international nature, where Eastern flavours and cooking subtly blend with Western recipes.

Golfers will love the courses in the area, offering challenges of varying degrees of difficulty. Lockerbie, Dumfries, Lochmaben, Powfoot and Moffat are all nearby. If shooting or stalking is more your scene, there are numerous large estates around Lockerbie offering facilities. For the fisherman, the Rivers Annan, Mill, Cree, Blanock and Penkiln all beckon. Within the space of a short drive you can visit the beautiful Galloway coast, Drumlanrigg Castle, Maxwellton House in Monaive, Threave Gardens and Castle near Castle Douglas and Thomas Carlyle's birthplace at Ecclefechan.

Lockerbie Manor Country Hotel
Boreland Road
Lockerbie
Dumfries and Galloway
DG11 2RG
Tel: (0576) 202610/203939
Fax: (0576) 203046

Alfred de Breanski **HIGHLAND PEAKS** *Courtesy of Rosenstiel's*

Southern Uplands

ENGLAND'S NORTH

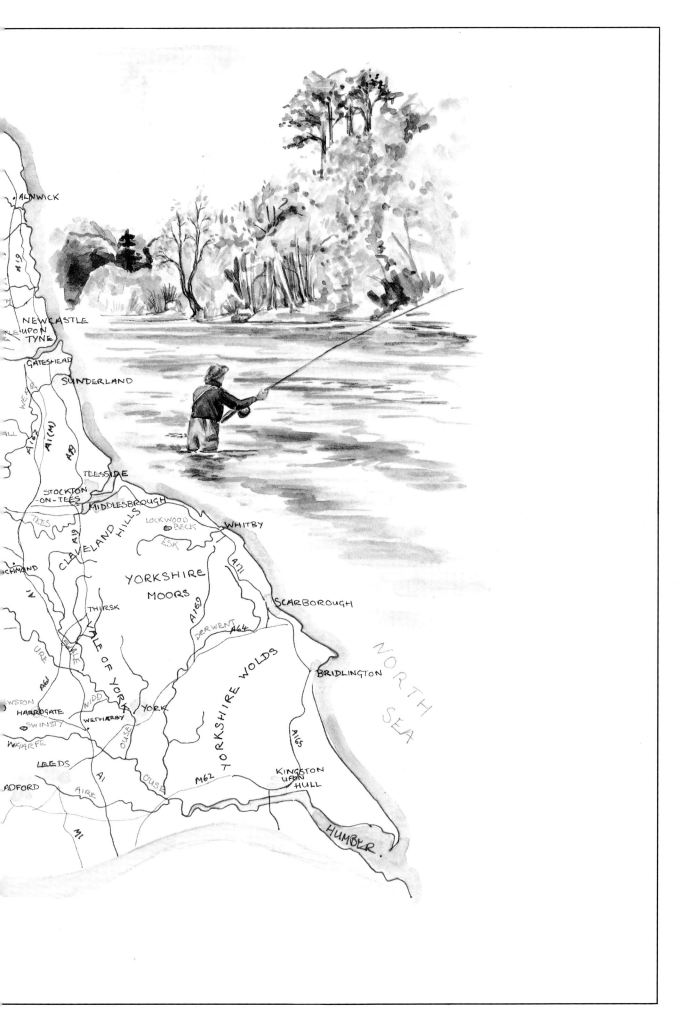

England's North

Cumbrian Lakes and Rivers

For many the North conjures up images of industrial slag heaps and pit villages. What they fail to appreciate is some of the most rugged and remote and the most beautiful scenery in the country. The North is not short on water—no drought here. In fact Northumberland actually exports this precious commodity to the Middle East. The Pennines, the Lakes, the deserted coastal areas and the wild moorlands all provide a haven for the angler. Fishing is here aplenty, and it is never dull. For our purposes northern England will take in the superb lakeland scenery with its steep fells, tarns and delightful villages. We will travel south to Lancashire where a number of excellent fisheries can be found. Crossing the Pennines, we struggle through the remote and rugged uplands to the contrasting areas of South and North Yorkshire. The dales and peaks of the white rose county make for stunning countryside. Heading north again through moorlands, we arrive in the vast expanse of Northumbria, the unspoiled and undeveloped hinterland contrasting with the cities of Durham, Sunderland and Newcastle-Upon-Tyne. From the Tyne to the Tweed we promise you an exciting and inspiring journey.

Cumbrian Rivers

North West Water, who control much of this area's waters are making commendable efforts to upgrade the waters in the region. Restricting netting on the Solway and banning the use of drift nets in the River Eden are just two examples of recent improvements. The hope is, clearly, to see increased runs of migratory fish and we wish them and the NRA all good fortune in this endeavour.

The Eden

The Border Esk, which in part marks the Anglo-Scottish border, has been considered in our Southern Scotland section and, as a result, the first great river we should consider is the Eden. The river runs for some seventy miles. At its estuary and for its first twenty miles there is some fine salmon fishing, but sadly the sea-trout fishing could only be described as indifferent.

A few miles south of Carlisle we find a productive stretch under the control of Warwick Hall. This stretch has done quite well for salmon in recent years, and as you can imagine, the fishing is extremely popular. There are two people who will be able to help you here; Don Haughin at Keeper's Cottage (0228) 560545 and Major Murphy (0228) 561918 at The Annexe. Both are situated at Warwick Hall itself. If you apply by November, Major Murphy will consider you for day rods the following season. The address is The Annexe, Warwick Hall, Carlisle, CA4 8PG

The Eden is particularly rich in natural food and another location where excellent cuisine can be found is in the Tufton Arms Hotel (0768) 351593. The performance of this stretch of the water is largely determined by water levels and, given a good period of rainfall, salmon run up to the Appleby area before the close of the season. Indeed, the spawning grounds are not usually reached until very late in the season. Appleby is one such spawning area but it is also good for brown trout. The remaining fifty miles of the river are dominated by some really excellent trouting. The Tufton Arms itself has good access to some first class water on over twenty-three

The River Eden   Cumbria Tourist Board

miles of river and salmon fishing can be arranged from here too. Fishing for guests of the hotel costs between £6 and £12 per day and you also have the option of fishing two picturesque tarns, which are well stocked with rainbows. The salmon and sea-trout fishing, on estate water lower down the river, ranges from £15 to £50 depending on the season and the beat. The Tufton Arms can arrange tuition aimed at both the beginner and the more experienced fisherman who is seeking to brush up certain aspects of his technique. These courses are a delightful way of enjoying your fishing, combining practical guidance with some fishing on the glorious Eden. For the racing enthusiast, the Greystoke Estate is now a renowned training centre for racehorses. Despite the many sporting attractions, we must also emphasise the natural beauty of the Eden Valley, which boasts a rugged charm and a wealth of wild life.

The Eden differs from many English rivers in that there are very few stretches retained for private use and a number of fishing clubs have access to good water. So it may be of help to indicate some useful contacts. The Upper Appleby fishings, which are controlled by John Pape, are well worth noting. This is a fine stretch for brown trout. It includes five miles of double and single-bank, with a maximum of four rods at any one time. The brownies here are wild and furious and a battle royal often ensues to the delight of all lovers of the sport. Permits are £12 per day and are available from Mr Pape's shop, Appleby Shoe and Sports (0768) 352148. Mind you, you'll be lucky to snare the man himself as he's a passionate practitioner of the sport, runs some superb practical courses for small groups and is also the local chiropodist!

While Appleby may be something of a centre point for those seeking to fish the Eden, Carlisle Angling Association have approximately seven miles of double-bank fishing as well as some tidal waters. There are two principal points to note here. Firstly the value is excellent. Secondly all legal methods are allowed. A permit for the season would cost in the order of £15 for brown trout and sea-trout. A day ticket for salmon fishing will cost £10 up until the end of August, when weekly permits are available at £20. All the necessary permits can be obtained from the excellent tackle shop McHardy's (0228) 23988 in South Henry Street, Carlisle.

The Lazonby Estate, a little way north of Carlisle, has approximately four miles of single-bank fishing which ranges from £10 to £25 per day. This comprises the lower and upper beats, both of which hold four rods. There is some good salmon fishing here. In 1990 a 29lb beauty was taken from the Hollingstown Pool on the lower beat. Bookings are taken in advance but you need to be quick off the mark to be successful. Please contact Mrs Boyd (06974) 72453 for further details. The Estate can also organise some delightful beck fishing and the moorland streams are also great fun, especially for the beginner. They also provide good sport in the middle of the summer when other fishing is less good. There is a lodge available for hire and guests here receive discounted rates on fishing. Those of you contemplating a move to the area should consider a seasonal rod, which gives you one day's fishing per week at a cost of £300 for weekdays or £350 for weekends. Spinning is permitted on the Skye Foot beat.

Returning to a somewhat more tranquil scene, we should

consider the Penrith Angler's water which is both varied and good. Some five different tickets are available here but perhaps the best value means of enjoying the fishing is to purchase a general weekly ticket. This costs in the region of £40, which covers two miles of fishing on the Eden and stretches of its tributaries, the Lowther, Eamont (also note Hornby Hall (0768) 891114 which has has 2½ miles single-bank on the Lower Eamont) and Petteril. Contact the Gun and Tackle Shop in Penrith (0768) 62418 for further details. Incidentally, the proprietor, Mr Rosling, is an experienced fisherman himself and also a mine of local knowledge. If you buy a couple of permits here you will be making a solid investment as this will hopefully give you the opportunity to pick his brains and receive some excellent advice. The Eamont is some twelve miles in length and joins the Eden just south-east of Penrith.

The Eden stretches through some really unspoiled land and the Kirkby Stephen and District Anglers Association has some super fishing upstream, some four miles from its source. Here, you find broad grouse moors and beautiful, if somewhat remote, open countryside. The Association's water is approximately twelve miles in length and provides a rich variety of fishing. Runs contrast with the many pools and the river itself changes tempo, flowing fast and free, then slowing to a more sedate pace. The average weight of fish ranges from a half to three quarters of a pound, but fish weighing between two and three pounds are not uncommon. There are some excellent lies to be found and trout and grayling fishing are both good at the confluence of the River Belah. Day tickets cost £15 per day and are available from Robinsons in Kirkby Stephen (0768) 371519.

The Eden is a marvellously scenic river yet there are many challenges to its depths. It is a real delight to those who class themselves in the true sportsman's league. The brownies are particularly tricky customers. They have been harried by mink, heron and other predators all their lives and have no intention of succumbing to your fly without putting up a good fight.

The Derwent

To the west is the River Derwent, a prime salmon water and one of Cumbria's most important river systems. It runs for some thirty miles and its source at Scafell lies amidst the most beautiful scenery. The river flows through the Borrowdale Valley, passing into Derwentwater and Bassenthwaite Lake before it reaches the Irish Sea at Workington. Poaching used to be an enormous problem on this water but the water bailiffs and the NRA have now got the situation pretty well under control. The best months for sea-trout tend to be July and August.

An excellent early start was made to the 1991 season with a 12lb fish being taken in early June. Salmon fishing seems to be at its best between July and October. The run may start in late June but this depends on the spring rains and the subsequent water levels. The average weight is in the 9lb region but usually a few fish are taken around the 24lb mark. In 1990 one rod successfully caught some forty-two fish in two splendid September days. The brown trout fishing is good and the bigger fish tend to be lower down the river. A large section of the river is owned by the Leckonfield Estate. The fishing is handled by their subsiduary, Castle Fisheries (0900) 826320. The Estate issues a limited number of permits for salmon, sea-trout and brown trout and the chap to talk to is the redoubtable Stan Payne. He has put some twenty years of service into the Estate and knows the scene intimately. The fishing is normally let to the same people. However, at the time of enquiring some weeks were available. There are six rotating beats of two rods per beat, the cheapest day rod is in the order of £35 and a weekly rod for a renowned time of year (September) would cost £850. Ghillies are also available at a cost of £25 per day. The Derwent is essentially straight forward to fish and wading is no problem. The more successful flies tend to be Stoats Tail, Garry Dog and Shrimp Fly.

There is also some town water, details of which can be obtained from the local tourist board (0900) 822634 in Cockermouth. The fishing is available on both banks and the right bank stretches from Derwent Bridge to Harris Mill Bridge and the left spans the water between High Sand Lane and Low Sand Lane and also from the junction of the River Cocker to the prominent N.W.E.B. pylon. The permit charge is £4.50 per week for visitor. Perhaps the best place to stay is the Trout Hotel (0900) 823591. The hotel have the fishing rights on the water behind them but acknowledge that the good beats are available through Castle Fisheries. Keswick Anglers Association have a two and a half mile stretch which runs from Portinscale to High Stock Bridge, in addition to water on the River Greta (a less significant salmon and sea-trout river.) Day permits for salmon are £20 and £5 is the charge for trout. Weekly tickets range from £80 to £25 for salmon and trout respectively. This section of the river flows through farmland which is surrounded on all sides by the Cumbrian Hills. The river can be quite fast flowing in places with good pools, allowing for some splendid wet fly fishing with traditional flies. Permits are available from Field and Stream in Main Street, Keswick (0768) 774396.

There are a number of stretches where your charm is as important as your casting ability. Workington Anglers Association and Cockermouth Anglers Association are essentially private clubs requiring you to be guests of members. We recommend you scour the local pub for that elusive catch. The fortunate fisherman will find water on a three mile stretch which runs from Carmeadow Bridge to the sea. If the water is below the two feet four inches gauge you must use a fly but if it rises to three feet, or the water is dirty or coloured, a worm can be used. Cockermouth and District Anglers Association allow members six guest days per year and they make use of a four mile stretch running through Cockermouth and wooded farmland. Cockermouth is the birthplace of two very different characters; the poet Wordsworth and the mutineer Fletcher Christian of The Bounty. A less renowned son of the area is Mr D.W. Lothian, who is a dab hand at fixing your clocks and also has a fair range of tackle (0900) 822006.

Hornby Hall

This seventeenth century farmhouse is situated just off the A66, 3 miles south-east of Penrith on the river Eamont. The house has recently been refurbished and furnished with antiques in keeping with the period of the red sandstone building. There are two en suite double bedrooms and three twin rooms. Up the original spiral staircase are two small single rooms. The sandstone flagged main hall is used as a dining room. Dinner must be pre-booked as meals are freshly cooked from local produce. Set menus Monday to Thursday, choice of menu on Friday and Saturday. There is a residential table licence. Splendid packed lunches are available. We have an excellent drying/boot room for all those wet clothes and boots! Dogs are not allowed in the main house, but may sleep in here. In addition, a self-catering flat is available which sleeps four.

The two mile stretch of fishing on the right bank of the Eamont produces good dry fly fishing. The Brown Trout season starts on 15th March, closing end September. The Salmon season opens on 16th January until 14th October. The best Salmon fishing is usually at the end of the season.

A wealth of other country pursuits are available in the area, from walking in the Pennine fells to sailing in the Lake District. Fishing and shooting parties can be arranged. Cycles are available for hire locally. Helicopter landing by arrangement.

Why not enjoy the privacy of your own house party at Hornby Hall by taking the whole house?

Tourist Board—Highly Recommended (2 crowns) RAC - listed. Highly Commended.

Hornby Hall
Brougham
Penrith
Cumbria CA10 2AR
Tel: (0768) 89114

The Cocker

The River Cocker is a significant tributary with good runs of salmon and sea-trout and some first class brown trout fishing. Tickets are available from the Gun Shop in Cockermouth (0900) 822058. The National Trust also have some water and information is available from Wordsworth House (0900) 824805. This is a super place to visit and, although fishing is not the best in the world, there are some opportunities. In addition, there are a number of becks in the Derwent system which offer a certain amount of free fishing. Coldale and Newlands Becks, which flow into Bassenthwaite Lake are super stretches, as are the River Greta and Mosedale Beck. You should always seek permission but, essentially, fishing is free and accessible, set amidst beautiful scenery.

The Ehen

A little way north of the River Calder, we come to the River Ehen which drains Ennerdale Water through Cleator Moor, flowing into the Irish Sea between Seascale and Nethertown. Egremont Angling Association runs about seven miles of desirable bank fishing and also has fishing on Ennerdale Water. A £30 permit allows reasonable salmon and some fine trout fishing. Salmon tend to be best from June to August and permits are available from the Rod and Gun Shop in Egremont (0946) 820368.

The Kent

The River Kent meanders steadily through from Kentmere Reservoir which is located north of Staveley. Its principal tributaries include the Gowan and Sprint. The river flows through some of the most beautiful countryside in Britain and is a delight to fish. Despite an unfortunate poisoning the river still provides the game fisherman with some quality sport. The better salmon and sea-trout fishing generally takes place later in the season—from September—and it is fair to say that the river is generally more renowned as a brown trout fishery. There are a number of stretches that can be fished by the nomadic angler, as well as some waters that become available—if you're lucky. There is a two to three mile stretch of private water owned by the Levens Hall Estate. The fishing is excellent here but there is a waiting list. What's more, only season tickets are issued. If you are interested, write to The Estate Office, Levens Hall, Kendal, Cumbria. Another private stretch of about one mile which offers some good value day permits (£3–£5 per day), is found a short distance below Lower Levens Farm. Permits here are available from Olde Peat Cotes, Sampool Lane, Levens, Nr Kendal, Cumbria.

Burnside and District Angling Association has some four miles on the main river which also encompasses the confluence of the River Sprint. Permits can be purchased from either the Burnside Post Office (0539) 726114 or the local boozer, appropriately named the Jolly Angler's Inn (0539) 732552. Although this stretch is some thirty miles from the sea, some impressive 30lb catches have been recorded in the area! All legal methods of fishing are allowed, but here's a tip for you; bright orange lures do particularly well.

Staveley is some eight miles from the Kent's source which flows from Kentmere Reservoir. Staveley Anglers Association has five miles of fishing available and permits are obtainable from D. & H. Woof in the Main Street, Staveley (0539) 821253. The cost of the permit is £10 for a week. This allows fishing for salmon, sea-trout and brown trout. The salmon run does not tend to peak until late October. A fine freehouse in which to hear some good fishing tales is the Eagle and Child, Staveley (0539) 821320. The tenant here is Lenny Sosnowsky, a keen fisherman of Russian descent, who has many a yarn, and pulls a fine pint and, furthermore, hosts the local Fly Dressers Guild. This celebrated fishing pub is situated at the confluence of the Rivers Kent and Gowan and is a splendid place to visit. Permits for about twenty nearby tarns of the Windermere and District Anglers Association are also available here.

The largest association on this fine river is the Kent Anglers with approximately eight miles of fishing—five miles stretching downstream of Kendal and three miles upstream, with free town water in between. This is available to visiting fisherman for between £15 and £20 per day and £40 and £60 per week according to the time of season. Fly, spin and worm are allowed, although most members prefer to fly. Other methods catch too many young fish! Permits are readily available from either Kendal Sports (0539) 721554, 30 Stramongate, Kendal or Mr V. Carlson at 64 Kirkland (0539) 724867. Kendal, home of the mint cake, is a lovely town from which to commence any outdoor pursuit. Interestingly, Kendal has one of the few surviving snuff mills and the castle is famous for being the former home of Catherine Parr—the last of the wives of Henry VIII, who actually outlived him.

The Lune

Closely stalking the direction of the Kent a few miles east is the River Lune. This is another river with a good reputation for sea-trout and salmon, running some forty-five miles from its source in Ravenstonedale Common, about six miles south of Kirkby Stephen, to its mouth at Lancaster. This important river passes through some celebrated scenery and the angler has the double delight of some fine fishing with a wonderful backdrop.

The Kirkby Lonsdale A.A. water near to Tebay and down to Kirkby is particularly well stocked with brownies. As the river becomes wider and deeper the fish become larger. Weekly tickets are available from the Tourist Information Centre in the Main Street (0524) 271437, next door but one to the Royal Hotel. Prices range from £35 to £50 per week.

There is also some good fishing for wild brown trout around Sedbergh. Lowis' in the Main Street issue weekly tickets. Although there are still nets in the estuary, there is some fine salmon fishing in the lower reaches of the river. Mrs Anne Curwen (0524) 770078 sells day tickets on behalf of the Lancaster and District Anglers Association. For salmon and brown trout, prices will vary depending on the day but are usually between £10 and £18. Visitors should note, however, that these permits are only issued on weekdays. This is not a major worry as there are all manner of other opportunities for fishing locally. Mrs Carwen also sells tickets for the NRA's Halton Fishery which cost £8 per night (8.00pmto 4.00 am). Mr Shallis at the Halton Stores and Off Licence (handy for all night vigils) can also supply day permits for the Halton beats and day and night permits for the Skerton beats.

This is excellent value fishing and sea-trout are, despite the ravages of UDN, well worth going for. The waters vary, with the upper beat sluggish in character, while below Forge Weir the river offers fast runs and a succession of rocky pools. If you are planning to fish at night it is critical to familiarise yourself with the nature of the riverbed and locals advise chest waders for all but a few of the pools. The best fishing runs from late June through July although, unusually, the lower reaches of the river have a run of fresh sea-trout until the close of the season in mid-October. The favoured salmon waters are the Halton beats at higher river levels, with two feet to three feet being the best for spinning. Fly and shrimp come into their own when the water is down to one foot. The lower beat is fly-only but the Toby and Koster are fine in heavy waters. The Garry Dog is popular in the spring and autumn, while the Stoats Tail and Munro Killer are effective in the summer and early autumn. The Mallard and Claret used on the dropper is another first class way of maximising your chances with the sea-trout. Do book up well in advance and hope for a good spate as algae can be a problem.

Cumbrian Waters

Despite the excellence of the river systems in Cumbria, there are a number of excellent fisheries and reservoirs, not to mention numerous tarns, becks and lakes. The border country is particularly well blessed and the countryside is delightfully unspoiled. Fell walking, riding, bird-watching and fishing are just some of the outdoor pursuits to be enjoyed. Border Game Fisheries Ltd are based in Longtown, Cumbria (0228) 791108 and have a number of fishing opportunities including day tickets for fishing on the Esk priced at £12 to £50, as well as a number of

other excellent stretches on other northern rivers. The company also has sixty acres of land with two lakes of ten and fifteen acres which make up Oakbank Fisheries. The attractive caravan/camping site by one of the lakes provides a peaceful opportunity for a longer stay. The bird sanctuary, game bird breeding unit and country museum provide additional interests for the family. Oakbank Lake is restricted to fly fishing from the bank but Barn Lake offers some boats and has some limited bait fishing. The waters are regularly stocked with rainbow and some browns and a catch and release policy has resulted in fish up to 8lb. Some two miles from Hadrian's Wall we find the New Mills Trout Farm, which although dealing essentially with catering and restocking also provides a pleasant excuse for some good fishing in picturesque surroundings. Finally, if you haven't caught anything in years, the Ford Pool is a place to lift the spirits.

Watendlath Fishery (07687) 77293 near Borrowdale is another for the shortlist. It is generally a late starter due to its location but is well stocked with fish, as well as having wild browns. The water is open from Easter to the end of October from 8.00am to dusk and there is a limit of twelve rods per day, so advance booking is essential. The scenery here is magnificent. Outside July and August the waters are often secluded, so the fishing is very peaceful indeed. The water is fly-only and boats are available at a charge of £9 per day and there is a bag limit here of four fish. Alternatively, a half-day ticket is priced at £9 with a bag limit of two fish.

Kentmere Tarn (0539) 822223 is situated on the floor of the Kentmere Valley. Surrounded by hills, this a beauti-

Lowes Water (Cumbria Tourist Board)

fully secluded spot. Deer and badgers lurk in the nearby woods and the wildfowl add further colour to the scene. The water covers a total of ten acres and is stocked with browns, although wild ones and the odd indigenous salmon can be caught in these twenty-foot depths. The season runs from mid March to the end of September and a charge of £15 a day is levied for the visiting angler. From the banks, anglers may fish with fly or bait and there is a boat for hire for fly fishing only. A similar summary can be applied to Pinfold lake at Raisbeck which once again is rich in flora and fauna. The lake itself is stocked with rainbow and is open all year. The water covers four acres and there is a four rod limit and a four fish limit too. The water may be fished by fly-only and the four fish day ticket is priced at £7 per rod. This lake is particularly convenient for the M6 motorway which is only five minutes' drive away—exit at junction 38. Despite the presence of this major road the area is unspoiled and peaceful. Tickets are obtainable from John Pape (07683) 52148 in the Market place at Appleby-In-Westmoreland.

The Lough Trout Fishery (0228) 576552 is yet another name that should most definitely not be ignored. Thurstonfield Lough is a large and scenic stretch of freshwater in the Northern part of Cumbria, west of Carlisle, and is surrounded by fifty acres of woodland that are designated an area of Special Scientific Interest. The Lough is stream fed and exceptionally well stocked with brown and rainbow trout. Day permits cost £15 and a boat costs a further £5. The fishing is complemented by six Scandinavian pine bungalows available for self catering rent.

The Lakes
Those of you keen to take the family on a sporting holiday should consider the Lake District—it offers some marvellous opportunities. But do not expect a peaceful holiday if you go in season as this is a very popular place for tourists. Bigland Hall Country Sports Ltd. (05395) 31361 offers clay pigeon shooting, archery, windsurfing, a riding centre and, most importantly, sixteen acres of fishing away from the madding crowd. The water is well stocked with rainbows, the record fish being 12lb. The number of rods is strictly controlled and you should endeavour to book well in advance. The day permit costs some £15 with an evening charge of £10.50. If you can't manage to pack your own then rod hire is £8.50 per day.

Esthwaite water is another for the short list. It lies amidst the more gentle hills of the southern lakeland and is unusual in that it is the only major Cumbrian lake commercially stocked with rainbows. The water is controlled by the Hawkshead Trout Farm (05394) 36541 and is popular with locals and visitors. The scenery is once again superb and the fish, often tending to congregate at the end of the lake, are great fighters—this may be due to the fact that the pike, for which this lake is renowned, are monstrously large. The browns, ever keen to avoid these

freshwater sharks are both elusive and fight like tigers when hooked. Day tickets are priced at £10 and there is a bag limit of four fish. Hire of a rod for the day can be had for a further £5. Weekly and season tickets are priced at £38 and £165 respectively. Those anglers may take two fish per visit. There are twelve boats for hire priced at £8 per day. You may fly fish, spin or use bait but no maggots are allowed. The fishery's record for a brown trout is 4lb 4oz and 12lb for a rainbow. The largest pike weighed in at 37lb!

Heading northwards, we arrive at Lamplugh and Cogra Moss (0900) 823638, a fourty-one acre lake which offers fly-fishing for the resident brown trout and stocked rainbows. The water is open daily from sunrise to an hour after sunset and tickets are available from West Lothian in Cockermouth (0900) 822006. Cogra Moss enjoys a perfect setting amidst hills and forests. There are several islands accessible to anglers, except one built by the RSPB for wild fowl and currently inhabited by nesting grebes. Season tickets are £75 with a limit of four fish per day. Day tickets cost £8 with a similar catch restriction.

There are a whole host of delightful small tarns, in fact a number all share the same name which is very confusing! These are often remote and rugged waters but are a delight to fish. Burnmore tarn is a two mile walk from the isolated village of Bouth. The sport, however, can be marvellous not to mention idyllic! Then there are the vast waters of Coniston. Tickets for these waters are available from the Tourist Centre (05394) 41533. Salmon are far from abundant in the water but the brown trout are quite prolific, as is the less common char, a landlocked relative of the salmon. The char generally inhabits deeper sections of the lake, which can be up to 180 feet in places. The popular way of fishing for these super game fish is to trail a small spinner from a light rod—great sport if you find the depth at which they are feeding.

Ullswater is another splendid large lake to fish. Trout here are generally free rising and drifts around Pooley Bridge and Howtown Bay can be especially productive. Night rises can also be excellent, given good weather on such an evening, you will surely be a happy chappie. It is a majestic lake and a splendid scene against the craggy backdrop of Place Fell. Boats are available for hire from Glenridding in the south or Pooley Bridge at the northern end.

Windermere is also good for fishing but it gets horribly crowded in the summer. However, despite all the distractions, brown trout fishing can be good and fish up to 4lb are regularly caught. The lake is effectively divided into two by Belle Isle and the Lake's several large islands are noted spots, indeed boat fishing tends to be favoured. Contact the Tourist Information Centre in Windermere for further details. This is an excellent lake and in the early morning and evening fishing can be memorable. Boats can be hired in Ambleside (05394) 33187 or Bowness on Windermere (09662) 3360.

The River Ribble probably deserves the prize as Lancashire's most prolific fresh water. However, Yorkshire, the county of the white rose, should also receive some acclaim, for the Ribble has its source in the North Riding on Cam Fell, some eight miles north of Settle. There can be no doubt, however, that the principle waters are in red rose country.

The Ribble

The best returns for the game fisherman tend to be upstream of the river's confluence with its two main tributaries the Hodder and the Calder. Few salmon or sea-trout journey beyond Settle and the water tends to be regarded as a good water at the back end of the season, with salmon still swimming upstream in October. The river is tied up with a number of fishing associations and some clubs have a guest day. Only limited water, however, is available to visitors. Some fishing is possible and the Ribble Valley Borough Council have two stretches above the bridge at Brungerley and at Edisford Bridge. Permits are available from Ken Varey (0200) 23267. Fishing costs £4.25 per day and £10 per week and there is a bag limit of three fish. The Mitton Fishery, which is controlled by the NRA, is a fine stretch to note. Tickets are available from Mrs Haynes at Mitton Hall farm (0254) 826281. There are ten permits available for salmon and sea-trout and prices vary between £6 to £11 per day. A brown trout permit will set you back some £3, but only four are available per day and there is a daily bag limit of six. The methods allowed tend to vary with the water level and fly-only fishing is permitted when the level is below the mark stipulated on Mitton Bridge. Fly and spinning are possible when the river rises over the mark. However, from the marker post at Hodder Foot to, and including, the River Calder's confluence spinning, fly and worm fishing can be carried out at all levels. The neighbouring stretch of water is owned by Townson Brothers (0200) 441542 who issue season tickets at £150. This section of the Ribble makes for a delightful scene and is an ideal spot for the fisherman. It runs through lush green pastures and the neighbouring farmland has both dairy and sheep farming—in short a peaceful place to escape to. Great Mitton itself is a charming village, with two friendly ale-houses at which to celebrate or quench your thirst. The Royal Oak, Settle (0729) 822561 is another splendid establishment. On this occasion, a former coaching inn dating from 1684. The hotel sells permits at £11 per day on the Settle Anglers Association stretch which is fly-only water and runs for approximately seven miles, five of which are double-bank fishing.

The Hodder

The River Hodder is a large tributary of the Ribble. The river starts life on Burn Moor, flowing through Stocks Reservoir before joining the Ribble at Great Mitton. The river is largely preserved which is a pity as some great sport is to be found. There are, however, some spots available—for instance a one mile stretch on the Slaidburn Estate. Permits are available from The Jam Pot in Slaidburn (0200) 446225 and are priced at £7 and £20 for a day and week respectively. This is another delightful spot in which to fish, surrounded by vast expanses of Lancashire moorland. The village pub, the Hark to Bounty is a fine place to whet your whistle. The Hodder Bridge Hotel (0254) 826216 is another hostelry to shortlist. It has a private 600 yard stretch and can organise good and inexpensive fishing on the Rivers Ribble and Hodder. The Inn at Whitewell (0200) 448222 overlooks, and has the rights to, approximately four miles of the Hodder. Costs vary significantly with the season. Day tickets are for residents only and range from £11 to £25. This is a beautiful part of Lancashire and the riverbank setting quite superb.

Lancastrian Waters

Bank House Fishery is situated in the picturesque Lune Valley at the edge of Caton Village, some two miles from the M6 (junction 34). This man-made water has been thoughtfully landscaped of late, with several secluded islands and a number of casting jetties. The water is well stocked with brown and rainbow trout and provides excellent fishing. Some five hundred yards away we find a more illustrious water, the River Lune. Rods are limited here which adds to the feeling of seclusion. The record rainbow weighed in at 13lb—so you can see the inmates are very large. There is a bag limit of four fish per day and two fish for an evening or for a half rod. The season runs from March to the end of October and a day ticket is £17 and £10 for an evening or half rod. You are advised to book in advance and can do so by contacting Bank House (0524) 770412. Stocks Fishery (05242) 61305 is another well run fishery in Clitheroe. Should you need to contact them after the start of the season in March then try the Fishing Lodge (0200) 446602. The fishery has a superb moorland setting in the Hodder Valley, close to the source of this celebrated river and as well as the trout, deer, rabbit and all manner of wildlife inhabit the environs. Bank fishing is permitted from 8.30am until an hour after sunset. Boat fishing is possible from 8.30am until sunset itself. The Lodge is located a mile off the Slaidburn to High Bentham Road. There are numerous charges here, but a day permit costs £10. Rowing boats and outboard motors can also be hired and tackle is available too. One of the delights of Stocks is the abundant wildlife and all visitors to the area are asked to tread with care! This is a well run fishery with an impressive catch rate.

The nearby Trout Fishery at Whalley (0254) 822211 is also worth noting. It is stocked with rainbows and has a number of wild browns. The fishery is open throughout the year for rainbows. Some fifty-five rods per day are available, and fly-fishing only is allowed with barbless hooks. There are some large fish here and a day ticket will cost £15 with a limit of four fish. A six-hour ticket is £9. There are three double boats available for hire at £9 per day and a single boat at £5. The fishery is situated amidst the shadows of Pendle Hill—witches and all—and the scenery is beautiful. The Pennine Trout Fishery (0706) 378325 is another extremely popular fishery with some monstrous fish lurking its thirty-foot depths. There are two lakes with a total surface of five acres. It is close to Greater Manchester but despite this bookings are generally only required for weekends or bank holidays. It is open twenty-four hours with night fishing by floodlight, which should suit all insomniacs. There is little chance of nodding off either—the thought of the 11lb brown or the 24lb rainbow which were taken here should have everyone on their toes. The Top Lake has thirty rods and the Bottom Lake twelve. Four hours here costs £11.00 and eight hours £16.75. There is a two fish limit for the shorter stint and three for the eight hours. If you catch an additional fish you may keep it provided you fork out an extra £3.75. If it's an eleven-pounder then that is good value!

Hurleston Hall (0704) 841064 is another fishery that merits attention. It is situated at Scarisbrick on the A570, Southport Road, a mile or so from Ormskirk. This is a place with a past and there are legends involving ghosts, civil war relics and tunnels for escaping prisoners. This is a haven for spooks and sportsmen alike and the rainbows range from a pound and eight ounces and fifteen pounds. The water is restricted to fly-only, barbless hooks (maximum size 8). A full day's fishing will cost £9, five and three hours are priced at £6 and £4 respectively. There are some good rates for juniors and rods can be hired for £3. All fish taken are costed at £1.70 per pound. Ironically, the water is known as the friendly fishery—one can only assume that the ghosties are similarly inclined!

Preston is well served by trout fisheries and Rawcliffe (0253) 700279 is one suggestion. The fishery lies some six miles from Blackpool and tickets are priced at £7 per half day or £4 for an evening. Barbless hooks are once again required and your prey will be rainbows or wild browns. The lake is small but well worth a peep. The Twin Lakes Trout Fishery (0772) 601093 at Croston is well worth a visit too. It comprises two six-acre lakes and the North Lake is fly-only. Opening hours range from 8.00am to dusk until October and thereafter from 8.00am to 4.30pm. Tickets cost £15.50 per day with a four fish limit and five hours is £9.50 with a two fish limit. Any three hours is £6.00 with a one fish limit. The lake is stocked three times a week with rainbows. The fish are often in double figures in weight and the fishery record currently stands at 15lb 4oz. Tuition is available by arrangement along with rod hire. There are excellent facilities, including a tackle shop and licensed bar—another good excuse for an afternoon's sport here.

Northern Waters (Hornby Hall)

England's North

Artist: **Don Vaughan**   *PEACEFUL MOMENTS*   *Courtesy of:* **Rosenstiels'**

What lovelier county could there be than Yorkshire, with its rolling hills, glorious dales and wild moors? As well as its natural beauty, the county also boasts a marvelous selection of stately homes, churches, gardens and famous houses. And here, of course, is some of the finest fishing to be found in England.

The Aire

The River Aire offers trout and grayling fishing in its upper reaches where it is a typical tumbling dales river. Heavy brown trout are recorded downstream of Gargrave and in the Skipton area. Keighley Angling Club has approximately fourteen miles of fishing and day tickets are available from various tackle shops in the area for as little as £2 per day. Willis Walker in Keighley (0535) 602928 and K. Tackle (0756) 794451 handle the permits for Skipton Anglers Association who have three miles of double-bank fishing. Saltaire Anglers Association has a further two miles, again all double-bank, and you should contact the Shipley Angling Centre (0274) 595726 for more information. It is fair to say that the Aire in its lower reaches is polluted, but the game fishing in its upper reaches is well worth sampling and, as you might imagine, the setting is somewhat more attractive in these remote parts too.

The Wharfe

It would not be too outrageous to suggest that fishing in the north and west of Yorkshire is somewhat superior to that in the south of this large county. The River Wharfe is a delightful and extremely popular river. The water has numerous fishing opportunities and the game fisherman will find some fine trout fishing. This is generally in the upper reaches of the river and around Bolton Bridge, Burnsall and Grassington. The Wharfe rises in Langstrothdale and in its upper reaches the water passes through dramatic upland country. It has fast, rushing waterfalls combined with long, slow glides and an abundance of tree lined banks. After Otley, it becomes an altogether more sedate water and thereafter, coarse fish are increasingly prevalent. The season spans the months of April, through summer to September. Linton, Threshfield and Grassington Angling Club control two miles of water, in the environs of the village of Linton. The Devonshire Arms Hotel, Grassington (0756) 752525 issues day permits at £15 for this fly-only water which is restricted to members only on Sundays. Between Grassington and the village of Barden we find seven miles of single and double-bank fishing. Day tickets are available from the Red Lion at Burnsall (0756) 720204. Fly fishing is permitted and there is a six fish limit. Brown trout costs £16.50 per day. Another splendid location is on the Duke of Devonshire's Estate at Bolton Abbey (0756) 710227. There are five miles of double-bank fishing here and the charge is £10 per day with a bag limit of four

fish. The average weight is one pound but fish of over twenty pounds have been known in recent years. The river at this point is still fast-flowing and strewn with rocks. The Estate have their own hatcheries and as a result the waters are well stocked. Tickets are also available for residents of the splendid Devonshire Arms Hotel (0756) 710441.

The Nidd

Some charming scenery can be found on many stretches of the River Nidd, another tributary of the Ouse System. The river's source is on Great Whernside, from where it flows to Nidderdale, past Pateley Bridge and Knaresborough. Most of the water is controlled by local angling associations but a number of day tickets can be found.

Great Whernside reveals bleak moorland akin to that of the Bronte novels. The river initially feeds two reservoirs and its character is shallow and rocky in its infancy. As the river flows from Gouthwaite Reservoir, it takes on an enlarged character. Here its steep banks are predominantly tree-lined and the scene is a real delight. Nidderdale Angling Club controls seven miles on both banks in the area of Pateley Bridge. Day tickets are available for £7 from the Royal Oak Hotel (0423) 780200 on the village green at Dacre, ten miles from Harrogate on the A59. Theakston's bitter is brewed in nearby Masham and adds further attraction to this delightful area. The York and District Anglers Association waters are not as renowned as those one finds further upstream. Nevertheless, day tickets can be purchased from the tacklist P. H. & J. R. Smith, High Street Knaresborough (0423) 863322, which lies opposite the Little Elephant pub. The staff here are extremely helpful and will advise you on various good waters in the vicinity. Some of the best water is retained by the Harrogate Fly Fishers but, sadly, the water is restricted to members and their guests. Such is life! There is some fine fishing available, a number of outstanding real ales to sample and some really tremendous countryside which the trout, as you will perhaps find out, are far from happy to leave!

The Ure & the Bain

The River Ure holds some good trout and stretches for some forty-five miles from Abbotside Common to its confluence with the Swale at Boroughbridge. Although trout are present throughout the water, they are more prolific in the reaches above Middleham where some 5lb brown trout are taken each year and a couple of 8lb fish have been reported, so be prepared! Wensleydale Anglers Association has some four miles of double-bank fishing on the Ure and day tickets can be obtained from the Rose and Crown Hotel (0969) 50225 on Bainbridge village green. Permits cost £6 a day and £12 a week and fishing can also be enjoyed on the River Bain. This is a delightful little river that provides some fine fishing for browns and grayling. Palmer Flatts Hotel (0969) 663228 some five minutes down from the wild Aysgarth Falls has a small stretch which is free to guests and some £2 a day for non-residents. Further good fishing can be purchased from Lewis Country Wear in Hawes (0969) 667443 who represent the Hawes and High Abbotside Anglers Association. Dry and wet fly as well as worm fishing is allowed from 24th March to October 1st.

The Swale

The River Swale shares many characteristics with its near neighbour the Ure. It provides an ever-changing scene with deep slow-moving bends and contrasting fast-flowing runs. The water is renowned for chub and barbel, but some good trout fishing can also be enjoyed in the upper reaches, particularly above Richmond. The Northallerton Angling Club have some five miles of single-bank available for non-members below Morton Bridge on the Northallerton to Bedale Road. Permits cost £3 per day and a 4lb brown trout was taken here in June 1991. Permits are obtainable from Angling (0609) 779140 in Northallerton. W. Metcalfe, Guns and Tackle, Richmond (0748) 822108 issues permits for the Richmond and District Angling Club for £12 a week and offers approximately eight to nine miles of double-bank fishing between Maske Bridge and Brompton-on-Swale.

The Esk

Despite its rural splendour and its many rivers, Yorkshire only lays claim to one salmon river—the Esk. As you can imagine, the Yorkshire folk are proud of this particular water, but they are not overly possessive and day tickets can be bought. In recent times the river has suffered from low water and some have even written it off as a salmon and sea-trout river. This seems a trifle premature and invariably some good fish are landed; particularly towards the end of the season.

The NRA have embarked upon a smolt re-introduction scheme which is producing good results and which augurs well for the future. As the environment continues to play havoc and the demands on the water supply become ever greater, the situation on the Esk will be fascinating to watch.

The Esk rises on Westerdale Moor and runs into the sea at Whitby. There are fine stocks of brown trout in the many moorland beats which flow into the Esk. The river is largely controlled by the Esk Fishery Association but a

number of very attractive stretches are accessible. The Egton Estate (0947) 85466 has a delightful one and a half mile stretch of double-bank fishing which holds three rods. There are some fine holding pools and the brown trout are prolific here. A day's fishing will cost in the region of £15.

Woodlands Hall (0947) 811180, some four miles from Whitby has some superbly scenic waters in the Yorkshire National Park. Permits can be obtained from £10 to £15. Always phone in advance as only two rods per day are permitted. The water includes two salmon pools and three trout runs. John Hobbs will help you with your enquiries here and the nearby Mallyan Spout Hotel (0947) 86206 is one for the notebook.

The North Yorks Steam Railway, which has a delightful journey through the Yorkshire woodlands from Grosmont to Pickering, is a quaint intrusion into a relatively quiet untroubled world. Danby Angling Club has some seven miles of double-bank fishing and the brown trout fishing here is good. Day tickets are available at a cost of £3 from the Duke of Wellington (0287) 660351, which stands proudly in the middle of Danby.

Although much of the fishing is kept on a tight rein and is closely preserved, the Ruswarp Pleasure Boat Company in Ruswarp (0947) 604658 leases one and a half miles from the Esk Fishery Association, from the weir at Ruswarp to Iburndale Beck. This allows some really good value fishing and the possibility that the salmon will return in ever increasing numbers in the years to come. Fingers crossed anyway!

Yorkshire Waters

The Recreational Department of Yorkshire Water have created some fine fishing opportunities in well-stocked reservoirs in the region. But beware. Coin-operated systems are used at many of the waters in the Yorkshire region, so take plenty of change with you.

Not all the fisheries are run by the Authority and the Cleatham Fishery (0724) 855972 is one such example. Although the fishery is a mere four miles from the M18 it is surrounded by agricultural countryside and woodland. The water has a popular catch and release system but four fish can be taken for £10. Heading westwards, we arrive at Hepworth and Heathcote Trout Fishery (0274) 877498. This is a delightful two acre lake set amidst ten acres of woodland. It is stocked with rainbows, brown trout and Arctic char. There is an interesting policy, as any fish over 4lb must be returned. The owner Mr Ted Heathcote-Walker believes that big fish are seldom eaten and often end up in the bin! The policy, therefore, is to leave them and let others enjoy the challenge as they become increasingly weighty. There are several big fish in these waters, one of which was 24lb 8oz. However, it was not a record as it was not killed. Tuition is available and the first lesson is free—an excellent idea. Recently, a blind person learnt to fish here and caught a twelve-pounder!

The Washburn Valley Fisheries (0943) 880658 are made up of four reservoirs including the excellent Fewston and Swinsty. Each water is in excess of a hundred and fifty acres and all are regularly stocked with brown trout and rainbows. The season can run from mid March until the end of October and the fisheries are open daily from 7.30am. Children under the age of fifteen may fish without a permit if accompanied by an experienced adult who does possess a permit. Fewston is easy to find, on the A59 road between Harrogate and Blubberhouses Moor. Fewston is restricted to fly-only fishing whilst

friendly introduction to fly fishing but the scenery is beautiful and there is a catch and return policy in operation at the lake. Tickets are available from the farm, shop for a full or half day's fishing. The waters are regularly stocked by the adjoining trout farm which also supplies the shop. As you can see, this will appeal to the casual fisherman. Furthermore, the 'Daleslife' Visitor Centre has a unique aquarium of freshwater fish which are beautifully displayed and labelled. The Fly Fishing in Wharfedale Exhibition provides a visual account of the sport in the area.

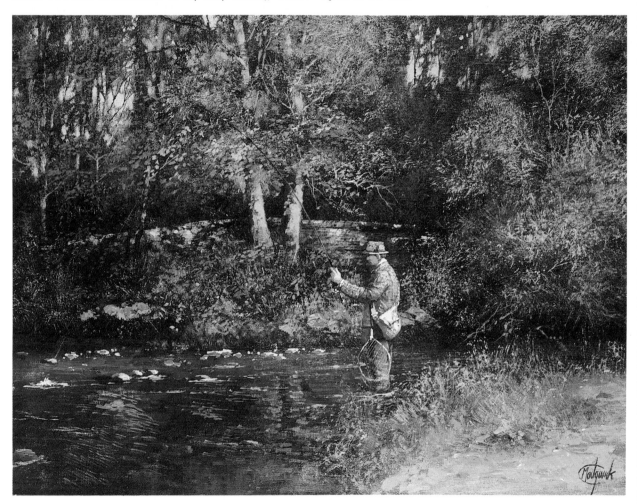

Artist: Clive Madwick TROUT FISHING Courtesy of Rosenstiel's

Swinsty allows some bait fishing. The Authority is endeavouring to encourage all manner of recreation on the reservoirs but this will not be allowed to detract from the fishing. Incidentally, Yorkshire Water controls a number of worthy fisheries, among them Thornton Steward reservoir, More Hall, and Scout Dike. Details can be obtained by telephoning (0532) 448201.

Another water which boasts a number of attractions is the Kilnsey Park Water (0756) 752150, which is set in the heart of the delightful Yorkshire dales. This is a relatively

Leighton Reservoir (0765) 689224 is another extremely popular fishery, situated on the edge of the windy Masham Moor. The water is controlled by Swainton Estate who have their own hatchery. Browns of 5lb and rainbows of 10lb are commonly caught. Season tickets are available and the fishery is open from late March to the end of November. A four fish day ticket (6.00am to sunset) will cost in the region of £10. There is a coin operated system here, too, so take plenty of change.

Northumbria has had a turbulent history, often at the hands of various conquerors, and it has an important place in the history of Christianity. It also includes some of Britain's most spectacular scenery. And fishing!

The Tees

The River Tees has a remote Pennine setting in Cumbria's Cross Fell. The brown trout is the prolific species of game fish to be found on the Tees and the best locations are generally in the upper reaches. The waters between Middleton in Teesdale and a short distance further downstream at Barnard Castle are particularly recommended. The grayling also revel in the faster flowing parts of the upper reaches and Barnard Castle is once again a popular location. Serious pollution in the industrialised areas of Middlesborough have restricted salmon and sea-trout runs, but there is much work being done to try and redress the balance. It will take time, effort and money but let us hope that this once notable salmon river recovers some of its esteem.

The Raby Estate Office (0833) 40209 has some good brown trout fishing on nine miles of the river. The fee is £6.00 per day with a bag limit of four. A week costs £18 and a season £45. The Estate office is located opposite the Teesdale Hotel and tickets can also be obtained from the High Force Hotel (0833) 22264. J Raine & Son (0833) 40406 in Middleton issue day tickets for the Strathore Estate who own the South Bank. The price is £4 for a day, £18 for a week and £45 for the season. The upper reaches are set amidst some delightful scenery and High Force is a celebrated landmark. If there is a good head of water, the falls are truly spectacular and well worth a detour.

The Wear

The River Wear rises on Burnhope Seat to the west of the county, amidst the delightful ragged fells where Cumbria borders Durham. It flows east, a distance of some sixty-five miles through Stanhope, Bishop Auckland and Durham, before it spills into the North Sea at Sunderland. Some serious anti-pollution work and a gradual re-stocking programme have ensured the river's renaissance and the game angler can now enjoy some fine sea-trout fishing. The salmon runs could not be described as substantial but they are progressing, which is tremendous to report. A twenty-two pounder was caught in 1993, and they average at around 12lbs.

Bishop Auckland and District Angling Club have approximately twenty miles available for day tickets, which range from £5 to £20 depending on the season. The higher price is naturally charged in the later months when the salmon and sea-trout fishing comes into its own. Assuming a good level of rainfall, the river fishes well,

particularly late in the season. Season tickets can be had for £93.50 (plus £23.50 joining fee) from the Secretary, J. Winter (0388) 762538 and day tickets from Windrow Sports in Bishop Auckland (0388) 603759. The Club also have one mile on the River Browney which joins the Wear at Sunderland Bridge; this tributary offers good brown trout fishing.

The Upper Wear behaves more like a spate river, and if there has been sufficient rainfall, sea-trout can be good at the back end of the season and salmon also come up to a mile or so below St John's Chapel, some forty miles from the sea. The Upper Weardale Angling Club has some six miles of water here and day permits can be obtained for £5 from the post office or the Golden Lion (0388) 537231, beside the cattle market. The sea-trout tend to be most prolific in September and October and dependent on summer rainfalls, which sometimes arrive earlier. In other words, keep in tune with the summer weather!

The Tyne

Energetic work in re-stocking and the closure of several collieries, together with an improved attitude to pollution by a number of industries has seen some great improvements to the Wear but it is still shadowed by its more illustrious and much improved sister, the Tyne. This is a tremendous credit to the water companies and all involved.

The North Tyne flows out of the massive Kielder Water and joins the South Tyne near Hexham. Thereafter, the Tyne flows through Corbridge, Prudhoe and Newcastle before arriving at the North Sea at Tynemouth. The river journeys through some delightful Northumberland scenery and there are a number of fishing opportunities for the visiting angler. Falstone Fishing Club have a good two mile stretch of double-bank fishing. Permits are available from the Black Cock Inn (0434) 240200. This charming 380 year old inn sits next to the church and is a fine spot if you happen to like real ale. A seventh-century cross was discovered here in the 1950s, so keep your eyes open for similar relics! Day tickets are £10. The George at Chollerford (0434) 681611 also has water on the North Tyne. The fishing here is excellent value for residents and the setting is absolutely enchanting.

The Northumberland Anglers Federation has three good stretches of approximately five miles which is well stocked with brown trout. Salmon were making a good showing in 1991. The only ticket that is currently available is a fourteen day permit which costs £42 and includes one and a half miles on the River Coquet. Permits are available from the Head Bailiff, Mr Bagnall, at

Thirston Mill, West Thirston (0670) 787663. There are a number of opportunities for fishing the Tyne, with a premier beat eight miles east of Hexham. This is a three mile stretch which can be fished from both banks, and there is some first class fishing here. The best months for salmon are from February to May and September to October with sea-trout fishing from May onwards, although September is the best month where both fly and spinning is permitted. Mr A.F. Pollard of Reeltime Fishing Services (0661) 843799 will assist with enquiries. Season rods offer one manned day per week and occasional day rods.

The North and South Tynes are generally fast running rivers which favour dry fly trout fishing. Deep pools near Haltwhistle can be found and trout in the 5lb bracket are lurking—so be prepared! The North Tyne has a number of fine beats: some five miles north of Hexham; Chollerford; up river between Wark and Simonhorn; above Wark, as well as various other beats. Salmon run from March onwards, with March, April and May being good months. September and October are also extremely good and are the two prime months for sea-trout which tend to run from June onwards. The beats are mainly let on a weekly basis and you should contact Mr Gaisford at J. M. Clarke and Partners on (0434) 602301 for all the details. The South Tyne has some quality association waters. The river requires good water and when in spate provides some fine fishing. The salmon run from May with August through to October being the favoured times. Sea-trout will run from June given good water but the best months are again September and October. Weekly permits are available and you are advised to contact Greggs Sports in Haltwhistle (0434) 320255 for further details. Finally, Haydon Bridge Angling Club offers visitors who are staying in the area weekly permits. Details can be obtained from the splendid Langley Castle Hotel (0434) 688888. If you are looking for good fishing in England, the Tyne provides a plethora of good opportunities. Further information on the Tyne, and on all of the region's waters, may be obtained from Northumbrian Water (091) 383 2222.

The River Rede is a tributary of the Tyne that is well worth exploring and two excellent places from which to plan your attack are The Percy Arms (0830) 20261 and The Otterburn Tower (0830) 20620—two extremely pleasant establishments in which to stay.

The Wansbeck

The delightful Northumbrian scenery reveals a number of other splendid rivers for the visiting angler. The River Wansbeck is tied up with private syndicates and clubs but there is a two mile stretch below Morpeth at Wansbeck Riverside Park. It is owned by the council and has produced some good trout in recent years. Day permits can be purchased for £2.70 from the Park Warden in Green Lane, Ashington (0670) 812323.

The Coquet

The River Coquet is a delightful water which rises in the wilds of the Cheviot Hills and flows through Rothbury and, after some forty miles, enters the North Sea at Warkworth. This is a good game fishing river with salmon, sea-trout and brown trout all to be found. The Coquet is generally regarded as a late river with a good run of salmon and sea-trout well into October. The Northumberland Angling Federation lease waters from the Duke of Northumberland and this comprises some eleven miles of fishing, which is spread along the river and includes a variety of waters. Recent reports for the river have looked good, with salmon and brown trout prolific. If you are seeking advice or information on the Coquet contact The Sports Shop in Fawcett's Yard, Morpeth (0670) 514760. For visitors tickets and salmon fishing contact Mr Bagnall at Thirston Mill, Felton (0670) 787663. The Whitton Farmhouse Hotel (0669) 20811, next to Whitton's Riding Stables, also issues fourteen-day trout permits for the NAF. The Angler's Arms Hotel (0665) 570655 at Weldon Bridge also has a small stretch which provides more fine brown trout fishing. Furthermore, in September and October, some great value salmon fishing can be had for £7.50 a day. The Angler's Arms is a classic coaching inn remotely situated beside the bridge where the A697 crosses the Coquet. It is a classic country pub and the nearest neighbours tend to be oyster catchers and goosanders.

Rothbury and Thropton Angling Club have three and a half miles of single-bank fishing. Permits cost in the region of £5 per day and are available from the Thropton Village Shop (0669) 20412, beside The Three Wheat Heads. Night fishing for sea-trout is also permitted here, should you be keen on night fishing, or if you are an insomniac.

Murraysport in Alnwick (0665) 602462 handle a good private beat on the Coquet, The Weldon Water, which offers two miles of mainly double-bank fishing and also has some fine pools. However, rods are limited to only two per day and day tickets cost £11 between February and August and £16 for the months of September and October.

The Aln

The River Aln is comparatively short and flows into the sea at Alnmouth. The Aln Anglers Association, who control a seven mile stretch downstream from Denwick Bridge, is a working trust and all monies are reinvested into the upkeep of the river, which is regularly stocked with one-pound brown trout. This is fly-water and includes some tidal waters where the sea-trout and salmon are most prolific. In 1989, a weighty seventeen-pound sea-trout was caught and four to nine pounders are regularly caught here. Iron Blue Dun is a recommended fly for the brownies and Garry and Viva Green Tail for sea-trout. Fish tend to run in February and March and September and October. The water also provides some fine brown trout sport and comes into its own in the late spring and summer months. There are only weekly or monthly tickets available and the weekly permit will set you back £25. There is no Sunday fishing for visitors. Permits can be obtained from L.K. Jobson (0665) 602135, beside the Hotspur Tower in Alnwick or from Murraysport (0665) 602462.

Northumbria Waters

Lockwood Beck is one of several waters in the Durhsand Cleveland area. It is pleasantly secluded, situated just north of the A171 Guisborough to Whitby Road. A total of five streams and three becks run into the reservoir, which is well-stocked with brown and rainbow trout. The area is set amidst some beautiful woods, and mallards, great crested grebes are among a number of frequent visitors. Curlew and woodcock also abound in the wooded area beyond. The reservoir is limited to fly fishing and is managed by Northumbrian Water Ltd.

One of the delights of reservoir fishing is that it often takes you to some wonderful places and Cow Green (0833) 50204 is no exception. Situated ten miles west of Middleton-in-Teesdale, this reservoir offers tremendous sport on a water that contains one of England's best natural populations of brown trout. A twelve fish bag limit is enforced, with permits available on a self-serve basis from the fishing lodge. This superb wild fishery is complemented by five stocked waters in Lunedale and Baldersdale. For the up to date 'Fisherman's Handbook' of the various options available in the north east you should contact the Northumbrian Water Recreation Department (091) 383 2222.

Tunstall Reservoir (0388) 527293 lies in the valley of Waskerley Beck, three miles north of Wolsingham in Weardale. The water is surrounded by mature woodland and is well stocked with brown and rainbow trout. Boats are available too and day permits can be purchased here. Another fishery which enjoys a Wear Valley setting is the Witton Castle Water which is bounded by the more famous Wear. The water is managed by the Bishop Aukland Angling Club (0388) 762538. The fishery is stocked with rainbow trout between 2lb and 12lb and there are also a number of brown trout, which should be returned if caught. The fishery operates a barbless hook rule. A day permit costs £15, the facilities here are very good and the isolated location ensures a peaceful day out.

Kielder Water is surely the 'Big Daddy' of all Northumbrian waters. The reservoir enjoys a memorable setting and caters for all manner of leisure pursuits. The water is massive and there is plenty of room for all. The fishing comes into its own in the evening and Kielder's wild brown trout are prolific. The reservoir is surrounded by rolling hills and lies in the heart of the Border Forest Park. There are some twenty-seven miles of bank fishing and boats are available for hire and can be reserved in advance by telephoning (0434) 250203. Kielder Water is a splendid place to get away from it all and a little bit of peace and quiet awaits you too!

Our final thought for this area is the Whittle Dene Reservoirs (0661) 853210 where a day's fishing will cost you £12 with a six fish limit. The water lies in close proximity to Hadrian's Wall and other Roman remains, surrounded by woodland and farming—a real delight. Boats can be hired from around £6 per day and permits will cost £8.50. There are a total of four reservoirs here, all well stocked and providing yet another good reason for visiting this part of the country.

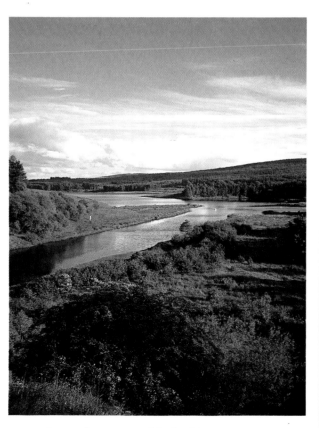

Late afternoon of Bakethin Reservoir, Northumberland (Northumbrian Waters)

Northumbrian Water Ltd. owns and manages 16 major trout still-waters in the counties of Northumberland, Durham and Cleveland. Each is unique in character and each is set in some of the most beautiful country in England. Management of the fisheries is co-ordinated regionally to ensure that a wide variety of sport is available, and as a result nine waters are stocked on a 'put and take' basis throughout the season, whereas others rely on wild fish to tempt the sportsman.

A brief description of each water follows, but to find out more fully the delights of what Northumbria has to offer the angler, a FREE regional guide is available either by telephoning 091 383 2222 or by writing to The Recreation Department Northumbrian Water Ltd, Abbey Road Pity Me, Durham DH1 5FJ.

Day, evening and Regional 'cast about' seasonal permits are on offer, and boat as well as bank fishing operates on four waters. Concessionary permits are available for senior citizens, under 17s and the disabled, who are provided for at several fisheries with special facilities.

In Northumberland lie Fontburn, Bakethin and Kielder Water. Fontburn nestles beneath the Simonside Hills near Rothbury and is a very popular worm and fly venue for anglers from Tyneside. A splendid Scandanavian style fishing lodge welcomes fishermen to the site, which is becoming legendary for the numbers of large fish taken from the dark peaty waters.

Bakethin and Kielder adjoin each other in the North Tyne Valley, in total offering more than 3000 acres of water with 27 miles of varied shoreline fishing and a fleet of 30 boats for hire.

Kielder is unstocked, but rapidly gaining in popularity due to high catch levels and very low charges. Neighbouring Bakethin caters for the fly fisherman. Both waters are surrounded by the spectacular scenery of the Border Forest Park and make an

ideal location for a fishing week. Luxurious Forest Cabin Accommodation is available at Leaplish Waterside Park (Tel: (0502) 500 500 for details).

In County Durham, both Burnhope and Tunstall lie in Weardale, the former high up in the hills and the latter, a wooded fly-only little jewel nestling in a side valley near Wolsingham.

In Teesdale, Cow Green is operated as a wild fishery for the purist, as it retains a wonderful head of indigenous brownies, some of the best natural stock in England. The setting of Cow Green is majestic, lying high in the Pennine Dales above the foaming cataract of Cauldron Snout on the infant river Tees.

Down the valley in Lunedale and Baldersdale lie five waters, one wild and four stocked, and all popular with worm and fly anglers alike. Grassholme, Blackton and Hury are surrounded by a patchwork of buttercup meadows in early summer and are bordered by a landscape of stone walls and Dales barns. Selset and Baldershead have less verdant surrounds with heather and moorland grasslands echoing to the cry of the curlew.

Further south on the edge of the North York Moors National Park are Scaling Dam and Lockwood Beck, fisheries close to the Guisborough to Whitby main road.

Scaling is a very popular stocked water regularly fished by anglers from Teeside, and Lockwood is a very beautiful small fly only fishery where boats are an excellent way to get the best from the fine stocks of brown and rainbow trout.

Northumbrian Water fisheries have a lot on offer. Write or telephone for your FREE 1993 guide and when next in the area why not give them a try?

In the old county of Westmorland, overlooked by the spectacular Howgill fells, The Black Swan is a charming country hotel tucked away in the village centre of Ravenstonedale. Here you find a welcome as warm as the open fires crackling in the grates - comfortable rooms, beds warmed by electric blankets, lots of magazines and books - even newspapers brought to you on the Sunday morning - in short, service where nothing is too much trouble.

The house was built of Lakeland stone at the turn of the century and therefore the sixteen bedrooms vary in size and aspect, with three at ground floor level suitable for the disabled. They are all tastefully furnished with direct dial telephone and lots of thoughtful extras and all with en suite bathrooms. There are also very comfortable public rooms, including a residents' sitting room with an open fire and a television which is rarely used, as there is so much to do in this beautiful part of the country. The quaint stonewalled lounge bar is popular with visitors and locals alike and in the summer months everyone enjoys the delightful garden, bordered by the village back.

The Kitchen is under the personal supervision of the owners

ensuring its renowned reputation for excellent cuisine as recognised in all leading food and hotel guides. Breakfasts are substantial - essential to enjoy your day in the country. Local produce is used whenever possible for dinner, including Westmorland beef and lamb, local game and traditionally made cheeses. There is a set five-course dinner and a small a la carte menu as well, together with a sensibly priced wine list.

For the energetic there is unrivalled walking in the area. The birdlife is plentiful and the call of the curlew can often be heard from the hotel garden on a summer's evening. Kendal and Penrith are both only half an hour to the west, giving easy access to the busier attractions of the English Lakes.Ten minutes in the opposite direction unfolds the gentler scenery of the Yorkshire Dales National Park. Also easily reached from Ravenstonedale are the Pennines to the north and Hadrian's Wall. Much closer at hand there is excellent fishing, with rods on a private stretch of the Bela and Eden, Association Waters on the Lune and private tarn - even a tennis court and golf and riding are nearby.

The Black Swan
Ravenstonedale
Kirkby Stephen
Cumbria CA17 4NG
Tel: (05396) 23204

Cumbria

Cumbria is renowned as one of the most scenic and popular of all England's counties. The lakes and the fells provide a stunning backdrop for the rivers which wind their way seaward. There are also hundreds of hotels in the area and all manner of pubs, inns and bed & breakfasts are scattered liberally throughout the region. The Tourist Boards are particularly helpful and will always point you in the right direction but the following thoughts should be of some help too.

The Eden is a marvellous water to fish and, in addition to the accommodation at the lodges of Estate waters, there are some splendid hotels nearby. The Crosby Lodge Hotel (0228) 573618 at Crosby-On-Eden is a relaxing place in which to stay. Newby Grange (0228) 573645 is another excellent hotel. Brampton is a picturesque little village and Farlam Hall (06973) 234 has to be one of the most delightful hotels in the area. It has a superb location and a restaurant of rare distinction. Tarn End (06977) 2340 is less grand but equally welcoming and the hotel enjoys a watery setting on the banks of Talkin Tarn. The restaurant serves a variety of excellent dishes and the bar snacks are to be recommended too. The Hayton Castle (0228) 70651 is also well worth considering with good facilities and friendly atmosphere.

Some way upstream, at Temple Sowerby, we find the seventeenth-century Temple Sowerby House (07683) 61578. More good cooking, log fires and ample character make this a local favourite, as indeed is Hornby Hall (0768) 891114 in Culgaith. Appleby-In-Westmoreland also reveals some excellent hotels in this pleasant Cumbrian

town. The Tufton Arms (07683) 51593 is an outstanding place to stay. The hotel has fishing rights and has recently been restored to provide both comfort and style for the discerning angler. The Royal Oak Inn (07683) 51463, dating back to the eighteenth century, offers good food and a traditional friendly atmosphere. In Kirkby Stephen's Market Place you will find the King's Arms (07683) 71378. This former coaching inn is a most enjoyable place to stay and ideally situated for exploring the upper reaches of the Eden.

The Derwent takes us through some delightful scenery from its source in Scafell through lakeland and sheep-filled valleys. Those of you wishing to visit the source should journey to Rosthwaite and the Scafell Hotel (059684) 208. This is a remote situation but the welcome here is warm and the scenery is, needless to say, wonderful. Journeying through Borrowdale and Derwent Water we arrive in Keswick. There are numerous hotels here; The Derwent Water Hotel (07687) 22538 has its own fishing and is continually being upgraded. The Grange (07687) 72500 also has a beautiful setting and is well recommended, while finally here we would recommend the stylish Brandholme Country House Hotel (07687) 74495, which boasts excellent cooking as well as all the comforts expected of a fine hotel. Turning our attention away briefly from the lakeside settings to Mungrisdale, we find the Mill (07687) 79659, a delightful unpretentious mill cottage bordered by a trout stream—a pleasant thought for an evening's entertainment. The Pheasant Inn (059681) 234 is another abode that exudes charm. This is an ideal base for a lakeland holiday with self-catering units also available. The inn lies between

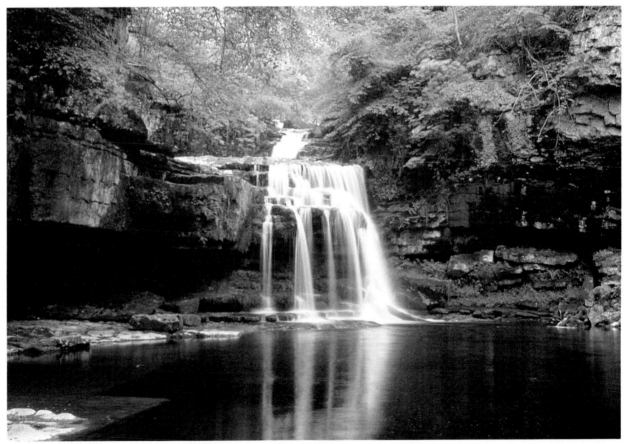

Janet's Foss, River Ribble *(NRA Leeds)*

Bassenthwaite Lake and Thornthwaite Forest in idyllic surroundings. Cockermouth also has its fair share of good hotels and The Trout (0900) 823591 in Crown Street is one to note. The gardens sweep down to the river bank, providing a truly delightful setting for such a hotel.

Ullswater, Coniston and Windermere are huge stretches of water and for many they are the most celebrated waters. Although crowds flock here in high season there is some good fishing to be enjoyed at the beginning and end of the season. Coniston has a number of hotels to consider including the Coniston Sun (05394) 41248 which is a comfortable hotel enjoying a marvellous location. The Coniston Road, a little way outside Ambleside, reveals another distinguished place in which to stay; Rothay Manor (05394) 33605. The Watersedge in Waterhead (05394) 32332 is another establishment to note; originally two fishermens' cottages the hotel is situated on the shores of Lake Windermere. This is a remarkably comfortable hotel where a day's fishing is followed by a first rate dinner. A little further afield, someway west of Ambleside, the Skelwith Bridge (05394) 32115 is another welcoming inn which enjoys a picturesque lakeland situation and is highly recommended. Troutbeck provides another good value inn, The Mortal Man (05394) 33193—an extremely pleasant place to stay.

Windermere itself has various good hotels, the biggest problem is choosing one to stay in. The excellent Miller Howe (09662) 2536 is quite outstanding and the proprietor, John Tovey's cuisine renowned. Lindeth Fell (09662) 3286 in Bowness is impressive too. Newly Bridge at the foot of the Lake has the Lakeside (05395) 31207, enjoying a pleasant setting and offering very comfortable accommodation. The Swan (05395) 31681 is also full of character and well worth considering, as is the Newby Bridge Hotel (05395) 31222 at the southern end of Lake Windermere.

Ullswater offers the Sharrow Bay (07684) 86301—one of England's finest country house hotels. The cuisine here is superb. This is for the fisherman who really likes to spoil his other half! However, there are a number of hotels which will happily organise fishing for you such as the Old Church Hotel in Watermillock (07684) 86204—a first class hotel. The Rampsbeck (07684) 86442 is another thoroughly charming country house with an excellent restaurant.

There are yet more superb hotels south of The Lakes in picturesque Cumbrian towns and villages. The Abbey House Hotel (0229) 838282 in Barrow-in-Furness is one such example. The rivers Kent and Lune are worthy of attention and a number of hotels are well situated here. Witherslack reveals the Old Vicarage (044852) 381, a superb hotel and a delight to stay in. In Kendal itself there are several hotels from which to choose. The Riverside (0539) 724707 sits on the banks of the River Kent, whilst the Westmoreland (0539) 723852 also exudes much charm.

The Lune ends its journey in Lancaster but the upper reaches flow through some delightful rugged countryside. In Ravenstone Dale, The Black Swan (0539) 632204 is most definitely worth a visit. Journeying south to Kirkby Lonsdale you will chance upon The Pheasant Inn (05242) 71230 and in the centre of the town is The Royal (05242) 71217.

Lancashire

The Ribble and the Hodder offer some first class opportunities for some excellent fishing forays. The Blackmoor Country House Hotel in Thornley (0772) 783148 is extremely welcoming as is the Shireburn Arms (025486) 518 in Hurst Green. Both have their own unique and charming character.

The Hodder winds through some beautiful scenery and its course also brings to light some excellent hotels. The Inn at Whitewell is set on the River Hodder and is a quite outstanding inn. In Slaidburn, there are two establishments from which to choose. The Hodder Bridge (0254) 86216 is extremely welcoming and has some good fishing while the Hark To Bounty (02006) 246 is another delightful place to stay. Finally, in this part of the country, the Royal Oak (07292) 2561 in Settle offers good food and comfortable accommodation in this peaceful village.

The Dales

Like the rivers, many of the better hotels are to found in North Yorkshire. A large number of hotels in the southern half of the county cater for the businessman rather than the holiday-maker or fisherman. There are, however, a number which have retained their character and

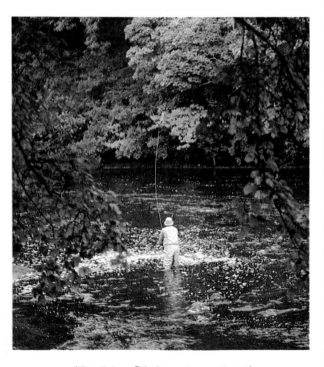

The Eden (Tufton Arms Hotel)

should be shortlisted. The Ouse system, which plays such a significant role in the make-up of Yorkshire's waterways, offers much good fishing, although much is of the coarse variety and therefore outside the bounds of this book. Some of the Ouse's tributaries do provide good sport and the Aire has worthwhile trout fishing in its upper reaches. A little south of Skipton we find the village of Kildwick and Kildwick Hall (0535) 632244. This is an excellent hotel and is held in high regard amongst Yorkshire folk. It is a fine building, extremely comfortable, and enjoying marvellous views of Airedale. A short distance away we find Haworth, Bronte Country. Amidst the moors and bleak uplands we find the sophisticated Rydings Hotel (0535) 45206—a very friendly place to stay.

Wharfedale runs through some delightful scenery and on its banks some pleasant village pubs and small hotels can be found. Although the Wharfe is the dominant water, there are a number of smaller streams and daleside waters which produce some good fishing too. The Black Inn in Buckden (075676) 227 is extremely pleasant as is The Racehorses (075676) 233 in Kettlewell, an eighteenth-century inn of character with a lovely riverside setting. Threshfield and Grassington both reveal celebrated hostelries. The former, the Wilson Arms (0756) 752666 is a comfortable inn and the latter, The Black Horse, (0756) 752770 serves good bar food.

Burnsall enjoys spectacular views of the Wharfe and the Red Lion (075672) 204 sits in the middle of the village overlooking it. Both the food and accommodation are recommended here. One of the best spots from which to fish the Wharfe is from within the grounds of the outstanding Devonshire Arms (075671) 441, a country house hotel of distinction. The grounds here are superb and the restaurant and accommodation of a very high standard. There are a number of excellent eating establishments in the environs of the Wharfe and Ilkley produces The Box Tree (0943) 816793, a restaurant renowned for its first class cuisine and charming atmosphere. People staying in the area should be happy at the Rombalds (0943) 603201, an extremely pleasant hotel.

Towards Otley, the game fishing tends to become less significant but, those seeking accommodation should sample the delights of Chevin Lodge (0943) 467818, surrounded by pine trees. Alternatively, in Linton, Wood Hall (0937) 67271 is set in over 100 acres of park and woodland and is a superb place to stay.

The Nidd also reveals some excellent establishments in which to escape the stresses of the twentieth century. The picturesque Yorke Arms (0423) 755243 in Ramsgill is a fine place to start one's journey and the restaurant has much appeal. The Yorkshire Dales are breathtakingly beautiful but on a bleak day the crackle of a log fire is a welcoming sight and there are plenty of those to be found in the many pubs dotted around this area. Throughout Nidderdale, there are many such good establishments but one which stands out is the Sportsmans Arms (0423) 711306, in Wath-in-Nidderdale. Here, the trout served in the restaurant may well be from the local river, and are always beautifully prepared. The bar here is also a very friendly place to enjoy a good Yorkshire pint. Those who seek a variety of sporting entertainment should consider Nidd Hall (0423) 771598, a magnificent country house. Another good hotel with excellent facilities but a less grand setting is the Dower House Hotel in Knaresborough (0423) 863302.

Anglers visiting the Ure should visit the Miller's House at Middleham (0969) 22630, an extremely well maintained hotel with comfortable rooms. Jervaulx Hall (0677) 60235 in Jervaulx is a hotel with a warm welcome and a charming setting—a stylish place to stay. Similarly, the elegant Simonstone Hall in Hawes (09697) 255 is a very fine base to use whilst fishing a number of local rivers, including the Swale. There are many other good hotels too. In Kirkby Fleetham, Kirkby Fleetham Hall (0609) 748711 is an imposing hotel which once again offers style and comfort, together with an impressive restaurant. If you wish to stay within a budget then the Nags Head at Pickshill (0845) 567391 is well worth considering—good value accommodation is found here and the atmosphere and facilities are excellent.

Northumbria

Journeying north into the historic county of Durham we find more beautiful countryside bordering the Tees and the Wear. In Middleton-in-Teesdale, the Teesdale Hotel (0833) 40264 is a former coaching inn and a friendly place in which to stay. Another charming village inn to shortlist is the Rose and Crown (0833) 50213, beside the Church and overlooking the village green. It is a tremendous hotel to use as a base for exploring the surrounding countryside. The Jersey Farm Hotel, Barnard Castle (0833) 38223 is another informal and friendly place to stay. There are some delightfully rustic areas here and a charming old inn from which to explore further is the Morritt Arms Hotel (0833) 27232—full of character. The Dickens Bar here will appeal to the more literary anglers!

The River Wear flows through some spectacular scenery, especially in its upper reaches and Weardale is quite beautiful. The City of Durham, dominated by the Norman cathedral and castle, has many good hotels and the city itself is one of the north's most attractive. Just outside Durham, to the east, we find Hallgarth Manor (091) 372 1188, a first class hotel, whilst Lumley Castle (091) 389 1111 in Chester-Le-Street offers some excellent accommodation in the castle which dates back to the thirteenth century. Bishop Auckland is the setting for the Park Head Hotel (0388) 661727, another quite charming hotel.

The Tyne's rapid regeneration is quite something and naturally this area is becoming more popular every year. There are numerous inns and hotels to consider in the area. The Northumbrian countryside is some of the most unspoiled and spectacular in the world despite its less glamorous image. The upper reaches of the Tyne consist of two tributaries; the South and North Tyne. The South Tyne rises in Cumbria and the Lovelady Shield Country House (0434) 381203 is a delightful hotel in which to stay. Those of you seeking a drink, or refuge from the weather, should consider the Milecastle Inn (0498) 20682, overlooking Hadrian's Wall. A Tyneside setting awaits those who choose to stay at The Anchor (0434) 684227 in Haydon Bridge. This former inn is very good value and enjoys a marvellous location. The General Havelock is also very pleasant, serving good bar snacks. Langley Castle (0434) 688888 is an hotel of great character and a pleasant place to stay in this area.

More Tyneside charm can be found at Riverdale Hall (0434) 220254, Bellingham—a really excellent place to rest your bags when fishing the local waters. More modest but still very comfortable accommodation can be found at Wark. Here, The Village Inn, Battlesteads (0660) 30209 is the place to earmark. Also, a really first rate hotel which offers a superb riverside setting, excellent cuisine and good value weekend breaks, is The George at Chollerford (043481) 611. Corbridge is a quaint market town and here there are too many hotels to be recommended, but one in the very centre of the town is The Angel Inn (0434) 632119. One final thought here is Laburnum House (0661) 852185 in Wylam. The restaurant is the focal point of this eighteenth-century house, which also has some pleasant bedrooms.

North of the Tyne, the Rivers Blyth, Wansbeck, Coquet and Aln are all near parallel veins running through some superb countryside in the upper body of Northumberland. The fishing varies somewhat but the scenery is generally superb. There are a number of places to consider if you are fishing these waters. Linden Hall (0670) 51611 at Longhorsley is a beautiful country house hotel set in its own wooded estate and a fine focal point for exploring the surrounding countryryside. Less grand, but with an equally splendid location, is Coquet Vale (0669) 20305 at Rothbury which is comfortable and good value. The same summary can be applied to The Granby Inn (066570) 228 in Longframlington.

In Alnwick, The White Swan (0665) 602109 and The Hotspur (0665) 602924 are both welcome retreats. A short distance north of this market town, we find Wooler and The Tankerville Arms (0668) 81581—a seventeenth-century coaching inn of great charm.

Although the Tweed is covered in detail in our Scottish Section, no game fisherman will wish to overlook the Tillmouth Park (0890) 2255, full of fishing memorabilia. The hotel is set in extensive grounds, three miles north east of the village. Boats and ghillies are available and there are few finer hotels for a fishing break.

The prime salmon fishing might be in Scotland, but the counties of Cumbria, Lancashire, Yorkshire and Northumbria provide some first class sporting opportunities.

The River Eden (Cumbria Tourist Board)

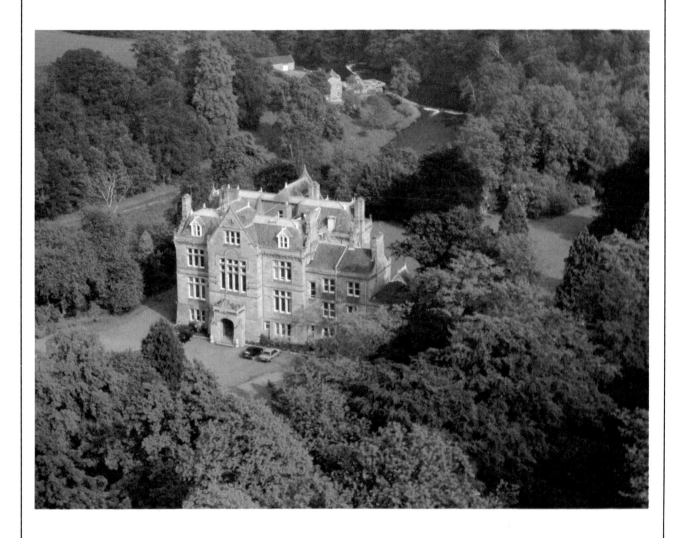

Built in 1882 by the famous architect Charles Barry, using stones from nearby Twizel Castle, Tillmouth typifies a more leisured age. A secluded mansion, set in fifteen acres of mature parkland and gardens, you'll feel yourself relax into it's atmosphere of a bygone age.

All of our thirteen en suite bedrooms are generous in size and individually furnished to the highest standard. The spacious public rooms are furnished with the same attention to detail and open log fires create a relaxing ambience.

Tillmouth Park is an ideal centre for country pursuits - fishing, shooting, riding and of course, golf. Spring fishing packages can be arranged on the river Tweed with all the fisherman's requirements catered for. There is also an abundance of excellent shooting in the Borders within 30 minutes drive of the hotel. Berwick-upon-Tweed and the Hirsel at Coldstream are just two excellent golf courses nearby. There are many stately homes to visit such as Floors Castle, Manderston and Paxton, ruined abbeys, Flodden Field and Holy Island are all within easy reach.

Our Library Restaurant offers fresh local produce imaginatively prepared and presented by our Head Chef David Jeffries. To match the superb food there is an extensive wine list and comprehensive range of over 100 malt whiskies.

You can be assured of a warm welcome in the Borders when you come to Tillmouth Park.

Tillmouth Park Hotel
Cornhill-On-Tweed
Northumberland
TD12 4UU
Tel: (0890) 882255
Fax: (0890) 882540

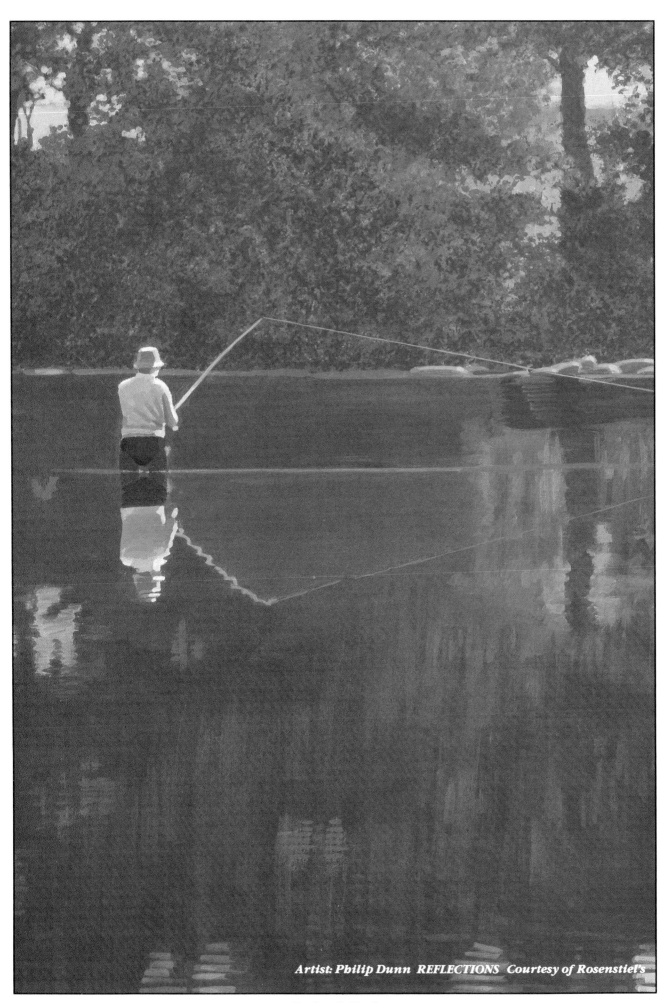

Artist: Philip Dunn REFLECTIONS Courtesy of Rosenstiel's

MIDDLE SHIRES

So what constitutes my ideal stillwater? I go fishing for fun and to relax, so it should be in pleasant surroundings. There should be a good amount of weed and bankside vegetation with woodland nearby, but not so close as to make casting a problem. This will ensure a good range of fly life both in and on the water which, being chalk stream fed, will be gin-clear. The water will be stocked with fish from one to five pounds and, because it is clear, I'll be able to stalk them. The level of stocking will be such that getting in a day's limit will be an achievement, but on the other hand one will not expect to return home empty-handed. The number of rods will be strictly limited so that I'll be free to try different places as I wish and feel that I'm on my own. Finally, the other rods will be kindred spirits so at the end of the day we can all go off and enjoy a drink and a chat in the excellent pub nearby!

Suffolk Waters

One might not think of East Anglia as a game fishing area, but there are good stillwaters and trout streams to be enjoyed here. A short distance off the A12 near Thaxted in Suffolk is the village of Walpole, and Valley Fisheries (098684) 488 have a two and a half acre spring fed lake which is regularly stocked with brownies as well as rainbows. A day ticket here for five fish costs £20. Near Bury St. Edmunds there is the two lake Larkwood Fishery (0284) 728612, while on the Norfolk, Suffolk border off the 143 near Harleston is Mendham Mill Trout Fishery (0379) 852328. Mendham offers four acres of fishing in lakes as well as the River Waveney Mill race and is set in the picturesque Waveney Valley. Locally-tied flies and tuition are available and a four fish day ticket costs £10. The number of rods is limited to sixteen a day so advance booking is recommended.

Norfolk Waters

Across the border in Norfolk is the Salmon and Trout Association's stillwater at Lenwade. This is a season ticket water only and you must be a member of the Association. Membership in 1992 cost £12 and can be obtained from Lt Cdr L. D. Temple-Richards (032878) 217. Nearby are the four acre Whinburgh Trout Lakes (0362) 850201 and near Kings Lynn are Narborough Trout Lakes (0760) 338005. These five lakes are well stocked and hold some big fish. North east of Aylesham, just off the B1354 are Bure Valley Lake Fisheries (026387) 666. The fishery's three lakes total ten acres and it has a mile of the River Bure. Salmon were introduced in 1992 and the fishery has been featured on ITV's *Go Fishing*. Downstream at Abbots Hall, Ingworth, members of the STA can enjoy a mile of double-bank fishing on the Bure for £8 a day or £60 a season. There is however, a waiting list for season tickets. Fakenham Angling Club have two miles of the River Wensum. Day tickets are available from Dave's

Tackle Shop at No 1, Rear of Norwich Street, Fakenham (0328) 862543. This river does tend to get heavily weeded from mid-summer so it is probably best to inspect the river first.

Cambridgeshire Waters

Close to Peterborough, in Cambridgeshire, is the Orton Water Trout Fishery at Orton Waterville (0733) 239995. Boats are available on this twenty-five acre water, which also holds brook trout and has produced a rainbow of 15lb 10oz and a brown of 7lb 4oz. It is set in the pretty Nene Country Park and is an ideal spot for a family day out, as other attractions include steam trains, horse riding and bird watching. There is an 18 hole golf course very near by, so watch out for sliced shots! A five-fish day ticket costs £10 and a father and son day is £12.50.

Grafham

The county that once bore the name of Huntingdonshire has sadly disappeared from the maps, but of course there is still the former county town of Huntingdon—its name well-known from the legends of Robin Hood. From a fishing point of view its chief glory is Grafham which is now in Cambridgeshire. The county of Rutland has also disappeared from the maps, but the locals strive to keep the name alive and Rutland Water helps to preserve its fame. I cannot help thinking that if the name of this fishery had been changed to something like East Midlands Fishery, it would have lost part of its charm.

The popularity of stillwater game fishing owes much to the celebrated status of Grafham Water (0480) 810531, the reservoir that celebrated its twenty-fifth anniversary in 1991. Grafham is a veritable giant among stillwaters for it covers 1569 acres and holds 13,000 million gallons of water. Over the years it has mellowed and now blends in with the local landscape. This is largely due to the care and conservation policies of Anglian Water. It is a Site of Special Scientific Interest (SSSI), and in recent years, has held nationally important numbers of wintering Great crested grebe, tufted duck and coot, while late summer sees significant numbers of moulting mute swan. There is a wide variety of bank-fishing and boats are available; details of costs etc. may be found from the fishery manager (0480) 810531. The world championships were held here in 1987 and the water has produced a 12lb 6oz brownie. Grafham is the sort of water that can always be relied on to produce good fish and the beginning of May 1991 saw a great bag of three brownies weighing 15lb 12oz, while a week later a magnificent brown of 10lb was recorded. An eight fish day ticket will set you back £11.

Rutland Water

I suppose its original title of Empingham reservoir would have been preferable to East Midlands Fishery, but thank goodness local pressure prevailed and it was called Rutland Water. I am sure the bells of Normanton Church, the well known local landmark, would have rung out in anger at any other name. Although comparatively new, the original detailed landscaping work of Dame Sylvia Crewe has ensured that it now blends in perfectly with the local scenery. Grafham is huge but Rutland is a monster, for it covers over 3000 acres—roughly the same size as Lake Windermere. Peace and quiet are assured here for, although sailing is permitted, intrusive sports such as water-skiing and power boating are banned. An eight-fish day ticket costs £11 and boats are available, further details can be obtained from the fishing lodge (0780) 86770. Part of the western end is a nature reserve and one of the richest reservoir locations for wintering and passage wildfowl in Britain. It is particularly notable for its numbers of mallard, shoveler, gadwell, teal, wigeon, pochard, tufted duck and goldeneye. Rutland co-hosted the 1987 world championship with Grafham and this is not surprising when you consider that over 50,000 anglers fish here every season and the total catch weight is over fifty tons. Both rainbows and browns of over 12lb have been caught as has an eight fish bag totalling 48lb, a record for any European reservoir.

Northamptonshire Waters

North from Kettering on the A6003 is Eyebrook Reservoir at Caldecott (0536) 770264. This 400 acre water is set in a natural valley and has very good weed growth with plenty of snacks; shrimp, sedge, midge and ceria. Not far away is the fifty-acre Elinor Trout Fishery (08015) 786 at Aldwincle near Kettering. Boats are available although the bank fishing is excellent. A few miles north of Northampton are two more well known Anglian Water Reservoirs, Ravensthorpe and Pitsford. Built in 1886, Ravensthorpe is a very mature water and, many would say, the most attractive of the Northamptonshire reservoirs. Further details can be had from the fishing lodge (0604) 770875. Pitsford (0604) 781350 is a 750 acre water whose popularity has increased enormously in recent years due to Anglian

Artist: W D Sadler A PEGGED-DOWN FISHING MATCH Courtesy of Rosenstiel's

Water's hard work in improving stocks and facilities. Unlike many reservoirs, Pitsford trout have a reputation for surface feeding and dry flies are usually very effective. A good range of coarses are on offer here and at Grafham.

Warwickshire Waters

With so many good fisheries in such pleasant surroundings it is hard to remember that the Midlands used to be called 'The Black Country'. However, local industry has seen a lot of changes and coal is no longer king. Many authorities have done a great deal of conservation work. At Bishop's Itchington near Leamington Spa are the Bishop's Bowl Lakes (0926) 613344, which hosted the final of the Troutmasters competition a few years ago. The lakes cover forty acres and are formed from old limestone quarries. The actual rocks are more than 170 million years old and contain a wealth of fossils. Quarrying in 1927 revealed the intact skeleton of a plesiosaur, an aquatic reptile often thought to be the identity of the Loch Ness Monster. This skeleton, which is eighteen feet long, can be seen in the Natural History Museum in London. There are three lakes here. White Bishop Lake is designed to be a 'quick catch' lake and is ideal for the less experienced. The five acre Mitre Pool holds bigger fish, as does Bishop's Bowl which has a great mayfly hatch, and both lakes are designed to appeal to the more experienced rod. A day ticket costs £6 and casting instruction is available.

Less than two miles away at Harbury is Chesterton Mill Pool (0926) 613235. The fishery is set in twenty acres, surrounded by lovely unspoiled countryside and woodland. The water mill, like the windmill, was built in 1620 by Sir Edward Peyto, then Sheriff of the county. The mill was used to grind corn right up to the 1950s when it fell into disuse. By 1976 the lake was so full of silt and overgrown with reeds that the water area was down to half an acre. Restoration work started in 1980 and the lake is now some four and a half acres and has just the right amount of weed and bank-side vegetation to ensure good fly life. A five-fish ticket costs £17.50 and the water is stocked with browns and rainbows. Severn Trent's 600 acre Draycote Water (0788) 812018 is near Rugby and an eight fish day ticket costs £11.40. In 1992 the proposed stocking programme was 49,000 mixed browns and rainbows. The rainbows were mainly around one and a quarter pounds, but there was a significant number of 4lb fish and some over 10lb. At Meriden, near Coventry, is Lord Guernsey's Packington Fishery (0676) 22754. There are three established lakes of twenty-eight, eighteen and six acres which are reserved for members, and three former gravel pits totalling forty-four acres on which day tickets are available. The lakes are stocked with rainbows and the minimum size is 1¼lb. The best rainbow of 1993 weighed in at 12lb 11oz. The fishery also has two miles on the River Blythe. A day ticket costs £14 and that will give you a bag limit of eight fish! The Blythe has rightly been called a sparkling gem as the entire river is an SSSI. The reason for this is that, botanically, the river is one of the richest in lowland England, with some sections containing as many species as the very richest chalk streams. The SSSI system operates in a similar way to the way buildings are listed and can be a bit of a headache for river managers and riparian owners, as any improvements they wish to make must first be agreed by English Nature.

West Midlands Waters

At Coleshill, in the West Midlands, is Shustoke Reservoir, the home of Shustoke Fly Fishers Limited (0675) 481702. The fishery consists of a main reservoir of ninety-two acres and a settling pool which can only be fished by members. Visitors can fish the main water where a five fish day ticket costs £12. An added attraction is the rather good pub within a hundred yards of the main gate. Patshull Hall at Burnhill Green, near Wolverhampton, was once the seat of the Earl of Dartmouth, but now stands empty. Patshull Great Lake, (0902) 700774, is occupied by many splendid hard fighting brownies and rainbows. The Great Lake covers some seventy-five acres and was designed by Capability Brown in the 1740s, the result being one of the most picturesque fisheries in the country. The fishery is particularly keen to support the disabled angler and boats have been specially adapted to take wheelchairs. There is easy access to the bank and there is a very popular annual fishing competition for the disabled. A six-fish day ticket costs £12 and a further £2.20 per fish caught. West of here and some four miles north of Kidderminster on the A442 are Shatterford Lakes (02997) 597. There are four lakes here ranging from half an acre to two acres, and a ten fish day ticket costs £6. The fishery is set in a delightful location on a hillside on the edge of the beautiful Severn Valley and has fine views over the Shropshire Countryside. There are herds of red, fallow and sika deer and a number of peacocks. There is a wealth of bird life including pied flycatchers and wild flowers such as spotted orchids.

The River Teme rises near Newton in Powys and its winding course takes it over the Welsh border into Hereford until it flows south to join the Severn at Worcester. There is an unusual way to fish the upper reaches of this charming little stream—all you have to do is stay in one of the houses in the Knighton area that do bed and breakfast and your fishing is free. Knighton stands half way down Offas Dyke and was described in A. E. Housman's *A Shropshire Lad* as one of the quietest places under the sun. G. H. Medlicott and Son, Solicitors, of Station Road, Knighton, Powys can provide more details about the fishing. The river and its feeders here are pretty small and you won't need anything bigger than an eight-foot rod. Suggested flies include Black Gnat, Black Pennell, Zulu, Red Spinner, Blue Dun, Coachman and Alder. At Lindridge, Mr Ken Powell (058470) 208, has one and a half miles of single and double-bank fishing near Tenbury Wells. This delightful gentleman has been fishing the river for over sixty years and welcomes day visitors to his water. The water was stocked with several thousand trout which have now reached a fair size. There are salmon here, too, and this beat has several pools including one of particular merit. A day in this delightful area can be had for the very modest amount of £2.

The Severn

The headwaters of the Severn are also in Wales and, having a course of over 180 miles on its journey to the Bristol Channel, it is the longest river in England and Wales. The upper reaches offer good trouting and although, in common with most other rivers, the salmon run is not what it was, the Severn is still not bad and produces some good-sized fish. The best part for salmon fishing is the middle reaches since the lower ones are mainly noted for their excellent coarse fishing. If you want to fish the headwaters, the Poachers Pocket Pub at Llanidloes (0686) 688233 issue day tickets which cost £4 for the Dinas Estuary Fishing, which is two and a half miles of well-stocked, double-bank trout water. Llanidloes Angling Association have approximately twelve miles of fishing on the Severn and its tributaries. Salmon are hardly ever seen this far up, except occasionally in a very wet season and afforestation schemes have caused drainage problems here. For a good days trouting, Mr Davis of the Association recommends a visit to Clywedog Reservoir, permits for which can be had from Mrs Gough at the Travellers Rest Restaurant (05512) 2329. Downstream at Caersws, the Maesmawr Hotel (0686) 688255 has one and a half miles of double-bank fishing which is free to residents, while visitors can buy a day ticket for £3.50. This is a beautiful part of the country and there is one particularly good pool on this water. Mike's Tackle Shop at Newtown (0686) 624388 is run by Mike and Carol Barber who can give you comprehensive advice on salmon fishing in the area. This friendly couple are both experienced anglers who welcome phone calls and visitors to the shop and can also introduce you to local fishermen, who will be pleased to show you their favourite waters.

With its medieval church spires, Norman castle, and beautiful Georgian and Tudor black and white houses, Shrewsbury must have one of the richest visible histories of any English town. It also has some good fishing, especially at the Weir and at Monkmoor. Further details can be had from the Council offices (0743) 231456. A must for any fisherman is a visit to Chris Partington's Vintage Tackle shop at 103 Longden Coleham in Shrewsbury (0743) 369373. Chris deals in tackle that spans four centuries and has also set up Britain's Angling Heritage Trust. He is a very experienced fisherman and generous with his advice on tackling both the Severn and the area generally.

Another interesting town lies about fifteen miles downstream. Ironbridge witnessed the birth of the Industrial Revolution, and the eponymous bridge still spans the Severn. A great deal of restoration has been done to the old buildings and factories in the last twenty years and the town now has a wealth of interesting exhibitions. Further downstream, at Stourport on Severn, day tickets can be had from John White's Tackle Shop (02993) 71735. Although salmon are caught here it is predominantly a coarse fishery and the game fisherman would probably prefer to cast his fly elsewhere.

Cheshire Waters

Returning north to Cheshire, Chester, with its half timbered buildings and old shopping area called the Rows, is another attractive town. A short distance away is Mickle Trafford and Meadow Fishery (0244) 300236. This fishery has two lakes of five and two of three quarter acres which are stocked with both brown and rainbow. A four-fish day ticket costs £18 and June 1991 saw a splendid 10lb rainbow, and a bag of twenty-two fish—someone must have been feeling rich!—caught in five hours with a best fish of 5lb 8oz. East of here at Mobberley, which is located between Knutsford and Wilmslow, is the Clay Lane Farm Fishery (056587) 3337. This is a one and a half acre spring fed water where a four-fish day ticket costs £18. Clay Lane has produced a brown of 9lb and a rainbow of 12lb. I am delighted to see that this is a fishery which states that barbless hooks must be used. Other Cheshire stillwaters include Brookside at Crewe (0270) 820528, Marton Heath at Macclesfield (0260) 224221, and Wall Pool Lodge (0260) 223442, also near Macclesfield.

Staffordshire Waters

Across the county border at Meerbrook, near Leek,s in Staffordshire is Tittesworth Fly Fishing (0538) 300389. We are on the edge of the Peak District here, and the reservoir has been called the Loch of the Peaks; indeed loch style drifts in a boat with a team of small, wet flies can be very successful. There are five miles of interesting bank fishing here. Lure specialists will enjoy the deep marks at Badger and Scar Hole, while nymph fishermen will have good sport in the shallower waters such as Fosters and Troutsdale. There is also fishing on the Churnet, which is one of the few rivers in the country where rainbow breed naturally. A six-fish day ticket costs £8. Other Staffordshire stillwaters include Gailey Fishery at Penkridge (0785) 715848 and Donkhill Fisheries near Burton-on-Trent (0827) 383296. Also near Burton is Severn Trent Waters Foremark Reservoir, (0283) 701709. A day on this well-stocked water can be had for £9.50.

The Derwent & the Wye

North of here is Derbyshire's Peak District with its heather-clad moss moors and dry stone walls. The source of the River Derwent is High Peak in the north of the county, from where it flows some sixty miles to join the Trent, below Derby. Its lower reaches are monopolised by coarse fish but the upper reaches of the river and its tributary, the Wye, are first class trout and grayling water. The Peacock hotel at Rowsley (0629) 733518 has a small stretch on the Haddon Hall water which holds two rods. The Derwent Hotel (0773) 856616 can offer a day permit for its own small stretch of the water for £2. This lovely virginia-creeper clad hotel is beside the bridge at Whatstandwell and fishing is free for guests. The Duke of Rutland's Haddon Hall Estate has six miles of double-bank fishing on the Wye which is let through the Peacock Hotel at £22 per day. The water is extremely well managed by two keepers who look after approximately twenty-two miles of river. The Head Keeper is committed to restoring the river to as close to a naturally re-generating river as possible, so that fishermen will pay for the good fishing and not for the limit of fish, which sounds highly commendable. Many fish are around a pound and eight ounces but five pounders have been caught in the mayfly season. There is a rather unique stock of natural rainbows. You can't mistake them—full finned, streamlined bodies and beautiful, vivid markings—hence their name! There is of course, a fair number of wild browns and a limited restocking programme. At this stage the Wye can be likened to an old fashioned wild river, meandering through open meadowland and coppice of alder and willow. The Duke of Devonshire's Chatsworth Estate owns six miles of which one mile is available to visitors. Tickets can be had from the Head River Keeper (0629) 87484. The Cavendish Hotel (0246) 582311 has access to the syndicated water owned by the Chatsworth Estate which has three rods on the Wye and three on the Derwent. A day's fishing—for residents only—costs £23.50. Darley Dale Fly Fishing Club (Secretary; Brian Jones (0457) 872967) has four and a half miles of the Derwent, downstream from Chatsworth Park. Darley Dale is a most attractive spot and both the

Derwent and the Wye have good natural fly life, such as olives, mayfly and cranefly.

The Dove

For a large part of its course the River Dove forms the boundary line between Staffordshire and Derbyshire. It is also rightly associated with Izaak Walton, but I wonder how many people realise it was his friend Charles Cotton who wrote the part about trout fishing? Among its many fine and interesting possessions the Flyfishers Club in London has got Walton creel and his casting hand. Leek Fishing Association stock and control the whole of the river. The Izaak Walton Hotel (0335) 29555 has a three mile stretch which holds four rods. Another hotel steeped in angling history is the Charles Cotton hotel at Hartington (0298) 84229 which has quarter of a mile, let out for £12 a day. Doveridge Sporting Club (0889) 565986 has one mile of excellent single-bank fishing and also has a well stocked lake. It is set in seventy acres and has a variety of clay pigeon traps. Callow Hall Country Club at Ashbourne (0335) 43164 has a mile of double-bank fishing for guests. The River Manifold is a tributary of the

The Peak district (Staffordshire Moorlands District Council)

Dove but the only fishing available is a stretch which is owned by the National Trust, who lease it to Mr Grindey of Wetton Mill Farm, of Wetton near Ashbourne (0298) 84341. He allows four rods on his water and the cost of a day is £1.25.

Derbyshire Waters

On the Staffordshire border, near the delightfully named village of Wincle, are Danebridge Fisheries (0260) 227293. The fishery has a two and a half acre lake in the pretty Dane Valley. You may think the lake small but it holds trout of 16lb and is regularly featured in the angling press. At the other end of the county in North Derbyshire, is Ladybower Reservoir (0433) 651254. The cost of a six-fish day ticket for this 504 acre water is £8.70.

Nottinghamshire Water

Residents of the city of Nottingham are fortunate to have Colwick Country Park (0602) 870785. There is a twenty-five acre lake for wind surfing, but the fishing lake is some sixty five acres and is just for fishing. At the end of a successful day you can have a pleasant drink in the Georgian designed Colwick Hall which now acts partly as a restaurant and bar.

Lincolnshire Waters

East of Nottinghamshire is the flat, rich arable land of Lincolnshire. There are not much in the way of trout streams here but there are some nice stillwaters. The River Witham here is good coarse fishing water while, above Grantham, it provides decent trouting. However, most of this is in private hands and the one or two clubs who have game fishing also have long membership lists. Among the stillwaters are Toft Newton at Market Rasen (0603) 7453. The fishery is a privately run reservoir that has been leased from NRA and I am pleased to see it has given up the salmon experiment and now puts brookies in. This forty-acre water is right next door to RAF Scampton. The aeroplanes are not too intrusive but you do get a free Red Arrow display every now and again. The fishery can sell you tackle and gut or smoke your catch. A four-fish day here costs £10.50. Hill View Trout Lake (0754) 72979 is at Hogs Thorpe near Skegness. This two-acre lake is in an attractive woodland setting with lovely views over the Lincolnshire Wolds and is only two miles from the sea. It's mainly stocked with rainbows but there are some browns; the best brown so far has been 6lb 8oz and Hill View has produced a great 12lb 8oz rainbow. Pheasant Tail and Montana Mymphs do well, as do Invictas, Hawthorns and Black and Peacock Spiders. A four-fish day ticket can be had for £10.50. Stemborough Mill Fishery (0455) 209624 is an attractive three and a half acre lake, set in open countryside two miles north of the Roman Centre of England near Lutterworth, and £12 buys you a six-fish day ticket. Other good Lincolnshire stillwaters include, Hatton (0673) 858682, Syston Park (0400) 50000, Red House Farm (052 277) 224 and Lakeside Farm (0400) 72758.

Lady Bower Reservoir (Seven Trent plc)

The Midlands of England may not traditionally have been a Mecca for game fishing but its huge city populations house many an enthusiast who delights in a day away from the metropolis. The scenery contrasts hugely; the delightful border country of Hereford and Worcester, the dales of Derbyshire and the more sedate fens and broads of Lincolnshire and East Anglia all make up a rich, varied picture. There are numerous stillwaters on the territory and if you are planning a day's fishing we hope the following suggestions will be of interest. They include several pubs, some with bedrooms, and a number of hotels—some of which are outstanding establishments. The type of place you go for a real treat, perhaps to keep the other half sweet!

Suffolk is a beautiful county with thatched villages and many a country tavern. Bury St. Edmunds is a marvellous town to visit and The Angel (0284) 753926 is an historic vine-covered inn which has welcomed visitors since the mid eighteenth century. It is a fine place to stay and boasts a very good restaurant. Visitors to Mendham Mill should consider the seventeenth century Scole Inn (0379) 740481 in Scole which provides a warm welcome. North of here, travellers to Lewade might consider the King's Head, East Dereham (0362) 693842 or The Buckinghamshire Arms, Blicking (0263) 732133—a really splendid pub with excellent food and ale as well as a number of cosy bedrooms. If you are fishing on the Bure or the Nar then the Boar Inn at Great Ryburgh (032 878) 212 is a really welcoming place to stay.

The Peterborough area has a number of good stillwaters and an inn of considerable charm is The Haycock at Wansford (0780) 782223. The hotel has a gorgeous riverside setting and its restaurant and bedrooms are of an excellent standard. An alternative recommendation is The Bell at Stilton (0733) 241066, an historic inn which has been recently renovated. These establishments are also well placed for Grafham, Eyebrook and Rutland Water.

If you are visiting this celebrated fishery then how about an equally splendid hotel or inn. Well, there are a good number of choices: The George of Stamford (0780) 55171 is one of the finest inns in Britain. It dates from the sixteenth century and combines historic charm with all the modern comforts of today—an outstanding restaurant makes the hotel yet more appealing. A similar summary can be applied to Hambleton Hall in Hambleton (0572) 756991. The house enjoys wonderful views from its grounds over Rutland Water. The hotel exudes quality and the restaurant is one of the finest in the country. The Whipper Inn (0572) 756971 is also first class and has a fine setting in Oakham's Market Place, once again, the restaurant is excellent. Other splendid establishments to add to this list include Barnsdale Lodge (0572) 724678 and Normanton Park (0780) 720315. The former is a coach-house which has been sympathetically restored. The latter, a former country farmhouse which offers every comfort and a high standard of cuisine. These hotels are all excellent but are also in the more expensive end of the range. Less pricey are the Rutland Angler (0572) 755839 in Oakham and the White Horse Inn (0780) 86221, with both providing a good standard of accommodation and some excellent bar meals. Good food can also be enjoyed at a number of nearby pubs, including the Berwicke Arms at Hallaton (085 889) 217. Visitors to nearby Eyebrook should visit Lydington, where there are a brace of hostelries, and those who are planning to stay

overnight should consider The Marquess of Exeter (0572) 822477, a sixteenth century coaching inn with a lot of charm. There are a number of hotels in the Oundle area and the Ship (0832) 273918 is good value and extremely comfortable. The Chequered Skipper at Ashton is also a fun pub to visit, while the Falcon at Fotheringay (08326) 254 serves excellent bar food. Those anglers visiting Pitsford or Ravensthorpe should also note the Fawn (060129) 200 at Castle Ashby, a pleasant hotel in a picturesque village, or the Red Lion (0604) 770223 at East Haddon.

Bishop's Bowl Lakes has a number of pubs in its environs. The Old Mint at Fouthern is particularly good as is The Falcon at Prior's Manor (0327) 605620. A friendly hotel to consider is the Easthorpe Park (0926) 632245 in nearby Easthorpe. Or south of here, at Charlecote, The Charlecote Pheasant (0789) 470333. Less grand but still a great place for a swiftie is The Plough at Warrington which is handy for the recently opened M40. In addition to these fine establishments, The Dunncow (0788) 810233 at Dunchurch is a delightful old inn—the building boasts a bundle of character and is a fine port of call. In Meriden, The Manor Hotel (0676) 22735 is a good place to stay for the Packington Fishery, and The Bear at Berkswellplace is a pub to note. Visitors to Shustoke should consider The Griffin, a fine pub in which to discuss the days exploits. Patshull visitors may well be out for a day in the country but people who want to have a sporting break should make a note of the Patshull Park Hotel (0902) 700100, west of Pattington; there is a fine golf course here as well. Shatterford is a lovely spot and The Black Boy at Bewdley (0299) 402119 is a cosy inn in the centre of the town in which to stay. Alternatively, The Little Pack Horse is a splendid pub to partake in a little liquid refreshment. Other lovely places to stay are The Crown at Hopton Wafers (0299) 270372 or The Talbot at Cleobury Mortimer (0299) 270036.

There are numerous streams and rivers flowing through Herefordshire, Shropshire and Worcestershire, and the Teme runs through gorgeous countryside and Hopton Wafers. There are numerous places to stay along its banks and in Knighton, the Milebrook House Hotel (0547) 528632 is a tremendous place, with fly fishing thrown in. Ludlow is a delightful town. The Angel Hotel (0584) 872581, and the marvellous Feathers at Ludlow (0584) 875261 are places to consider here. Those who happen to want an excellent spot for dinner should try Poppies at the Roebuck Inn (058472) 230 in Brimfield—it is outstanding. There are some comfortable bedrooms here as well. In Tenbury Wells, The Ship is well worth visiting for good food and some comfortable accommodation. If you are looking for a superb hotel in which to stay then The Elms (0299) 896666 at Averley enjoys superb views of the Teme Valley and is an outstanding edifice in every way. The Manor Arms at Abberley (0299) 896507 is also welcoming, though a little less grand.

Returning westwards to the Severn, we travel through some delightful border country before encroaching again on Welsh soil. The game fishing, although improving, is not of the highest order and talk of a barrage on the water puts the fear of God into those that still enjoy fishing it and its abundant tributaries. Those who wish to fish the Severn should consider staying at the friendly and comfortable Red Lion (05512) 2270, not grand but most convenient, or the equally welcoming Elephant and Cracke (0686) 626271, a Severn side hotel and the birthplace of Robert Owen. Upstream, The Lion at Berriew (0686) 640452 is an extremely comfortable hotel and is well worth considering.

Chester is another delightful town and its surrounding countryside, though dotted with urban life, also offers some fine scenery and some delightful pubs. Stillwater trout fishing can also be found and for those anglers who enjoy nothing more than a fireside chinwag at the end of a day the following ideas may be of interest. The Bells of Peover in Lower Peover (0565) 722269 is an elegant, wisteria-clad pub with excellent bar food. The Golden Pheasant in Plumley is also pleasant and has some accommodation, while The Dun Cow at Ollerton is another welcoming pub which is ideal for your fireside chat. There are many other splendid pubs in the vicinity, ensuring a wonderfully complete day.

The Peak District offers some of the most delightful scenery in England and there are a number of hotels here that fair take the breath away—several of which also have fishing. The Peacock Hotel (0629) 733518 offers an excellent restaurant and some good accommodation. Fishermen should note the aptly named Derwent Hotel (0773) 856616 where they will be thoroughly well looked after. Some outstanding accommodation and culinary delights can be found at the Cavendish Hotel (0246) 582311, which has a glorious setting overlooking the Chatsworth Estate. The fishing it offers is a bonus and the hotel is thoroughly recommended. Those of you

who are less inclined to stay around should consider at least one of the excellent pubs in the area. The Chequers at Froggatt Edge (0433) 30231 or the Bull's Head at Wardlow (0298) 871431 both have simple accommodation, or alternatively the splendidly named Lazy Landlord at Foolow (0433) 30873 provides excellent bar food.

The Dove is another sporting river on which to cast the old fly. Callow Hall is a wonderful hotel with excellent bedrooms as well as game fishing for guests. Dovedale reveals a celebrated fishing hotel, The Izaac Walton (033529) 559. The hotel enjoys splendid views up the Dove Valley and it was here that Walton penned much of the material for his celebrated fishing work. His great friend and co-author Charles Cotton also has a hotel named after him. The Charles Cotton (0298) 84229 in Hartington has a Peak District location and offers simple but comfortable accommodation. The popular Jug and Glass (0298) 84224 is a fine ale pub to consider. Visitors to Ladybower, east of Sheffield will find some fine scenery and a pub or two to sample. The Derwent at Bamford (0433) 51395 is convenient and a pleasant place for a leisurely drink. Bedrooms are also available. Lovers of the historic pub will enjoy the Strides Inn, handy for the reservoirs and offering tremendous views, this pub also has modest bedrooms.

Much of Lincolnshire is given over to agriculture and its fishing opportunities are somewhat restricted. Pubs are also fairly thin on the ground. The Priory at Louth (0507) 602930 is a welcoming, comfortable hotel in which to stay and The Leagate at Coningsby (0526) 42370 is a pub that is well worth a visit. There may not be the abundant game fishing opportunities offered to those who live in the middle of England or northern Scotland, but there are a number of waters that provide satisfactory sport and, in many cases, there are pubs and hotels aplenty where one can enjoy a relaxing day or two, free—even temporarily—from the pressures of modern day living.

Artist: D F Dane EARLY MORNING Courtesy of Rosenstiel's

Nestling in some of the most beautiful countryside in Britain, while still within easy reach of the A1, this seventeenth century coaching inn retains all its country charm. The character and history of the building is reflected in the decor with plush, rich fabrics in warm hues complementing the ancient oak beams. Local links with equestrian and country pursuits are a theme carried through to the naming of the rooms and the hotel—the whipper-in is the person in charge of the hunt beagles.

The bedrooms are all beautifully restored and decorated with a unique collection of prints, paintings and antiques. Designed by internationally recognised interior decorators, each room has thick carpets, fresh flowers and sparkling luxurious bathrooms with thick fluffy towels and deep baths. Each bedroom has direct dial telephone, remote control colour television, trouser press, hairdryer and tea and coffee making facilities.

The Whipper-In Restaurant has deservedly won a reputation for providing some of the finest food available locally. Chef Carl Bontoft produces menus on a daily basis—each one reflecting the best in English and French cuisine and making full use of the abundant local natural produce. The wine cellar is well stocked with the highest calibre wines to suit all tastes and budgets.

The Whipper-In Bar is an ideal spot for a snack or an informal meal. Guests can enjoy a range of filled croissants, pies and traditional English food beside the log fire in this peaceful bar.

The two specially designed conference rooms both have natural light, easy access and offer a comprehensive meeting facility. Both rooms are equally suited to parties or private dining and can be transformed from efficient meeting rooms to sophisticated party venues in a short time.

The hotel is located in the heart of Oakham, the capital of the ancient county of Rutland and yet is only minutes away from Rutland Water, the largest man-made lake in Europe, and the endless leisure activities available there. Close by are Burghley house, Belvoir Castle and all around is the stunning Leicestershire countryside.

Whipper-In Hotel
Market Place
Oakham, Rutland
Leicestershire LE15 6DT
Tel: (0572) 796571
Fax: (0572) 757759

Clive Madgwick Fishing Scene, Loch Earn Courtesy of Rosenstiel's

SOUTHERN ENGLAND

The South of England owes much of its prominence in fishing circles to legendary chalk streams such as the Test, the Itchen and the Kennet, together with stillwaters from Bewl Water in Kent to Blagdon and Chew in the west. A day on these gin-clear and beautifully maintained waters is a unique experience. One of the delights of fishing a chalk stream is the abundance of fly life. Many a fisherman's preferred natural fly is the mayfly, for this is the trout's favourite delicacy to which he rises without thought or care. The mayfly hatch is around the first two weeks in May and is often referred to as 'duffer's delight', because the trout rise so freely that beginners will strike lucky. Old fishing books are full of stories about the excitement the news of a hatch brought.

The Houghton

Before the improvements to the A303 I always used to take the A30, for not far from the M3 motorway the road winds down a hill to the small town of Stockbridge. At the Grosvenor Hotel here is that most exclusive of fishing clubs, the Houghton, which has been so ably served by three generations of the Lunn family. Looking over the bridge to the far end of the town, one can see the clear water with its inviting patches of weedy shelter and the trout swimming lazily against the current. Several of the houses have little feeder streams running past their gardens and here, where only two or three feet separate the banks, there can be trout of up to two pounds, fat on tit-bits from their human neighbours.

The Kennet

Another good place for trout watching is Hungerford, which is not far beyond Newbury and is a few miles away from the M4. This small town is the antiques capital of the area; there is a large range of shops from an indoor antique market to the most exclusive, dealing in top quality Georgian furniture. At the bottom of the town there is a bridge under which flows that delightful stream, the Kennet and close by is the recently restored Kennet and Avon canal. Walking though the meadows alongside the river one can see trout lying in wait for those appetizing morsels that the river brings to their larder. You can fish the Kennet for free as some of the old buildings have fishing rights and shooting rights on the common.

The Frome

Dorset is a sportsman's paradise. While the hunting may not be as good as Leicestershire, the shooting as good as Norfolk nor the fishing as good as Hampshire, few other counties can boast such a good overall standard of all these sports. The best known river in Dorset is the Frome whose source is near Evershot. This river has been described as a miniature Test, with chalk hills on either side and rich meadows in between which the river meanders over its gravel bed on its way through Dorchester to Wareham and Poole Harbour. The upper reaches are good for trouting while below Dorchester it used to be regarded as one of the best little salmon rivers in the south of England, at the turn of the century regularly producing forty-pounders! I have heard of salmon as far up as Maiden Newton where the river is no more than a few feet across, but it holds some nice wild trout.

Downstream at Frampton, there used to be marvellous trout fishing in the days of the Great Edwardian sportsman, Squire Brinsley Sheridan—a descendant of the famous playwright. In 1907 the Vicar, the Rev. Filleul, hooked a notable trout just above Dorchester. Having played his fish he eventually bought it to the bank but it was too big for his net. Luckily a servant was passing on her way to the Manor and she was asked to bring him a washing basket! The fish was successfully landed in the basket and found to weigh 12¾lb. The Frome holds the record for a sea-trout caught in the British Isles at 24lb. The salmon fishing suffered a setback about thirty years ago when the army dumped a large quantity of lead-based paint in the river. However, the Frome has recovered well and has produced a forty-two pounder in the last decade, while fish of between fifteen and eighteen pounds are not uncommon.

The Piddle

The other main river is the Piddle which is mentioned in the Domesday Book and whose name is of Saxon origin. From its source near Alton Pancras to its mouth at Poole Harbour, near that of the Frome, the river is some twenty two miles long. The names of some of the villages through which it flows were bowdlerized by the Victorians, who felt that Piddle offended their sensibilities for, after flowing through Piddletrenthide and Piddlehinton, the prefix changes to puddle and the river reaches Puddletown and then on to Tolpuddle of 'Martyrs' fame. The river is smaller than the Frome and produces only the occasional salmon and sea-trout, but these can be big fish. A salmon of 34lb and a sea-trout of 14lb have been caught within the last fifteen years. The Piddle and its feeders offer good trout fishing with fish weighing up to 3lb.

Nearly all the fishing on the rivers is privately owned and difficult to get on, but help is at hand from Richard Slocock's Wessex Fly Fishing at Tolpuddle (0305) 848460. First class tuition is available here as are bed and breakfast and self-catering cottages. There is a comprehensive tackle shop and a wide range of courses from one hour casting lessons to four day courses. Fishing for guests can be arranged on both the Frome and the Piddle, with day tickets available to non-residents. The fishing on the Piddle is on a catch and release basis with barbless hooks and a maximum of ten fish may be caught in a day.

Wessex Waters

Wessex also has lakes stocked with brownies and rainbows up to 10lb. Mr Harry Maddocks of Wool Bridge Manor (0929) 462313 has one and a quarter miles of single-bank fishing below East Burton on the Frome. Salmon here are around 16lb and the grilse run between July and September and are between 7lb and 10lb. 1990 saw 28 fish caught on this water and in 1991, eleven had been caught by July. This beat has two rods and a day permit costs £25.

Another good stillwater fishery is Flowers Farm (0300) 341351. This fishery is not far from the village of Cerne Abbas with its famous prehistoric giant cut into the chalk hillside and is situated on the edge of Batcombe Down, with views over Blackmore Vale. There are five spring-fed lakes here, all of a smallish size. A four-fish ticket will cost £16 per day. Half day and evening tickets are available too. Day tickets start at 5.30am. Completely different in character is Wessex Water's 142 acre reservoir at Sutton Bingham. This is just off the A37 Dorchester to Yeovil road on the Dorset Somerset border. It is a very attractive situation and much work has been done recently to remove the silt from the southern arm of the reservoir, which should also improve the fishing both in that area and generally. The lodge is designed to cater for the disabled fisherman and boats can be hired from the Ranger, Ivan Tinsley (0935) 872389.

The Avon

Any county would consider itself fortunate to have one river as famous as the Test, or the Itchen or the Avon. Hampshire has all three! The Avon rises near Devizes in the Vale of Pewsey and its course runs close to Stonehenge. At Salisbury it is greatly enlarged by its tributaries, of which the Wylye and the Nadder offer the best trout fishing. From Salisbury the river runs due south to enter the sea at Christchurch in Dorset. The Avon used to be one of the most famous mixed fisheries in England; the Upper Avon is a typical chalk stream and offers first class trouting for those lucky enough to fish it. The middle Avon has salmon, trout and coarse fish, while its lower reaches offer salmon, trout and superb sea-trout fishing. The river has good weed growth throughout its length which makes for good insect life and, while it may not be a prolific salmon river, its deep pools are renowned for producing heavy fish. Once again, however, this is another water that is little more than a shadow (or puddle?) of its former self; several of its tributaries above Salisbury are dry and the wet winters relied upon by the water boards are, at present, failing to materialise.Salisbury and District Angling Club has some excellent varied chalk stream fishing. Their twelve miles of the Avon is prime trout and grayling water and some of the lower stretches offer the chance of salmon. The Club's fishing stretches from Durnford, two miles north of Salisbury down to Burgate and also includes some fishing on the Bourne and three quarters of a mile on the Wylye. The Club has a relatively open membership and your first annual subscription will cost £47 plus a registration fee of £15. Further details are available from John Eadies, 20 Catherine Street, Salisbury (0722) 328535.

Broadlands (Broadlands Estate)

A few miles south of Braemore, on the B3347 is the village of Winkton and the Winkton Fishery, whose two and a half miles of double-water fishing is divided into two beats. In the old days this used to be a spring fishery but the season now extends until the end of July. Day rods are occasionally available and if you are interested in fishing either this water or the Bisterne Fishery you should write to Major J. M. Mills of Bisterne Manor, Ringwood, Hampshire. Alternatively, for Bisterne you could try the Tyrrells Ford Hotel (0425) 72646 or the Fisherman's Haunt (0202) 484071 for Winkton. This used to be a favourite pub for fishermen but in the opinion of the keeper now caters more for the yuppie crowd!

At Christchurch is the famous Royalty Fishery which has two miles of water. Bridge Pool is particularly good for sea-trout and June 1991 saw a fine fish of 14lb caught here. Fishing starts at 6.00am and most rods start the day with a fly, before changing to bait during the day and returning to fly in the evening. Only two rods are allowed and the price for them, including a punt, varies between £60 and £75 according to the season. Rather less expensive is the stretch of river above Bridge Pool where a day's salmon fishing costs £24 and sea-trout between £7 and £11. The Compound at the top weir tends to only fish well in good water levels, while the holding pool, Parlour, does well in low water conditions. Two rods can fish the pool for between £46 and £64 a day. Further details may be had from the owner, Lt Col Ransley of West Hampshire Water Company, Water Mill Road, Christchurch. Day tickets are also available from Davis Tackle Shop (0202) 485169 at 75, Bargate which is almost opposite the Royalty Inn (used to be the Red Lion), known locally by some as the 'spud pub' for its large variety of baked potatoes.

The Wylye & the Nadder

The Wylye and the Nadder are both first class chalk streams. The Marquess of Bath's Estate at Longleat has the uppermost two and a half miles of the Wylye dry fly water. Season tickets only are available at a cost of £450 plus VAT and can be obtained from T. R. W. Moore Esq. of the Longleat Estate (0985) 844400. Day tickets can, however, be bought for the Sutton Veny Estates water (0985) 40682 which is the next main fishery downstream, at a cost £25 per week day or £30 at weekends. Tuition and tackle can be arranged for guests but prior notice is required. The estate has three and a half miles of double-water fishing and the average brownie on this stocked water is 1¾lb. Both the Wylye and the Nadder flow through Wilton Park. Wilton House is famous for its cube and double cube rooms designed by Inigo Jones and there is a delightful Palladian Bridge over the Nadder. Tisbury Angling Club has a good stretch of approximately four miles on the Nadder. This water has a good stock of wild brown trout who average around 1¼lb. The Club is keen on its grayling fishing and has many imports from other clubs anxious to limit their numbers of this prolific breeding fish. Membership costs £20 a year with a £4 joining fee and further details are available from the Secretary, Mr H. J. Haskell of The Forge, Fovant, Nr Salisbury (0722) 714203.

The River Itchen (Winchester Tourism)

The Test & the Itchen

The Test is probably the most famous chalkstream in the world. Talk to fishermen as far apart as the Shores of Lake Taupo in New Zealand or on the banks of a trout stream in Montana and the Test is *the* English trout stream. Although fishing books have spread its fame, its glories have been known to fishermen for hundreds of years. Many famous fishermen have stalked its banks and peered into a pool or a likely lie. Here, at Longparish, that veteran of Wellington's Peninsular Campaigns, Colonel Peter Hawker, killed forty trout in three hours and over twelve thousand trout in fifty years. I purposely used the word 'killed' as this great sportsman only killed fish of over 3¾lb and returned far more than he took. In Stockbridge is the Grosvenor and, above its portico, is the Houghton Club, founded in 1822 and the most famous fishing club in the world. Here is Compton, the home of the late Sir Thomas Sopwith, the designer of the pioneer fighter plane, the Sopwith Camel, who would not allow his guests to fish in the evening and who, with his wife, killed twenty-one salmon in a day in 1954. Broadlands used to belong to Lord Mount Temple and here is Lady Mount Temple, fishing the special place where monster trout lurk. In the morning she has seen a large fish and determines to try for him in the evening. She hooks him and brings him safely to the net but he is not the one she spotted earlier on so he is returned although he weighed 11lb. The pool is rested and she tries again with a special lure, for these trout are more accustomed to dining on exotic morsels such as liver rather than flies! There is a fierce tug. It's the fish, and after a gallant fight he is landed and found to weigh 13lb. Many famous fly-tiers have walked these banks and observed the hatches and the trouts' ensuing banquets. Here are Francis Halford and George Marryat of the Houghton Club who helped to pioneer dry-fly fishing and G.E.M. Skues who tied many a fly but is probably best known for his pheasant-tail nymph which also works so well in stillwaters.

The twenty-five mile course of the Itchen which Skues knew so well, offers superb trout fishing along its length, from its source near New Alresford down to Southampton. Like the Test, it has an abundant weed growth and hence a wide and varied insect life with prolific hatches of mayflies, olives, hawthorn, damselfly and sedges. Similar to its famous sister, salmon and sea-trout are caught on its lower reaches. The Test may be better known but I know several friends who would prefer to fish the Itchen, just as the many excellent small streams like the Meon are overshadowed by the better known waters. Fishing on the Test and the Itchen is very sought after to say the least! As a result, they are difficult to get on and very expensive when you do! Mrs Howlett of the Rod Box in King's Worthy, Winchester (0962) 883600 may be able to help you as the company rents, or acts as agent, for approximately forty miles of fishing on the two rivers. Prices start at £65 per day on the Itchen, and £200 for a two-rod day on the Test. Bookings can be made on a seasonal basis on a named day of the week either as a full or half rod, the latter being one day a fortnight. There is a waiting list. The Greyhound Hotel at Stockbridge (0264) 810833 has a third of a mile single-bank fishing on the Test, which is adjacent to the hotel and just downstream from the Houghton Club's Grosvenor Hotel. This beat holds two rods and, although hotel guests have priority, day tickets are sometimes available and cost between £40 and £50.

Mr Robin Gow of Orvis at Nether Wallop (0264) 781212 can arrange a day for you on the Itchen near Abbots Worthy. This half mile beat is mainly stocked and dry fly and upstream nymphing are the permitted methods. The trout average 2¼lb and the cost of a day is £270 for three rods and includes a ghillie. Mr Gow also has access to beats on the Test such as Timsbury 5 and 6 which are below Kimbridge and the famous Ginger Beer Beat at Kimbridge, four miles upstream from Romsey. This prime beat comprises half a mile of shallow pools and deep runs. It has four rods and costs £375 per day. At Broadlands, the home of the late Lord Mountbatten, there is over two miles of the Test which is divided into three beats. A season's salmon fishing for two rods on a named day costs £780 while half a rod is one day a fortnight and costs £395. The comparative costs for trout fishing are £950 for a full rod and £500 for a half. Day tickets are available at between £355 and £75 per day with further information obtainable from the Estate Office (0703) 732354 and the indefatigable head river keeper, Bernard Aldrich. Roxton Sporting Agency (0488) 683222 let days on the Compton Manor Estate water, which comprises some six miles of prime fishing on the Test divided into ten beats. Two of these beats will be let by the day at a fixed cost of £1000, plus agency commission. This price includes fishing for four rods, lunch and the services of a ghillie.

Hampshire Waters

For those of us with more modest means, there is excellent stillwater fishing to be had in Hampshire. Avington Trout Fishing (0962) 779312 is near Itchen Abbas and offers fishing on three lakes, which are stocked on a daily basis, and a chalk stream feeder of the Itchen. The fishery is open all year, including Christmas Day and New Year's Day, and is renowned for its big rainbows. Several 14lb to 20lb fish have been caught here and the record is a superb fish of 23lb 10oz. A day here costs £35. At Sandleheath, near Fordingbridge, there is the Rockbourne Trout Fishery (0725) 3603. The fishery has six spring-fed lakes which have good hatches of fly and three beats on the Sweatford water which is a tributary of the Avon. The lakes are stocked on a daily basis with rainbows which average 2lb 8oz and a five-fish day ticket costs £28.00. A comprehensive range of flies and tackle is available from the fishery office. In 1990, ten percent of the fish caught here were over 4lb, the best rainbow was 13lb 12oz and best brownie 6lb 14oz. An added attraction is that the fishery has a licensed bar with meals and snacks.

There are two good stillwaters in the Andover area, Rooksbury Mill and Dever Springs. Rooksbury Mill (0264) 352921 is set in sixteen acres on the outskirts of Andover and has two lakes of six and a half acres and two and a half acres as well as one mile on the river Anton, which is a tributary of the Test. The fishery shop has a comprehensive range of tackle including its own range of carbon rods. Expert tuition is available as is a smoking service. The fishery can also organise corporate days for parties of more than twenty rods and will prepare breakfast and lunch. A five fish day ticket costs £25.

Wiltshire Waters

If it's big fish you're after then I suggest you visit Dever Springs (0264) 72592 at Barton Stacey, which is just off the A303 some six miles east of Andover. The fishery has two lakes totalling six acres and a half mile stretch of the Dever, a tributary of the Test. The minimum stocking size is 3lb and the average is 4lb 8oz. Double figure fish are taken most days on this water which has excellent fly life including an abundant mayfly hatch. Casts with a breaking strain of under 6lb are prohibited which is not surprising since the Dever has produced a rainbow of 22lb 15oz and a brown trout of 18lb 2oz. The chance of catching one of these big fish on a four-fish day ticket costs £45. Among other good stillwater fisheries in Wiltshire is Avon Springs (0980) 53557. This fishery is at Durrington on the A345 and just a few miles north of Amesbury. There are two spring-fed lakes of two acres and five acres which have excellent mayfly, sedge and olive hatches. The water is stocked on a daily basis with fish from 2lb upwards. The fishery also has a stretch of the Avon which is dry-fly and upstream nymphing water and only barbless hooks are permitted. A four fish day ticket on the lakes costs £28. The 1993 season saw a best bag of 32lb 10oz and a best fish of 15lb 6oz. Perhaps more significant is the high average weight of 3lb 2oz and the rod average of 3.4 fish. Some ten miles further west on the A303 is the junction with the A36 and less than two miles south on this road is the village of Steeple Langford and Langford Fisheries (0722) 790770. The fifteen-acres lake has excellent insect life and in particular has spectacular evening rises to hatching buzzers. The average fish is around 2lb 4oz, while the record rainbow is 17lb and brownie is 8lb 5oz. A five fish day ticket will cost you £23. The fishery can also arrange corporate days when tuition by well known experts can be arranged. It is in the beautiful Wylye Valley and is unique in that it is also an officially recognised nature reserve. Zeals is the most westerly Wiltshire village on the A303 and here, Zeals Fish Farm (0747) 840573 has a two acre lake stocked with rainbows of up to 14lb. The record is 16lb 8oz. A day ticket costs £20 for four fish and it is nice to see that barbless hooks are preferred.

Fly-tying by Mike Sugg

After twenty years fly-tying part-time commercially, Mike and his wife stated a full-time business in Dorset where they produce flies and fly-tying materials for leadng retailers and private clients in many parts of the world. Tiny dry flies to exhibition salmon flies are tied to order using high quality, and, in the main, home-produced materials. They use fur and feathers dyed to the correct shades and quality hackles from their own flock of poultry which they have built up over a number of years. A fine collection of fly-tying materials was obtained while living abroad and—with the aid of a good 'library'—flies can be tied to customers' requirements. Mike has fished in many parts of the world for a wide variety of fish and is always pleased to help with suggestions for fly selections. Trade enquiries are also welcome. For further information please contact:

Mike Sugg
Homecroft
Sandford Orcas
SHERBOURNE
Dorset DT9 4SD
Tel: (0963) 220335

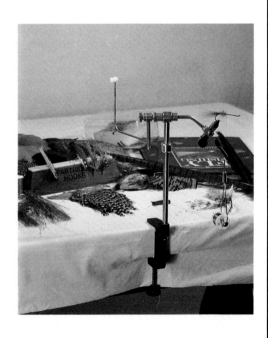

Fly-tying bench (Mike Sugg)

Bristol Waters

West of here are the well known Bristol Waters Fisheries of Chew, Blagdon and Barrow. Blagdon was the first reservoir to be opened to the public for trout fishing. In 1904 this was regarded as a daring venture, but soon gained popularity. The precedent has been followed by many other reservoirs. Over the years, the fishery has mellowed and now has all the appearance of a natural lake with varied marsh vegetation, wild-flowers, rich meadows and mixed conifer and broad-leafed woodlands. Twelve rowing boats, including one adapted for the disabled, are available on this 440 acre water. Chew is nearly three times the size of Blagdon and is surrounded by unspoiled meadows and woods. There are some seven miles of bank fishing and twenty six motorboats are available. John Horsey, the resident professional here, is on record as having said he takes around eighty per cent of his fish uing a dry fly! Something of a revelation, and you might like to bear this in mind. Barrow consists of three small reservoirs of sixty, forty and twenty-five acres and the average fish is around a pound and ten ounces, slightly less than Blagdon and Chew where the average is two pounds. The total yearly catch on these waters is over 50,000 and there are many better fish of 4lb and over. The company is actively concerned with conservation. There is a nature reserve at Herriotts Pool on Chew where of islands have been created to encourage nesting ducks, and in the twenty acres of parkland which are managed by the Nature Conservancy Council, there are green winged orchids. A day costs £11 and permits can be obtained from the lodges which also sell tackle and flies. There is a wide range of help on offer to beginners. There are free casting lessons or you can pay for more comprehensive tuition given by NAC qualified instructors. For under eighteens, there is a special £1 permit for the first five visits if accompanied by an experienced fisherman. Also on offer are special beginner's days when experienced local anglers will help you to have a go at trout or bank fishing. Further details can be had from the company's Woodford Lodge Office (0275) 332339 and from Veals Tackle Shop, 61 Old Market Street, Bristol (0272) 260790.

Gloucestershire Waters

There are several stillwater fisheries in the disused gravel pits around Cirencester in Gloucestershire. They tend to be quite deep and having only recently been converted, lack the maturity of Blagdon and Chew. North of here at Upper Swell near Stow-on-the-Wold is Donnington Fish Farm (0451) 30873. The lake is stocked with browns and rainbows and an unusual feature is that two fish are guaranteed on a day ticket. The shop sells both hot and cold smoked trout and a very good smoked trout pate.

The Coln

The River Coln is a typical Cotswold chalk stream and has long been prized for the availability of its trout fishing. The Bull Hotel at Fairford (0285) 712535 has one and a half miles of single-bank fishing which takes six rods.

Hotel residents pay £9.50 for a two fish day ticket and the charge for non-residents is £15. The water is stocked with browns and rainbows which average around 1½lb. At picturesque Bibury, the Bibury Court Hotel (0285) 740337 has got just under a quarter of a mile of river which is available to guests only and costs £10 per day. Also at Bibury is the recently refurbished Swan Hotel (0285) 740204 whose six hundred yards hold three rods. There is a three fish limit and in 1988 an 11lb fish was taken here. This part of the river is a popular tourist attraction and although requested not to, people often throw bread for the trout. However, they will take a fly and early morning and evening are the best times.

The Lambourn & the Kennet

East of here are the Lambourn and the Kennet. The Lambourn is a delightful little chalk stream with a good stock of brownies and a two-pounder on this small water is a good fish. The course of the Kennet covers some forty-four miles from its source near Marlborough Downs to where it joins the Thames above Reading. The lower reaches are a combination of river and canal and are not of interest to us, but the stretch from above Marlborough to the Hungerford area has long been famous as some of the finest chalk stream fishing in the country. The Town and Manor of Hungerford bought their fishing from King James I in 1617 and, as a result, enjoy fishing on two miles of the Kennet, half a mile of one of the carries and a mile on the Dunn. A full time keeper is employed on the water which has both brownies and rainbows. Two-pounders are caught regularly and there are fish of up to five pounds. Season tickets only are available and cost £957. Further details may be obtained from Colonel Macey (0488) 682770.

Some of the best small stream fishing you could wish for can be found at the Denford Fisheries (0488) 684179 which has two and a half miles of carriers and a short stretch on the Kennet itself. In 1990 there were 1100 rainbows and 110 brownies caught here and of the rainbows 98 were over 2lb, 53 over 3lb. Dry-fly only is the rule until the end of June, after which upstream nymphing is permitted. The water holds six rods and a day's fishing costs £32.50, except in June when it is £35.00. The reason for this is that early June sees a fine Mayfly hatch.

At Kintbury is Mr Edward Hill's Barton Court Fishery (0488) 58226 which has three miles of double-water fishing on the three main streams and some carriers. This area of the Kennet used to be marshland until it was drained by French prisoners of war in Napoleonic times and now offers many types of water. A four fish day ticket on this brown trout water costs £25, with a season weighing in at £600. It is regularly stocked and the stocking size is a pound to a pound and eight ounces. The best fish here was seven pounds and July 1991 produced one of five pounds ten ounces. Downstream at Newbury, the Millwaters Hotel (0635) 528838 has half a mile of fishing and a stocked lake which is available to residents only. This though, is on the Lambourn which, like the Kennet, flows through the hotel's gardens.

Oxon Water

North of here, at Abingdon, near Oxford is Millet's Farm Trout Fishery (0865) 391394. The fishery has two spring-fed lakes on limestone which total seven acres. There is an abundance of natural water life such as nymphs, shrimp and corixa. Flies and refreshments can be obtained from the lodge and professional tuition is available. The water is stocked with the powerful fighting shasta strain of rainbows which average 2¼lb. A five-fish day ticket costs £20 to £50 and half days and evening tickets are also available.

Capital Waters

There is a wealth of trout fishing within easy reach of London. Church Hill Farm (0296) 720524 at Mursley, near Winslow in Buckinghamshire is only fifty miles away. The two spring-fed lakes total ten acres and both are alkaline and very productive of natural lifeforms. The water is regularly stocked with brownies and rainbows of between 1½lb and 12lb. The fishery has a particularly fine clubhouse which is a converted eighteenth- century barn. Nymphs such as damsel, mayfly and montana are particularly successful and the best fish caught here was 17lb ½ oz. The price for a four-fish day ticket is £23.

Also in Buckinghamshire are the Latimer Park Lakes (0494) 762396 which are sited in the Chess Valley on the south eastern side of the Chilterns. The lakes, which are eight acres and four acres, are well over two hundred years old and the fishery can also offer chalk stream fishing on the river Chess. The lakes are chalk stream fed which ensures a prolific food supply and are restocked on a daily basis with rainbow and brown trout that are reared on the premises. Around 10,000 fish are caught here every season and over half of them are larger than 2lb. A four fish day ticket will set you back £23, with a complimentary evening ticket given to anyone who has failed to catch a fish during the day. At Slough, is the Queen Mother Fly Fishery (0753) 683605. A day ticket on this 475 acre water costs £10. There have recently been improvements here, including thirty-three new boats and ninety-six casting platforms and the water is now stocked with brookies as well as browns and rainbows. The Chess, sad to report, has almost disappeared in places, with other stretches of one of the country's best chalk streams reduced to stagnant pools. The stretch of the river that runs through Chesam is worst affected, with fish moving downstream, and the NRA are praying for substantial rainfall to restore both water levels and the chalk bed itself.

If you live in East London or Essex, a wide range of still-water fishing is available. Near Chelmsford, is the Essex Water Company's Hanningfield Reservoir (0268) 710101. Boats are available on this six hundred acre water which is stocked with 65-70,000 of the company's home-reared rainbows every season. The fish average between 1¼lb and 2½lb and a six-fish day ticket costs £13.50. The whole area of the reservoir is a wild bird sanctuary which adds to the tranquillity of an excellent day's fishing. Near Colchester is the well known Ardleigh Reservoir (0206) 230642 which in 1991 hosted the European International Trout Fishing Competition. The average weight is just under 1¼lb and the record is 4lb while the best brown is 9lb 12oz. An eight fish day ticket is priced at £13.30. Expert tuition is available as are locally tied flies and bed and breakfast can be arranged. Among the good, privately-owned waters are Aveley Trout Lakes (0708) 868245, Chelmer's Fisheries at Thaxted (0371) 3595, Chigboro at Maldon (0621) 57368 and Cooks Farm at Brentwood (0277) 72265.

South of the Thames, there is the excellent stillwater and river fishing in Surrey, Kent and Sussex. In the Tillingbourne Valley, near Guildford in Surrey are the Duke of Northumberland's Albury Estate Fisheries (0486) 412323. They are set in a 3,000 acre estate which has pleasure grounds and terraces laid out by the seventeenth-century diarist John Evelyn and offer a wide range of fishing. The Park Fishery has two lakes and three beats on the river Tillingbourne which is predominantly chalk

Small Lake Solitude (Chalk Springs Fishery)

water, and can be fished on a season ticket basis only. The Powder Mills Fishery is a lake of nearly four acres and is designed to appeal to the experienced fisherman. The water provides excellent buzzer fishing and is stocked with rainbows. A less experienced fisherman might prefer the Weston Fishery which has wide banks and easy casting. The main lake is some four acres and there is a smaller one which is ideal for dry fly. A four fish day ticket for either Weston or Powder Mills costs £20. One of my favourite fisheries is Willinghurst (0483) 275048 which is just off the A281 Guildford to Horsham Road. There are two main lakes and four smaller ones which are set in woodland. It is a delightful country setting with not a house in sight. Other good Surrey stillwaters include Crosswater Mill at Churt (0251) 254321, Enton Lakes at Godalming (0428) 792620, and Gatton Manor at Dorking (0306) 79555.

At Lamberhurst, Kent, is Bewl Water Reservoir (0892) 890352 which attracts over 20,000 fishermen a year. Six fish, brace and evening tickets are available. Boats and tackle can be hired and there is a tackle shop at the Lodge. A range of courses are designed to cater for the beginner as well as the more experienced fisherman. Nearby, is the excellent sixteen acre Bayham Lake Trout Fishery (0892) 890276. This lake is one of the most prolific trout fisheries in the country; it is stocked with rainbows averaging 2½lb and running up to 12lb and more. The fishery includes double-water fishing on the River Teise which has a series of beautiful and very prolific waterfalls and pools downstream from the lake. Instructors are on hand to help and advise if required and you can also try your hand at clay pigeon shooting in the nearby woodland. Bayham can also provide superb lunches, which are served in the former boathouse which has a promenade deck overlooking the lake. A six fish day ticket costs £28. The River Teise rises near Tunbridge Wells and covers some twenty miles on its journey to join the Medway near Yalding. The upper reaches are well stocked with brown and rainbow trout and offer good dry-fly fishing. Just below Bayhams water, is the Hoathly Fishery which has 1½ miles of the Teise and a similar amount on Bartley Mill. A day here is priced at a modest £3 and tickets are available from Bassett's Garage in the village. Other stillwaters include Chequertree at Ashford (0233) 820383 and Tenterden Trout Waters at Tenterden (0580) 763201. Tenterden has three lakes totalling five acres of water and is situated at Coombe Farm which is about a mile outside the town. One lake is for dry fly and nymphing only and the water is regularly stocked with brownies and rainbows of between 1½lb and 10lb. The fishery has a unique basket system which allows continuous fishing with no restriction on the number of fish caught, though fish not required must be returned at the end of the day. A three fish day tickets costs £15.

The Rivers of Sussex are best known for their coarse fishing but the lower reaches of the Arun, Western and Eastern Rother, Ouse and Adur all have runs of sea-trout which are generally larger than in Hampshire. There are a number of good stillwaters in the county too. At Burwash, near Heathfield, is Lakedown Trout Fishery (0435) 883449. This is owned by Roger Daltrey of 'The Who' fame. Game fishing is popular in the music business and Eric Clapton is also a very keen fisherman. The fishery is set in a delightful valley and has four lakes and a well equipped lodge. North of here, just off the A267, is

the Yew Tree Trout Fishery at Rotherfield (0892) 852529. The fishery consists of three beautiful lakes surrounded by fields and woodland. The price of a four fish day ticket is £16 and tuition is available. At Flimwell, on the A2115, the Spring Wood Trout Farm (0580) 87525 consists of three lakes totalling more than five acres and is set on the peak of a hill overlooking Bewl Water. Two lakes are dry fly and nymph only and the water is stocked with brownies and rainbows. Bed and Breakfast is available at the farm house and a four fish day ticket costs £20 with reductions for morning and evening only tickets. Corporate Fishing Days can also be arranged.

West of here on the A24 London to Worthing Road some ten miles south of Horsham is Ashington Trout Farm (0903) 893066. This is a new fishery set under the famous Chanctonbury Ring at the base of the South Downs. The water is fed by chalk streams and stocked with rainbows and, consequently, has some double figure fish. Overnight accommodation is available and a four fish day ticket costs £16. Another newish fishery, not far from West Meon on the A32, is Meon Springs trout Fishery (073087) 249. Although only one and a half acres, the fishery occupies an attractive location and is well stocked with rainbows and brownies. Further west at Arundel, on the Duke of Norfolk's Estate, is the delightful Chalk Springs Fishery (0903) 883742. The four spring fed lakes total five acres and a four fish ticket costs £24.50. The water is very clear and gives you the opportunity to stalk rainbows and brown trout which run into double figures in weight.

The Hastings Flyfishers' Club (0580) 880407 was formed as a limited company in 1932. The club has the fishing on two reservoirs; Darwell which is 165 acres and Powdermill at 54 acres. Southern Water have plans to extend the former, to cater for increased water demand, and details of trout fishing on both reservoirs can be obtained from Mr D. E. Tack on (0424) 33957. Rowing boats are available on both waters which are very attractive and well established. Powdermill is so named because it used to drive the waterwheel of a gunpowder works which blew up! The waters are well stocked, mainly with rainbows, but there are some natural and stocked browns. A six fish day ticket costs £12.50 and the average size is around 1¼lb but fish of up to 6lb and more can be expected. Southern Water also manage the Weirwood reservoir (0342) 822731 in Forest Row, the only mixed reservoir fishery in the area, which incidentally is also an SSSI. A final suggestion is Colin Godman's Trouting (0825 74) 322 near Uckfield in East Sussex. This private syndicate has three lakes covering seven acres in attractive scenery and is well stocked with rainbows and natural brownies. A few rods are occasionally available at £370 or £210 for a half rod.

Set at the lower end of the Hampshire Avon which then runs on into Christchurch Harbour and to the sea, lies one of the South of England's most famous fisheries. Granted into private ownership by the Crown around the Magna Carta period, this part of the river is noted for its combination of coarse and game fishing. Spring and summer salmon run regularly and sea trout are prolific in the revered Bridge Pool in the centre of the town.

Anglers also find a wide choice of coarse species including barbel, chub, carp, roach, bream, pike and perch. The easy access to the banks makes it a favourite with visitors from all over the country. Juvenile anglers are also encouraged and there are one or two areas which offer anyone who may be disabled a chance to fish.

Permits are readily available from both Davis Fishing Tackle Shop at 75 Bargates, about a hundred yards from the main fishery car park, where there is ample parking space; and from the Bailiffs Office at the Fishery House, 2 Avon Buildings. The price of a permit does not include the National Rivers Authority rod licence. The quoted price of the permit includes VAT.

Christchurch itself is very handy for shopping, restaurants, pubs and entertainment. There are a number of hotels in the area, including The Kings Arms which is conveniently adjacent to the Bridge Pool, as well as guest houses only a few minutes from the fishery, catering specifically for the needs of fishermen. Bournemouth is a ten minute car drive away if the rest of the family is not addicted to the piscatorial skills. Caravan and camping sites abound in the area.

Details of permit prices can be obtained in a brochure available from:
The Manager, Recreation Services
West Hampshire Water Company
Mill Road
Christchurch
Dorset BH23 2LU
Tel: (0202) 499000
Fax: (0202) 499100

Just as your fishing in this part of the world most often needs to have been planned well in advance if you are to stand a chance of getting on to your favourite stretch, so it is usually ess6ential to book accommodation—fishermen are not the only ones who are out and about in this very popular tourist area. Not to be overlooked are the companies who can organise package breaks for you. UK Field and Stream (0527) 66344 and Fishing Breaks (071) 281 6737 are two examples, but for those wishing to organise their own get away, here are a few good suggestions.

The rivers Frome and Piddle weave their intricate pattern through much of Hardy's Wessex. This is a delightful part of England and, whilst much has changed since Thomas penned his first epistle, it remains very picturesque with sleepy villages nestling in the English countryside. Near the source of the Frome we find an hotel of outstanding quality; Swanner Lodge (0935) 83424 in Evershott. It is small but well kept with superb grounds and a first rate restaurant. Dorchester offers the King's Arms (0305) 65353 which has its roots in the eighteenth century and is a popular spot for fishermen. More outstanding value and character can be found at Cerne Abbas. Here, The New Inn (03003) 274 dates from the eleventh century (it was refurbished in the seventeenth) and is a tremendous place to stay, full of character. This fine establishment is very conveniently situated for the Flowers Farm Fishery.

Both the Piddle and the Frome arrive at Poole Harbour in the vicinity of Wareham, and here we find The Priory (0929) 552772. Beautifully maintained gardens reach down to the River Frome and the hotel has a number of contacts who can arrange some excellent fishing for guests. If you want to spoil yourself, this is an excellent place in which to do it. The Piddle is responsible for some of the most delightfully named villages; Affpuddle, Puddletown, Tolpuddle and even Piddletrenthide to name but a few. The latter is home to The Old Bakehouse (03004) 305—a very comfortable hotel. Those considering a trip to Sutton Bingham Reservoir, which is only a short distance from Evershott, will be pleased to hear that they are surrounded by pleasant pubs. One such beauty is the Rose and Crown (0935) 850776. There is no accommodation here but the food is good. People wishing to stay in the area should try The Four Acres at West Cocker (093586) 2555 or the sixteenth- century King's Arms (093582) 2513, a former coaching inn. While the majority of the River Avon runs through Hampshire territory, the folk in Wiltshire and Dorset can also lay claim to its sparkling waters. The upper reaches, which boast such fine trouting, offer relatively few hotels, largely because the river here flows through the remote expanses of Salisbury Plain. However, Salisbury does have a number of hotels and the Red Lion (0722) 23334 is an historic inn in which to stay, as is the Rose and Crown (0722) 27908 in Harnham. The conservatory here enjoys a fine view to the River Avon. Although some of the Wylie is the reserved water of the historic Wilton Fly Fishing Club there remain opportunities available on

parts of the river. Two selections, both near Warminster, are The Dove at Corton (0985) 50378 which offers superb fayre and secondly, the Bishopstow House (0985) 212312. This is a majestic hotel in which to stay where guests can enjoy some free fishing on the hotel water or, alternatively, may fish the nearby estate water for £35 per day. Those prepared to travel a little further should consider the Longleat Arms (09853) 308 which is a pleasant village pub with good food and accommodation. For those fishing the Nadder, Fovant reveals a brace of pubs with more modest, but essentially very comfortable accommodation:- The Cross Keys (072270) 284 and The Pembroke Arms (072270) 201 which was formerly the shooting lodge of the Earl of Pembroke. Alternatively, the Lamb at Hindon (074789) 573, formerly a smugglers' haunt, is a good place to take shelter and the food here is very good.

Returning to the Salisbury area, we can recommend another outstanding food pub—the Silver Plough (0722) 72266 at Pitton, a really superb establishment but unfortunately with no accommodation. A less elaborate, but still a welcoming pub, is The Radnor Arms (0722) 29722. Fordingbridge offers the Ashburn Hotel (0425) 652060, a quiet but no less engaging abode which is well worth considering. South of here, at Stackton, lovers of fine cuisine should earmark the Three Lions (0425) 652489, an extremely sophisticated and very good restaurant. Journeying through the Ringwood Forest we have two suggestions to make. Firstly, the Moortown Lodge (0425) 471404, and secondly, the Struan Hotel (0425) 473553 in Ashley Heath. A little way south is Tyrells Ford Country House (0425) 72646. The hotel is situated on the edge of the New Forest and is an excellent base for those who are fortunate enough to be fishing in the area. It is extremely comfortable and has a choice of menu as well as good bar food. The Fisherman's Haunt (0202) 484071 may be a popular haunt with the upwardly mobile but it remains well worth a visit. The Avon runs alongside the grounds and trophied fish add to the character. There are a number of bedrooms here which are spotless and very comfortable.

The Test and Itchen are truly celebrated chalk streams. For much of their length they run parallel and are only a few miles apart. As a result, there are a few hotels that will serve both waters. However, let us start with the Test. Hurstbourne Tarrant is conveniently situated for the upper reaches of the Test and lovers of style should try Esseborne Manor (0264) 76444. Charm happily blends here with comfort and luxury; accommodation and cuisine are both of a high standard. Journey towards Stockbridge and you find the Pleasant Mayfly (026474)

283 pub in Testcombe. The Test flows through its garden making it a delightful spot for lunch. Further down the valley we arrive at a hotel which is a mecca for serious fishermen; the Grosvenor Hotel (0264) 810606 in Stockbridge, the home of the Houghton Fishing Club. The hotel. is now owned by Whitbread Brewery but in keeping with tradition, fly fishing tackle adorns the walls. However, you should note that the hotel is well equipped, comfortable and offers good food. The White Hart Inn (0264) 810475 and the Greyhound (0264) 81033 are also worth considering. A short distance west of Stockbridge we find the charming Wallops, that is to say Nether Wallop and Middle Wallop. The latter houses the Fifehead Manor (0264) 781565 which is very comfortable and dates back to the Middle Ages. The welcome here is warm and a visit is highly recommended.

Venturing through the villages of Houghton, Horsebridge and Timsbury, we trace the Test to Romsey where the White Horse (0794) 512431 is an historic hotel to try. Alternatively, lovers of outstanding cuisine should sample the Old Manor House (0794) 517353 in Palmerston Street. Our final port of call is the excellent Lee Park (0794) 517888 which is, by virtue of its Broadlands associations, able to provide good fishing as well as outstanding hospitality. The Test may be tricky to fish but it is not impossible as many visitors to Lee Park can testify. Midway between the Test and the Itchen stands the village of Crawley. The Fox and Hounds (096272) 285 is a splendid red-brick built pub which is very cosy. This pub has good food and a few rooms should you wish to stay in the area. Sparsholt is similarly sandwiched between the two rivers and handy for Lainston House (0962) 63588—a really outstanding hotel to try. It is lavishly decorated and, furthermore, has its own fishing on the Test for guests. As you can imagine, this is an extremely popular place so contact the hotel well in advance of your proposed trip.

Artist Terrence Gilbert FLY FISHING, VIRGINIA WATER Courtesy of the Artist

A little south of Eastleigh is the village of Hedge End. Here we find a hotel that will please the fisherman. It's not set on the Itchen but it is a well run, beautifully situated hotel and convenient for the lower reaches. In Winchester, an historic town, we find a number of excellent hotels; The Wykeham Arms (0962) 52834 has a fine restaurant. The Bush Inn, on the Itchen at Ovington (0962) 732764 is a delightful pub and a superb place to stop for some liquid refreshment. Alternatively, try the Tichborne Arms (096273) 3760 in Tichborne, further up the Itchen Valley—a pub with a good atmosphere and excellent bar food.

Although the fishing on the Test and the Itchen is often excellent, if expensive, Hampshire also provides a number of stillwaters. Those of us who enjoy a weekend away at such a venue will hopefully find the following thoughts of interest. Avington Trout Fishery is well served by the pubs recommended for the upper waters of the Itchen. Some distance away is The Wheatsheaf (0256) 398282 in North Waltham which offers good weekend breaks. Visitors to the Rockbourne Trout Fishery will find a number of opportunities neighbouring the Avon and slightly further up field, The Horton Inn at Horton (0258) 840252 and the Langton Arms at Tarrant Monkton (025889) 225 provide excellent pub accommodation and a friendly atmosphere. A similar summary can be applied to The King's Arms at Fonthill Bishop (074789) 523 where you will find good food and accommodation.

If you are venturing further westwards to Zeals, The Old Ship, Mere (0747) 860258 is an historic inn with comfortable bedrooms. This is a friendly and informal establishment. The Barrows Fishery, Blagdon Lake and the Chew Valley Lake are all within a few miles of Bristol and should you wish to stay in this area, the Carpenter's Arms (07618) 202 at Wick is worth a try. The Penscot Farmhouse, Shipham (093484) 2659 is very welcoming and provides good value accommodation. Grander accommodation in Shipham can be found at Daneswood House (093484) 3145, an Edwardian house with a wooded setting in the Mendip Hills. Our final thought is Chelwood House (0761) 490730 which is the perfect base if you are fishing the nearby Avon.

Although the stillwaters of Gloucestershire lack the maturity of their southern cousins, the Cotswolds provide some of the most spectacular scenery and charming hostelries in England. Visitors to the Donnington Fish Farm at Upper Swell are positively spoilt for choice. A splendid place at which to stay is Lords of The Manor Hotel (0451) 20243—a delightful hotel with a well stocked trout lake in the grounds. In Lower Swell, The Old Farmhouse (0451) 30232 is a convivial place to stay and is particularly good value. The Grapevine Hotel (0451) 30344 is another to note—a thoroughly well maintained

and welcoming hotel. If you prefer a pub-type environment then two gems to try are the Horse and Groom at Boulton On The Hill (0386) 700413, a splendid village inn and the Black Horse at Naunton (04515) 378; more wonderful countryside, modest accommodation and excellent bar meals. Not so very far away, the clear waters of the Coln flow by and fishing here can be tremendous fun. In Fossebridge, we find the Fossebridge Inn, an ivy-clad building standing on the Fosse Way where it crosses the River Coln. The Bridge Bar dates back to the eighteenth century and is delightful, whilst the rooms are comfortable. This is a good value hotel with much charm. More excellent hotels from which to organise your fishing trip can be found in Bibury. Bibury Court (0285) 740337 is a fine place with a beautiful setting and a well recommended restaurant. The Swan Hotel (028574) 204 has its own spring which feeds into the River Coln. It is another lovely setting to inspire all fishermen. Moving on to Fairford, we come across The Bull (0285) 712535 with a cosy beamed bar, log fires and friendly atmosphere.

Lambourn Downs offers the Lambourn River, much of which is preserved. However, if you are lucky enough to arrange a day's fishing here then a pub which might interest you is The Pheasant (0488) 39284—a good place for some bar snacks. In Kintbury, The Blue Boar (0635) 248236 has some comfortable rooms. Those who prefer more luxury should head for the Royal Oak, Yattendon (0635) 201325 nearby, a delightful mix of pub and inn with an outstanding restaurant. Many of these establishments will also be convenient for those who are fishing the Kennet, as is the Millwaters Hotel (0635) 528838 which has the benefit of fishing as well as over thirty rooms. Elcot Park (0488) 58100 has recently been refurbished and is very appealing. In Hungerford itself, there are several hotels and pubs. The Bear (0488) 682512 is the best known and is very popular with visitors and locals alike. The John O'Gaunt (0488) 683535 is a pleasant pub with good bedrooms and excellent bar snacks. The Bell (0672) 20230 at Ramsbury is a good, friendly free house to visit and reflect on your day. Marlborough is another delightful town and hotels to try here include the Ivy House (0672) 515333 and The Castle and Ball (0672) 515201 on the High Street.

There are a number of excellent trout fisheries in the London area and the neighbouring home counties and small hotels and pubs may appeal to the fisherman who is seeking an early start, or anticipating a late night. The tremendously named Dog House (0865) 390830 in Frilford Heath is certainly one for the notebook. Accommodation alongside the Thames can always be found. Jerome K. Jerome mentioned the historic Barley Mow at Clifton Hampton (086730) 7847 which remains a welcoming hostelry. In Abingdon itself, another hotel which boasts an historic waterside setting is the Upper Reaches (0235) 522311. If you are visiting the Welling

Trout Fishery then The Swan Diplomat at Streatley is outstanding and once again has a marvellous Thameside setting. Similarly, the Beetle and Wedge in Moulsford (0491) 651381 is a delightful hotel and restaurant, whilst those seeking a first rate hotel should try Pennyhill Park (0276) 71774 in Bagshot. This has a very good restaurant too. Visitors to Church Hill Farm should consider the Bell at Windslow (029671) 2741, a delightful bar and some very cosy bedrooms make this an ideal stopping place. The Bricklayers Arms at Flaunden is a pleasant place for a pint and The Greyhound at Chalfont St Peter (0753) 883404 is also popular and has some satisfactory accommodation. In Chenies the Bedford Arms (09278) 3301 is a fine hotel for those who are seeking good value accommodation.

Essex has a number of well stocked waters and Hanningfield Water which is situated due south of Chelmsford, is surrounded by some good pubs. The Hoop in Stock is renowned for its good value bar food and well kept real ales and The Gardener's Arms in Loghton is also popular. Good value accommodation is less easy to find but the Haybridge Mont House in Ingatestone (0277) 355355 is extremely well run and has a pleasant atmosphere. Better value perhaps is Ye Old White House at Burnham-on-Crouch (0621) 782106. Visitors to Ardleigh should visit the Marlborough Head (0206) 323124 in Dedham, an outstanding hotel, or for real sophistication try Le Maison Talbooth (0206) 322367—an outstanding hotel and restaurant. Alternatively, The Angel Inn in Stoke by Nayland (0206) 263245 is a beautifully restored village inn with pleasant bedrooms and excellent bar food. Visitors to Chelmes should consider The Swan at Thaxted (0371) 830321 while visitors to Cooks Farm should note The Oak House, Axbridge (0934) 732444.

Surrey also has a number of good fishing opportunities for the resident members of the stockbroker shire and the capital. Although many consider Surrey to be a suburb of London, it does have some beautiful countryside. It also has numerous good pubs. The Crown at Chidingfold (042879) 2255 offers some pleasant bed and breakfast accommodation, as does The King's Arms, Ockley (0306) 711224. Another good base for the numerous stillwaters is Lybble Hill Hotel (0428) 51251 in Haslemere which is a superb former farmhouse converted to a welcoming hotel. The Lamberhurst area is something of a mecca to many fishermen and there are many good pubs in the area with rooms too. Two excellent ones to note are The Rose and Crown, Mayfield (0435) 872200 and The Bell Inn at Burwash (0435) 882304. Good food can be enjoyed at the appropriately named Brown Trout in Lamberhurst (0892) 890312 or The Bull at Ticehurst (0580) 200586. People looking for rather more style and some excellent cuisine should note the Spindlewood Country House Hotel (0580) 200430, an altogether grander affair.

South east of here, is Tenterten, a pretty Kentish village, where all lovers of good food should try the Three Chimneys at Biddenden (0580) 291472 or The Bell at Smarden (023377) 283 which also has pleasant rooms. Finally, The White Dog Inn at Eashurst Green (058083) 264 is an extremely pleasant place to stay when in this area.

If you are heading for the Arundel area, once again you have a good choice of establishments but The Spread Eagle (0730) 816911 in Midhurst or The Norfolk Arms at Arundel (0903) 882101 are both excellent.

Artist: Spencer Coleman FISHING FROM THE BANK Courtesy of Rosenstiel's

Lakedown is a premier still water trout fishery. Situated in a secluded Wealden valley with scenic views and no visible habitation, the fishery consists of four picturesque lakes covering an area in excess of 20 acres, specifically designed for fly fishing. Each lake is well stocked with rainbow and brown trout with sizes ranging from 1 1/2 lbs to 20lbs. Fishing is from 8.00 am to sunset with day, half day and evening tickets available. The catch limit is five fish on a full day ticket. All fish are to be killed.

No fish should be returned to the water once caught.

Also available for self catering fishing trips and vacations is a four bedroomed Scandia Hus with lounge, kitchen, utility room, bathroom, shower etc. which sleeps eight people. The Hus is situated within 50 yards of the lakes, overlooking the fishery and set within woodland.

Minimum hire period is for three nights and four anglers. Anglers are charged £65 per night (which includes a five fish day ticket). All non-angling wives are free.

Lakedown is within easy driving distance of Brighton (30 miles), Eastbourne (20 miles), Hastings (18 miles) and is one hour and 15 minutes from central London. Lakedown is available for hire all year round.

All bookings for fishing or accommodation please contact: Alan Bristow or Dove Grant
Lakedown Fishery
Swife Lane
Broad Oak
Heathfield
East Sussex TN21 8UX
Tel: (0435) 883449

SOUTH WEST PENINSULA

South West Peninsula

149

For all the trials and tribulations that can be attributed to the advent of motorway driving it has to be said that it makes getting to places like the South West much easier, providing of course there are no road works to hold things up! It is perfectly possible for anyone living in London or the Midlands to be on Exmoor in three and a half hours or less. After leaving the M5 at Junction 27 one can afford to drive at a more leisurely pace and take the A396, which follows the course of the Exe and then north of Bampton a left turn on to the B3222 will take you to Dulverton and on to the heart of Exmoor.

The Exe & the Barle

Serious fishing on the Exe begins at Dulverton. In recent times it has become rather a summer and autumn river with September being the best month. The Exe has become predominantly a spate river and summer fishing especially this far up depends on rain but can be very good, with grilse averaging around 5lb and salmon between 8lb and 12lb. Flies such as the Black Great, Tupps, Greenwells Clergy and Blue Nun are popular choices.

The Carnarvon Arms Hotel (0398) 23302 has five miles of fishing on the Exe and its main tributary, the Barle. It has been a sporting hotel for many years and looking at an advertisement in the *Anglers Diary* for 1928, little seems to have changed apart from the telephone number which in those days was Dulverton 2 ! It still has a billiard room and livery stables as it had then. These days it can also offer guests a day's shooting and the West Somerset Polo Club plays on the hotel meadows. Set in the midst of Negley Farson country, both the Exe and the Barle are typically moorland rivers with clear and bright shallow runs between the pools. The wild brownies are usually excellent fighters and average two or three to the pound. Salmon range in size from 3lb grilse, to the 8lb-12lb summer and autumn fish. Fished on a strict rota system, the different beats offer a wide variety of fishing to suit all age groups and abilities. Salmon fishing on the Exe costs from between £12 and £25 per day and £100-£130 per week for residents of the hotel. Non-residents can get permits but the prices are doubled. Whilst the droughts of the last three years have affected catches, last year's numbers represented a slight improvement on the previous year. Trout fishing on both the Exe and the Barle costs between £7 and £12 per day, with any fishing beyond four days provided free. Non-residents can fish for £20 a day. Popular flies include Black Gnat, Pheasant Tail and Kite's Imperial.

The Barle is the most important tributary of the Exe and flows through the heart of Exmoor Forest. The Exmoor Forest Hotel at Simonsbath (064383) 341 can offer guests fishing on eight and a half miles of the Barle and a small stretch of the Bray. Fishing for non-residents costs £8 a day. Some of the fishing takes some getting to and it is rather rocky in places so good boots or stout shoes are essential. However, like all things that require an effort, it is well worthwhile. South Molton AC also has water on the Bray with a day's fishing costing £5.

Downstream just above Hawkridge are the picturesque Tarr Steps which appear on so many calendars and boxes of chocolates, but this is not surprising for they capture the spirit of English countryside at its best. The Tarr Steps Hotel at Hawkridge (0643) 85293 has three miles of fishing, most of which is double-banked and free to guests. It is good to hear that salmon catches are on the increase and 1992 the best recent year, saw ninety-three fish grassed from this water. The proprietor, Mr D. Keane, can also arrange fishing on the Exe and shooting for guests. The Fishing Tackle shop in Dulverton's High street can steer the under sixteens towards some free water exclusively for them. An NRA licence is required but no grown-ups is the rule and that includes Peter Pans! John Sharpe of J.S. Sporting has seven miles of fishing on the Exe and the Haddeo and a nice one and three quarter acre lake stocked with rainbows. The Haddeo is the small river that drains Wimbleball Reservoir and compensation flows help to keep a reasonable water level. The cost of fishing on this stretch of the Middle Exe is £10 for trout and between £18 and £25 for salmon according to season, with tuition also available.

By the time the Exe reaches Tiverton the valley has widened out and from here to the sea the river, which is the longest in the area, strolls through rich and fertile parkland until it flows into the estuary near Exeter and finally into the sea between Exmouth and Dawlish Warren. The Tiverton Fly Fishing Club owns half a mile of the Exe and leases a further half-mile from the NRA where the cost is £3.30 a day, with August being the best month for salmon. The club also has three and a half miles of fly-only trout fishing on the Knightshayes Estate Water. This concession was granted by the late Sir John Amory to residents within Tiverton Borough. The estate however retains the salmon rights.

Five miles or so south of Tiverton is the village of Bickleigh where the Fishermans Cot (0884) 855289 has a quarter of a mile for guests. The NRA own three miles of the Exe and the Exeter Angling Centre (0392) 436404 will be able to give you further information about this water. Exeter City Council also own some water but it has to be said that it is not of the very highest quality, besides with so much fishing in lovely countryside being readily available, I would rather fish there than near a town.

The Teign

The Teign begins its life as the North and South Teign high up on Dartmoor. These small streams join forces just west of Chagford and between there and Steps Bridge the river tumbles through a wooded gorge. Fingle Bridge is a popular beauty spot and vantage point from which to see the river. Down to just south of Mortonhampstead the river is referred to as the Upper Teign and from there down to Newton Abbot is the Lower Teign. It is not a big river and so easy to cover and is also one which will delight the spring fisherman for at that time of the year the banks are thick with daffodils particularly around Clifford Bridge. There is good brown trout, sea-trout and salmon fishing to be had here. Permits for the Upper Teign Fishing Association's water may be had from the Anglers Rest at Finglebridge (0647) 21287 or James Bowden and Son of Chagford (0647) 433271. Chagford Weir provides a good holding pool and it is essential to book as only two permits a day are issued. A combined salmon and sea-trout ticket costs £12 and a permit for brown trout costs only £3 a day. Sea-trout offer particularly good sport here and many fishermen mark the fish in daylight and return to stalk them at night.

The Mill End Hotel at Chagford (0647) 432282 has just under half a mile, which is free to guests and fishing can also be arranged on six miles of the Upper Teign Fishing Association Water. The Great Tree Hotel (0647) 432491 have access to a two and a half mile stretch of the Teign for two to four rods. This stretch is excellent for sea-trout, and the hotel has a 'REFIS' indtructor for beginners and advanced! Mrs C. Thatcher (0647) 52805 at the Ryecroft Fishery issues evening, day, weekly and season permits. This one mile stretch of double-bank fishing is first class and it is advisable to book as it is very popular. A day's permit for the Lower Teign Fishing Association's water can be had for £10 (£5 juniors) from the secretary, Mr P. Knibbs of Shaldon (0626) 873612 and from Drum Sports in Courtenay Street, Newton (0626) 65333. The Salmon season runs from 1st February to 30th September and the Seatrout season from 15th March to 30th September.

The West Dart

The West Dart's source is on the moor above the famous prison at Princetown. It joins the East Dart at Dartmoor and much of the river is owned by the Duchy of Cornwall. Below Dartmoor the river tumbles down a wooded valley and leaves the moor at Buckfastleigh to flow to its estuary at Totnes and the sea at Dartmouth, under the guard of the famous naval academy. This is good fly water and its tributaries also fish well. There is a delightful reach on the Blackbrook, a tributary of the West Dart which can produce pre-life hatches of duns where you can have the fun of fishing to rising trout, though success, of course, depends on whether you can match the hatch. The Prince Hall Hotel (0822) 89403 issues permits for the West Dart as does the Two Bridges Hotel (0822) 89581 where the river runs through the hotel grounds.

Below Dartmeet at Holne, the Church House Inn (03643) 208 issue NRA licences and Duchy permits and make a point of putting visitors in touch with experienced locals. This is particularly helpful as there is a lot of water and advice on likely spots and flies will save you a long walk and a boring day. Just downstream at Ashburton the Holne Chase Hotel (0364) 3471 has a nice stretch of just over a mile of single-bank fishing upstream from Holne Bridge, which has five pools and is free to hotel guests. This is fast flowing water which fishes best on the fall after a spate. This fishing is in a wooded valley and the ability to spey or roll cast will save you a lot of time from trying to retrieve flies from trees.

The Perfect Spot (South West Water)

The Dart

There are many, especially those who live in the area, who consider the Dart to be the most beautiful river in the South West. It is a spate river whose occasional floods can scour the banks of vegetation, but this of course is on the upper reaches and below Dartington Hall the river is much more sedate. This is another river which alas suffered the ravages of UDN and the spring run is sadly now almost non-existent and July onwards is the best time. It is particularly good sea-trout water however. The Dart Angling Association has five and a half miles of good sea-trout water. A day's salmon fishing costs £12 and sea-trout £10 while the charge for brown trout is £8. Weir Pool is a local favourite and in 1992 permits were available from C. Harris of Prismatic in Totnes (0803) 867154, though it is worth checking with the Totnes Information Centre (0803) 863168 as permit issuers do change. From a family point of view, there is the added attraction of a ride on a steam train for the Dart Valley Railway runs close to the river between Totnes and Buckfastleigh.

The Avon

West of here, entering the sea at Thurlestone, is the Avon, one of the better, what I would term 'minor league', rivers in the area. It is the sort of water that produces fifty or more salmon and around two hundred sea-trout a year. The Erme produces a handful of migrating fish but the Plym and Tavy are another matter. The Tavy rises in Cranmere Pool, that strange spot which also sees the start of the Dart and that good tributary of the Torridge, the Okement. The Plym produces under fifty salmon a year but it averages over three hundred sea-trout a season and some years have yielded double this amount. The Tavy is slightly better averaging around four hundred sea-trout and over a hundred salmon. All these rivers are very good dry fly waters.

Fishing for sea-trout on these rivers is great fun. The water is crystal clear and requires a very careful approach, as it is very easy to put them down. A thorough reconnaissance during the day is essential and with polaroids and a stealthy approach you can see the fish and mark the lies. It also gives you the opportunity to work out how you are going to fish the water at night. Casting at night confuses many a fisherman as it is impossible to see what is going on! There is a natural tendency to bring the tip of the rod back too far which can lead to lost flies. To cast too quickly will cause the line to land in a heap and make for wind knots in the cast. Night fishing is no different from day fishing in that to be successful the fly has got to be presented in the right manner and the best thing to do is to practice away from where you will be fishing. Once you have mastered the

art, the memory of a successful night's sea-trout or peal fishing as they are locally known will cheer many a winter's evening. Numerous tacklists in the area can be of help and supply day permits for the Tavy; for example, Barkells in Tavistock (082261) 2198. The cost for the fisherman is £10 per day and trout fishing is £3 per day.

The East Lyn

On the north coast of Devon is a small river of just some six miles in length that fishes very well and is inexpensive whilst set in beautiful countryside. What more could you want apart from knowing its name! It is the East Lyn and until recently seems to have been a well kept local secret. The river is formed by several small Exmoor streams. Weir Water and Chalk Water continue to form Oare water which is joined by Badgworthy Water at Malmsmead and this is the start of the East Lyn. It is very much a spate river which drops and clears very rapidly after rain and as with any river of a similar character it is all a matter of hitting it at the right time. From Brendon Bridge down to Rockford through a deep wooded gorge, which, though a local beauty spot, is no place to wander about at night and for sea-trout it is advisable to pick a good pool before the light goes and stay there. This part is the Glenthorne Fishery while below Rockford down to Lynmouth is the Watersmeet Fishery which has the best salmon fishing. This belongs to the National Trust and like Glenthorne is administered by the NRA. This white water tumbles from pool to pool, some of which are quite large and others pocket handkerchief size. The spinner and worm are the most successful methods and the fly only really works on the large slower pools. There is a daily limit of two salmon and six sea-trout and permits can be had from the Brendon House Hotel at Brendon (05987) 206.

The Taw

Driving south west from Lynmouth on the A39, is the road to Barnstaple and the much better known Taw. This river which rises on Dartmoor is, at fifty miles, one of the longer ones in the region. It and the neighbouring Torridge have long been regarded as the most important Devon salmon rivers. Indeed they are recorded in the Domesday Book where they were valued at 25 shillings a year. In the 1950s, rods were accustomed to taking 2000 salmon a year while a further 3000 were netted. Sadly, catches have declined since then but they are both good salmon and sea-trout waters as is the Taw's main tributary, the Mole at Eggesford near Chumleigh. The Fox and Hounds (0769) 80345 has seven miles of fishing on the Taw and also has some water on the Little Dart. The cost of a day's salmon, brown-trout and sea-trout fishing is £18.50. To help get beginners started the hotel has a three quarter of an acre novice pond which is well stocked.

Downstream at Umberleigh there is the well known Rising Sun (0769) 60447 which has been looking after anglers for many a year. Its three and a half miles are divided into seven beats which produce good numbers of summer sea-trout and autumn salmon and a fair few fish in spring, although the spring run is not what it was. Day tickets for residents are priced at £17.50 and for non-residents £25. The West of England Centre of Angling (0805) 23256 also has water on the Taw, upstream of Umberleigh at £25-£30 for a daily ticket. Lower down is the Barnstaple and District Angling Associations water which extends to some two miles and it also has trout fishing on the Yeo. Four permits are issued a day but not for weekends or Bank Holidays and they can be obtained from the Secretary, Mr A. J. Penny (0271) 73241, or the Devon Angling Centre in Barnstaple (0271) 45191.

The Torridge

The source of the Torridge is not far from the picturesque seaside town of Clovelly near the border with Cornwall. After a tortuous course, full of bends and loops, the river doubles back on itself and flows into the Taw estuary at Bideford. Throughout its length it flows through rock rolling farmland and in spring its banks abound with daffodils and primroses. This river also has a famous sporting hotel at Sheepwash, the Half Moon Inn (040923) 376, which has twelve miles of very good fishing. Spinning is allowed in spring—which has seen fish of up to 19lb but fly only is the rule after May 1st. It is not a large river and an eleven-foot rod will enable you to cover the water. Popular salmon flies are the Yellow Torrisch, Silver Doctor and Thunder and Lightening while the Silver Butcher, Peter Ross and Connemara Black are favourite choices for sea-trout. The fishing is easy to get at as the banks have been cleared on all beats. It also offers excellent trout fishing and its waters are stocked with good brownies of around the one pound mark.

Group Captain P. Norten-Smith (08053) 317 owns the Little Warham Fishery at Beaford. This one and a half mile stretch of single-bank fishing is divided into four beats and there are four named pools on each beat. This, like the Half Moon's stretch, is prime water. However, for those wishing to fish the upper reaches both the Devil's Stone Inn at Shebbear (040928) 210 and the Woodford Bridge Hotel at Milton Damerel (040926) 481 have their own water. Simon Gawesworth (0805) 23256 provides tuition and expert advice in conjunction with the hotel, which has some fishing rights on the hotel. A few miles south of Beaford on the B3220, is Winkleigh and the Stafford Moor Fishery (08054) 360. This well known stillwater consists of two lakes of fourteen acres and eight acres and produces some very big rainbows. A stillwater of a larger size at forty-one acres is Wistlandpound Reservoir (03987) 372 which is north east of Barnstaple, and a day costs £5.50.

The Tamar

The A30 is the main road to Cornwall and its sandy beaches and sailing creeks. Just east of Launceston this road passes through the village of Lifton. To the casual driver there is nothing remarkable about it, houses line the road on both sides and on one side is a pleasant looking hotel. This ivy-clad building is the Arundell Arms (0566) 84666, which is known to fishermen around the world as a hotel for fishermen run by fishermen. Anne Voss Bark has fished the hotels waters for many years. Expert tuition is on hand and the hotel runs many courses. There are courses for beginners, advanced salmon and trout casting, fly fishing and refreshers to brush up your technique. In winter, the hotel can arrange a day's shooting, including driven snipe. The Arundell Arms has twenty miles of fishing on the Tamar and its tributaries, the Lyd, Carey, Wolf and Thrushel. The salmon that run up the hotel's water on the Tamar and the Lyd average 10lb but there is always the chance of a twenty-pounder, while the average sea-trout is between 3/4lb and 1lb 8oz, but there are a number of larger fish up to 6lb. There is very good trout fishing to be had here and dry fly works particularly well. The trout average two or three to the pound but are genuinely wild and are prime fighters. When the rivers are in spate, excellent sport can be had on the hotel's Twynhay Lake. This three acre water is just down the road from the hotel and is stocked with rainbows and some browns up to 9lb. The water is clear and quite deep and nymphing with a long leader is often a productive method.

The beautiful Endsleigh House at Milton Abbot (0822) 87248 is set in seventy acres and is owned by a syndicate; the Endsleigh Fishing Club. For most of the year it is run as a hotel and guests can fish the hotels nine miles of double-bank on the Lower Tamar. The cost of a day varies between £20 and £42 and fly is the most successful method. The seven year average for this water is two hundred and twenty-eight fish.

The Lamerhooe Lodge Fishings on the Lower Tamar have recently been bought by the River Beauly Fishings Company Ltd. (0463) 782215. This delightful beat is set in a beautiful wooded valley and consists of one and three quarter miles of double-bank fishing with eighteen named pools. It has been in private hands, with only three owners since the sixteenth century and the fishing has always been retained for them and their guests. The Beauly team have made substantial improvements to the river and the pools and fly only is the rule. The fishing is now available to let to four rods who can stay at the company's Lammerhooe Lodge which has five double bedrooms and is set in sixty acres. A ghillie is on hand to help guests.

The Bude Angling Association has trout fishing on the upper reaches of the Tamar and the River Claw. Permits cost £3 a day and can be had from Bude Sports (0288) 352943. The Tamar is a small river this far up as it runs through rolling farmland and produces fine trout of about ten or eleven ounces and the odd grayling in winter. Nearby, for those who enjoy stillwater fishing, is Upper Tamar lake. This is a natural stocked fishery and provides fine fishing and excellent value for money.

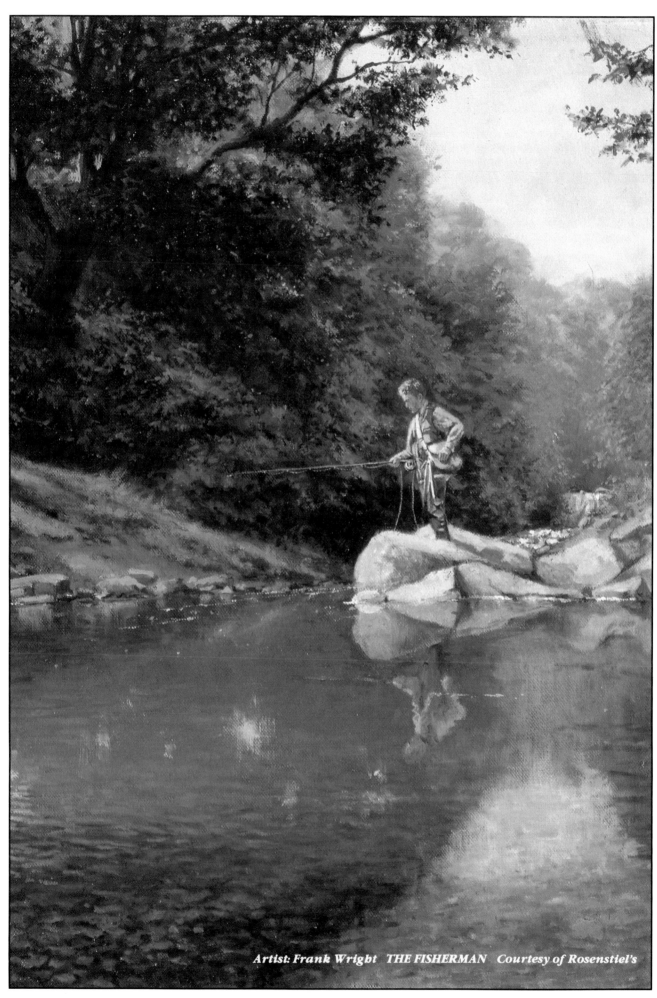

Artist: Frank Wright THE FISHERMAN Courtesy of Rosenstiel's

The Fowey

The best sea-trout water in the area, and indeed in the South West, is the Fowey. Although like every river the last year or so has been disappointing, in the past it has yielded between 1500 and 2000 or more fish in a good year, including around 300 salmon. On this small river, which has few pools and tumbles down wooded valleys, fly fishing can be difficult, though a flashy fly which resembles a small fish such as the Silver Invicta may be very successful. Most rods however, will be spinning and Rapallas are a popular choice. The river flows through the ground of the National Trust's beautiful property, Lanhydrock House and permits for here cost £5 a day or £15 a week and can be had from the Trust's regional office or Lanhydrock (0208) 74281. Slightly more expensive at £7 a day or £25 a week is the water belonging to the Liskeard and District Angling Association, but they do have six miles of it. Indeed, the Association has some twenty five miles of fishing in all, including stretches of the Camel, Lynhea, Inny, Looe and Seaton. Permits for here and the two miles controlled by the Lostwithiel Fishing Association can be had from Ken Raymond's Fishing Tackle in Liskeard (0579) 47324. The Fowey produces big sea-trout that can be up to 8lb, while its average salmon is between 8lb and 12lb, although in 1990 a thirty-eight pounder was found dead, beached on a bank.

At Bolventor is the Jamaica Inn of Du Maurier fame and from Fowey West we are in the romantic hidden creeks of Cornwall, which the author also immortalised. It is an area which abounds in picturesque place names like St Just in Roseland, Praze-an-beeble, Nancegollan, Mevagissey and Indian Queens, so called because the tragic Red Indian Princess Pocahontas, stayed there. On the north coast is the River Camel, which hit the headlines after aluminium sulphate was inadvertently released into the domestic water system and then flushed out into the river. As a result, a large proportion, 60,000 was the estimated figure, of the young fish stock were killed. Time will tell how badly this has affected the river. Accidents by their nature are chance happenings, but like the 1991 spillage of 25,000 gallons of slurry into the Tamar, a very short time can undo many years' work. In 1990, the level of rod caught salmon was relatively normal and saw three fish of over 20lb. This river is the converse of the Fowey for it is a better salmon water than it is sea-trout, though those that are caught are large fish.

The Camel

The Camel rises near the Fowey and this clear, fast-flowing river has a course of some twenty-five miles before reaching the estuary at Padstow. The best fishing is from

Lamerhooe Fisherings (Beauly Fishing Company)

Trecarne down to the tide and there are about a hundred and fifty pools in this stretch. This is a river for winter fishing with a good salmon run from October through to December. Wadebridge and District Angling Association has four and a half miles which is best suited to spinning. Mepps always do well, as do a local creation called Muppets. Permits can be had from North Cornwall Angling Centre in Wadebridge. Bodmin Angling Association (0208) 75513 has eleven miles of the Camel and a short stretch of the Fowey. The scenic Camel Trail runs beside the river for several miles from Padstow to Wenford. This smooth sanded path is the track of the former Bodmin to Adebridge railway line. Further down the coast at St Mawgan, which is just above Newquay, trout fishing can be had on the River Menalhyl.

Smaller Rivers

To the east of here are several good small rivers. The Lynher rises on Bodmin Moor and joins the Tamar estuary opposite Plymouth. The twin rivers, East and West Looe, have their sources near Liskeard and join shortly before reaching the sea at Looe. Still smaller is the Tiddy which enters the sea near Devonport. These rivers produce the occasional salmon and good brownies, but their main claim to fame is that they are excellent sea-trout fisheries so don't ignore them! The Tavy is one of the several rivers that have their source in Cranmere Pool on Dartmoor and flows through Tavistock on its way to Plymouth, where in the estuary it meets up with the Tamar. It is an excellent salmon and sea-trout water.

South West Waters

Just the other side of the A396 from Dulverton is Wimbleball Lake. This is the third largest reservoir in the area and is administered by South West Water, whose dedicated team of rangers do a great job running all the company's fisheries. They have a busy life, as several of their waters have over 100,000 visitors a year, drawn by the nature reserves and sailing as well as fishing. Wimbleball is fairly new, having opened for fishing in 1980, but has built up an impressive reputation and the Benson and Hedges competition heats are held here. Near the dam wall it is 160 feet deep, but the best fishing is to be held at the shallower northern end and Cow Moor is a favourite spot. Boats are available and there is one which is specially equipped for handicapped anglers. The lake's 374 acres have a natural stock of brownies which run up to 4lb and are regularly stocked with rainbows, for which the current record is 10lb 4oz. Before setting out it is worth calling Bob Lunk, the ranger, to ensure that it is not a competition day. Nearby is the Exe Valley Fisheries (0398) 23328 which has been a trout hatchery and rearing farm since 1885. This is a put-and-take water which is just the place for a beginner. The cost of a five-fish day is £5.50 plus £1.30 per pound of fish caught and they will clean, smoke and freeze your fish if you want.

The village of Oakford is not far from Bampton and is just off the main road to Barnstaple and here you will find Bellbrook Valley Trout Fishery (03985) 292. Peter Swaby's fishery is as pleasant a stillwater as you could wish to find. Its three lakes and two pools are in a beautiful valley and the old Iron Mill Stream and adjacent woodland supply an abundance of natural feed for the fish. Professional tuition is available as is bed and breakfast accommodation at the fishery farmhouse. The cost of a day on this noted Troutmaster Water is £20 with a four fish limit. Half-day tickets are available, or you can pay less and then pay £1.50 per pound of fish caught. One lake is for large fish only, the minimum weight is 3lb and you can have a half day for £17 with a two fish limit, or a full three fish day for £25, or a four fish limit day for £30. These big fish are fine fighters and not like the underweight submarines found on some fisheries. To give you some idea of what may be in store, Bellbrook holds the South West record with a superb 17lb 12oz fish taken in 1988.

A fifteen minute drive south west of Chagford will take you into the heart of Dartmoor and Fernworthy Reservoir. This is a beautiful away from it all spot where you will only meet fellow fishermen or ramblers. The seventy-six acre water is very established, having been created fifty years ago and with its moorland setting will remind many of a Scottish loch. It is stocked on a regular basis with brown trout which go up to 4lb and may succumb to the allure of a Hawthorne early in the season, while Daddies, Black Marilous and Sedge Patterns work well later on. The cost of a day with a four fish limit is £13 and if you want to book a boat it is advisable to ring the ranger, Mr John Baker (0647) 432440, in advance.

Approximately ten miles east of Fernworthy and a quarter of an hours drive north of Bovey Tracey, are Kennick and Tottiford Reservoirs where £11 buys you a six-fish day ticket. This is another beautiful but remote water and is regularly stocked with rainbows and has a stock of native brownies. The best rainbow to date is 5lb 14oz and there are rumours of brown trout of just under double figures. Hawthorns and Daddies do well here as do Montanas and Vivas. This water is only twenty-three feet at its deepest/widest point so it is possible to fish all of it.

If you prefer big fish on a smaller and more private water you should try John Hern's Watercress Farm Trout Fishery at Chudleigh (0626) 852168 which is about seven miles north of Newton Abbot. The three gin clear lakes are fed by springs and stocked on a daily basis with rainbows of between 1¼lb and 15lb. Day tickets are available but booking is essential as the number of rods is limited. A day's fishing will cost either £18.50 with a five fish limit or £6.50 plus £1.55 per pound with a six fish limit. Other prices and variations are also offered.

Among other stillwaters in this area are the Avon Dam and Meldon reservoirs, where fishing is free to NRA licence holders—although I can't help feeling that this reflects the quality of the fishing. If you enjoy reservoir fishing the 150 acre Burrator Reservoir near Yelverton is likely to be more productive, and a day ticket costs a modest £3.50.

With over 730 acres of water, Roadford Lake is set to become one of the country's leading brown trout fisheries. This magnificent, meandering stretch of water has been stocked with fingerlings which have grown on to become as near to wild fish as is possible. Brownies in excess of 3lb have regularly been recorded and are all perfectly proportioned. The vast reaches of shallow water will offer the cream of this crop, and with over half the fishable bank side consisting of such water the challenge for the sports fisherman is obvious. The A30 passes within half a mile of the lake. The season here is from 14th April to 12th October, fishing is fly only and there is a bag limit of four fish over ten inches. Any smaller fish must be returned. A day here will cost £12.50.

Heading west from Launceston the A30 takes you through the heart of Bodmin Moor. Just before you reach Bolventor there is a small turning on the left which will take you to Liskeard. This minor road follows the upper reaches of the Fowey over Smallacombe Downs and Siblyback Reservoir is close at hand. This 140 acre water is widely considered the second best of South West Waters' first class stocked rainbow fisheries. Every year sees some good trout caught here and the current record is 13lb 2oz. There is a natural head of brownies and permits can be had from the Ranger, Reg England (0579) 342366, who can also advise you on flies and where the fish are! Reg also looks after neighbouring Colliford which is brown trout only and has many pleasant bays.

Porth is a thirty-eight acre stocked lake near Newquay. Not far off the A394, south of Penryn, is Stithians Reservoir. Permits cost £5.50 and can be had from the water sports centre or the shop in Stithians village.

Artist C W Crocker THE FISHERMAN Courtsey of Rosenstiel's

Scattered throughout the beautiful landscape of the South West peninsula are a wide range of reservoirs and water parks, ranging from Argal near Falmouth, set among rolling hills near the coast, to the wild moorland setting of Fernworthy on Dartmoor and Wimbleball on Exmoor.

These varied and beautiful waters offer a wide choice of top quality fishing.

The company's Ranger service manages these waters to ensure that you get the most from your visit.

Fishing from boat or bank is available at lakes such as kennick, Fernworthy, Wimbleball, Siblyback, and Argal. Roadford Lake, near Okehampton, has recently been opened and offers superb bank fishing for wild brown trout in magnificent surroundings.

Our aim is to provide a wide choice of trout fishing across the region.

Stocked rainbow trout provide lake fly fishing at affordable prices. Fish are trickle stocked throughout the year from top quality fish farms to ensure fish are in tip top conditions at all times.

Sizes of fish stocked average 1lb plus, with occasional stocking of larger fish up to 4lbs plus.

Budget trout water provide a challenging day's sport at low prices. Fish stocking takes place to enhance and improve natural stocks.

A 'catch and release' scheme gives anglers greater flexibility enabling smaller fish to be returned, and the whole day is used to reach the bag limit.

Our premier brown trout fishing is stocked brown trout at Fernworthy, where loch style fishing is offered in the grand surroundings of Dartmoor.

A leaflet giving further information.
South West Water Leisure Services
peninsula House
Rydon Lane
Exeter EX2 7HR
Tel: (0392) 443362

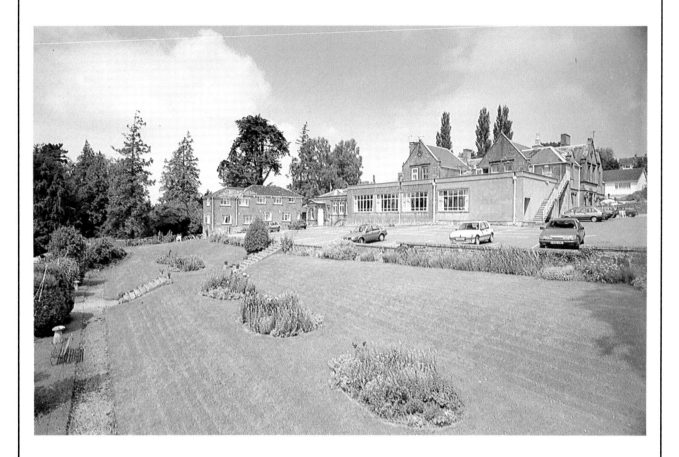

This is a hotel that looks after its guests in the finest country house tradition. For the fisherman everything is provided right down to the packed lunch to be enjoyed at sea on the hotel's own boat, the 'Little Shrub'.

Note well: guests desiring a safe return to the shore should note that the food will more than likely have been prepared by their skipper the hotel chef. Parties ideally four to six in number are handsomely rewarded with a fine day out and rods and bait can be provided by the hotel if required.

The journey to and from Lyme Regis, where the 'Little Shrub' is moored (courtesy of hotel mini-bus) is a well travelled route in the history of the hotel. The present building has its origins in 'Crosses' a private house dating back to the seventeenth century and it was around this edifice (now the imposing Victorian house) that the hotel as it stands today was created by H.H. Shepherd who bought the house in the 1850s. It is believed that the finance for this work came from the export of Hessian and Jute to both sides in the American Civil War, materials from Shepherd's factory on a site now occupied by Clarks Shoes! The sea also played its part in finishing the

house with ornate Italian marble courtesy of a Lyme Bay shipwreck.

The decline of the Hessian and Jute industry heralded a change in fortune for the house and it lay unoccupied for three years, reopening in 1932 as the West Country Club. Today's owners Stuart and Liz Shepherd may be no relation to the entrepreneurial H.H. Shepherd, but they have brought in their own way a great wealth of hospitality and service to the Hotel, which they have managed for thirty years. During this period and particularly recently, there has been much refurbishment work and the addition of extensive banqueting and conference facilities. This has, however, not been to the detriment of the personal service and attention lavished on residents of the hotel's fourteen bedrooms.

Modern facilities and a reputation for high standards of cuisine are two further factors to be considered when selecting a base to tour from in this area and the Shrubbery does not disappoint on either score. With an atmosphere best described as both 'relaxing and vital' this former Victorian gentleman's residence is perfect for the modern traveller.

The Shrubbery Hotel
Ilminster
Somerset
TA19 9AR
Tel: (0460) 52108
Fax: (0460) 53660

The craggy coastline of Cornwall has little in common with the moorland scenery of inland Devon, but both counties have stunning countryside. The fishing found here is both accessible and often excellent, and for the fishing fraternity who have not yet discovered this area, with its remote beauty, you are urged to visit. Some of the finest fishing hotels are situated within the compass of the south west, so let us consider these fine establishments, and a few others besides that will offer a friendly welcome after a day on the moors. The Exe, which rises in Exmoor, flows through some stunning moorland and we start our journey with one of its well known tributaries, the Barle. Simonsbath reveals the Simonsbath House Hotel (064383) 259, a tranquil spot and extremely comfortable. The Royal Oak Inn, Withypool (064383) 506 is also on the shortlist. It is a cosy hotel and a delight in which to stay. Log fires and a good restaurant all add to the ambience of this friendly establishment. The inn does not have its own water but can arrange fishing through contacts. The Tarr Steps (064 385) 293 at Hawkridge, near Dulverton is a fine place to stay for fishing on the Barle.

North of Dulverton, we find another gem, The Royal Oak (064385) 455, a delightful inn which dates back to the twelfth- century and sits in one of the most beautiful of Exmoor's many pretty villages. There is a great atmosphere here and, although fishing takes a back seat, the vast Wimbleball Lake is not far away and makes for an excellent day trip.

At Exbridge, the Anchor Inn (0398) 23433 only has a small stretch of the Exe but should not be forgotten. It is a very comfortable hotel with a friendly welcome and marvellous views of the river. It was tremendous to hear of some good salmon running in 1991 in these flowing waters. The hotel is also well situated for the Bellbrook Trout Fishery. South of Tiverton, a welcoming pub to put in the equation is The Trout at Bickleigh which has some accommodation.

The Teign also enjoys an immensely beautiful journey and once again a number of good opportunities arise for fishing. In its upper reaches, the river tumbles through the grounds of Gidleigh Park (0647) 432367, surely one of our finest hotels and restaurants. Fishing can be arranged by the hotel and if you are prepared to part with considerable amounts of hard earned cash you will enjoy a really wonderful stay. Chagford has a number of pleasant hotels. The Great Tree (0647) 432491 is an excellent place to stay and sample home grown produce from its own gardens. The Mill End Hotel (0647) 432282 also has delightful gardens which lead down to the Teign.

This hotel is thoroughly recommended. It is also convenient for Fernworthy Reservoir as is the Ring of Bells (0647) 40375 in North Bovey, a thirteenth-century inn with great character and some good value accommodation from which to explore the delights of Dartmoor. It is also very convenient for a visit to Kennick and Tottiford as is the Riverside Inn (0626) 832293 in Bovey Tracey, a welcoming and unpretentious establishment. In Kingsteignton, two fine establishments can be found: The Passage House (0626) 55515, which overlooks the Teign Valley, and the Old Rydon Inn (0626) 54626 which are both splendid.

The Dart is another delightful water. It flows through breathtaking scenery and travels through tree-bound territory and the wilder terrain of the upland moors. Here, amidst the bleak landscape of Dartmoor, we find The Prince Hotel (082289) 403 and The Two Bridges Hotel (082289) 581. Both hotels are comfortable and command breathtaking views of this marvellous scenery. Near to Holne there are two further possibilities. Firstly, the Church House, Holne (03643) 208—a listed medieval building with a truly beautiful setting. This is a superb place to stay when fishing the upper reaches of the Dart. The Holne Chase Hotel (03643) 471 is an attractive house with another superb setting. Some good fishing can be arranged here and the hotel is well worth visiting. Less grand but equally welcoming, is the excellent Sea-trout (080426) 274. Fishing on the Dart can be organised from here and the lounge bar will delight fishing enthusiasts. If you are planning a fishing trip in south west Devon, the Bedford Hotel in Tavistock (0822) 613221 is welcoming and a real pleasure to visit.

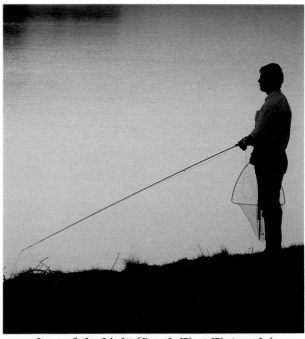

Last of the Light (South West Water plc)

North of Tavistock, we find a whole host of waters and the Tamar is just one celebrated example. Endsleigh House is also a good place to stay for those who are fishing the Tamar. The river cuts its way north through some beautiful scenery on the way to Launceston and nearby Lifton, so do visit the Royal at Horsebridge, a thoroughly unspoiled pub. The bridge, from which the river takes its name, was the first built over the Tamar and dates from 1437, a fascinating spot for a swiftie or two.

There are several celebrated fishing hotels in the country but there are very few that have the reputation and renown of the Arundell Arms, Lifton (0566) 84666. Rivers seem to congregate at its very door step and a splendid selection of fishing opportunities can be found here. The hotel has excellent facilities for the fisherman and inside, flagstones and rugs add to the friendly but unfussy atmosphere. This is an hotel that all fishermen should visit—it is a real treat. Not a fishing hotel as such, but another tremendous place to stay or to dine is the Lewtrenchard Manor (056683) 256, situated midway between the Thrushel and the Lyd.

The Taw and the Torridge are yet two further rivers for the angler to inspect. The Taw volunteers the Fox and Hounds Hotel (0769) 80345 which offers a great welcome to those planning many fishing forays. The Rising Sun at Umberleigh (0769) 60447 is a comfortable inn catering for the fisherman. Highbullen (0769) 540561 at Chittleham Holt is a sporting hotel which offers all manner of excellent sporting opportunities in addition to 1000 yards of fishing on the River Mole. The fishing is free to guests staying at the hotel.

The Black Horse at Torrington (0805) 22121 is an ancient public house and it is allegedly haunted. The Half Moon Inn at Sheepwash (040923) 376 not only has excellent fishing opportunities but also a delightful atmosphere and great character. Our final thought for Torridge is the Woodford Bridge Hotel, Milton Damerel (0409) 26481. Tuition and expert advice are available from the hotel, which has some fishing rights on the Torridge. The hotel has recently been upgraded, which has added to its charm whilst retaining its character. Assuming you feel, as we do, that a fishing foray on the Fowey is a good idea, you may be seeking a place or two in which to stay. The following ideas may be of help. The Punch Bowl Inn at Lanreath (0503) 20218 is a cosy place to stay, while lovers of history and intrigue will no doubt make a beeline for Jamaica Inn, a popular inn and tourist attraction. They should also consider the Royal Oak at Lostwithiel (0208) 872552, which has smugglers associations as well as good food and bedrooms. The Cormorant Hotel (072683) 3426 is a welcoming place and the bar has splendid views overlooking the river—an ideal base for any trip to this part of England.

The Camel, despite its pollution problems, runs through some delightful scenery and if you are wishing to stay nearby, The Cornish Arms (0208) 880263 with the Pendogget restaurant is a charming location. The Malsters Arms (020881) 2473 is also recommended for its good bar food. There are numerous hotels to be found in and around Newquay and if you are journeying this far down the country, perhaps for a family holiday, you should contact the local tourist board. Indeed, it is worth emphasising that the tourist boards are generally extremely helpful and a mine of useful local information.

For those interested in sea-fishing, the Shrubbery Hotel (0460) 52108 at Ilminster offers the finest accomodation and has its own boat—the Little Shrub..

Little Shrub (The Shrubbery Hotel)

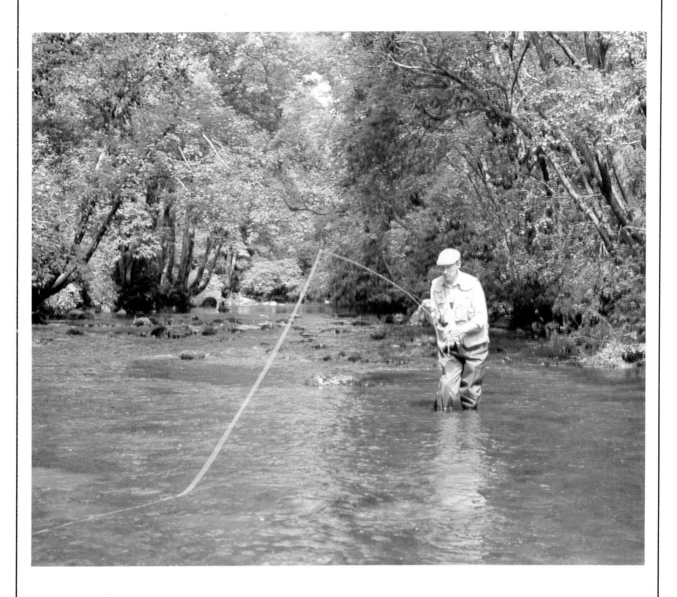

The River Teign flows through some of the most beautiful and unspoilt countryside in Devon. The fishing the Teign has to offer is varied. Between Chagford bridge and Steppes Bridge the angler can fish for moorland trout. Salmon and Sea trout begin to appear in the Upper Teign waters from about April, with greater numbers becoming available from the middle of June until the end of the season on 30th September. The hotel can arrange fishing for its guests on about fourteen miles of brown trout water and six miles of salmon and sea trout water.

The Mill End Hotel is a superb base for fishing. Immediately adjacent to the hotel are 600 yards of private bank and four pools for salmon and sea trout. Fernworthy and Hennock reservoirs, stocked with rainbow trout, are within easy driving distance. Mr Roddie Rae, a local expert and Upper Teign water bailiff, is available to tutor the inexperienced or act as a ghillie to skilled fishermen.

The Mill End hotel was formally a flour mill and its wheel still turns in the peaceful courtyard. Converted in 1929 the hotel has an atmosphere of a comfortable private house. All rooms have a private bathroom, telephone, colour television, hairdryer and other practical comforts.

To complete your day a superb dinner with fresh ingredients, carefully prepared on the premises the day you eat them - is the Mill End promise. An award winning cheese selection includes several local favourites as well as many from France. There are over a hundred wines listed and an interesting selection of Cognacs and Malt Whiskys.

For the non-fisherman Mill End is ideally situated for exploring Dartmoor. There is an excellent 18 hole golf course near by and opportunities to ride and shoot. There are many delightful walks on Dartmoor and National Trust properties to explore.

Mill End Hotel
Sandy Park, Chagford
Devon TQ13 8JN
Tel: (0647) 432282
Fax: (0647) 433106

This delightful country house was originally the Georgian Rectory of Hawkridge. Standing in over eight acres of slightly wild gardens and grounds, 800 feet above sea level, it commands extensive views of the river Barle and its valley.

The hotel takes its name from Tarr Steps, a cyclopean bridge of unhewn stone believed to date from the Bronze Age which is within 200 yards of the hotel. Three miles of trout and salmon fishing on the river Barle (both banks) are available free of charge to residents and the hotel offers three day beginners courses on fly fishing. The hotel also arranges shooting parties and riding, golf, squash and tennis are all available locally.

Every effort is directed towards maintaining an atmosphere of privacy, quiet luxury and friendliness. All principal rooms have a southern aspect with uninterrupted views of river, moor and woodland.

One can relax in a comfortable sitting room in front of an open log fire and enjoy a homely atmosphere. In the Georgian dining room we offer excellent food from a selective menu that changes daily. The food is tastefully served and of a consistently high standard. Our wines are carefully chosen and of good quality with value having been kept in mind. There is also an attractive, well stocked bar.

The sea is only three quarters of an hour drive from the hotel and the hotel enjoys a delightful situation for walkers with miles of uninhabited countryside in every direction. The Barle Valley is one of the most beautiful parts of Exmoor with an abundance of wildlife and rare flowers.

For those who wish to escape from the humdrum of life to the peace of the countryside, these settings provide the hotel with an unusual, almost unique atmosphere.

Tarr Steps Hotel
Hawkridge
Nr Dulverton
Somerset
TA22 9PY
Tel: (064 385) 293
Fax: (064 385) 218

The Two Bridges Hotel

Situated in the centre of Dartmoor there is arguably no more beautiful hotel on the moor. Nestling alongside the West Dart River there is excellent fishing to be had throughout the hotel's sixty acres of grounds. Here the traditional pleasure of the country can be enjoyed along with modern comforts in a Hotel where the best of both worlds are to be found.

Just to enter the Two Bridges is to embrace the feel of Olde England with huge log fires and the gleam of copper and brass. Outside the history of the area is revealed in stone circles, ancient encampments and by abandoned villages. The areas bounds with places of historical interest, cathedrals, abbeys and castles are all close by, as is the solitude of the moor, a walker's paradise, though guests preferring to explore on horseback can also be accommodated.

Returning to the hotel, the well appointed bedrooms and sumptuous bathrooms will satisfy the more demanding guest. So, it is hoped, will the cuisine which attracts Devonians from far and wide for Sunday lunch and weekend carveries, with, of course a vegetarian selection.

The elegant furnishings, first-class service and idyllic setting also combine to make the Two Bridges a perfect environment for that away from it all meeting or conference.

Whatever your pleasure enjoy it to the full in the company of Lesley and Philip Davies at the Two Bridges.

The Two Bridges hotel
Dartmoor
Devon
Tel: (0822) 890581
Fax: (0822) 890575

Set on a south facing hillside 700 feet up in the Dartmoor foothills in eighteen acres of its own woods and gardens, the Great Tree Hotel enjoys an idyllic, delightfully quiet and secluded location. There are spectacular views from the lounge which looks out across the gardens to the surrounding woods and hills, a view shared by most of the bedrooms.

The building was constructed originally as a hunting lodge about twenty miles away from its present position but was moved to the Great Tree estate in 1909 where it was used as a private residence for many years. The building still retains much of the colonial character of the original tea planter owners. A wide ornately carved oak staircase leads down from reception to a large and comfortable lounge with log fire and cosy adjoining bar. An elegant restaurant where the cut glass on the tables glints magically in the candlelight, serves a five course table d'hote dinner each evening. The menu which contains plenty of choice, is changed each day, is traditional in style and uses much local produce and vegetables from the hotel's own gardens. There is an extensive wine list very realistically priced to encourage guests to expand their experience of the vigneron's art. The whole ambience of the hotel is relaxed and informal and is a delightful place in which to unwind.

The river Teign is only a mile away and the hotel has leased a two and a half mile stretch of single bank fishing on the river below Fingle Bridge, a beat which has a very good record for sea trout and where there have been some very worthwhile salmon catches too. There is plenty of other fishing available nearby, the hotel can sell you tickets for the Upper Teign Fishing Association waters, and there is good fishing to be had at Fernworthy and Kennock reservoirs. Expert assistance in the form of a REFFIS instructor or a ghillie is on hand should you be starting on your first tentative steps as a game fisherman, need to improve your technique or just wish to learn the how, when and where of our local waters.

In addition to the fishing, there are excellent golf courses nearby; we can arrange clay or rough shooting and deer stalking either with a gun or a camera and there is riding at nearby stables. Should the weather gods fail to co-operate, there are drying facilities available at the hotel.

Modern roads have made the Great Tree Hotel quick and easy to reach by car. Motorway and dual carriageway via the M5 and the A30 lead to Whiddon Down where a turn onto the A382 leads to the entrance drive just two miles to the south.

Great Tree Hotel
Sandy Park, Chagford
Devon TQ13 8JS
Tel: (0647) 432491
Fax: (0647) 432562

Fishing in Calm Waters – George Cammidge. Courtesy of Rosentiel's.

WALES

Wales is a land of vivid contrasts—spectacular scenery and a rich industrial heritage. It is also a country which boasts several fine rivers weaving intricately through largely unspoiled mountainside and wooded countryside. It may not be a game fishing mecca but it has a number of excellent salmon rivers, as well as some engaging streams where the brown trout fight like demons.

Sewin (Welsh for sea-trout) fishing is, like rugby, a passion amongst the Welsh. Sea-trout are prolific here and tend to move in pairs or threes, often reaching 8lb to 10lb. Sewin fishing is a real game fisherman's delight and only starts properly at twilight when the world around is quiet. Make no mistake, these fish fight and good judgement and planning are essential if you are to have any chance of success. Unlike brown trout, the sewin will journey within the river system, so the visiting angler must, therefore, endeavour to track them down before embarking on an evening that can hold its own alongside game fishing to be found almost anywhere. One tip here, it is always worth visiting the local hostelry in search of some essential tips for the battle ahead. The locals will tell you that colour and depth of presentation are two major keys to your success. Fishing a good pool will achieve little if you are unable to offer your fly on a plate, so to speak. Mind you, when you feel that monumental tug, prepare for chaos. The sewin plunges to the depths and occasionally, unbowed, he will leap skyward. This is a celebrated fish and, pound for pound, it will give you a fight equal to the wildest salmon.

As in many places, the salmon fishing is not as good as it once was. Salmon fishing can nevertheless still be found in all rivers although the runs do vary radically from year to year. The River Wye is particularly excellent. Autumn runs tend to be more productive than those in the spring when the salmon dart up the river in good numbers. This is the sport at its best. Brown trout fishing is also good in Wales and this crafty fish will test all your skills.

The River Wye
The River Wye is probably the best known river in Wales and one of the most famous of Britain's salmon rivers. It crosses the border between England and Wales and is often referred to as England's best salmon river! The Wye rises on the south side of Plynlimon and rushes as a boulder-strewn stream down river—a delight for brown trout. As the river grows, so the trout gain stature. Around Rhayader a number of important tributaries join the Wye, including the Irfon of which we will have more anon. Through careful conservation and control of nets the salmon catch is impressive. Although much of the river is privately owned there are several hotels and associations with rights to the water.

Many people who fish the Wye will take advantage of some of the splendid opportunities afforded by Harris and Stokes (0432) 354455 who have reminded me of a Scottish fishing custom. On the first day of the season, a half bottle of whisky should be poured into the water to bless, and, hopefully, intoxicate the fish. You must be sure to keep a half bottle nearby, not only to celebrate your catch but also to keep you warm. It can be very

cold on the Wye as the last two seasons have proved. Demand remains high for the prime beats and lettings are far from cheap, but some lesser known beats are good value and the fishing is still very good.

Another point that Roger Stokes makes is that the economic recession is effecting the take-up of certain beats and, if you haven't been too badly effected yourself, then you might just be able to acquire some rods here. Harris and Stokes have in excess of 400 salmon rods to let each year, principally on the Wye and the Usk, but can also arrange fishing in the smaller rivers.

The Wye from Chepstow to Builth Wells is made up of large bends and loops and the water glides in leisurely fashion, in striking contrast to its infant pace. There is some one and three quarter miles of fishing, some double-bank, such as at Lydbrook five miles below Ross-On-Wye, with season tickets still available. Ross itself has some town water available to visiting anglers and G. & R. Sports (0989) 63723 will provide you with all the details. It is also worth mentioning that trout streams abound here; the Monnow, Lugg and Garron are particularly good and landowners sometimes do consent to fishing them. The Birmingham Anglers Association have a number of excellent opportunities here as well as on other waters in Wales. Hattons (0432) 272317, who are based at St Owen Street in Hereford, also issue day licences and permits. The visiting fisherman may often be referred to the splendid Red Lion Hotel (0981) 500303 at Bredwardine, who own eight miles of the Wye and, assuming the water is good, provide excellent fishing. The water is made up of nine beats which run consecutively and hold two rods per beat. The fishing has been much improved in recent years and the brown trout have been much in evidence. The hotel sells and lends tackle to residents and day tickets can be purchased for £28. Permits and tackle, along with some good fishing, can be obtained from H. R. Grant (0497) 820309 in Castle Street, Hay-On-Wye. As well as issuing permits for town waters they have one mile of their own single-bank fishing.

The Swan Hotel (0497) 821188 also offers some good water. The Swan is a member of a syndicate which owns a four and a half mile stretch of single-bank fishing on the Wye. Excellent salmon fishing here. The Old Black Lion in Hay (0497) 820841 does not have its own water but has good local contacts who can provide fishing on one and a half miles of single-bank and about eight good pools. This water is understandably available to residents only, who must bring their own tackle. Two weeks' notice is also required. This is a very friendly place to stay and if you are seeking a bit of local advice then a ghillie can be hired at a cost of £25 per day.

The Irfon

The Wye has numerous tributaries and one of the most celebrated is the River Irfon, in which good trout and salmon fishing can be enjoyed. The Grove Park and Irfon Angling Club have water available on both the Wye and the Irfon, as well as Caer Beris Stillwater Fishery. Tickets are available from Mrs Morgan (0982) 552759. Caer Beris Manor (0982) 552601 at Builth Wells have some thousand yards of the Irfon with access to some excellent fishing on the Wye and some lake fishing at Caer Beris. The brown trout on the Irfon are fighting fit and provide tremendous sport. They usually weigh in at under a pound but there are a few wily fish who are considerably larger. The salmon fishing can also be good and 38lb 8oz record fish is a testimony to this. The hotel offers a package which includes dinner, bed and breakfast and free fishing for two nights for £95 per person—excellent stuff!

The Lake Country House Hotel (05912) 202 also has private fishing on the Irfon available to guests. This spans four and a half miles of single-bank fishing. The hotel is situated at Llangammarch Wells and you have to inspect your map closely to find it at all. The river is a typical Welsh stream, which runs over a hard stone bed of layered rock, resulting in some delightful pools. In other locations the river is wide and shallow, but always take care when wading as it is easy to slip over here. The wild trout are supplemented by the Lake Hotel (05912) 202 and its charming companion the Cammarch Arms Hotel (05912) 205, also in Llangammarch Wells. The proprietor of this establishment, Mr Alan Tansley has made a considerable effort to keep these waters and his care has most definitely reaped dividends. Incidentally, in the vicinity lies the only barium spring in Britain, considered to be a cure for gout, heart disease and rheumatism. Any afflicted anglers will therefore have a second good reason to make a trip here.

The Cammarch Arms' water is divided into three sections spanning three and a half miles of single-bank fishing, available to non-residents as well as guests. The hotel also has a mile of the Wye and three and a half miles of the Cammarch and Upper Dulas. Further upstream, we find real `trout country'. In Rhayader, you will find the newsagents have excellent value day tickets and licences, sold on behalf of the Elan Angling Club, who own a one mile stretch of double-bank fishing. This is the place where a 10lb trout was caught—that should give you food for thought. There have been a number of efforts made to stock this part of the river but the fishing is likely to take some time to regenerate itself, despite all efforts made. Indeed, the water bailiffs believe it may be as long as five years before the likes of Llangurig see fish of any consequence again.

The Usk

The River Usk is regarded as one of the finest fisheries in the United Kingdom and it is certainly one of the finest trout rivers in the principality. It is also a fine salmon

Pontsticill Reservoir (Welsh Water plc)

water. The river affords some spectacular scenery and the wild native brownies offer a challenging duel. The best fishing is in April and May, during the prolific fly hatches.

The water starts its journey some 2400 feet above sea level from Carmarthen Fan and travels through limestone and sandstone outcrops. Much of this water is preserved, but the visitor can still fish on the town water and Jean Williams at Sweets Fishing Tackle (02913) 2552 is perhaps the best person to talk to. Tickets are £7 a day and a licence can also be obtained here. The Bridge Inn (0873) 853045 is situated on the river and on occasion, when the river floods and breaks its banks the hotel is in the river! The water is particularly good and comprises calm stretches which break into rapids and changes again into deep pools. Trout tickets are available from The Bridge at a price of £6 per day or £15.50 per week. Salmon fishing will cost you £11.70 per day and £32.50 per week. One of the best spots from which to enjoy the Usk is from Gliffaes Country House Hotel (0874) 730371 who hold two attractive stretches. Gliffaes owns a mile of water and has two thirds of a mile double-bank fishing a few miles upstream. The Usk is extremely susceptible to changes in the water level. However, when the waters are up the river is a delight to fish. The Usk is renowned for its early start and fine sport can be had in March and April. The hatches tend to occur in the morning during March and the rise gradually occurs later through April and May until the evening hatch in June. Traditional wet flies work well and this is also good dry fly water. Naturally, each individual has their own preferred methods and the Gliffaes offers local advice on the most successful methods and flies. Beats are rotated

each day. In recent years salmon catches have dwindled significantly due to a number of factors. There is some reason for optimism, as sea nets are being restricted in Ireland and the estuary nets are also being more stringently controlled. The average size of the salmon tends to be about 10lb to 12lb but there are some bigger fish to be taken and the largest caught at Gliffaes was 35lb. Gliffaes offer trout fishing at £11 per day and salmon at £16 per day. Non-residents are welcome but guests do have preference.

The Vine Tree Inn (0873) 810514 at Llangattock issues tickets on behalf of the Crickhowell and District Anglers Association waters, which comprise three separate stretches. One is a mere 100 yards from the inn which is great value at £2 per day. The other stretches are a little further away and consist of three quarters of a mile of double-bank water and one and a half miles of single-bank fishing. Trout fishing is priced at £12 per day and salmon fishing at £17. The fishing is good provided the water is not too low. Returning downstream, The Bell Hotel (0873) 810247 at Glangrwyney has a few hundred yards of single-bank, predominately trout water, which is priced at £5 per day. At Abergavenny, permits for the Town Water, at £6 for a day's trouting, can be obtained from PM Fishing Tackle (0873) 853175.

River Towy (Glanrannell Park Hotel)

Talybont on the Usk offers a variety of waters and one of the most accessible to the visiting angler is the three quarters of a mile stretch of single-bank fishing available at the Usk Hotel (0874) 87251. This water includes four good salmon pools and is also some of the best brown trout fishing in the vicinity. Fishing is available for residents only. The hotel has a number of shooting opportunities available too, including grouse, pheasant, partridge and duck.

South Wales Waters

There are a large number of stillwaters in south east Wales and the angler who crosses the Severn in the hope of a good catch will surely not be disappointed. Lladegfedd (04957) 55122 covers a huge area and is located in the lowlands among wooded, rolling hills between the Usk and the valleys of South Wales. The water is restricted to fly-only and there are numerous opportunities available to the visiting angler. Day tickets are priced at around £9 and season tickets £250. The season runs from mid-March to mid-October. The fishery opens at 10.00am and boats may be rented from 8.00am onwards. Closing times vary from month to month in accordance with the daylight hours. There is a six fish limit per day and if you wish to explore the water to its full extent, then a motor boat will set you back £15 and a rowing boat £6. They can be reserved in advance by telephoning the fishery. In the closed season, the water is a haven for wintering wildfowl. Two fisheries to the south of here

are Llanishen and Lisvane (0222) 618919 which are joined by a central embankment and cover some eighty acres in total. They are situated a short distance outside Cardiff on the southern tip of the Welsh Hills in attractively wooded and open countryside. Lisvane is another reservoir which is popular with wintering wildfowl as well as local fishermen. The reservoir is stocked with rainbows and browns. Day tickets are priced at £10 and the waters are open from sunrise to an hour after sunset.

There is some fine sewin fishing in South and West Wales. The stillwaters are also useful when other waters are out of condition. Before we examine the delights of the major rivers, a glance at one or two less well known ones is well worthwhile.

The Ogmore

The River Ogmore has fishing opportunities for trout, sewin and salmon and the Ogmore Anglers Association which has just celebrated its centenary year, owns eighteen miles of double-bank fishing of this good water. Weekly tickets are available at £25 which represents good value for money. The Association bye-laws stipulate that you may only fish if you are introduced by a member of the club. In reality, the extremely friendly Mr Protheroe, Secretary, (0656) 861139 will merely sound you out on the telephone.

River Cothi (Glanrannell Park Hotel)

The Tawe

The River Tawe flows through some superb scenery in its upper reaches and the sewin and salmon fishing is very much improved, although some parts of the river still suffer from pollution. Mainwarings in Dillwyn Road, Sketty (0792) 202245 sell licences and permits for the Pontardawe Angling Club who own eight miles of double-bank fishing between Pontardawe and Morriston. Assuming conditions are in our favour, the fishermen can enjoy some fine sport and day tickets can be purchased for £8.

The Towy & The Cothi

The River Towy (or Tywi) rises in the Cambrian Mountains and flows thence from the Brianne Reservoir to Carmarthen and the Bristol Channel. Although the reservoir has been blamed for many ills in the water, it does act as a potential safety fuse for surges of water and consequent flooding. This generally ensures some good, easy fishing. It is excellent sewin water and the fish generally run from the first day of the season in March. The association waters are available but some of the water is understandably retained for private use. However, the Land and Leisure Group (0874) 623181, a subsidiary of Welsh Water, have a large amount of opportunities for sewin and to a lesser extent salmon. The Group also have some water on the River Cothi, a rocky stream which can prove quite difficult to fish. This tributary of the Towy has some excellent sewin fishing from June onwards. Prices are available on application. The Forest Arms (0267) 202339 in Brechta also have a mile on the Cothi. The locals are generally delighted to share their expertise and permits are available for £8 and £5. The Forest Arms also doubles as a good value bed and breakfast for people who wish to stay a day or two. The Tackle Shop at Felingwm Uchaf (0267) 290207 sells permits and can also arrange fishing on the Treflyn Estate some distance away near Tregaron. This comprises some six and a half miles of double and single-bank fishing on what is delightful water. The Estate also rents cottages by the week, which may appeal to the many fishermen who enjoy the freedom of self-catering.

Returning southwards we arrive at Llandovery. Mrs Thomas at Tonn Farm has a short half a mile stretch which is good for trout fishing enthusiasts. Mrs Barbara Leech, who runs the antique shop (0550) 20602 sells tackle as well as licences for Llandovery Anglers Association who have a good stretch on the Towy. Permits cost £7.50 for a day and £20 per week for the lower water, and £15 and £70 respectively for the upper water. The proprietor is most helpful and will be delighted to assist you. Llandovery AA also have three miles of the River Bran, an excellent trout stream. Although much of the water is in the hands of Land and Leisure, The Golden Grove Arms Hotel (0558) 668551 has a three quarter mile stretch of single-bank which is excellent for sewin and salmon. The hotel bar is well frequented by locals who are happy to offer good advice on the area, especially if you are buying.

Carmarthen and District Anglers Club (0267) 231945 is currently in the care of Mr Evans. The Club has six miles of mixed bank fishing on the Towy as well as a stretch of the Cothi. Permits on most waters are £12 a day. Lyric Sports, King Street in Carmarthen (0267) 237166, will supply tickets for these waters and also for the Carmarthen Anglers Association waters. These comprise some six and a half miles of predominantly double-bank fishing on the Towy and two and a half miles on the Cothi. The Club Secretary (0267) 237362 is also extremely helpful and you should note that a £50 season ticket will allow you to fish any of the Club's waters, which also includes stretches on the Gwili and Taf.

The better salmon fishing tends to take place toward the end of the season and the sewin will provide some thrilling sport earlier in the year. There will be few fishermen who will not delight in the varied opportunities that are afforded by the River Towy.

The Cleddau

The River Cleddau has two limbs, one which stretches east and the other west. Both then journey north through parts of unspoiled Wales. The Pembrokeshire Anglers Association have fifteen miles of fishing, much of which is double-bank. Salmon tend to run from March to the end of June and sewin from mid-June onwards. In league with the NRA, the Association have also an extensive cleaning operation underway to improve the banks and habitat of the Western Cleddau, creating some five or six new pools to add to the many already existing. County Sports in Haverfordwest (0437) 763740 issue permits, and licences at £6 per day or £32 a week, together with an extensive range of tackle. Maps are issued with the permits which is often the case in Wales—just as well as some of the pools are in remarkably remote settings. The Chairman, Mr Tony Summers (0437) 763216 is extremely helpful and is happy to advise you on currently favoured flies and the better times to fish. This is a common trait amongst the Welsh fishing fraternity who could not be kinder, but obviously visitors should be respectful of privacy.

The Eastern Cleddau is mostly taken up by private syndicates, but the Slebech Estates (0834) 860905 have one and a half miles of double-bank fishing which offers good opportunities for salmon, sewin and trout fishing. The water is restricted to fly-only, a twenty-four hour permit will cost you £17, and a day pass in the order of £12. The Estate also rents riverside cottages to visiting anglers, which sounds very promising. Try and contact Jim Brown around meal times!

Those anglers fishing in south west waters should make a note of Llys-y-Fran (0437) 532273 which is an attractive reservoir on the edge of the Preseli Hills and provides bank and boat fishing. Fishing takes place from 8.00am to half an hour after sunset. The reservoir which is situated near to Haverfordwest, has good quality fishing for rainbow and brown trout. If you are looking for a family day out this is a good place as there are picnic tables, walks and nature trails. The price of a day ticket is £8 and there is a six fish bag limit. Boats may be hired for £15 per day and a superb wheelie boat is available for disabled anglers free of charge. Another fishery which also provides additional activities is located at Mynyddcerrig near Pontyberem. The Granffrwd Trout Fishery (0269) 870539 provides riding and shooting as well as some fine fishing that has been acclaimed by the angling press. Day tickets are £18, there is a four fish limit and if you don't manage to catch anything you can have your money back! The fishery enjoys a wonderful setting just nine miles from Camarthen. Canadian Pine Cabins with bathroom and kitchen make for an ideal family holiday.

The Lake is a riverside country house set in 50 acres of beautiful grounds with sweeping lawns, woods, riverside walks and a large well stocked lake. The hotel offers spacious and luxurious accommodation, enhanced by log fires and antiques. Excellent imaginative food, prepared from fresh local produce, is served in the elegant dining room, accompanied by one of the finest wine lists in Wales. The Lake has been awarded the Restaurant of the Year by Johansens for 1991 and has also received a Rosette for food from the AA for the last two years. The Lake offers all that is best in country house hospitality and satisfied guests return again and again.

For the golf enthusiast there are four full size courses in close proximity, with Builth Wells Course only 10 minutes away, an attractive parkland course of 5386 yards, par 66, the hotel can organise concessionary tickets here.

It is a fisherman's paradise with a lake covering 2 1/2 acres, within the grounds and a 4 1/2 mile stretch of the River Irfon running through the extensive parkland of the hotel. The trout in the river are mostly wild fish and run up to 5lb, with some larger. Our water is divided into six beats, a maximum of two rods being allowed on each. **The Wye** provides good trout fishing, specimens up to and over 1lb are not uncommon. The number of rods per beat is restricted. **The Irfon** is likely to produce salmon almost anytime in the season, but really comes into its own in the latter part. There are also a number of Welsh Water Authorities Reservoirs within easy reach. Our gillie is on hand to give fishing instruction at a very reasonable charge.

The region is well known to birdwatchers and is an ideal centre for walkers and also a haven for wildlife, including badgers and red kite. There are spectacular drives in all directions. Clay pigeon shooting and horse riding are available. AA and RAC 3 Stars and Merit Award. Children welcome. Dogs by arrangement.

The Lake Country House
Llangammarch Wells
Powys
Wales LD4 4BS
Tel: (05912) 202/474
Fax: (05912) 457

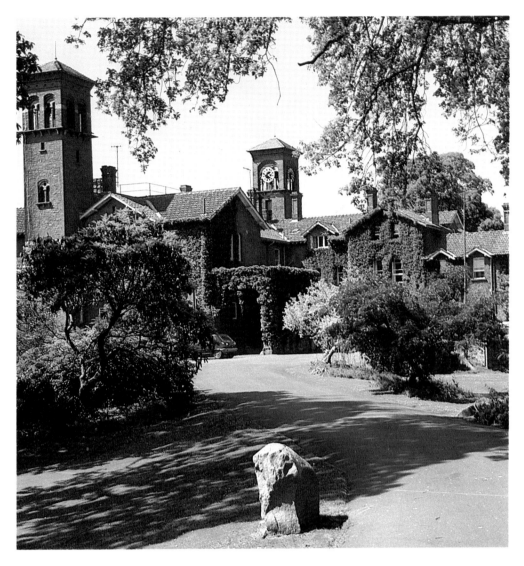

A thoroughly charming Victorian country house hotel, Gliffaes boasts fine gardens and parkland, situated in the National Park yet only one mile off the main A40 road. It offers peace and tranquillity as well as being easily accessible.

The house, which faces due south, stands in its own 29 acres in the beautiful valley of the River Usk, midway between the Brecon Beacons and the Black Mountains. Built in 1885 as a private residence, it has been ideally adapted to provide spacious comfort in the country house tradition. There are 22 bedrooms with private bathrooms or showers and all are individual in decor and furnishings, including three in the converted lodge.

The downstairs rooms include a large, comfortable, panelled sitting-room which leads into an elegant regency style drawing-room. From here, french windows open into a large conservatory with double doors on to the terrace. The dining-room and comfortable bar also open on to the terrace, with the glorious views of the surrounding hills and River Usk one hundred and fifty feet below. The billiard room has a full sized table and provides an additional sitting-room with something of a club atmosphere.

Breakfast is served from a sideboard, lunch is a cold buffet with soup and a hot dish. Dinner is either table d'hote or a la carte. In fact, country house standards of the old order are carefully maintained by the resident owners; the Brabner family have held sway here since 1948.

External facilities include fishing for salmon and trout in the part of the Usk which the hotel overlooks, tennis, bowls, putting and croquet. There is an extensive range of short walks in the vicinity and a nearby riding and pony trekking establishment where horses and ponies can be hired.

The hotel is justly proud of its in-house cooking and remains open from the middle of March to the end of the year.

Gliffaes Country House Hotel
Crickhowell
Powys
Wales NP8 1RH
Tel: (0874) 730371 Fax: (0874) 730463

On this site, fourteen hundred years ago, the Welsh Parliament stood; at least according to legend. Inspired by this, the celebrated architect, Sir Clough Williams-Ellis transformed the largely Jacobean mansion he found here into the great country house it is today. Llangoed Hall was completed in 1918 although parts of the South facing wing, including the panelled library date, from 1632. Inside it is the Laura Ashley genius that is most striking, that ability of interpreting the past to bring comfort and beauty to the present.

The intention of Sir Bernard Ashley, when he decided to convert the hall, was never that of the usual hotelier. Having decided to return to the idea of entertaining guests, rather than patrons, he worked hard to re-create the style and atmosphere of what it once was, a great Edwardian country house where visitors could stay and enjoy the way of life it once stood for. Thoughtful luxuries abound, personal touches make all the difference; fresh fruit; a decanter of sherry or mineral water ready to pour; plenty of books in the bedrooms fleecy robes and luxurious oils in the bathrooms a tray of famous Welsh afternoon tea of scones and home-made jam, shortbread and cream-filled meringues and local Bara Brith served in the Morning Room to welcome you on arrival.

The dining room is handsome with yellow and cornflower blue, a perfect complement to the menu of one the finest young chefs in Britain; always insisting on fresh local produce; Welsh lamb, Wye salmon and traditional laverbread; vegetables and herbs collected from the hotel's own gardens. All to be enjoyed with a choice from some of the 300 superb wines assembled from the greatest wine regions of the world.

For the sportsman, three superb golf courses are within easy driving distance; all 18-hole with breathtaking scenery. In addition to the hotel's own all-weather tennis court and croquet lawn guests may fish for salmon and trout on the Upper Wye and River Irfon. The countryside, rich in wildlife, offers a variety of rough shooting and bird-watching. Riding can be easily arranged and the magnificent Brecon Beacons have much to offer both the serious and casual walker; not to mention the fascinating surrounding countryside, from Wordsworth's beloved Tintern Abbey to the ancient castles of Raglan and Caerphilly.

Conference facilities are, naturally, extensive, with a variety of rooms available, from the panelled, book-lined library to separate dining room, the Flower Room. For all guests a chauffeur-driven car is available for day-to-day touring or collection from rail and air terminals, and helicopters may use the south lawn by prior arrangement.

Llangoed Hall
Llyswen
Brecon
Powys
Wales
LD3 0YP
Tel: (0874) 754525
Fax: (0874) 754545

Whether you are fishing at nightfall or early in the morning in hopeful anticipation of your lunch, you will find a wealth of good sport in Wales. In this age of pollution, grinding mechanisation and awesome technology you will find places where seemingly time has stood still. These are charming villages in idyllic surroundings, providing a perfect excuse for a timely excursion into some of Britain's most remote and unspoiled reaches. Here, you can pause from fishing as otters plunder the waters. Here, you are accompanied by birds of prey and many wildfowl. The Welsh Water Authorities are doing a tremendous job promoting these waters without sacrificing their intrinsic charms. If you are keen on fly fishing then a journey to all corners of Wales must be high on your list of forays.

The Teifi

The River Teifi rises in Lyn Teifi near Strata Florida in the Cambrian Hills not far from the source of the Towy. The river is often titled the Queen of Welsh Rivers and this is hardly surprising when one reflects on the sport available. The river flows south west and then westwards, entering Cardigan Bay south of the town. There are a number of opportunities for the visiting fisherman and fishing is at a premium for sewin in July and August, particularly from dusk until dawn. The Cenarth area holds good salmon and at Cilgerran one can see historic Coracles. The river runs through enchanting scenery including the Caron Bog, a renowned nature reserve. Salmon and sewin tend to dominate in the lower reaches while trout naturally tend to predominate in the upper reaches and the tributaries.

The Teifi concludes its journey a little south of Cardigan. Mr Cliff Jones (0239) 710405 is Secretary of the Teifi Trout Association and is something of a Welsh wizard on the area when it comes to fishing. The association has some fifteen miles of the Lower Teifi. One bank offers continuous fishing, the other has four beats in and around Newcastle Emlyn and permits can be obtained at £10 a day or £35 a week from Andrew Sports in the town (0239) 710349. Cenarth Falls is the last site of historical coracle fishing for salmon. The Castle Malgwyn Hotel (023987) 644 in Llechryd have a mile of fishing which is available to guests as do the Llwyndywys Mansion Hotel (023987) 263. These waters both have trout, salmon and sewin fishing.

The Llandysul Anglers Association has some twenty-two miles of the middle waters of the Teifi and this is an extremely popular stretch of the river. Salmon run in the spring months and again from August through September, while sewin are prolific from July onwards. Mr Artie Jones (0559) 362317 is the secretary and permits are available from Alma Stores in Llandysul (0559) 363322, just beyond Barclays Bank.

The Llanbydder Anglers Association has some five miles on the Teifi and Bill Wilkins (0570) 480038 is the man at the reel, so to speak. Tickets are available direct from him or David Morgan, Siop-y-Bont, Llanybdder (0570) 480980.

The Tregaron Anglers Association controls several miles of the Upper Teifi and Mr D.L. Evans (0974) 298304 is the Association's Honourary Secretary. There is some fine brown trout fishing available on these stretches. Wet fly fishing tends to be the most favoured in March and April with dry fly coming into its own in early May. Salmon will run up this far if the water conditions are favourable, particularly later in the season. Permits can be purchased from the newsagents in Tregaron or from the post office in Pontrhydfendigaid (try asking for directions to this village!) There are also good value day tickets available here for trout fishing only. The Talbot Hotel (0974) 298208 have good contacts with the local association and are delighted to arrange fishing for their guests. The water bailiff is also a helpful chap as are so many of the association officials. This may be a queen of rivers but it is one of the most accessible as well as one of the most beautiful in the area.

Finally, if you are endeavouring to fish the seven mile stretch of Llyn Gynon you will find the Visitors Centre in Glan Village (0597) 810880 a mine of useful information. Permits are also available from the centre. Access to this water is difficult but well worth making an effort for. The wild brown trout fight like tigers. Day tickets are priced at a reasonable £3. If you happen to be sitting at home with little to do, reflect on the River Teifi. Imagine, if you will, the morning quiet or the evening solace, the flow and the ripple.

The Aeron

There are many reasons for going fishing; the solitude, the scenery and the challenge. The River Aeron is a relatively small but still attractive river with an excellent run of sewin from June onwards. The lower reaches are generally the most productive and are controlled by the Aberaeron Angling Club. Permits are available from Cei Lee Sports in Bridge Street, Arberaeron (0545) 571123. Local residents are given priority and pensioners and juniors even better treatment. Visitors who live two or more miles away from Aberaeron are required to pay £60 for a year's fishing. Please contact Geoff Parry, West Winds, Wellington Street, Aberaeron for further details. Night fishing for sewin in this area is often excellent. Upriver the water flows through farmland but the waters are still often fishable by virtue of the local farmers who allow fishermen onto their land. The Post Office in Abraeron generally has a list of farmers who are welcoming. The banks are often overgrown here, but in the later weeks of the season the sewin fishing is phenomenal. The Butcher and the Silver March Brown are two popular flies used locally.

The Rheidol

There are numerous streams in Dyfed and the Rheidol is one that is well worth your attention. The sewin that run up-river in May are of top quality and the middle reaches, which have long glides suit wet fly fishing for sewin. The level of water often fluctuates dramatically by virtue of the fact that the Nant-y-Moch and Dinas Reservoirs are used for hydro-electric power generation. Although the increased levels may aid fishing, the changes in water temperature make it doubly difficult to tempt the devious sewin which are so prolific in these waters. The Aberystwyth Anglers Association own all the water and some eight lakes in the district. Permits can be obtained from the Aberystwyth Tackle Shop (0970) 611200 and prices are in the region of £12 per day or £55 per week. There are some excellent sewin lurking, which will give you some great sport should you be lucky enough to catch one. It is a good idea to use both a floating and a sinking line to counteract the changes in temperature that follow any fluctuation in the water level. Equipped with wet fly you should be fortunate to have a lot of fun amid the pools and deep glides of the River Rheidol.

The Dovey

The Dovey is one of the finest waters in Britain and its sewin fishing is outstanding. The thirty or so miles of water starts amidst mountainous terrain and hereafter the waters wind their way in a south westerly direction to Aberdovey. This spate river also has some three hundred and fifty miles of feeder tributaries which offer some fine trout fishing. The New Aberdovey Fishery Association (0654) 702721 controls twenty-eight miles of river and, as you may imagine, rods are somewhat hard to come by. Indeed, no day tickets are available to visitors, although weekly permits at £80 are available. The lower beats are almost impossible to get on and you must book well in advance to stand any chance here. The upper beats are less popular and you may well be able to purchase a weekly ticket from the post office in Cemmaes. The sea-trout tend to range from 2lb to 8lb and salmon from 8lb to 10lb. In June 1991, a 30lb fish was taken—the largest since 1930. There are numerous pools of note; Rhiwlas, Tank, Glandwr and Cottage are some of the most celebrated. Equally notable is the Haslan Fly which has made a reputation for itself on this water. The Brigands Inn (0650) 531208 is an historic establishment in which to stay. It dates from the eighteenth century and has welcomed anglers to the area for a hundred years. The inn owns two miles of predominantly double-bank fishing on the Dovey which is almost entirely reserved for residents. Eight rods are allowed per day and these are priced at £17 The hotel arranges special fishing breaks and you should contact them for further details. We have received very positive reports on the sea-trout fishing in this stretch and in 1990 a 24lb fish topped the scales here. Salmon are also reported to be on the increase. This is a first class river and if you are able to fish it you are extremely fortunate

The Vyrnwy & the Tanat

The River Vyrnwy runs from the lake of the same name to the north of Powys and offers some fine trout and salmon fishing as well as some good coarse fishing. The Vyrnwy is a tributary of the Severn and whilst it is not a classic salmon river, it has given up some 30lb fish in recent seasons and is well located for the many anglers of the Midlands who are not so spoilt in their choice of good game fishing rivers. The sport has been restricted of late by low water levels here, but when the river rises the clear waters are a delight to fish. A mere £8 covers the cost of a season ticket here—tremendous value. Tickets are available from Sundore Fishing Tackle and Leisure in Shrewsbury (0743) 361804 or direct from Oswestry and District Angling Society (0691) 772045. This is a wonderfully unspoiled area and awaits your attention.

The River Tanat is a tributary of the Vyrnwy and is a good trout river which will appeal to those living on the border. Much of the water is owned by syndicates but two inns offer good value fishing and provide an excellent base for exploring this delightful countryside. Llan-y-Blodwel finds the Horseshoe Inn (0691) 828227 which has three rods available per day for fly fishing only. The Green Inn in Llangedwyn (0691) 828234 has three quarters of a mile of single-bank fishing, again with three rods available (the other bank is too steep to fish from).

The Mawddach & The Wnion

The River Mawddach rises on a remote hillside between Bala and Trawsfyndd Lake, holds salmon, trout and to a lesser extent, sea-trout. Although much of the water is preserved, there are two excellent hotels from which to enjoy the fishing. The Tyn y Groes Hotel, Granllwyd (034140) 275 has a mile and a half of single-bank fishing available for guests. This is predominantly salmon water and licences can be obtained from the nearby post office. Permits are available at the hotel and are priced at £10 per day. The proprietor, Barry Rithwell, has access to other rivers as well as a splendid knowledge of the Mawddach. The delightful Dolmelynllyn Hall (034140) 273 is a true haven and the hotel can provide guests with some twelve miles of fishing on the Mawddach and its best known tributary the River Wnion. This is a tumbling, often turbulent water. Guests can enjoy the fine fishing here for free. Permits are available to non-residents for £15 although they should always enquire in advance as to availability. Licences can be purchased in the local village. An encouraging thought for the younger, aspiring anglers is that in 1992 the first salmon, a seven-pounder, was caught on this stretch of water by a fourteen year old boy. Further information is also obtainable from Dolgellau Angling Club (0341) 422906 who control much of the association waters. They are particularly well organised and have in the region of twelve miles of salmon and sea-trout fishing on the Mawddach and Wnion at Dolgellau in addition to the recently acquired Storehouse waters. Both rivers are stocked with salmon and sea-trout from the Mawddach Hatchery. Weekly permits are well priced at £26 and day permits are £9 (river and lake combined). Tickets can be purchased from the Seafarer (0341) 280978, a tackle shop in Barmouth.

The Dysynni
Journeying westwards, we find the River Dysynni which rises in Llyn Cau on the towering Cader Idris. The water falls rapidly via Dol-y-Cau and into the picturesque Tal-y-Llyn. Emerging from the lake it flows westwards as a small upland river but grows ever deeper as it carves its way through the valley to enter the sea at Cardigan Bay, a mile or so to the north of Tywyn. The river offers interesting trout and sewin fishing and in the late summer the occasional salmon will be encountered. The Estimaner Angling Association owns three miles of the lower river and seven miles of its upper reaches and the Peniarth Estate has a further four miles. This is one of the most picturesque rivers you are ever likely to fish and permits are available from Abergynolwyn Post Office (0654) 782635 in the Square, opposite the Railway Hotel. Day tickets cost £9, weekly tickets £12. The Sports Shop in Tywyn (0654) 710772 also has permits for sale. If you are looking for an escape in superb scenery then this fishing is first rate.

Central Wales Waters
Central Wales reveals some interesting lake fishing, all of which offers good daily forays for brown trout and rainbows. Bag limits are usually around six fish per day and tickets start at £6 for a full day's fishing. Dinas and Nant-y-Moch Reservoirs are both under the ownership of Powergen (097084) 667 and are part of the Rheidol Hydro-Electric Power Scheme. They are both very popular and the fisherman landing the largest fish wins a season ticket for the following year. If you happen to be fishing the Rhayader, then surely a visit to Elan Valley Fisheries is in order. In fact, it is a good idea even if you're not in the area. The interlinked reservoirs of Caban Coch, Garreg Ddu, Graig Goch and Pen-y-Garreg are controlled by Elan Trout Fisheries and provide 850 acres of excellent trout fishing in a beautiful setting. Permits can be bought from the Elan Valley Visitors Centre (0597) 810898, take the B4518 from Rhayader.

One of the most renowned stillwater lakes in Britain is Lake Vyrnwy. It spans 1100 acres and is 800 feet above sea level. The rights to this water are owned by the Lake Vyrnwy Hotel (069173) 692, a delightful place to stay. The lake is surrounded by moorland, meadow, mountain and forest, which all provide a stunning backdrop for the casting fisherman. The lake is restricted to fly fishing only from the hotels boats which are available with or without engines. Tackle can be hired and licences can also be purchased from the hotel. Late in the season when the water level drops, bank fishing is also possible. The lake is well stocked throughout the season with brown, rainbow and American brook trout to comple-

ment the indigenous population of brownies. For groups, tuition is available and the services of a ghillie can be arranged. The price of day tickets is in the region of £6, with boat hire costing £10.50. An engine will cost a further £9.50 and there is ample room for two people in a boat. There are a whole host of other permits obtainable from the hotel and this is an ideal place to stay and enjoy some good fishing in a superb natural environment.

Gwynedd offers a number of fishing opportunities. The Lakes of Blaenau Ffestiniog number twenty and offer some first class fishing for wild trout. Here, the fishing is managed by the local angling association and if you like being well away from the crowds then these lakes are for you. The Dolgellau Angling Association (0341) 422706 control the waters of Llyn Cynwch as well as first class river fishing. The lake is situated near the renowned Precipice Walk and all around are stunning views of Cader Idris and the Mawddach Estuary. The lake is stocked every three weeks with brown and rainbow trout and has natural brown trout too. The record fish is an impressive 10lb. The northern section of the lake is fly-only but the remainder is open fishing. Tickets for the lake are priced at £7 and for the views that come with it, that seems like good value!

South of Dolgellau we find another hotel which provides superb lakeside fishing. The Tynycornel at Talyllyn (0654) 782282 provides fishing on one of the most beautiful waters in the principality. The management also control the fishing on Bugeilyn, a truly marvellous setting in the hills above Llanbrynmair, where boat fishing for the wild brown trout will provide a feast of memories.

Snowdonia not only has wonderful scenery but some delightfully unspoiled mountain lakes too, gouged out by glaciers many thousands of years ago. One such lake is Llyn Crafnant (0492) 640818. Formerly the exclusive territory of the wild brown trout, these wild fish now share their home with rainbows which are stocked weekly, including a former record fish of some 17lb. The lake is signposted from Trefriw on the B5106 which is in the Conway Valley some five miles north of Betws-y-Coed. Day tickets are priced at £10 and can be purchased from the Lakeside Office. There is also some cottage accommodation available.

The Dwyfawr & the Glaslyn
Venturing ever northwards, one has a choice between the wilds of Snowdonia or the coastline, dotted with small fishing villages and larger resort towns. There are numerous streams in Gwynedd and the Dwyfawr, Glaslyn and Erch are three which flow from the Lleyn Peninsula and attract quality fish. The locals love their fishing here and when the sewin are running everyone knows! However, in recent years numbers have been substantially reduced. This is an area of quite stunning scenery, much of which can be enjoyed with fishing rod in hand. Most of the Dwyfawr is in the hands of Criccieth, Llanystumdwy and District Anglers Association and permits, licences and tackle can be purchased from Pritchards (0766) 522116. Mr Goodman Jones is a member of the Club and is very helpful. Permits are priced at approximately £75 for a season or £30 for a week. A day's fishing will cost you £10. There had been a decline in sea-trout here in recent years, but reports for 1993 were actually very encouraging. Salmon, moreover, have increased in number. The Glaslyn which rises in Llyn Conwy and runs along the valley floor to Portmadog is

another sewin river although the Glaslyn Anglers Association owns much of the river. Monday to Friday tickets are £10 and are available from the Angling and Gun Centre (0766) 512464. If you wish to fish at the weekend you must hold a season ticket which is priced at £50. Once again, the surroundings are perfect and the river is well known for its early run of Sewin.

The Conway

The River Conway (Conwy) rises in Migneint and flows through the Carnarvonshire countryside, through Betws-y-Coed and Llanrwst and into Conway Bay. The upper part of the Conway Valley takes in some celebrated unspoiled countryside and much of the land is in the care of the National Trust. Permits are available for a number of stretches of the river between Conway Falls Bridge and Rhydlanfair. In total, the National Trust (0492) 860123 handle four beats and weekly tickets are available at £10 or £3 per day.

Although the trout are small, they fight well and the scenery is quite breathtaking. Tickets are also available from Bob Ellis (0690) 710567 and from The Old Library Newsagent and Tackle Shop (0492) 641 477 in Llanrwst at £45 for a weekly permit. It is also worth considering the National Trust on a number of other fishing opportunities, and also Conway Valley Fisheries (0492) 650063,

who have day and season tickets available on a two acre spring fed lake.

It is difficult to consider such beauty and at the same time pay sufficient attention to the worries over pollution and acid rain, but the Conway is susceptible to both these problems. As a result, trout fishing was in trouble here a couple of years ago. Since then, however, things have taken a definite turn for the better. Salmon still run the river and average between 9lb and 12lb. The Betws-y-Coed Angling Association (0690) 710618 has some four and a half miles of mixed bank fishing as well as three lakes on the river. The Committee have passed a ruling that no day or weekly tickets are to be issued after August each year but prior to that, day fishing is available at £15 and weekly tickets at £40 (Monday to Friday). A season ticket is priced at £105. Mr Melvin Hughes, the Membership Secretary, is happy to hear from prospective members (after 6.00pm please). Permits and maps are obtainable from Gareth Parry at the Tan Ian Restaurant, Betws-y-Coed (0690) 710232.

Those wishing to fish later in the season might be advised to stay at one of the nearby hotels. The Maenen Abbey (049269) 230 have one mile of single-bank fishing available to guests and there are a number of locals who frequent the bar with useful knowledge and advice! The Gwydyr Hotel (0690) 710777, Betws-y-Coed has about six miles of double-bank fishing. Tackle is also available for hire, but only guests can fish for salmon at £55 per day or £140 per week between March and May, and £235 per week for the latter part of the season. Night fishing for sea-trout is possible at a price of £18.50 or £110 for a weekly permit (residents only). Two of the Conway's chief tributaries are the Lledr and the Llugwy. Betws-y-

First Class Fishing (Brigand's Inn)

Sea-trout Flies: Bloody Butcher, Black and Teal, Connemara Black (Mike Sugg)

Coed Anglers Club has permits for the latter, whilst Dolwyddelan FA has one and a half miles double-bank fishing on the Lledr. Daily tickets, costing £20 a week for trout and salmon, are available from Dolwyddelan Post Office (0690) 6201 if you are staying in the village.

The Clwyd

The Clwyd, which meets the sea at Rhyl, is predominantly controlled by clubs and associations which restrict the waters to members only. However the St Asaph Angling Association have two beats available to day visitors from Monday to Friday. The fishing, which includes salmon in the summer and autumn is priced at £5 per day. The Club also has two miles of excellent trout fishing on the River Elwy. Permits are £3 per day—great value indeed! Foxon's Tackle (0745) 583583 in St Asaphs sells permits for the waters and will help with any information. The water is good below Ruthin and the Ruthin Castle Hotel (08242) 2664 has rights to the water which is free to guests. It is fly-only and guests may fish for salmon, brown and sea-trout.

The Dee

Unlike the Clwyd, the River Dee is far easier to fish and the visitor will not only find good value but also a delightful setting. In an age when the price of a beat is extremely high and fish harder to find, the Dee is a real treat. It is well cared for by the associations that own much of this water. The nature of the valley is varied, sometimes deep, and on other sections bordered by meadows. As you will appreciate, access is not always possible. The River Dee rises in the Cambrian Mountains and threads its way to Chester, flowing through Bala, Corwen, Llangollen and Overton. The river holds trout, salmon, sewin and grayling. The grayling in particular are top quality and offer good sport when other game fish are out of season. The insect life is staggering and your fly box will have to be well filled to compete. Membership of the principal clubs such as the Corwen and Llangollen is excellent value. The Llangollen Angling Association has some six and a half miles of double-bank fly fishing and recently hosted the 10th World Fly Fishing Championships. D. M. Southern in Chapel Street, (0978) 860155 Llangollen sells permits at £3 a day for trout and £10 for salmon. Weekly permits are priced at £15 and £30 respectively. Mr Southern can also sell permits for Midland Fly Fishers Syndicate who have three miles of double-bank fly-only water, priced at £4 for trout and grayling fishing.

The Bryn Howel Hotel (0978) 860331 has access to the Llangollen Anglers Association waters and issue permits for trout at £3 per day, and salmon at £10 a day. As we head towards the Corwen Anglers Association waters we should pencil in a visit to the Berwyn Arms Hotel at Glyndyfrdwy (0490) 83210 which has two miles of single-bank fishing. There is a tackle shop at the hotel and the owner, Mr Gallagher, fishes regularly. Permits for trout and grayling cost £5 and salmon is priced at £12 per day. The trout fishing is fly-only. Corwen and District Angling Club controls most of the trout and grayling fishing on the Rhug Estate. Permits are available from local tacklists and a visit is thoroughly recommended. Pale Hall at Llandderfel (06783) 285 have bought some ten rods on the Dee, using Bala Association water and covering several sections of the Dee, Towyn and a mountain lake. There is some good salmon fishing here and tackle is available should you wish it. Fishing is reserved for guests only and is free. A licence can also be purchased at the hotel, should this be required. In Bala itself, Siop Yr Eryr, Sports and Tackle (0678) 520370 has an excellent range of tackle and the proprietor, Mr Evans, is a member of the local association and, as something of an expert, he is also generous with his advice. Mr Evans is a specialist in fly-tying and has some good examples of old eighteenth and nineteenth century Welsh patterns.

North Wales Waters

North Wales has a number of stillwaters rich in fish. Llyn Brenig (049082) 463 is situated high on Denbigh Moors and offers fly fishing for rainbow and brown trout. It is particularly notable as a boat fishery and hosted the World Championship in 1990. Day permits are £9 and boats can be hired for £15. Fishing takes place from mid-March to the end of October and between 8.00am until an hour after sunset. The water is located off the B4501 and is well worth a visit. Other waters to note include Felin-y-Gors (0745) 584044, which offers ten acres of fly fishing and four spring fed lakes in secluded surroundings. The fishery which opens from 9.00am to 10.00pm hires out tackle and also has some pleasant self-catering accommodation for people wishing to stay in the area.

The cost of fishing varies with the duration of your stay and the longer you are here the more fish you may keep. Four hours will cost £8, maximum two fish, whilst a day ticket costs £22.50 with a six fish limit.

Journeying to the Moelfre Hills, we find the Tan-y-Mynydd Trout Lake (0745) 823691 on the B5381, St Asaph to Conway Road, just three miles outside Abergele and three and a half miles from the coast. There are ten self-catering cottages on site and a licenced bar and restaurant too. The tariffs and bag limits vary according to the number of hours you wish to spend here. There are a total of five small lakes which cover three and a half acres and each lake is stocked with rainbows, American brook trout and brown trout.

The Usk (Gliffaes)

Built in 1870 for a wealthy railway engineer, Palé Hall has recently been converted to a luxurious and exquisite hotel. It has, however, retained all its finest original Victorian features.

The most interesting of all of these must surely be the original baths and adjoining bedroom used by Queen Victoria during her stay at Palé Hall for a short time after Prince Albert's death. Then there is the 'boudoir', a beautiful interior boasts a magnificent hand painted dome ceiling and the Corwen Bar where one can see the unusual bar made from the marble fireplaces that have been removed from the bedrooms.

Each of the seventeen bedrooms are individually designed and finished to compliment their own particular features. It is this fine attention to detail that make

Palé Hall so interestingly unique. Despite its strong historical identity, however, it still provides all the home comforts of the present day subtly blended into this fine regal setting.

The restaurant and its cuisine is also of an exceptionally high standard. Interestingly, breakfast and morning coffee is served in the Bala Kitchen, which is still enhanced by its original cooking range from the late nineteenth century.

From the building and its grounds, spectacular views can be enjoyed. Here you can walk in solitude, sail serene waters, shoot, fish or enjoy a round of golf. Whatever your interests the Welsh hospitality will ensure a relaxing visit.

Palé Hall
Llandderfel
Nr Bala
Gwynedd
Tel: (06783) 285
Fax: (06783) 220

Glanrhyd-y-pysgod is set in beautiful woodland surroundings situated in unspoilt countryside in the lovely Teifi Valley, midway between Newcastle Emlyn, Lampeter and Carmarthen. This alone makes Glanrhyd-y-pysgod an ideal place for a fishing holiday or even just a relaxing break away from it all.

For those who wish to explore the beautiful countryside, Glanrhyd-y-pysgod is an ideal touring centre for Cardigan Bay and the Gower peninsula with Cenarth Falls only 16 miles away. Wildlife enthusiasts will find the area a particularly rich source of interest.

Accommodation consists of four attractive one and two bedroom cottages which sleep anything from two to six people.

These tastefully furnished stone-built cottages are self-catering and fitted to a very high standard, amenities include barbecue facilities and televisions.

Glanrhyd-y-pysgod has its own mile long stretch of private salmon and sewin fishing, incorporating 8 holding pools on the river Teifi. Access to the river, which is only a hundred yards from the cottages, could not be easier and once there, fly, spinning and worm fishing can all be enjoyed.

Also running alongside the cottages is Glanrhyd-y-pysgod's own trout lake covering an area of approximately three acres and stocked with rainbow trout, giving excellent fishing for the beginner as much as the enthusiast.

Glanrhyd-y-pysgod Farm
Maesycrugiau
Pencader
Dyfed SA39 9LX
Tel: (055 935) 253

Monmouthshire to Pembrokeshire

There are numerous hotels in Wales and many offer a warm welcome and some splendid fishing too. Visitors to Wales are seldom very far from beautiful countryside and if you have not yet considered a trip here then we would advise you to do so. There are many places in Wales where time has seemingly stood still.

Firstly, we consider the waters of the Wye which manage to sneak into England too. Around Chepstow, there are several superb hotels to consider. The St Pierre Hotel (0291) 625261 has outstanding leisure facilities, including a championship golf course, whilst lovers of tradition will enjoy the Castle View Inn (02912) 70349. This timber clad hotel stands directly opposite the historic fortress.

History continues in Tintern where we find the Beaufort Hotel (0291) 689777 which has marvellous views over the ruined abbey. The Royal George (0291) 689205 dates from the seventeenth-century and has delightful gardens through which a trout stream cascades into the River Wye. Another good value establishment on the Wye is Parva Farmhouse (0291) 689411. The Crown at Whitebrook (0600) 860254 is to be recommended for its fine restaurant and cosy bedrooms, whilst Clearwell Castle (0594) 32320 is an impressive neo-Gothic castle and the proprietor is happy to arrange some fishing for his guests.

In the Monmouth area, the Kings Head (0600) 712177 is a good place to stay and at Symonds Yat, where the Wye is fast and furious, is the Royal Hotel (0600) 890238 on the banks of the river. In nearby Goodrich, the well named Ye Hostelrie (0600) 890241 is situated in a quiet rural setting, ideally placed for the Wye and a fishing foray!

Like Monmouth, Ross-On-Wye and its environs offer up many good hotels, inns and bed & breakfasts. A small selection for you to ponder would include Pengethley Manor (098987) 211, four miles north of the town and with impressive views over Herefordshire. Similarly impressive is the Wharton Lodge (098981) 795, a Georgian property which stands in fifteen acres of parkland in Weston-Under-Penyard. This is another outstanding establishment. The Bridge House (0989) 62655 is worth a visit as is our final selection here, the Kings Head (0989) 763174, a fourteenth-century inn and a delightful place to stay. The whole area is particularly well endowed with old inns and The Green Man (0432) 860243 at Fownhope dates from the fifteenth-century and is quite splendid with open fires, beams and that sort of thing.

The Wye spans many miles and Hereford reveals yet more delights. Netherwood Country House Hotel, Tupsley (0432) 272388 is a charming Victorian house which once belonged to the Baskerville family. Travelling towards Hay-On-Wye, the visitor may chance upon another fascinating establishment; The Ancient Camp Hotel (0981) 250449, built on the site of an Iron Age fort which has panoramic views of the river. Hay-On-Wye also reveals a number of hotels to use as a base for your fishing holiday. These include the Old Black Lion (0497) 82084 and the Kilvert Court Hotel (0497) 821042 another friendly establishment. The Swan Hotel (0497) 821188 has good fishing and offers superb fishing breaks.

As the Wye gently meanders its way through the valley it has carved so majestically, we chance upon some delightful villages with pubs a plenty and numerous inns too. The Three Cocks (04974) 215 stands in the village from which it takes its name and here you can enjoy some pleasant bedrooms and an outstanding restaurant. Naturally, prices vary throughout the region but those with deeper pockets could consider a visit to Llyswen and the Llangoed Hall (0874) 754525. Sir Bernard Ashley has restored this superb building and if you enjoy gracious living then this is one for you. The restaurant here is also first class. Those with less loot should not be unduly worried as the Griffin Inn (0874) 754241 is a lovely establishment offering good value for your money.

Heading relentlessly upstream, following the A470 northwards, we arrive at Builth Wells where we find several good hotels and inns. The fisherman will be well aware that in addition to the Wye there are numerous other waters in the vicinity and Caer Beris Manor (0982) 552601, an attractively restored country house hotel in peaceful grounds, takes advantage of such a position close to these waters. In the market town of Builth Wells and near the Wye we find a hotel in the traditional sense with plenty of character, The Lion (0982) 553670. Shortly after Builth Wells the Wye is joined by two tributaries; the Ithen and Irfon. Those journeying north eastward should perhaps earmark Penybont. Here an historic inn, the Severn Arms (059787) 224, will fit the bill, while those journeying further on, following the course of the Wye, should earmark Newbridge-On-Wye and the extremely popular New Inn (059789) 211, a comfortable village inn which is thoroughly recommended.

Many fishermen will, however, be heading for the Irfon and in particular the delightful fishing village of Llangammarch Wells. This is an ideal location to use as a base to enjoy the spectacular surrounding scenery. The visitor faces a difficult choice between The Cammarch (05912) 205 or the Lake Country House Hotel (05912) 202. Both have contributed enormously to the excellence of the fishing here. The former is an unpretentious fishing hotel providing excellent value for money and great character. The Lake, however, is for those who prefer a little more style.

The Wye runs through some outstanding areas of natural beauty yet not to be outdone, the Usk reveals its own delights. If you are seeking an hotel of great style and excellent leisure facilities then The Cwrt Bleddyn Hotel (063349) 521 is one to try. Less grand, but no less worthy of a mention, is the Glen-yr-Afon (02913) 2302, situated on the very edge of the Usk—a pleasant and convenient place to stay. Abergavenny is one of the principal towns on the Usk and the Llanwenarth Arms (0873) 810550 nestles on the riverbank to the west of the town enjoying stunning views across the valley. Those who enjoy fine eating should consider the Walnut Tree Inn (0873) 852797 in nearby Llandewi Skirrid. Although the first impression is that of a country pub, this is a renowned restaurant and one of the finest in the country.

Crickhowell is another notable town and here we find The Bear (0873) 810408, an inn of real class and character which has some lovely rooms and a marvellous bar. A little outside the town we find a celebrated fishing hotel, Gliffaes (0874) 730371. The grounds here are magnificent and this is an elegant but friendly hotel in which to stay. More good fishing can be found at Talybont at the Usk Hotel (0874) 87251 which offers excellent value. The Aberclydach House (087487) 361, some two miles south west, is set in a wooded valley within the Brecon National Park and is also a charming place to stay. A final thought is the truly excellent Ty Newydd Country Hotel (0685) 813433 in Hirwaun.

Hotels of character are not as plentiful in the industrial areas of Wales and we shall therefore skip hurriedly down the M4 corridor towards Dyfed which has some wonderful scenery and fine fishing. The Tywi reveals some suitable contenders; The Plough Inn (0267) 290220 in Felingwm-Uchaf, is a splendid restaurant which also has some good bedrooms and is well placed for those wishing to fish the Twyi or the Cothi, its principle tributary. A similarly well located hotel is Ty Mawr (0267) 202332, a charming establishment. The Forest Arms Hotel (0267) 202339 is a friendly hotel too.

Returning to the main stream, there are some fine watering holes well worth inspecting when fishing the Tywi. The Golden Grove Arms at Llanarthney (0558) 668551 is a popular spot and has good value accommodation, too. Further upstream, we find The Cawdor Arms in Llandeilo (0558) 823500, an elegant place to stay. Crugybar is another location to head for, where we find the Glanrannell Park (0558) 685230, nestling in the hills between the Brecon Beacons and the Cambrian Mountains. This is a small country house hotel and a popular place for those wishing to find a rural retreat away from it all.

The waters of Eastern and Western Cleddau can not only be justified in fishing terms but also for those who delight in the beautiful scenery which can be found in the Gower Peninsula. In Haverfordwest, the Hotel Mariners (0437) 763353 is an ideal base from which to explore Pembrokeshire, while in nearby Wolf's Castle, the Wolf's Castle Country House Hotel (043787) 225 is an extremely pleasing place to stay.

Teifi to the Dee
The Teifi will surely be the destination of many a fisherman eager to catch a sewin or two and there are some excellent opportunities to enjoy some good hospitality too. The Castle Malgwyn Hotel (023987) 644 has some

good value breaks available. The Black Lion Hotel in Llanybydder (0570) 480212 is also well worth considering—more good value and a friendly Welsh welcome. Glanrhyd-y-Pysgod (055935) 253 offers comfortable self-catering cottages with access to the river only 100 yards away. Permits available from the nearest village.

Heading further upstream, we arrive at Lampeter and the Falcondale Country House (0570) 422910, a charming mansion set in fourteen acres of parkland. Our final thought here is the Talbot near Tregaron (0974) 298208, a cheap and very cheerful establishment.

Should you be touring the country, then waters you might perchance also be considering are the Aeron, the Rheidol and the Dyfi. There are several hotels to consider en route north, however, and these include the Gwesty Ffern Penbontbren Farm (0239) 810248, a delightful hotel predictably set on a farm. The restaurant here is one to note. The Conrah Country Hotel (0970) 617941 in Chancery, a few miles from Aberystwyth, is a distinguished hotel for those who are venturing to Rheidol and its waters. Hotels which don't have specific rights on the river but still provide a worthy establishment in which to stay include the Ynyshir Hall (0654) 781209 at Eglwysfach. This hotel will appeal still more to lovers of bird life as the RSPB's Ynyshir Reserve neighbours the hotel. If you are fishing the Dovey then you might consider Dolguog Hall (0654) 702244 in Machynlleth. The Hall dates from the seventeenth-century and is the focal point for a small holiday centre. Meanwhile, in the centre of this market town, The Wynnstay Arms (0654) 702941 is a popular meeting place. Beside the river lies Llugwy Hall (0654) 791228, a mile or so outside Pennal which offers charming accommodation.

An hotel which combines both fishing and a good welcome is the fifteenth-century Brigands Inn (0650) 531208 in Mallwyd. This is a very popular hotel amongst the fishing fraternity. The bar snacks, warming fires and pleasant bedrooms all add to the charming atmosphere. Another hotel with a picturesque setting is Buckley Pines (06504) 261—a fine place to stay and enjoy the delights of the local sewin fishing.

Journeying ever northwards, progressing around the coast and through the stunning inland scenery, we find Tal-y-Llyn and the Tyn-y-Cornel Hotel (0654) 782282, which has welcomed anglers for over a hundred and fifty years. This is a delightfully comfortable abode and, in addition to some superb fishing, you will enjoy fine cuisine and views that will last long in your memory.

While we are on the subject of hotels with lake fishing we should consider Lake Vyrnwy Hotel (069173) 692 which is another excellent establishment. If you enjoy fine food, good fishing and marvellous countryside then this is the place for you. The Minffordd Hotel (0654) 761665 may not perch alongside a lake but it boasts impressive views as it lies in the shadows of the mighty Cader Idris. Dolgellau fronts the Mawdach Estuary and has a number of good hotels in which to stay. Abergwynant Hall (0341) 422238, formerly part of a large sporting estate, has marvellous views of the estuary and, similarly, Borthwnog Hall (034149) 271, a splendid Regency house dating from the 1670s, looks out over the estuary. These three hotels are part of a select group of establishments called Welsh Rarebits (0686) 668030 who have a marvellous selection of country house hotels throughout Wales.

The Coed-y-Brenin Forest reveals another fine place to visit; Dolmelynllyn Hall (034140) 273 in Ganllwyd. This is a delightful Victorian house restored to all its former glory, set amidst some breathtaking scenery. Fishing can also be arranged by the hotel for their guests.

Although the sea-trout fishing may have declined somewhat recently it is still worthwhile, especially in North Wales. The River Dwyfawr and its environs offer a number of good establishments. Plas Bodegroes (0758) 612363 is one such example—a delightful restaurant with rooms awaits. A little north of busy Criccieth one finds Llanystumdwy, famous for its Lloyd George connections. Here, the Gwyndy (0766) 522720 is a place for you to consider when trekking through these parts. There are numerous lakes and streams that one can fish and a charming hotel to shortlist is the Royal Goat Hotel at Beddgelert (076686) 224; a welcoming hotel amidst spectacular scenery in the heart of Snowdonia National Park. In addition to the views, the hotel is an ideal base from which to fish or enjoy all manner of other attractions. In Llanrug, midway between Caernarfon and Llanberis, we find yet another outstanding hotel, Seiont Manor (0286) 673366 in Snowdonia, which has fishing in its grounds—a veritable haven for keen fishermen.

Although the Conwy (Conway) is not an easy river to fish it does offer several opportunities. Conwy itself is a busy resort with numerous hotels. However, it may be preferable to journey south through the majestic scenery of the Conwy Valley to find some fine brown trout waters and good hotels. Glyn Isa (0492) 650242 is a quite charming hotel and has the added advantage of being near Conwy Valley Fisheries. A small establishment with first class catering is located in Trefriw. The Hafod House (0492) 640029 is a wonderfully rustic place to stay.

Llanrwst also reveals a number of good hotels which overlook the valley. The Plas Maenan (049269) 232 is one such example while the Maenan Abbey (049269) 247 is an impressive hotel with pleasant gardens and some fishing rights on the Conwy. In Betws-y-Coed, the Gwydyr (0690) 710777 has some excellent fishing and some good value mini-breaks can also be arranged. The centre of the village also reveals the Royal Oak Hotel (06907) 710219, a former coaching inn which stands on the River Llugwy, the second major Conway tributary. There is some good eating to be enjoyed here and comfortable accommodation.

Another riverside setting, on the Lledr this time, reveals Plas Hall (0690) 710206—a really delightful place to stay. The Clwyd and Welsh Dee are other first rate rivers to visit, more gorgeous countryside and a number of pleasing dwellings in which to find accommodation. In St Asaphs, The Plas Elwy (0745) 582263 is a busy and popular hotel full of character, with a respected restaurant. In Ruthin, The Ruthin Castle (08242) 2664 has some twelve miles of fishing available and also boasts some fine grounds and facilities.

The Dee has some excellent fishing in the Llangollen area and there are some equally good hotels in which to stay. We would urge you to try Bodidris Hall (09788) 434, a really delightful place which has a trout lake and some first class shooting. The West Arms Hotel (069) 176 665, in Llanarmon Dyffryn Ceiriog, enjoys a splendid setting and a reputation of equal renown. Bryn Howel (0978) 860331 enjoys panoramic views of the Dee Valley and is a hotel which is thoroughly recommended to the game fisherman. Upstream in Glyndyfrdwy, one finds another fishing hotel of note, The Berwyn Arms (04903) 210—good value and exceptionally welcoming. The Dee is a fine river and the Tyddyn Llan Country House Hotel (049084) 264 is a majestic place to make the most of it. The bedrooms are pleasant and the cuisine mouth-wateringly good. At Pale Hall (06783) 285, in Llanderfel, near Bala, there are good fishing opportunities and some public rooms full of character.

These last two hotels and the spectacular waters of the Dee are a fitting way to conclude our brief journey through Wales. When you consider Wales, do not think of mines or rugby (both are currently in the doldrums in the valleys). Instead, consider some superb fishing, marvellous scenery and a Welsh welcome to remember. Our recommended hotels are often outstanding in every way and can therefore be fairly pricey, but there are numerous less expensive establishments not mentioned and the local tourist boards, as ever, will provide lists of bed and breakfast, guest house and self-catering accommodation. Always get in touch before you make up your mind. Whatever you decide, we wish you good sport in a delightful and relatively unspoilt country, a rarity in this day and age.

Dating back to the fifteenth century, The Griffin Inn is believed to be one of the oldest sporting inns in Wales. That tradition endures today, under the ownership and management of the Stockton family. A keen fisherman himself, Richard Stockton aims to ensure that visitors to The Griffin are able to enjoy a rewarding variety of game fishing.

The Griffin Inn is able to offer excellent salmon fishing along some twenty miles of the lower, middle and upper Wye. There is also superb trout fishing - both for wild brown river fish, and for rainbows in a nearby well-stocked private pool.

Recently, The Griffin embarked on a complementary new enterprise - Griffin Field Sports, incorporating a world-class fishing and shooting school under the personal direction of one of Britain's foremost exponents of both arts: Crawford Little. Throughout the season, the Crawford Little School of Country Sports offers a variety of residential courses in salmon and trout fishing - structured for complete beginners, competent enthusiasts and accomplished sportsmen and women.

The courses range from a broad introduction to fly-fishing, to specialised tuition in the most sophisticated salmon fishing techniques - including Roll and Spey-casting. From basics such as the selection of tackle, to the finer points of salmon line and fly control, all the courses have been carefully devised by Crawford Little to encourage the development of fishing skills - at every level. The School's facilities also include private tuition on a half-day or daily basis - mainly for those wanting to improve a particular aspect of their fly-fishing.

The Griffin itself exudes all the warmth and welcome to be expected of a hostelry where enthusiasm for country pursuits is shared by all the Stockton family, regulars and visitors alike.

Game fishing is very much a theme of The Griffin - the attractive cottage style bedrooms are all named after famous fishing flies, while the bar features a fascinating collection of cased flies, fish and maps of the River Wye.

The unspoilt Fisherman's Bar of The Griffin deserves special mention. Dominated by a huge inglenook fireplace and decorated with traditional simplicity, it has a timeless charm - a haven in which to enjoy good ale, good food and good company, where conversation naturally tends to turn to country matters, in particular, game fishing and shooting.

The Griffin has a well-established and far-reaching reputation for serving outstanding meals - country-style cooking at its best, always prepared from fresh local produce. The Inn's sporting interests are, not surprisingly, reflected in the menu. Depending on the season, it will generally include fresh salmon, river trout or game, invariably well prepared and attractively presented in either the restaurant or bar.

There is residential accommodation for sixteen guests, a comfortable residents' lounge with separate TV room and an attractive dining room. A free house - and incidentally the first 'Logis' in Wales - The Griffin Inn is on the A470 Builth Wells road, 9 miles from Brecon and 7 miles from Hay-on-Wye.

Further details are available from: Richard & Di Stockton:

The Griffin Inn
Llyswen
Brecon
Powys ID3 OUR
Tel: (0874) 754241
Fax: (0874) 754592

The Emerald Isle

Ireland is separated from Great Britain by only the fifty miles of St George's Channel, but to arrive in Ireland is to feel on the other side of the world. Ireland has three great assets; its countryside, the Irish themselves and the fishing! Everyone has heard of the description of Ireland as the Emerald Isle. Indeed, so often does the phrase crop up in advertisements and tourist brochures that you probably begin to wonder what the fuss is all about. Naturally, the only way to find out is to go there!

I well remember my first visit, which was to stay with friends in Tipperary. My friends met me at Dublin and in a very short time we had passed the Curragh and were heading west. Fields of lush, emerald green pasture succeeded each other, broken only now and then by cornfields. The green really is of a much deeper and richer hue than that of its English counterpart. One of the big surprises is the lack of traffic. Even on the main roads it is a fraction of what we have to put up with and if you turn off onto one of the country roads, you can drive for miles without seeing another car. Motoring is a real pleasure and you have ample opportunity to admire the magnificent scenery. The Irish have been conservation minded for a long time and the city of Dublin is a fine example of this. Many fine Georgian terraces had, by the 1950s, fallen into decay. Instead of pulling them down and erecting monstrous high-rise blocks, the Government has restored them and the modern buildings, such as they are, have been designed to fit in with their surroundings.

The Irish are justly renowned for their charm and hospitality. They are also famous for their love of sport. Horse racing is a passion for the Irish and everyone seems to know of a 'likely' horse. 'Likely' is a much used word and capable of many interpretations, as punters will know. Fishing is a sport which has a national following and the Irish are always keen to offer help and advice to the visiting angler.

I remember on one occasion being asked if I had fished Lough Corrib, some sixty miles away. Answering in the negative, I was assured that it would be a shame to return without having fished such a grand water. I thought no more about it and stumbled up to bed. However, at breakfast the next morning, my host announced that he had organised two days for me on the Corrib and would be coming too. We had a great two days, during which I was introduced to the art of dapping and was lucky enough to return with some fine sea-trout.

I have received the same hospitality and friendship whenever I have gone fishing on my own. On one holiday, I stopped at a garage to fill up with petrol. When the proprietor noticed the rods in the back of the car he asked if I was there for the fishing. We got talking and he asked me if I could spare a day as he knew of a small lough which held some fine trout. The following day his son was left in charge of the garage and we set off. The lough was miles from anywhere and I would never have found it on my own. My new-found friend gave me some flies he had tied the previous evening which resembled no pattern I had come across—but did they work! Within an hour and a half we both had two brace of fine brownies, the best being over 4lb.

If this all sounds too good to be true, I know of many others with similar tales and urge you to go and try for yourself! If you would prefer to explore Ireland on a more organised basis there are several operators who can organise fabulous holidays: Gillaroo Angles (0232) 862419 and Rod and Stream plc. (0704) 501450; to name but two.

Please note that telephone numbers quoted for Northern Ireland are national and those quoted for Eire are international. To call a number in the south from the British Isles it is necessary to drop the 0 from the code and use the prefix: 010 353.

Delphi Fisheries (Delphi Estate)

Ireland
190

Artist Clive Madgwick TROUT FISHING, COUNTY MAYO Courtesy of Rosenstiels

Ireland
191

SOUTH OF DUBLIN

Dublin City, its environs and the Counties Wicklow, Meath, Kildare and Louth make up the naturally beautiful Eastern Seaboard. Dublin Bay makes a glorious sweep northwards to Howth Head Peninsula, where there are spectacular views across the bay from the cliff walks, and southwards to the picturesque Dalkey, and its island with Benedictine ruins, then on to Killiney, where it is said that the view south compares with that over Naples. The Georgian city of Dublin was the European City of Culture in 1991 and its heritage trail around the old medieval parts of the city allows the visitor an insight into the nature of the Irish and also gives them the opportunity to sample some of Ireland's more modern culture—in the pub! The Irish are world renowned for their hospitality and in Dublin you will not be disappointed. There is no such thing as a quiet pint in Ireland, as you will inevitably be drawn into conversation by the locals.

The Boyne

With early Christian monuments scattered around the Boyne Valley to the north, the Newgrange burial chamber dating from 3000 B.C., some fine stately homes and gardens at Kilruddery and Mount Usher to the south, there is much to see and do. To the west of the city is the mecca for Ireland's other great passion—horseracing. Here, on the flat open plains of County Kildare, some of the best racehorses in the world are bred, trained and raced at the nearby Curragh. The River Boyne rises near Edenderry and flows for about seventy miles through County Meath to enter the sea near Drogheda, north of Dublin. Leave Dublin to the north-west, on the N2, where the imposing Slane Castle dates from 1785—the road from Dublin to the castle was supposedly straightened to hasten George IV's visits to his mistress! Here we find the fine limestone fishery with good runs and some deep pools. Unfortunately, due to low water levels, in recent years fewer fish have been taken, but some large salmon have been caught and this fishery really deserves a better reputation. Once a river of note for salmon, the arterial drainage scheme has lowered the water table and this has affected the runs up river. Brown trout are prolific in certain areas and come to wet and dry flies as well as spinners and worms. However, the river does tend to weed up from late July onwards. Sea-trout on the lower reaches are good in the autumn but generally the river is better known for its brownies. Local knowledge is absolutely essential and can be gleaned from any of the fourteen angling clubs or landowners who control the water.

The Trim, Athloy and District Angling Association (046) 31487 have a beat on the Boyne, and Gerard Lee wil be happy arrange a day's fishing on their behalf for IR5. This is fly-only water, and there is a bag limit of nine fish. A 5lb trout was caught here in 1993. Among the better flies for this stretch of the river are March Brown, Greenwells Glory, Sherry Spinner and Black Midge.

In recent years, some of the best fishing has been between Navan and Drogheda, with the lower stretches having good runs of grilse and sea-trout. The Kells Blackwater and Lough Ramor have also produced some good trout, averaging 2lb, especially during the mayfly hatch and in the evenings. The season runs from 1st February to 1st September for salmon and 1st March to 14th September for trout with permits priced at around IR10 per day.

The Navan Anglers' Association, Abbey Road, Navan, has fourteen miles of mixed bank fishing with excellent wild brown trout, and both wet and dry fly fishing is permitted. Michael Connor (046) 29007 is the man to contact. Permits for the Navan Club Waters only are available from the Sports Den (046) 21130 in Tringate Street, Navan.

Drogheda and District Anglers control one mile of the tidal section near the town which is good for sea-trout, and three miles up river which is particularly good for brownies around mayfly time. Salmon can be caught here too depending on the height of the river. In addition, the Club controls the rights to two reservoirs at Killineer (fly-only) and Bernattin, where you can use any method. Both are put and take reservoirs and are stocked with brownies and rainbows. The club also has the rights for the nine mile long River Nanny nearby, well stocked with brown trout.

Sean Keenan, The Military Connections (army surplus and tackle shop) (041) 34371, 8 Lawrence Street, Drogheda, sells permits for the Drogheda Angling Waters and Shane and Rosslin Anglers' Association, who have stretches of mixed bank fishing on the Boyne totalling two miles. These adjacent waters have a good mixture of deep pools and fast flowing waters with a couple of weirs. Sean Keenan will be happy to advise you as he fishes these waters himself.

The Liffey

The source of the River Liffey is around thirteen miles southwest of Dublin in the Wicklow mountains, but it winds its way through Poulaphouca, Golden Falls and Leixlip Reservoirs before reaching the sea eighty miles away at Islandbridge. It is essential to check the river before beginning to fish, as artificial floods do affect fly fishing and there are few salmon above Leixlip Bridge. The lower stretches are much better.

The Liffey is controlled by the Federation of Liffey Angling Clubs, (045) 33068 which co-ordinates all the clubs' fishing. The river is either club or privately owned with no free fishing anywhere on the eighty mile stretch. The season here runs from February to September, with the best salmon fishing from February to April, and sea-trout and grilse from July to September. The first hatches of dark olives begin in late March, the hawthorn and iron blue dun in early May, mayfly in May and June and various sedges throughout the summer. The Clubs welcome visitors and the cost of a day's fishing should be around IR5.

Dublin and District Anglers' Association; Pat O'Molloy (01) 6558594 at 16 Whitehall Crescent, Terenure, controls fisheries at St Raphaels, Celbridge, Avondale and

Islandbridge. Rory at Rory's Tackle Shop (01) 6772351, 17a Temple Bar, Dublin 2, fishes all over Ireland and is also a member of the North Kildare Trout and Salmon Association. He is happy to advise on the Liffey and elsewhere. The North Kildare Association has around thirty miles of mainly double-bank fishing stretching from Millicent Bridge to Kilcullen, with good salmon in September and an excellent stretch for trout near Millicent Bridge. Tom Walshe, also a member of North Kildare, can be contacted at John Cahill & Sons (045) 79655, and is happy to offer advice on all matters.

Dublin Trout Anglers' Association have fisheries at Clane and Straffan and contact should be made with Mr J. R. Miley (01) 6902163. Michael Casey of the Clane Trout and Salmon Anglers Association (045) 68995 can arrange day permits for approximately four miles of the Liffey for IR5. Dry-fly is the most productive method here. Worm and spinning for trout is allowed but not encouraged. Salmon are taken either spinning or with worm. (You should note that white maggots are banned on all salmonid rivers in Eire). This stretch of the middle Liffey runs slow and rich and has all of the flies familiar to chalkstream anglers. Early season sees falls of hawthorn flies and hatches of spring olives. The most important fly, the grey flag, appears in mid-May and can provide exceptional sport although it has declined in recent years. There is good evening sedge fishing and an abundance of blue-winged olives which provoke consistent rises to the sherry spinner in the evening and into the dark. There is a good mayfly hatch in late May. It should be noted that there is an electricity power plant on the lake at the top of the river and heavy floods occur. These can be dangerous to an unwary angler as they can appear at any time with no warning although they are fairly infrequent in the peak angling season. Dan O'Brien, New Road, Blackhall and Sye Gallagher, Reeves, Straffan—both County Kildare—can provide you with day permits. Tom Deegan (01) 6980222, of the Ballymore Estate Anglers' Association also controls some stretches in this area. Leixlip Anglers have a good salmon pool but it tends to be very heavily fished. Garnetts and Keegans in Dublin can supply you with all the necessary tackle.

Artist: G D Armour   **SALMON FISHING—COMING TO THE GAP**   *Courtesy of Malcolm Innes Gallery*

Four picturesque river valleys wind their way to the Irish Sea; the Suir, the Barrow and the Nore at Waterford and the Slaney at Wexford. This is the sunny south east corner of Ireland with long stretches of sandy beaches along the south coast. It is the home of the world famous Waterford crystal and is one of the most beautiful areas of the country. Of great historical importance, the National Heritage Park at Wexford traces the history of man and here we find the medieval Kilkenny, with the imposing castle on the bank of the Nore.

The Suir

The Suir has some of the finest trout fishing in the country for virtually its entire 130 mile length, from its source on Devils Bit Mountain near the border of County Tipperary and County Offaly to Carrick-on-Suir where it meets tidal waters. A 57lb salmon was taken here in 1874, but today (unfortunately) the average weight for fish taken here is around 7lb and trout are far more abundant than salmon. The season runs from March to September with fine fly-fishing in May, June and September. The Suir is a rich limestone river with several shallow and deep glides, only occasionally interspersed with shallow riffles. At Templemore, where the river is about fifteen feet wide, many trout are taken at around the 2lb mark.

Downstream from Thurles, the River Drish joins the Suir near Turtulla Bridge, where Michael Mockler (0504) 22493 is Secretary of the Thurles, Holycross and Ballycamas Anglers' Association. There is some free fishing on this stretch where good trout are taken and further information on the best water can be gleaned from the locals here, who are only too happy to offer help and advice. Further downstream, Ardmayle House (0504) 42399 is four miles west of Cashel on the L185 and has one mile of double-bank fishing which is free to guests staying at this comfortable hotel. The water is quite slow in parts here, and deep, but good for brownies. The owners can also organise fishing on other stretches both up and downstream.

At Camas Bridge, the river becomes wide and shallow, with some spring salmon. The grilse run is in July and August. The Cashel Golden and Tipperary Anglers Club control both banks up to the delightful Suir Castle and share the west bank to New Bridge with the Cahir and District Anglers' Association. Permits are available to fish this peaceful and secluded stretch, set in beautiful rolling green countryside, from Breeda Morissey at Morissey's Bar (052) 41516 for IR5 a day. Permits can also be obtained from Breeda for the Ara and Aherlow tributaries. The bar is a favourite haunt for many fishermen and is an excellent place to pick up good local tips as well as to hear some very entertaining stories.

Downstream from Cahir, fly fishing only is the rule. The waters here are shallow and free flowing as they glide under the walls of the beautiful Cahir Castle, standing on the banks of the River Suir. Good stocks of trout are found in this pretty stretch of water. Kilcoran Lodge

(052) 41288, set in twenty acres of landscaped gardens on the slopes of the Galtee Mountains, has a nine mile stretch of the Suir and eight miles on the Aherlow.

The Tar

In the beautiful Knockmealdown Mountains, the Shanbally and Duag join forces to form the River Tar, with good-sized trout found in the deeper pools. The Tar enters the Suir upstream from Newcastle, but for much of its length the fishing is free and also readily accessible, as the river runs close to the main road to the west of Newcastle. The Ardfinnan Anglers Club do control some of the Suir around this area and contact should be made with John Maher (052) 66242, the Club Secretary, Green View, Ardfinnan (the corner house beside Maher's Foodstore).

The Nire

The bubbling, fast-flowing River Nire winds its way from the Nire lakes through tree-lined glens and enters the Suir downstream from the town of Newcastle. The river varies in width from between fifteen to fifty feet and contains a good stock of brown trout. All legitimate methods of fishing are allowed here. As the Nire enters the Suir it widens to forty yards and comprises fast flowing shallows interspersed with long glides. Frans Beckers (052) 36433 and Eileen Ryan (052) 36141 control a four mile stretch of water on the Suir and seven miles on the Nire. Fishing here is fly-only and the cost for a day ticket is IR5. Salmon fishing here has seen a downturn of late. Nevertheless, as if proof were needed that this glorious part of Ireland was attractive to overseas visitors, Jean Loup Trautner of the Marlfield Fisheries (052) 25234 has an answering message in French!

Downstream from Clonmel, the Rivers Anner, Clashawley and Moyle meander peacefully through the Tipperary countryside past Anner Castle, to enter the Suir upstream from Kilsheelin. The Glencastle Fishery's water (052) 33287 is one and a half miles long and is very well stocked to provide some of the best fishing on the Suir, with deep pools and gentle glides, although it is barely two miles upstream from tidal waters. Fly fishing only is the rule and day tickets can be purchased for IR5. Mrs Long organises self-catering accommodation right on the river—perfect for a fishing holiday.

At Carrick-on-Suir, in a spectacular setting lodged between the Slievenamon Hills and the rolling slopes of the Comeraghs with their small mountain loughs, there is good salmon and trouting on what has become a splendid stretch from the Devils Bit Mountain.

The Nore

The Nore lies between the Barrow and the Suir and runs into the same estuary towards Waterford. Trout are regularly restocked and the sport is excellent. Mountrath and District Anglers Club (0502) 32540 offer day permits for IR1, a week for IR2. A season's fishing can be had for IR4. Four boats are available for hire. Thomas Watkins is the Honorary Secretary of the Association, and recommended flies are Red Butcher, Green Olive, Black Midge and May Fly. The association recommends that all unwanted fish are returned. Thomastown Anglers Association (056) 24363/24378 have eight miles on the Nore. A twenty-pound salmon was caught here in 1993 and a day permit will cost IR8, or IR3 for trout. No prawns or shrimps are allowed and flies and worms only for trout.

The Munster Blackwater

From its source in the Killarney Mountains near the Cork border with County Kerry, the Munster Blackwater (sometimes referred to as the Irish Rhine) meanders slowly eastwards through the scenic Blackwater Valley, before turning sharply south at Cappoquin to enter the sea at Youghal Bay through an estuary which stretches for fifteen miles. This is probably the most famous salmon river in Ireland and consistently provides fishermen with excellent sport and excitement. This great river has to be fished—even if it is the last thing you do.

The salmon and sea-trout season begins on 1st February and brown trout on 15th February and runs until 18th September. Sea-trout tend not to go up the main river but rather swim up the River North Bride, although they may occasionally be caught in the tidal section of the Blackwater River. The river runs through some twenty-five miles of the most beautiful countryside from its source, to be joined by the Rivers Dalau and Allow at Kanturk. Salmon predominate these waters with good brown trout in the tributaries and permits are available from John O'Sullivan (029)50257 at the Tackle Shop in Kanturk. The Assolas Country House (029) 50015 is an elegant manor house set on the banks of the river. This family-run establishment, near to Kanturk, has a well known restaurant where the Bourkes use freshly prepared local produce. The hotel can organise fishing for their guests on the nearby Blackwater and you should contact Mr Bourke for further information. Downstream, there are more good stretches of salmon fishing, some of which is free, but details on the waters are available from Dick Willis (022) 21057 at the Bridge House Bar in Mallow. Day tickets for this six mile stretch are priced at IR5 for brown trout and IR10 for salmon if the water level is high enough, and are available form the tackle shop in Mallow (022) 20121.

Blackwater Castle (022) 26333 is an imposing twelfth-century fort, built to protect the Holy St Patrick's Well which stands high above the Awbeg River at Castletownroche in County Cork. It provides excellent accommodation and has a fine gourmet restaurant. The Castle can also offer guests fishing on the Awbeg in one of the most scenic parts of the Blackwater Valley.

The Careysville Fishery, three miles downstream from Fermoy, consists of two miles of double-bank fishing with good pools and provides some of the most productive beats in Ireland. There is an excellent run at the start of the season below the Weir, with good salmon fishing throughout the fishery until May. June sees the grilse run, with good catches taken downstream peaking in July. The fishing remains good throughout the latter part of the season. The average weight in recent years for salmon has been 10lb with some rare fish weighing as much as 50lb. Details for the fishery can be obtained from the Estate Office, Lismore Castle, County Waterford (058) 544244, who also sell sea-trout and brown trout permits. The Ballymaquirk Fishery run by Julie O'Conner at Greybrook House, Waterfall, County Cork, has a good stretch of water upstream from Mallow. Peter Dempster Ltd. (058) 56248 in Conna has approximately nine miles of fishing for clients at IR30 per rod per day. Tackle and tuition are also available. Ballyduff Trout Fly Angling Association (058) 60201 have five miles of the Blackwater. The Secretary is Eamon Bolger, the brown trout avcerage around 8oz and a week's permit is available for £6. The Blackwater Lodge Fishery (058) 60235 at Upper Ballyduff is a high-yielding stretch with fifteen miles divided into seventeen beats downstream from Ballygarrett near Mallow. Again, there is a good spring run of salmon in February and March and the grilse run starts in May and peaks in July. The autumn run in late August and September generally sees some heavier fish. In recent years 1500 fish have been taken in a season, up to 25lb in weight. The most popular methods have proved to be spinning and worms. In 1993 permits were available for between IR28 and IR35 per day and ghillies can also be arranged through the lodge. The Blackwater Lodge is owned and run by Ian Powell who is happy to advise all his guests on one topic—fishing! The lodge stands on the south bank of the Blackwater in an ideal location for the fisherman. The Cappoquin Salmon and Trout Anglers Club (058) 54317 have five beats on the Blackwater. All methods are allowed and a day permit can be had for IR12.

Longueville is set in the centre of a 500 acre private wooded estate, overlooking one of the most beautiful river valleys in Ireland, the Blackwater - itself forming the Estate's southern boundary, famous as one of Ireland's foremost salmon and trout rivers.

Longueville is three miles on the Killarney road ex Mallow; Killarney itself in the heart of scenic Kerry being less than one hour away. Cork airport is 24 miles distant and Shannon airport is 54 miles away. Guests can make day trips to the Dingle and Beara Peninsulas. Blarney, Kinsale and the Vee Gap are all less than one hour's drive. For stay-at-homes, Longueville offers three miles of game fishing on the famous Blackwater river. There is horse-riding at nearby stables and golf at a dozen courses closeby including Premier Championship courses at Killarney, Ballybunion and Tralee.

A games room with full sized billiard table is in the basement. The estate is quiet and peaceful for walking or jogging with idyllic paths through wooded ways and water meadows.

Built in 1720, Longueville is the ancestral home of your hosts. Their aim is to maintain the friendly atmosphere of a home rather than a hotel. The centre block and two wings were added in 1800 and the Turner Curvilinear Conservatory was added in 1862.

Inside, Longueville offers many beautiful ceilings, doors and items of antique furniture in the public rooms and bedrooms - but in the latter, whether it be antique or otherwise, the acme of comfort is the bed. All bedrooms have en suite bathroom, colour television, radio and direct dial telephone.

The aim of Longueville's hosts is to have guests relax and feel completely at home in the comfort of their beautiful house, a classic Georgian country house. Central to all this is the kitchen, the heart of Longueville, over which the O'Callaghans' son William, a French-trained chef, presides. In here three lovingly prepared meals a day are made, using only the fresh produce of the estate's river, farm and gardens.

To match the superb food, Longueville's cellar includes over 150 wines, both from the Old and New World. The family's interest in wine has led them to plant their own three acre vineyard - unique in Ireland - produced in years of favourable climate.

Longueville House & Presidents' Restaurant
Mallow
Co Cork
Republic of Ireland
Tel: (010 353 22) 47156/47306
Fax: (010 353 22) 47459

When not looking after their guests' every need, proprietors Ian and Ute Powell enjoy nothing more than showing off the day's catch at the Blackwater Lodge.

It's a cosy, relaxed, informal, family-run hotel overlooking the famous Munster Blackwater—one of Europe's most beautiful and spectacular salmon rivers. The Lodge has exclusive rights on fifteen miles of the river, divided into seventeen premier beats, with a strict maximum of four rods per beat.

Very accessible
Only 155 kms from Rosslare ferryport and 50 kms from Cork airport, it's not surprising that the Blackwater Lodge attracts a large and loyal contingent of overseas anglers. They come not only for the quality of the fishing, but also for the unique atmosphere that's refreshingly 'no nonsense'. As one guest put it, 'more jeans than plus-fours'. It's something you'll sense right through the Hotel - from the excellent restaurant, to the well stocked tackle shop, to the chat-filled bar.

All about fishing
Beats are rotated on a daily basis and you're given your beat the night before. With your beat comes a detailed map of how to get there and a diagram of the beat with all pools and runs marked with helpful hints on tackle and water conditions. For even more detailed advice, our team of experienced ghillies are only too happy to help.

Back in the evening and we can treat your catch as you wish—with our own smoking, freezing and vacuum-packing facilities.

Hotel or self-catering
In addition to the Hotel itself we have a number of self-catering cottages in the hotel grounds. These are ideal for the larger group—especially if there are non-anglers in the party. For them, the surrounding area offers many attractions. Fabulous sandy beaches at Youghal; tennis; swimming; golf; horse riding and pony trekking are within the catchment area.

Ian and Ute Powell believe that a good holiday is a hassle-free holiday, so once you get in touch they are quite happy to organise everything for you—hotel, beat reservations, ferry tickets and even car hire. They'd prefer you concentrated on catching what could be the fish of a lifetime on one of the most beautiful rivers in Ireland.

Blackwater Lodge
Upper Ballyduff
Co Waterford
Ireland
Tel: (353) 58 60235
Fax: (353) 58 60162

Counties Cork, Limerick and Kerry, with their warm gulf breezes, provide a conducive climate for exotic and sub-tropical species of plants and vegetation. To the west of the area lie picturesque river valleys contrasting with the mountain ranges, deep loughs and rugged coastline. In Cork itself, lies the famous Blarney Castle and Stone. One kiss and you're immediately bestowed with the Irish gift of the gab!

The Lee

The River Lee drains Gouganebarra Lake and flows fifty-three miles to Cork Harbour through rugged mountains and rolling moorland, through two large dams used to create hydro-electric power. There is a feeling amongst the locals that the introduction of the dams has had a detrimental effect on the fishing here, but not everyone shares this view. However, game fishing on the Lee now seems to be concentrated on the seven miles or so between the dams and the city of Cork. The salmon season runs from February to the end of September. Mid March is the best time for spring fish and September fishing is also good, if the water levels are right. The trout season runs from 15th February to 12th October and licences are not required. Although more noted for its salmon, the Lee is also a first class trout stream. Anglers should contact the local angling clubs as there are voluntary restrictions operating with regard to the minimum length (seven inches) and size of catch.

The South Western Regional Fisheries Board (026) 41221 in County Cork can advise you on where to fish and will also issue you with some useful local maps. Immediately below the dam is the Inniscarra Fishery, controlled by the Board, which consists of three quarters of a mile of double-bank fishing, noted for its spring fishing and grilse run in June and July. Both spinning (Yellow Belly or Toby) and fly fishing (Hairy Mary or Shrimp) have proved very successful in recent years. The Board's fisheries are manned by keepers and bailiffs and permits can be obtained from the fishery. However, advance booking is strongly advised. The Lee Salmon Anglers (021) 342511 (Brendon O'Flaherty) have about three miles of the lower River Lee, below the dam, and sell daily and weekly tickets at IR10 and IR40 respectively. The Cork Salmon Anglers (021) 872137 (John Buckley) also have about three miles of mixed bank fishing here, with several salmon pools on their stretch. Day tickets can be obtained from the very helpful Mr Buckley at T.W. Murray and Co. (021) 271089 in Cork. There is also free fishing from the footpaths along the river above Waterworks Weir.

Downstream, the Lower Lee Fishery at Thomas Davis Bridge (also a Fisheries Board stretch) is one and a half miles of water with a fine, deep pool which is best fished around high tide with shrimp or prawn. The Tackle Shop, Lavitts Quay (021) 272842 will take bookings and give advice on all other matters regarding the fishing here.

The Bandon

Rising some fifty miles to the west, the River Bandon flows through this beautiful part of County Cork to enter the sea at Kinsale. The season for salmon and trout on the Bandon runs from 15th February to 30th September. February through to May are considered the best months for salmon, especially if it rains, and there are reasonable runs in August and September. Sea-trout and grilse run in June and brown trout fishing is good all season.

From just below Cork, down to the coast, the river becomes tidal and so the fishing is largely free. However, it is advisable to check locally beforehand. Mr Lee (023) 41178 at the Saddlers and Tacklist in Cork regularly fishes the river and is very happy to advise you on the appropriate flies to use. Michael O'Regan, 21 Oliver Plunkett Street, Bandon (023) 41674 of Bandon Anglers' Association controls eight miles of double-bank fishing on the Lee. Salmon fishing costs between IR10 and IR15 a day and IR50 a week. Trout fishing costs IR5 a day or IR25 a week. Contact him directly for further information. David Lamb (023) 47279 at Kilcoleman Fishery in Enniskeane can arrange self-catering accommodation in a lodge or part of a larger house, with one rod included in the accommodation fee. The brownies here are excellent. Accommodation is also available at Blandfield House (021) 885167 which has access to a mile of single-bank fishing on the Bandon, with good salmon in February and August. The Innishannon Hotel (021) 775121 owns eight miles of the tidal Bandon and fishing is free for guests and within the hotel's own grounds. The hotel also has access to five miles of water controlled by Bandon Anglers Club. Trout is fly-only and fishing is best from June to the end of the season. Any legal method is permitted for salmon.

Smaller Rivers

Argideen Anglers control the best three miles of sea-trout fishing on the Argideen, which enters the sea at Tinoleague. Visitors tickets are available for night fishing from the Fishery Office at Inchy Bridge. Peter Wolstenholme (023) 46239 may be able to help you here.

Several small salmon rivers, principally the Roughty and the Sheen, discharge into the Kenmare river and its deep lough, where the spectacular coastline and picturesque valleys are a delight. March is the best time for spring salmon, with grilse starting their run in July and August.The Sheen Falls Lodge (064) 41600 in Kenmare is situated on the River Sheen and the hotel enjoys seventeen and a half miles of water which is reserved for residents only and the fishing is free. The fishing is limited to fifteen rods per day with ghillies also available from the hotel. The two mile stretch immediately adjacent to the hotel is the best stretch for salmon. Mr Jan O'Hare (064) 41499 runs an electrical shop in Kenmares Main Street but he is more than willing to give interested parties a guided tour of the local fishing—by phone! He also sells tackle, licences and permits for a one and a half mile stretch of the River Roughty belonging to Artully Castle Salmon Fishery (064) 41447 run by Michael Harrington, just five miles outside Kenmare on the Code Road. The river is about fourteen miles long and the stretch owned by the Artully Club has some fabulous holding pools. Much of the river runs through open farmland and permission must be obtained from the local farmer or landowner. There is also some good sea-trout here, but few brown trout in the Roughty or the Sheen. There are a number of small loughs in this area, and the Kenmare Trout Anglers Club, Secretary John Dewey (064) 41676 can offer day permits for £3.

Lough Currane

Lough Currane in County Kerry, often referred to as Waterville Lake, is linked to the sea by the short Waterville river. The lake is generally considered to be one of the best game fishing loughs in the country. Near to the village of Waterville, it yields more sea-trout than any other fishery in the country, usually over three thousand each year, with some of the fish weighing over 10lb. A few years ago sea-trout numbers were down. The

Waterville Anglers' Association began some extensive work cleaning up spawning grounds, putting new gravel down and, with the new salmon hatchery up and running, there is much less pressure on the sea-trout for spawning beds. The best fishing is from May to the end of the season in mid-October. In addition to the sea-trout, however, there is excellent spring salmon from January through until June and the average weight is 10lb.

The grilse run in the lough is best in July and August. It is an excellent water for the beginner and expert alike and the fishing is free except for the cost of your state licence. Boats may be hired through the Waterville Anglers' Association. Michael O'Sullivan (0667) 4255 is more than happy to offer advice on the waters in the area and he can be found at The Lobster Bar and Restaurant in the centre of Waterville. There is also a Waterville Hotel (0667) 4310, now owned by Club Med, which testifies to the area's popularity with European visitors. Possibly one of the best known hotels in Ireland, the Butler Arms Hotel (0667) 4156 looks out over the Atlantic. The Huggards provide a warm welcome to all guests and keen anglers are able to make use of the hotel's four privately owned lakes, set high in the mountains, where boats and fishing are free to guests. The hotel will also arrange ghillies on request. Non-residents are charged IR15 per day for fishing which includes a boat. The hotel will also be happy to arrange a day's salmon fishing on the River Inny at a cost of IR10.

Artist: Roger Desoutter SEPTEMBER MORNING Courtesy of Rosenstiel's

Lough Namona

Lough Namona, connected to the Currane by the Cummeragh River, holds a good stock of brownies but is fished for the large sea-trout, as is Cloonaghlin Lough. Also part of this system is Derriana Lough, set high amidst the most spectacular scenery and fishes well for salmon, sea-trout and brown trout which are taken from the bank. Towards the end of the season, you must try the Coppal Lough which drains into the Currane at the east shore via the Coppal river. If you are not staying at the Butler Arms permission will be required for these four loughs.

Glencar Lake & the Caragh

Driving north-east across country from Waterville will bring the intrepid fisherman to another great Irish lough—Caragh. Set at the mouth of the magnificent Glencar Valley, Caragh is often called Glencar Lake and is noted for its spring salmon and grilse. For some unexplained reason the fly is not a method often used and most salmon are caught towards the southern end of the lough on the troll or by spinning. Sea-trout are caught from July and, historically, the best area has been around the mouth of the outflowing Lower Caragh. Brownies are small but on light tackle the sport is very thrilling. Fishing is free and for boats and boatmen contact the Glencar Hotel (066) 60102 which owns Loughs Acoose, Cloon and Reagh. Acoose will provide a great day for the trout fisherman who might find himself battling it out with a small salmon. The trout are small but quite free rising and many a local lad has been broken-in on this water.

The River Caragh completes the system flowing north into Dingle Bay. Mr Pat O'Grady (066) 68228 has been fishing this corner of Ireland for years and is very happy to advise newcomers to the area. He also issues permits for two miles of double-bank fishing on the Lower River Caragh, some private boats on the nearby River Laune, and day tickets for some rainbow stocked lakes. Mr O'Grady lives six hundred yards outside Glenbeigh on the Killarney road. His house is called Ferndale Heights. The Glencar Hotel (066) 60102 has a good seven miles of double-bank fishing on the Upper Caragh costing around IR200 per week. After July 1st, day tickets are available for IR30. The hotel is owned by a Swiss-German partnership and bookings made during the season are handled by Mrs Doppler in Kssnacht, Switzerland (01- 910) 3662. Bookings made out of peak season are done directly through the hotel. Salmon are from 1st February to mid-July.

The Shannon & Lough Derg

Wild brown trout, sea-trout and Atlantic salmon lie in the rivers and lakes of the Shannon region, which comprises the Counties of Clare, Tipperary, West and South-west Offaly, Limerick and North Kerry.

The River Shannon is the largest, longest river in Ireland and Great Britain. It stretches from its source three miles south of Blacklion, running for two hundred and twenty miles through central Ireland, to enter the Atlantic via a very long estuary. Mainly a slow-running, limestone river with an abundance of weed and insect life, the active fishery management have, to a large degree, rescued the river from the devastating effects of an hydro-electric scheme introduced in the 1940s.

South of the Shannon estuary and Limerick lies County Limerick and North Kerry. Numerous rivers and loughs enter the estuary with the productive River Feale often yielding over three thousand fish each season. The Loobagh and Camogue join the River Maigue, which enters the estuary west of Limerick, with good stocks of brown trout. Bunratty Castle stands on the banks of the Bunratty River at the river's estuary and there is some easy fishing from the river banks with sea-trout best in June and July.

Chris Meehan (061) 361555 at Shannon Development, Shannon Town Centre, County Clare, controls the fishing in the Shannon region and is very helpful with up to the minute information about the state of the river and the best stretches to fish.

At twenty-two miles long, Lough Dergh is the largest lake on the Shannon, with the best trout fishing during the mayfly season, which can start as early as the end of April. Dapping is popular here. Artificial flies such as the Spent Gnat and Grey Wolff are popular, with trout averaging 2lb although much larger fish are regularly caught. Historically, Derg was one of the great trout fisheries but has not lived up to its reputation of late. However, many anglers still make the pilgrimage during the mayfly season. This is a large lough and a boat is something of a necessity. There are boats available from points all around the lough and Chris Meehan will be able to give you a contact for wherever you wish to fish.

South Offaly and North Tipperary stretches from the River Brosna, with its small run of spring salmon and good grilse in early July, to Limerick in the south. Contact Jim Robinson (061) 414900/377666 at his shop in Limerick or Castleconnell for licences, permits, ghillies and boat hire. The best salmon fishing is on the Lower Shannon at Plassy. You will also find good salmon on the Mulcair, a twenty mile spate tributary at Castleconnell, where the salmon are fabulous and the season extends from March 1st to the end of September.

Elsewhere on the Shannon, the season starts on February 1st for salmon and February 15th for trout, ending on September 30th. Jim Robinson can also arrange private beats at Castleconnell for IR25 a day and boats on his own trout fishery—stocked with browns and rainbows at the fifty-five acre Lough Bleach.

The Fisheries Office, E.S.B. Hydro Group, Ardnacrusha, near Limerick (061) 345588 and The Limerick Sports Store, 10 William Street (061) 345647 can make all the necessary arrangements for anglers around Parteen, Plassey, Castleconnell and the Mulcair. Good trout fishing is possible at Killaloe, especially during May and in the autumn. This is where Lough Derg drains into the Shannon and the people to contact are McKeoghs in Ballina (061) 376249.

Shannon Region Fisheries restock Pallas lake, eighteen miles east of the river, with rainbow and brown trout. Here, the season starts late on 1st May and runs until 12th October, with good bank fishing. Further information is available from Jim Robinson.

Lough Ree, 25,000 acres, at Athlone, is stocked with trout by the local angling association and good trout fishing is available here in June. Through County Roscommon, Longford and Leitrim is Lough Allen, the most northerly lake on the Shanon, where large trout and pike are often taken. This is, in fact, a reservoir supplying Limericks power station and the water levels rise and fall, leaving dangerous rocks exposed.

The Shannon Regional Fisheries Angling Centre (049) 36144 overlooks Chambers Bay on Lough Sheelin. Reached by heading north east from Granard on the M55 and following the small signpost. Take the turning off to the right towards the lake shore, which serves Mullaghboy Guest House, Kilnahard Boat Quay and the angling information centre. Sheelin is one of the great Irish limestone loughs with a high-pH, ensuring a rich stock of natural food for the sizeable and excellent quality trout. In fact, fishery scientists have estimated that the lake has the greatest trout carrying capacity in Ireland and supports approximately 100,000 trout! Crover House (049) 40206 sits on the northern shore, providing fine views down the lough and has excellent accommodation. This two hundred year old manor house is run by the friendly O'Reilly family. Set in ninety acres, this hotel has its own airstrip and a boat pier with fifteen boats and ghillies available. A permit costs just IR2 for a day from the angling information centre and the fishery officers can give you all sorts of useful advice. Please ring first before you go.

Glencar Hotel

For two hundred years now the Glencar Hotel has been providing its own brand of warmth and open hospitality. Framed by 3000 feet of Macgillycuddy Reeks—Ireland's highest peaks—it rests in the heart of Co Kerry, probably the most charming and delightful of Irish landscapes.

Near the banks of the River Caragh, the hotel is perfect for the ardent salmon angler. As one of Ireland's best salmon rivers it is not surprising that it yields up hundreds of them every year for guests who fish the twelve and a half miles of running water and three loughs that the hotel owns sole rights to. All the pools have easily accessible banks and cabins for rest and shelter. For an interesting variation, seven rowing boats with outboard motors are always ready. Drying rooms and workshop are maintained by the hotel, complete with scales and deep-freezing facilities. A ghillie, expert with fish flies, is always on hand to help and offer advice and ladies with a guest angler can fish free of charge.

Most of the hotel's bedrooms have their own bathroom and the comfort continues down into the lounge and dining room where the kitchen serves home cooked fayre. Afterwards, why not retire to the bar and have a Guinness or a whisky by the open fire, with the possibility of live Irish music.

Glencar Hotel
Glencar
Co. Kerry
Tel: (010 353 66) 60102
Fax: (010 353 66) 60167

Many fishermen are drawn like magnets to the same stretch of water each year and to some this may seem odd. However, familiarity and fond memories are a draw for the angler wherever they fish. Stick with your week in Devon or Scotland, in the area you know, but do also consider fishing in Ireland. Once you've experienced it, I for one will be surprised if you do not return time and time again.

The Shannon Fishery Region is particularly well organised and this is just as well, due to size of the water, not to mention the many tributaries. Its significance as a coarse fishing water should not be underestimated but we intend to isolate several locations where the game fishing comes to the fore. The area is well served by Shannon Airport and the Shannon International (061) 61122 is extremely handy for those flying in and out of the area. County Clare reveals a number of superb hotels but before we embark on these, spare a quick thought for Limerick and County Kerry. The Listowel Arms (068) 21500 is a well equipped and convenient for the River Feale, while the modest but welcoming Leens (068) 31121 is an outstanding hotel in which to stay. It is pricey but excellent in every way. The Dunraven Arms (061) 396209 is less expensive but is still a very comfortable hotel.

Incidentally, it is worth emphasising that the Irish Tourist Board are extremely helpful and will provide lists of self-catering accommodation and bed and breakfast establishments.

Bunratty Castle is a beautiful example of Ireland's heritage and its situation, overlooking the River Bunratty, is quite stunning. The Fitzpatrick's Shannon Shamrock (061) 361177 is by contrast a more modern edifice, but a comfortable hotel nonetheless. Wending our way northwards up the Shannon, we find Castleconnell. The Castle Oaks House (061) 377666 is well thought of here. The Lakeside (061) 376122 at Killaloe is also well worth a visit. Further north still, and we arrive at Athlone County Westmeath. The Royal (0902) 72924 is a very friendly hotel in which to stay when in this vicinity.

Visitors to Lough Sheelin will be well catered for and the splendid views from the northern shore of Lough Sheelin are best appreciated from the two hundred year old Crover House (049) 40206, run by the friendly O'Reilly family. In this idyllic setting, every need of the fisherman is catered for with twelve comfortable bedrooms, its own airstrip, a boat pier with fifteen boats and ghillies if required. There is a fine restaurant too, and the chef will cook your own catch!

The capital and its surroundings boast a combination of culture and wild scenery which will fascinate the visitor. Those who are planning to stay in the city for the night are spoilt for choice. The Berkeley Court (01) 6601711 is an hotel of international acclaim but there are, however, numerous establishments, all extremely good, from which to choose. For help and advice, the Dublin City Tourist Office (01) 6747733 is always a good place to start. Outside the city, in Navan, the Ardboyne Hotel (046) 23119 is modern and comfortable. A more traditional and cosy establishment is Bearpark (041) 24207 near Slane. The Conyngham Arms (041) 24155 is also a relaxing hotel from which you can enjoy the Boyne Valley. Another jewel of an hotel which offers fishing too is the Red House in Ardee (041) 53523. You should definitely book in advance for this establishment and expect a very high standard. It is a wonderful place for the sportsman.

While in Kells, The Headfort Arms (046) 40063 is a friendly establishment in which to stay. Our final thought for the area is the Boyne Valley Hotel in Drogheda (041) 37737, a handy place from which to enjoy the fishing on the lower reaches of the Boyne

The Liffey flows through the Wicklow mountains and Kildare before it reaches Dublin. Tulfarris Hotel (045) 64574 overlooks Poulaphouca Lake and is lovingly sheltered by the Wicklow Mountains, which rise at the rear of the hotel. Ringwood (01) 6288220 is a splendid Georgian house in 65 acres of farmland and is another good place to stay whilst visiting this area. The Springfield in Leixlip (01) 6244925 should also be considered when planning your trip, as should the Setanta House (01) 6271111 in Celbridge, which is convenient for the river.

Cork is a friendly city and well worth a visit. It is also easily accessible and has both a ferry terminal and airport. The River Lee is one of the better local rivers and there are numerous hotels to choose from while staying in the area. The Arbutus Lodge (021) 501237 dates from the eighteenth century and has some superb grounds which run down to the Lee. The restaurant is first rate and very popular.

Fishing the River Bandon can prove tremendous fun and the Innishannon Hotel (021) 775121 is a superb base from which to conduct your fishing foray. The hotel has a parkland setting with riverside gardens. It boasts a friendly atmosphere and a fine cellar. In Bandon itself, lies the Manster Arms (023) 41562, which offers some good value accommodation.

County Kerry has some of the most beautiful scenery in Europe. Here you will find a range of scenery lovingly crafted by nature and a delight to behold. There are a number of small but worthy salmon waters in the area and no further excuse should be needed for planning a

trip here. In Kenmare, there are hotels to suit all budgets and the fisherman is again spoilt for choice. The Sheen Falls (064) 41600 has more glorious fishing opportunities and is obviously high on the list but there are several other options. The Park Hotel (064) 41200 is a palatial establishment with an excellent restaurant. More modest, is the Lansdowne Arms (064) 41368, a welcoming hotel in which to stay. Many will seek to fish Lough Currane and the sport here is good. The Butlers Arms (0667) 4144 has an idyllic setting on the Ring of Kerry overlooking the Atlantic. The Glencar Hotel (066) 60102 is another excellent place to stay, with fishing on the river Caragh..

North of Waterville, we find Caragh Lake, where a number of good hotels are to be found. Ard-Na-Sidhe (066) 69105 is an attractive creeper-clad house set in delightful gardens on the lakeside. This is an ideal place to stay and enjoy the surrounding countryside. Caragh Lodge (066) 69115 has a pretty run down to the lake too, and this well kept Victorian hotel offers a friendly welcome to its guests. Glendalough House (066) 69156 also enjoys panoramic views of the lake, albeit from a greater distance.

The south east of Ireland is very reachable from England, with flights into Cork and Waterford and the ferry docking at Rosslare. The River Suir reveals a number of first rate fishing opportunities as well as several first class hotels. In Thurles, one finds numerous guest houses and The Anner Hotel (0504) 21799 is a good place to stay in town. Many of Ireland's more significant hotels are located near here. These often tend to enjoy remote settings as they were formerly the homes of wealthy merchant families.

Ardnayle House (0504) 42399 is excellent value and an obvious choice for anglers. The Cashel Palace Hotel (062) 61411 is a Palladian mansion with stylish interiors and very comfortable bedrooms. In Dundrum, The Dundrum House Hotel (062) 71116 has a fine situation in acres of parkland through which the river flows, ensuring every game fisherman can be kept fully occupied. Bansha House (062) 54194 is also well worth considering, as is Aherlow House (062) 56147 in Aherlow. Midway between Cahir and Tipperary we find the delightful Lismacue House (062) 54106. The house has been in the family for over 180 years and is a classically beautiful dwelling, boasting all the tradition of Ireland. Trout fishing is available on the estates own river and salmon and trout fishing are available on the Suir some four miles away. A fine fishing hotel near Cahir, is Kilcoran Lodge (052) 41288, a former hunting lodge which overlooks the Suir Valley. Twenty or so bedrooms with all modern facilities are found here and the hotel has its own pub too. Nearer to Clonmel, Knocklofty offers the Knocklofty House (052) 38222 which once again enjoys a superb setting overlooking the River Suir. The interior is elegant and the hotel offers numerous leisure facilities. The Hotel Minella (052) 22388 also stands on the banks of the river and is worth noting.Waterford Castle (051) 78203 is often referred to as Ireland's most outstanding hotel. It is certainly a luxurious establishment with sumptuous bedroooms and elegant public rooms. The cuisine here is also first class.

South of the Suir, we find another river of great repute, the Blackwater River. At Kenturk, The Assolas Country House (025) 50015 has an extremely friendly atmosphere with cosy log fires in winter and some very comfortable

bedrooms to complete the picture. Fishing is also available, organised by the hotel. This is a peaceful, elegant establishment and a visit is highly recommended. Another fine hotel is Blackwater Castle (022) 26333 at Castletownroche. This is a tremendous hotel for the fisherman and enjoys a delightful setting. Longueville House (022) 47156 is a Georgian house and an ideal base for touring the countryside. It is a first class hotel and one of Ireland's best. The Blackwater runs through the 500 acre estate and both salmon and trout fishing are available to guests. The President's Restaurant here is renowned and is adorned with—you guessed it—paintings of past Presidents.

A small hotel of great charm enjoying a marvellous setting overlooking a wooded gorge cut by the River Arweg, is Creagh Castle (022) 24105. This is an hotel with tradition and is highly recommended. Similarly popular, is Ballyvolane (025) 36349, surrounded by farmland and woods. Guests here can enjoy fishing on eight miles of the River Blackwater. Our final thought for this area is The Blackwater Lodge (058) 60235—an angler's dream hotel. The enthusiasm for fishing here is almost on a par with the service and this hotel is a charming place to stay.

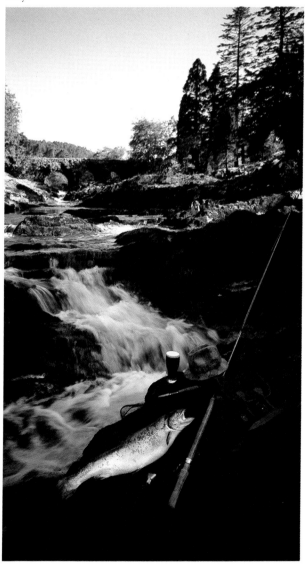

Fishing (Sheen Falls Hotel)

NORTH OF
DUBLIN

Ireland
207

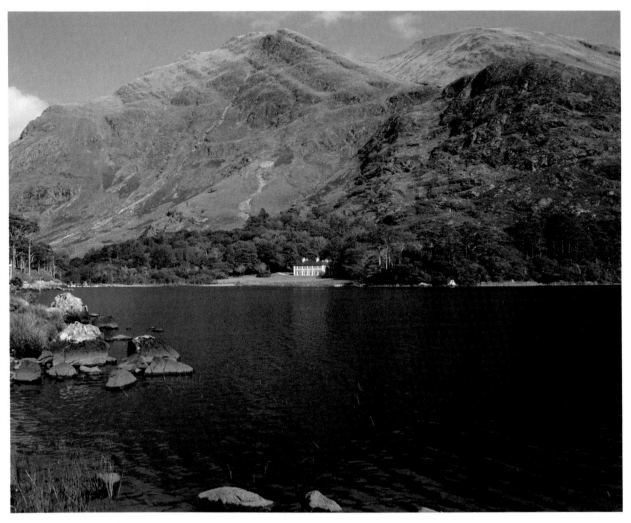

Delphi Lodge is one of the finest sporting lodges in Ireland. A magnificent 1830s country house which exudes a rich history and tradition. With fine antique furniture, beautiful decor, roaring fires and excellent food and wines, the Lodge is elegant yet totally informal and relaxing.

As an alternative to the lodge, four charming country cottages surrounded by a network of traditional dry stone walls, tumbling streams and rich vegetation, form part of the famous Delphi sporting estate. Beautifully restored in recent years, the cottages are comfortable and full of character. Antique country pine furniture, large open fireplaces, traditional stone floors downstairs and rich carpeting upstairs, all combine to give a wonderfully cosy atmosphere to these ancient cottages. The perfect setting for a relaxing country break.

The Delphi Fishery itself is a gem of Connemara. Set in a wild, unspoilt and stunningly beautiful valley, it offers gin-clear water, towering mountains, abundant wild life and total peace. It's the perfect haven for the discerning salmon and sea trout angler.

Delphi's sensational setting and prolific sporting fish have attracted generations of anglers from all over the world. With spring salmon, summer grilse and sea trout, it has long been recognised as a fly fisherman's paradise.

Delphi offers a wide variety of fly fishing over an unusually long and interesting season. Three fascinatingly different lakes, one and a half miles of tumbling river and the ideal fishing climate - all combine to offer relaxation, challenge and opportunity for expert and novice alike.

For centuries the sporting estate of the Marquis of Sligo, Delphi was acquired in 1986 by a young fisherman, Peter Mantle, who has ensured that the fishery and its facilities - from experienced ghillies to top quality flies, from helpful fishing maps to excellent drying facilities - are second to none. A unique fishery, managed superbly for the future.

The Delphi Estate
Leenane
County Galway
Ireland
Tel: (010 353 95) 42211
Fax: (010 353 95) 42296

The quality of Ireland's game fishing is superb. To many visiting anglers it presents an entirely new experience—fishing for wild salmon and trout in their natural undisturbed habitat. There are three main species, the majestic salmon, the gamey sea trout and the challenging brown trout which can be found, to a lesser or greater extent, in almost every stream, river and lake in the country.

Such quality fishing does not happen by chance. It requires continuing protection and prudent management against the encroachment of agricultural and municipal developments. Ireland's Central and Regional Fisheries are charged with securing the more effective conservation, management and development at our coarse, game and sea angling resources.

The Fisheries Boards have overall responsibility for all game fisheries whether public or privately owned. In addition, they have acquired and manage prestigious salmon fisheries such as the Galway Weir Fishery on the Corrib which offers both spring and grilse fishing (5 year average of 1091) and the beautiful Erriff Fishery in Connemara, a small spate river with a good grilse run (5 year average of 571). The Erriff also has attached the Aasleagh Lodge which offers excellent accommodation. Recently, the Board have acquired the River Blackwater in Co Kerry which is a grilse river and, what is probably Ireland's most productive fishery, the Ridge Pool on the Moy in Co Mayo.

The Boards manage several other salmon fisheries such as the Carrownisiky, Bunowen and Glenamoy in Co Mayo, the Owenea, Eany and Lough Eske in Co Donegal, the Lee and part of the Laune in Co Kerry.

A state licence is required for salmon and sea trout angling. Prices range from £25.00 yearly to £3.00 daily and a £10.00 licence caters for the holiday maker who may wish to fish for up to three weeks. A permit is also required for most salmon fisheries but not on Loughs Corrib and Conn in the west and Loughs Leane and Curraun in Co Kerry. Lough Curraun is also one of Ireland's premier sea trout fisheries.

Brown trout angling does not require a licence though there may be some local charges. The Fisheries Boards have developed over 150,000 acres of lakes and 1,000 miles of river for brown trout fishing. Many of the more important fisheries are under the Boards' control—Loughs Sheelin, Owel and Ennell in the midlands and the great trout lakes of Corrib, Mask, Carra and Conn in the west.

In some areas where there is a shortage of readily available trout fishing, the Fisheries Board operate managed fisheries. These are maintained at a very high standard by regular stocking with brown trout. Permits are required on very few Irish trout fisheries but it is always best to enquire.

Several Regional Boards have produced game angling guides to their own areas and a new national Central Fisheries Board Guide to Game Angling in Ireland is now available.

The Central Fisheries Board
Balnagowan
Mobhi Boreen
Glasnevin
Dublin 9
Tel: (0103531) 379206/7/8
Fax: (0103531) 360060

The Western Fishery Region comprises almost all of County Galway and part of County Mayo, stretching from Hog's Head in Galway Bay to Pidgeon Point in Westport Bay and taking in the great limestone loughs of Corrib, Mask and Cara.

The Corrib

Only 4½ miles long and 150 yards wide, the River Corrib runs through the city of Galway into Galway Bay, draining the vast 41,000 acre Lough Corrib—the Republic's largest lough. About two and a half miles of the river is suitable for salmon and sea-trout fishing, depending on the time of year. Don't forget your state licence as no local permits are required. Licences, tackle and advice are all available from Freeney's in Galway's High Street (091) 68794. It is the only tackle shop I know of that has a bar right next door (with the same name and owner), providing a ready-made audience for those tall fishing tales! Another rich vein of local information, offering all manner of advice and assistance for the visiting angler, is Gillie Angling (092) 48165.

Lough Corrib, or 'The Corrib' as it is generally known, stretches some thirty miles north from Galway to Maum Bridge. With its numerous tiny islands, bays and inlets it is perfectly suited for good brown trout—the larger fish tend to be taken in the southern part of the lough, although salmon have also been taken here. February 15th signals the start of the salmon season with trolling particularly popular at this time of year. Flies are also quite successful, even this early in the season. Mid-March sees hatches of chironomids, whilst olive hatches are best in April, May and September. From around the second or third week in May, the mayfly season allows you to fish for trout by dapping the natural mayfly, using both wet and dry flies. Some five thousand trout are usually caught in this period which lasts for approximately four weeks. Right up to the end of the season, daddy-longlegs and grasshoppers can be dapped and wet fly fishing is also successful. As no permit is required, fishing is free on this vast expanse of water. Recently, good catches have been taken in the Cornamona, Greenfields and Cong areas, generally using dapped mayfly or wet flies, the best being Hackled and Winged Mayflies, Green Peter, Olives and Bibio.

Detailed maps and information on fishing, boats, accommodation and other necessities are available from the Angling Officer of the Western Regional Fisheries Board at Weir Lodge, Earl's Island, Galway (091) 63118 for the southern end of the lough. For information on the northern end, contact the office at Cushlough (092) 41562. Currarevagh House, Oughterard (091) 82313 is a splendid Victorian manor set in 150 acres of park and woodland overlooking Lough Corrib and will provide boat, gillies and tackle for hire at around IR40 per day.

Lough Mask

The mysterious Lough Mask has several underground outflows where you can hear the water leaving. There is also a canal which has been constructed connecting Loughs Mask and Corrib, which only flows in times of high water in the winter months. The water levels between summer and winter can vary here between seven or eight feet. This 20,000 acre limestone lake holds large brown trout, with the larger fish normally caught by trolling. Rapallas are always popular but there are many excellent lures to use and if you have success with one—the advice is to stick to it! Traditional wet flies that do well are Connemara Black, Invicta and Olives.

The Mask has a similar season to the Corrib and anglers are free to use their own boats, although it is possible to fish from the lough shore. The annual World Cup Wet Fly Angling Competition is held here. Open to everyone, it normally attracts around four hundred entrants, including some of the sport's more famous names. Sponsored by Guinness, the first prize is a boat and outboard motor. Further information on the competition is available from the Western Regional Fisheries Board Information Centre, Cushlough, Ballinrobe (092) 41562 and the Fishery Board Officer, Joe Cusack (092) 41180, will also be willing to help. The information centre is a new bungalow-type building on Lough Mask's shore in Cushlough which can be reached from a tiny, dead-end track from Ballinrobe. The centre is open from 8.30am until 5.00pm but it is best to try to get there between 8.30am and 9.30am. There are numerous public access areas but anglers are asked to be cautious, due to the dangerous shallows.

Lough Carra lies in the shadow of Lough Mask (it shares the same information centre) and covers an area of over 4,000 acres. Tiny in comparison to Lough Mask, this limestone lake is one of the most picturesque in the country; with perfectly clear water over a white marl bottom the trout are easily seen when rising to take the fly. The season here lasts from March to September and the lough is stocked with brownies each year by the Fisheries Board in order to supplement the native wild brown trout. An 18lb trout has been taken in the past but the average is nearer 1¼lb. The mayfly season can produce good catches by dry fly, wet fly and dapping. Although standard patterns, including Green Drakes, are popular it is the Spent Gnat dry fly that produces the best results at all times of the day. In the summer and autumn, lake olives, murroughs and small sedges are the main fly hatches, with artificial flies such as Claret, Murrough, Invicta and Bibio being the most popular. A boat is essential for fishing Lough Carra and hire can be arranged through the Western Regional Fisheries Board at Cushlough (092) 41562 and other local outlets.

Western Region Waters

The Lough Inagh Fishery is set in a beautiful valley between the Twelve Bens to the west and the Maumturk Mountains to the east. Lough Inagh and Derryclare Lake combine to make up the Lough Inagh Fishery. The N59 and N344 run along the east side of the fishery and enquiries should be made to the Fishery Manager (095) 34670 at the Lough Inagh Fishery, County

Galway. At four miles long and up to three quarters of a mile wide, Lough Inagh offers quite splendid fishing.

Fine sea-trout fishing is available at Corloo, where the outflow from the Inagh tumbles through the Trout Pool. There is excellent fishing for sea-trout at night at the Derryclare Butts, where the river enters the lake. Glendollogh Butts, on the south east of Derryclare Lake provides good fishing, with the well known Pine Island a favourite spot for salmon and sea-trout. At the outfall from the lake, the angler can take both salmon and sea-trout from an area known as Green Point. April and May are the best months for salmon here, with fish averaging 10lb. June and September are generally the most productive times for grilse, whilst sea-trout are traditionally summer sport. However, last year saw a very slow start to the sea-trout season. Wet fly and dapping are both successful with Blue Badger, the Shrimp and Red Daddy flies best for salmon; Bibio, Delphi, Silver and Green Peter recommended for sea-trout. Boats and tackle are available at the fishery office, with ghillies normally required to be booked in advance. The clarity of the waters and the clean, crisp air, together with the number and size of fish make this a veritable haven for the fisherman.

Another fishery worthy of serious consideration is Galway Salmon Fishery (091) 62388, where a full day ticket ranges from IR12 to IR25, depending on the season. This unique fishery is situated on the river Corrib, practically in the centre of Galway. The season usually opens in February and closes in September.

The Delphi Fishery is situated in south County Mayo, on the R335 Leenane to Louisburgh road. The Delphi Estate is idyllic, set in a lovely valley with a magnificent mountain backdrop. The crystal clear waters afford the most perfect and tranquil setting for the fishing. The one and a half mile long Bundorragha River drains three main loughs and four main rivers to the sea at Killary Harbour.

From high in the beautiful hills at Lough Cunnel, where brown trout thrive, the Glencullin River tumbles into the lough of the same name, one of the most peaceful in the country, with steep mountains rising from the shore. Here at Glencullin Lough, is a boat to cover the half mile of lough, with good sea-trout taken on the fly from July onwards. With three boats, nearby Doolough is well known for exceptionally large sea-trout and some

salmon. Fly-only is the rule here, although some trolling for salmon may be possible in the early part of the season.

The Delphi Lodge and cottages overlook Finlough, where two boats cover the shallow picturesque water with its fine stock of salmon, grilse and sea-trout. Just a couple of miles east of the Delphi system is Tawnyard lough, the beautiful principal lough on the Erriff System, famous for salmon and sea-trout taken on the fly. Please note in particular the Erriff Fishery (095) 42252, which offers salmon and sea-trout fishing on the Erriff, one of the major salmon fishing rivers in Ireland, and on Tawnyard Lough. Derrintin Lough, a small hill lough, is also worth a visit, and sea angling is available in Killary Harbour, aboard the 'Aasleagh Lady'. However, possibly the best river in the west of the country, with plenty of white water and nineteen pools, is the Bundorragha River, which is semi-spate and is most productive after heavy rain. Again, fly fishing only here, with salmon taken throughout the season and sea-trout from June to August. All enquiries regarding accommodation, boats, ghillies and state licences should be made to Peter Mantle (095) 42213. A daily permit for the Delphi Fishery costs between IR40 and IR50, with cottages available at peak season for IR300 per week.

Recommended flies here include the Delphi Silver and Badger, Green Peter and Hairy Mary but again, it is worth spending some time chatting to Mr Mantle who is full of useful tips on the local waters. The long season, the variety of fishing, the perfect setting and the water's excellent record, averaging 100 salmon and 1000 sea-trout annually, make the Delphi Estate the ideal location for the keen fisherman.

It must be said that Delphi, like most of Ireland and the British Isles, has experienced the depressing disappearance of the sea-trout. In fact, the renowned Zetland Fishery closed in 1991, but the lovely Zetland House Hotel (095) 31111 is still thriving as there is much to do in this part of Connemara. Fishermen in the area could, of course, cast a fly on nearby Lough Shannaghcloontippen (nineteen letters, to save you counting!).

Enniscoe House

Enniscoe House is a fine Georgian home on the shores of Lough Conn which has recently been described as the 'last great house of North Mayo.' Declared a Heritage House of Ireland, it is owned and managed by Susan Kellett, a descendant of the original family who settled on the lands in the 1660s.

The house, which is lovingly and carefully maintained, retains its family portraits, antique furniture and welcoming open fires. In this setting, good food and wine contribute to a pleasant and relaxrd atmosphere. The main bedrooms which have a canopy or four posters beds and private bathrooms, have attractive views of parkland and the lake.

The 150 acre estate, which has its own farm and gardens, presents a tranquil setting for the house in mature woodlands through which paths run to the lake.

There are attractively renovated self-catering units in the stable yard and some old farm buildings have been taken over by the local Historical Society where a Heritage and Family History Research Centre was opened by President Mary Robinson in April 1992.

Enniscoe House, which has a long fishing tradition is the ideal base for the keen fisherman. Situated on the shores of Lough Conn, it has a private landing stage, boats and engines toghether with a rod and drying room on its own shore and within easy walking distance from the house. The Fishery Manager provides advice, tackle and tuition as well as arranging boats, engines and ghillies for the guests.

Lough Conn is renowned for its wild brown trout and spring salmon fishing. For a varied fishing holiday, the Fishery Manager can also arrange fishing on other local lakes and rivers including the River Moy as well as estuary and sea fishing.

In addition to its fishing attractions, North Mayo is a fascinating though little known area. The nearby North Coast has unspoilt and clean beaches at Ballycastle and Lacken, while further along the coast there are great cliffs overlooking the Atlantic where stone age settlements at Ceide Fields are being excavated.

Nephin Mountain, which overlooks the area, presents a challenge to the hill climber and at the base has a range of relatively unexplored small lakes, forests and boglands. There is also Achill Island to the south and Sligo Yeats Country to the north, both within easy driving distance of Enniscoe. Golf is readily available, as isd horse riding and bicycle hire.

You will find Enniscoe House an ideal base for an enjoyable and varied holiday.

Enniscoe House
Castlehill
Nr Crossmolina
Ballina
Co Mayo
Tel: (010 353 96) 31112
Fax: (010 353 96) 31773

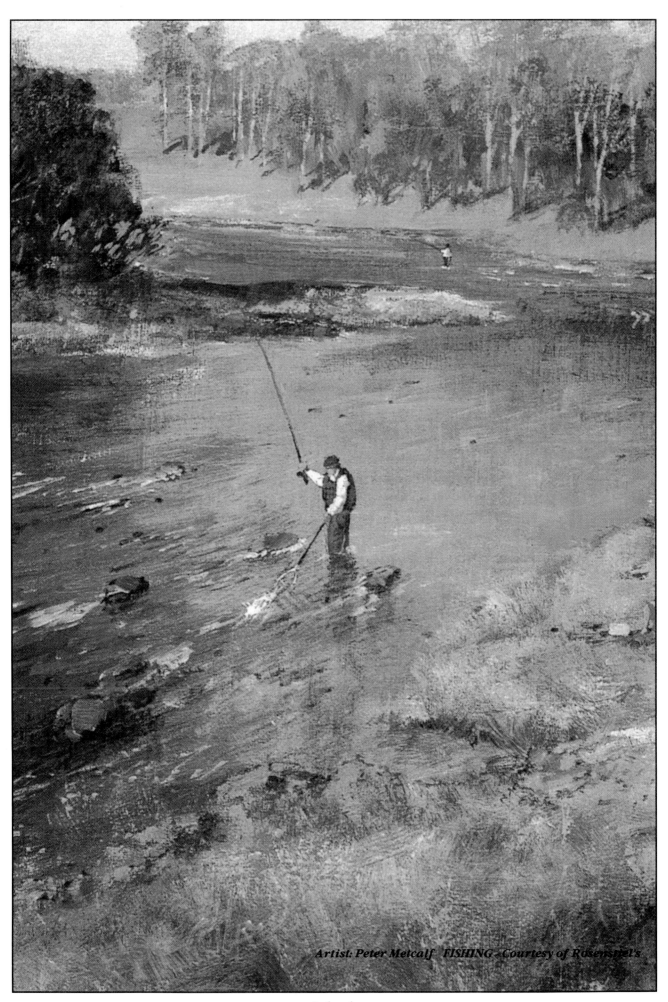

Artist: Peter Metcalf FISHING - Courtesy of Rosenspiel's

The North Western Fisheries Region is made up of the majority of County Mayo and parts of County Sligo, County Leitrim and County Roscommon. From Pidgeon Point, County Mayo, around the coastline to Mullaghnmore Head, County Sligo, the area encompasses all the rivers and loughs which flow into the sea between these two points. Without a doubt, the best known water is the River Moy with its principal lake, Lough Conn, forming a link at Pontoon to Lough Cullin. In addition, good runs of salmon and sea-trout are to be enjoyed at the Newport River and Lough Beltra system and at the Owenmore and Owenduff Rivers, together with the Burrishoole Fishery. Lough Cull, off the Mulraney to Achill road and Loughaun, set in picturesque Achill Island, may just surprise the dedicated angler, not only with the delightful setting but also the quality of the water.

Lough Beltra & the Newport

Lough Beltra and the Newport River can be found in south County Mayo, south west of Castlebar off the R311/R312. Lough Beltra is three miles long and one mile wide and is drained by the Newport river running into Clew Bay at Newport. Over seventeen miles long, with seventeen good holding pools, streams and glides, both the river and lough get a good run of spring salmon from the end of March (opening day is 20th March), grilse in June and sea-trout from mid-June. Unfortunately, there is no real brown trout fishing here.

Newport House in Newport (098) 41222 overlooks the river's estuary with the hotel gates facing you as you come into Newport from Castlebar. The house is set between Achill Island and the mountains of Mayo and the wild, unspoiled splendour of Erris and Connemara. The house owns the west side of the lough with five boats and five ghillies available for hire. The boats fish one side of an invisible line, although they can cross with permission, and generally the boats for hotel guests have priority. In addition, guests also have priority on an eight mile stretch of the river, which completes the Newport House fishery and there is a boat for use on Lough Furnace. Newport House can also arrange fishing on the Moy system should you wish to test those waters.

The east side of the Beltra is owned by Glenisland Co-op (094) 21302, where fishing costs around IR8 per day, plus IR10 for a boat for two people and IR6 for an outboard motor. Five boats are available for hire here and the salmon fishing is good, but due to lack of numbers, any sea-trout caught must be returned to the water. Late March, April and May tend to be the best fishing but this depends on the water level and weather conditions. An average of eighty to ninety salmon are caught on this side during the season, some up to 20lb in weight.

Lough Furnace & Lough Feeagh

Burrishoole Fishery is now owned and managed by the Salmon Research Agency of Ireland and comprises the tidal Lough Furnace and the freshwater Lough Feeagh. One of Ireland's few productive tidal loughs, Lough Furnace, rises and falls two feet each day. Both loughs are often referred to as spate loughs as they have a catchment area of approximately one hundred square miles and after heavy rain, the levels can rise very sharply. During hot, dry spells Furnace can become quite brackish and fish have to adjust to fluctuating salinity levels of between eight and twenty parts per thousand. Furnace has two separate stocks of fish; a natural stock and a supplement from the agency's ocean ranched salmon. The season runs from 10th June to 30th September, with July being the best month when all the fish are fresh. However, September may give larger bags with the autumn run. Salmon are to be found at both the Salmon Leap and the Millrace, and also at Long Shore, Duffys Point and Fahys Bay. For sea-trout, try Black Stone and Blacksod Bay, although they are currently subject to a restrictive byelaw and any caught have to be returned. Furnace also has excellent mullet fishing—so don't be surprised if you land a mullet, or a bass for that matter!

Lying in a deep valley, Lough Feeagh, although best known for salmon, holds good stocks of sea-trout and brown trout and the agency records the number of fish passing up into the lough through the counter. Again, June and July are the best months for salmon, particularly around the mouth of the Black River and Glenamong River. The best water for sea-trout is the area towards the lower lough, around Schoolhouse Bay.

Furnace and Feeagh are set in the beautiful countryside of Nephin Beg, easily accessible from Newport. Permits are available from the Manager's Office at the Burrishoole Fishery (098) 41107 at Farran Laboratory, Furnace, Newport, some two miles outside Newport on the south shore. Bank fishing is not allowed here and only five boats (with engines) are allowed on each lough. Fly only is the rule, with Green Peter, Daddy, Bibio, Black Pennell, Fiery Brown and Delphi recommended. The average weight for salmon from this water is around nine pounds and for sea-trout three quarters of a pound.

Bunarella Lough, managed and partially owned by the agency, is a good brown trout lough just ten miles north of Newport and enjoys a lovely tranquil setting. Trout are small, averaging about 8oz, but provide great fun on light tackle as they are quite free rising, especially during the summer hatch of sedges. In addition to the standard lough patterns, try Greenwells Spider and Glory and Connemara Black on the east and north shores.

The agency has recently opened up a new fishery at Ballinlough, two or three miles north of Westport on the N59. Generally speaking, this is the only lough run by the agency to allow bank fishing. It is very rich in limestone and well stocked with rainbows and browns, with 4oz fish growing to 4lb in two years. Visitors are advised to book well in advance for the whole fishery, especially for June, July and September and a ghillie is recommended. Permits are obtained from the office situated on the southern shore of Furnace, approximately two miles outside Newport. It's a signposted turning off to the right.

Carrowmore Lake

Situated twenty-eight miles west of Ballina and two miles north-west of Bangor Erris in County Mayo is Carrowmore Lake. Four miles long and approximately three miles wide it is primarily a brown trout fishery with occasional salmon and sea-trout. This is probably the last of the truly wild lakes as it has never been stocked. Owned by a syndicate in Dublin and controlled by Bangor Erris Angling Club, permits can be obtained from Seamus Henry at the post office in Bangor Erris (097) 83487 for around IR10 a day. There are twenty-five boats available and these are recommended, as bank fishing is not very productive. The post office is adjacent to the West End Bar—surely a recipe for disaster with regards to writing postcards! Mr Henry will also issue permits for the club's stretches on the River Owenmore and is happy to advise on both fishing and accommodation. Cloonamoyne Fishery (096) 31112, attached to the Enniscoe Hotel at Lough Conn, can also arrange fishing at Carrowmore. The Oweniny river flows into the Owenmore and then enters Carrowmore Lake before reaching the Atlantic at Blackrod Bay. On Carrowmore, the traditional fly patterns at Herritys and Derreens Islands on the north shore and the mouth of Glencullin River are the ones to use.

The Moy

The River Moy is one of the top salmon producing rivers in Ireland, flowing from the Ox Mountains to Killala Bay at Ballina. Its tributaries drain an area of some eight hundred square miles over its full sixty-three mile length and there are over thirty miles of double-bank fishing. Around eight thousand fish are taken from its waters every season, with stretches to suit fly fishing and spinning. The season starts on 1st February but it is more usual for serious fishing to start towards the end of the month. The main grilse run starts in May and peaks in June with an unbelievable number of fish in the river. Angling on the Moy is reasonably priced and available in spring and summer through to the autumn. Sea-trout can be taken from boats in the seven mile long estuary from Ballina to Killala Bay. The Moy Fishery Office (096) 21332 at Ridge Pool Road, Ballina controls some of the best beats on the river, including the famous Ridge Pool, where sixteen fish were taken in two days in June 1991. Prices range from IR8 to IR60 for two rods, boat hire and a ghillie in high season for the Ridge Pool. Advance booking is essential. The Ballina Angling Centre (096) 21850 at Dillon Terrace, Ballina is run by Michael Swartz who claims to be able to organise everything. Certainly permits, tuition, ghillies and general information are available here pertaining to the fishery which stretches out on both banks, from the Weir to the confluence with the Corroy river

The Downhill Hotel (096) 21033, Ballina is set in beautiful landscaped gardens overlooking the River Brosna, a tributary of the Moy. Mount Falcon Castle Fishery, between the Corroy and Foxford, controls seven and a half miles of double-bank fishing with good fly and spinning

Artist: Spencer Coleman HOPING FOR A BITE Courtesy of Rosenstiel's

stretches. The Mount Falcon (096) 21172 is four miles from Ballina on the Foxford Road, set in one hundred acres of beautiful parkland. The Alpine Hotel (096) 36144 overlooks Killala Bay some fifteen miles away, where guests have priority over one mile of left bank fishing, just upstream from the junction of the Rivers Yellow and Moy.

The Armstrong Family are one of the few Irish families that own a piece of the Moy. The cost to fish here is IR10 per day or IR50 and you are advised to book in advance for this one and a half mile stretch. The Armstrongs (094) 56580 live almost on the river, down a track off the Ballina Foxford Salmon Anglers control both banks immediately to the south of Foxford and anglers should contact Jack Wallace (094) 56238 at Swinford Road, Foxford. Cloongee Fishery permits can be purchased from Michael Ruane (094) 56634 in Cloongee for fishing on both banks where Lough Cullin enters the Moy. The East Mayo Anglers' Association control the Moy from around Cloongee House by the Ballylahan Bridge, to beyond the point where the Gweestion river joins the Moy. Permits cost IR12 per day and are available from Mrs Wills at Ballylahan Bridge (094) 56221 and Bolands Lounge, Bridge Street, Swinford (094) 51149. In addition, a short stretch downstream of Foxford Bridge offers free fishing.

Lough Conn

A few miles west of the Moy is the infamous Lough Conn. At around 13,000 acres, this beautiful lake provides the fisherman with an excellent challenge in stunning surroundings. Nephin, rising to almost two and a half thousand feet, dominates the western horizon. A limestone water of about nine miles in length and two to four miles in width, it has vast areas of relatively shallow water that sustain a huge population of wild trout. During fly hatches, trouting is excellent and with the many attractive bays and islands, Conn remains a firm favourite with all fishermen. The angling season begins in March with traditional wet fly fishing over shallow water. Brownies average just over the pound mark but three pounders are not uncommon. The chronomids hatch throughout the first half of the season but the fun really begins when the mayfly starts to hatch in mid-May. The latter is extensive and lasts until the end of June with the lesser hatch extending until mid-August. Sedges hatch towards the end of the season and so do not forget your sedge patterns at this time of year. Salmon are also present in fair numbers and are mainly taken by trolling from the end of March to July. Historically, the best areas have been at the northern end—try Masebrook, Cornakillew and Castlehill Bay. Access is not difficult and all your needs can be organised through the Pontoon Bridge Hotel, Foxford, (094) 56120. There are several people who have boats to hire and it is recommended that, even if you do not wish a boatman to accompany you, a guide of some sort would make a difference to the size of your bag. At the very

least, on a blank day, you can exchange jokes! Michael Schwartz in the Angling Centre, Ballina (open 7.00am to midnight) (096) 21850 can also help you here. On the northern shore Enniscoe House (096) 31112 stands alone amongst its gardens and parkland. Just off the N59 Crossmolina to Ballina road, this lovely Georgian house is the place to stay for all that is splendid. Barry Segrave is the fishery manager and can organise an impressive fishing package.

Lough Cullin

Lough Cullin is connected to the southern tip of Lough Conn at Pontoon. This 2000 acre lake holds a good stock of brown trout up to about 4lb and also has a good run of salmon. In fact, all the fish must pass through Cullin to get to Lough Conn and its feeder rivers. The narrow inlet that joins the two lakes is a favourite haunt of the salmon fisherman. Salmon are often caught by anglers fly fishing for trout. So, if it is trout you are after, use a slightly heavier leader than normal. In addition to the contacts for Lough Conn, you might prefer to speak to Healy's Hotel, Pontoon (094) 56443.

Lough Arrow

Lough Arrow is drained by the river of the same name. Only fifteen miles in length, the River Arrow is not widely fished. Access is awkward, with many overhanging trees and after June ends, the weed growth becomes too thick to cast a fly. There are, however, large trout in this river but they are not often seen as they feed deep down. Guests of Coopershill, Riverstown, County Sligo (071) 65108 are welcome to fish it but the O'Haras would prefer to organise fishing for you on Lough Arrow. This fine Irish water is one of the best mayfly fisheries in the country and is situated close to the border of County Sligo and Roscommon. At just over 3000 acres this rich limestone lough is small by comparison to some but brownies are here in good numbers and fish to 6lb and 7lb are caught on the fly every year. There are significant hatches of duckfly, olives, murroughs and even Green Peter. The season runs from March to September and all fishing is free. Before you start, though, ring or pop into the N.W. Fisheries Board Information Centre (079) 66033 in Ballinafad, beside the cemetery, for a fishing report and advice. First thing in the morning is the best time to catch a fishery officer; or contact Tim McGrath at the Rock View Hotel (079) 66073.

Fermanagh's loughs and rivers, tree-lined glens and islands, stately mansions and ruined castles form the perfect accompaniment to the spectacular fishing to be found in Loughs Erne and Melvin. Here, in the south west corner, are two of the best trout loughs in the land. The Upper and Lower Lough Erne is over fifty miles long with the medieval town of Enniskillen dividing the lough; and Lough Melvin, straddling Fermanagh's border with the Republic.

Lough Melvin

Approximately five thousand acres, eight miles long by nearly two miles wide, Lough Melvin is unique. It is scientifically accepted that there are four genetically distinct trout in this lough—brown, ferox, gillaroo and sonaghan. This rare salmonid displays the normal attributes of sea-trout—powerful tails and hard fighters, although much darker in colouring than sea-trout. They only grow to about 1½lb and are typically mid-water feeders of daphnia and emerging insects. The gillaroo is very similar to a brown trout but with more spots and a yellow belly. They feed a lot on the bottom in shallow water but do come up for the dry fly in the evening. Ferox are usually caught by trolling the deeper sections of the lake and char are caught at even greater depths. Brownies are best caught fishing a team; with a dark pattern on the point, a traditional wet fly, such as an Invicta, on the dropper and a local favourite, like a Gosling or Dabbler, on the bob. These latter two are based on patterns from two hundred years of fly-tying experience passed down through the years. Local fly-tyers still tie in the traditional way—hooks held in the hand without help from a vice!

One word of caution, Lough Melvin is scenic but can sometimes cut up rough and dangerous as it is very exposed to the prevailing westerlies. A good man to speak to for local advice is Terence Bradley (072) 54029, whose house, Eden Point, is situated on the east shore, the first house on the left as you leave Rossinver on the R282. Gillaroo Angles (0232) 862419, based in Newtownabbey, are also able to organise fishing forays throughout this area and the man to contact here is John Todd.

The Drowse

The River Drowse drains Lough Melvin and provides some spectacular sport when the salmon are running in the spring. Thomas Gallagher (072) 41208 owns the fishing rights on this short six mile river. There are fifty two named pools that yielded eight hundred fish in the first seven months of 1991. March produced over one hundred and fifty fish alone, with half caught on the fly. A tip here—use size 8 to 10 doubles for spring salmon, which have an average weight of 10lb, and size 10 to 12 for the grilse, which average 5lb. Mr Gallagher charges a very reasonable IR7 per day or IR30 per week, operating from the Kinlough end, and also hires boats for the lough. February to July is best for salmon here. Also in this area, the National Trust properties at Florence Court and Gardens and the Palladian Castle Coole are well worth a visit.

Lower Lough Erne

Picturesque Lower Lough Erne is a huge expanse of water (37,000 acres), twenty six miles long, running north west from Enniskillen to Rosscar viaduct, where the River Erne enters the ocean at Ballyshannon. The whole Erne system provides superb brown trout fishing in clean unpolluted waters containing plenty of fish. Trout

up to 20lb in weight are caught every season, usually on the troll in spring, whilst duckfly fishing begins in earnest in April. The numerous islands, rocky outlets and secluded coves and bays make for an idyllic setting for the fisherman to enjoy whilst pursuing his sport. Near Enniskillen, try St Catherine's and Rabbit Island where mayfly sport is particularly good for the trout, when fish of 6lb can be taken. Trout fishing naturally tends to die away in late June and early July but returns with a vengeance in August with the arrival of the daddy-longlegs and sedges and you may even pick up a salmon, which are now returning in larger numbers. The season generally runs from 1st March to 30th September, with some minor extensions, and details of permits and State licences can be obtained from John Richardson (0365) 322608, 9 East Bridge Street, Enniskillen, who also has holiday cottages to let on Lusty Island.

For those anglers keen to try their luck with the salmon, the stretch from Rosscor viaduct to Belleek has been good in August and September in recent years and Michael McGrath (0365) 658181 at Carlton Cottages, Belleek is an excellent source of local knowledge. The scenic Ballinamallard and Colebrooke, which are feeder rivers for the lough, get a run of large brown trout during August and September which provide great sport. Permits are also available from the following sources:- Bailey D. Blainey Service Station (03656) 634, Dickie and Sons (0365) 322165, Erne Marine (036582) 267, Home, Field and Stream (0365) 323481, Lochside Cruisers (0365) 324368 and Manor House Marine (03656) 28100.

The Foyle System

Managed by The Foyle Fisheries Commission, the Foyle System is unique in that it extends into Donegal in the Republic, as well as Derry and Tyrone. It was once the best salmon fishery in Western Europe but the ravages of UDN and overfishing, both legally and illegally, took their toll, although there are signs that things are improving. Consisting of Lough Foyle and the Rivers Finn, Strule, Derg, Mourne, Glenelly, Owenkilliew, Carnowen and Drumragh, the Foyle System has some superb fishing in this area on private, semi-private and association waters. Mr Ronnie Kerrigan at the Commission (0504) 42100 is very helpful and will give you advice on all areas to fish.

Classic fly fishing is available on the Mourne which like the Tay and Spey, fishes best in low to medium water. Good spring fishing can often be found on the Finn, but it is usually mid June before there is any consistency. Most of the other rivers are of a spatey nature and therefore require a good deal of rain. This is not usually a problem as Ulster's lush countryside testifies! Patrick Bonner (06487) 65920 is a very helpful water bailiff who fishes all over Northern Ireland and he can be contacted after 11.00am. (He is out fishing until midnight!)

The Rivers Roe and Faughan are part of the Foyle System and often yield first class salmon and sea-trout, with stretches on the Roe controlled by Roe Anglers' Association and Dungiven Anglers' Association. Sea-trout of up to 4lb are not uncommon and grilse between 4lb and 10lb are regularly caught here. Salmon from these waters tend to weigh around 8lb to 10lb.

For further information on fishing in Northern Ireland contact the Department of Agriculture which is responsible for the public waters and can give advice on angling permits, stocking and other matters. They can be contacted at The Department Of Agriculture, Fisheries Division, Hut 5, Castle Grounds, Stormont, Belfast. Telephone (0232) 63939. Licences are available from either the Fisheries Board or the Foyle Fisheries Commission.

Lough Neagh

Lough Neagh is the biggest lake in the British Isles and its main rivers are the Upper Bann and Blackwater to the south and Moyola to the west, and the Maine and its tributaries to the north. The system drains a vast area of central Ulster. The Lower Bann drains the lough to the north, through Lough Beg to the Atlantic near Coleraine. All these rivers enjoy a reasonable run of salmon from July to October and produce an indigenous population of brown trout from a quarter to one and a quarter pounds. Dollaghan, a big lough trout, sometimes over ten pounds, can be taken during the autumn. Similar to sea-trout in colour and size, they are best caught at dusk but, unfortunately, do not put up the entertaining resistance of the sea-trout.

The Blackwater

The River Blackwater is the largest of the rivers but, according to the locals, is virtually unfishable due to the Department of Agriculture's arterial drainage scheme. The last seven or eight miles of the upper part of the river in the Benburb area has some reasonable trout fishing and a few salmon. Permits are available from Hamiltons (06487) 63682. Around Blackwatertown there is a one and a half mile stretch of right bank fishing with good trout fishing here run by the Department of Agriculture. Permits should be purchased from Cahoon, 2 Irish Street, Dungannon (0867) 22754.

The Upper Bann

The Upper Bann rises in the Mourne Mountains and meanders and tumbles through the delightful County Down countryside to Lough Neagh. Between Banbridge and Hilltown, the Department has two ten-mile stretches of water. Brown trout and some late season salmon are taken from the banks between March and October.

The Ballinderry

The Ballinderry river is about thirty miles long and flows east to enter the lough near Ardhoe Cross. About two thirds of its length yields good brown trout and some dolaghan. Permits are obtainable from Cookstown Angling Club.

The Moyola, the Maine & the Lower Bann

From the Sperrin Mountains in South Derry, the Moyola river twists and winds its way to the north west corner of the lough, yielding some brown trout and a few salmon in the latter part of the season. This is private land and anglers must seek the landowner's permission to fish these waters. Principally a brown trout river, with some big lough dolaghan, the Maine flows south from

Glarryford Bogs. Several angling clubs and the Department of Agriculture own stretches on the river. Cullybackey has two and a half miles of the best trout waters, with day tickets obtained from local newsagents in Cullybackey. In recent years there have been some very good runs of salmon in the Maine and its tributaries, the Braid and Glenwhiry, providing the angler with excellent sport. The Lower Bann, which is the largest river in the British Isles in terms of water volume, is a slow running river which drains Lough Neagh. The water is owned by Bann Systems but most of the river can be fished without day permits although there are several private stretches fished by syndicates on Monday to Thursday and only available to day visitors at weekends. Although expensive, up to £160 per day, the salmon fishing can be fantastic below the weirs and lockgates, where fast-running waters can produce many salmon. Portna and Culiff rock are good stretches. Possibly the best, however, is Camroe where the number of fish taken is quite phenomenal, although this is a restricted stretch. There are several small rivers feeding into the Lower Bann which can yield some good salmon in their own right. From Coleraine to the river mouth there is some very good sea-trout fishing, especially from boats. Contact Bann Systems Ltd at Coleraine (02657) 31215.

The Bush

Wholly owned by Bann Systems Ltd., the thirty mile River Bush flows from the Tievebulliagh, through Bushmills village and distillery—one of the oldest in the world—to the Atlantic near the Giant's Causeway. The owner of Bann Systems, Sir Patrick McNaughton, sells day tickets on two miles of the river at the mouth where the fishing is mainly restricted to salmon, although there are some trout to be had. The remainder of the river is leased by the internationally-renowned Research Station of the Department of Agriculture, who allow fishing only on the strict understanding that anglers co-operate with the research project's progress by returning day tickets with details of the catch and whenever possible, submitting salmon for examination. It is particularly important to recover fin-clipped fish (those from which the adipose fin has been removed) as these individuals may contain minute tags which can only be detected using specialised equipment at the hatchery. All fish will be returned to anglers immediately and a reward is currently payable for each salmon submitted. Anyone catching a fin-clipped fish outside office hours or at the weekend is asked to retain the fish's head and report the catch on a returned day ticket or by telephone at their earliest convenience.

Angling on the river has been deliberately divided up so as to give the best sport to as many people as possible and to cater for varying desires, but the river is of a flashy nature and does not remain in top class order for extended periods. When in form, however, it can be excellent. At present the season lasts from 1st March until 30th September. Advance booking is essential for these waters and contact should be made with the Department. Ask for form ARB1 and bear in mind that applications are dealt with on a first come first served basis. Rods for spring and September go in a day as it is reputed to be bursting with salmon. If you can track down Sean Fleming (02657) 32422 at the Tackle Shop in Bushmills, he will be happy to advise you on all waters in the area. Permits are also available from Barry Jones (02657) 31435 at the Hatchery Office in Bushmills.

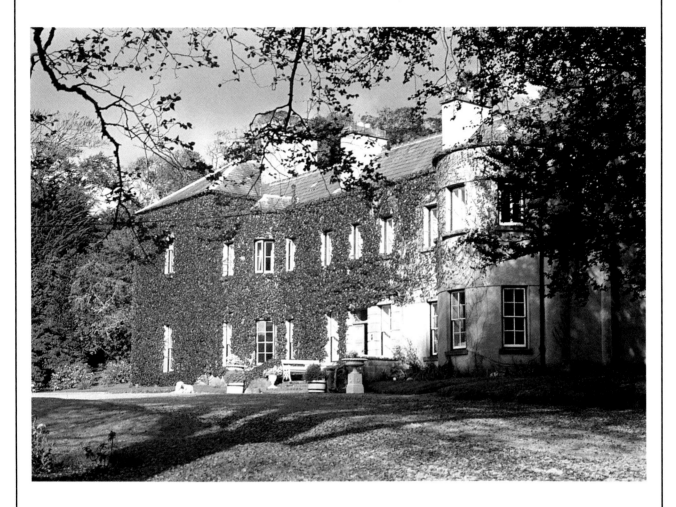

Adjoining the town of Newport and overlooking the tidal river and quay the impressive country mansion of Newport House stands guard over the centuries of history that form the backbone to its grounds and the surrounding countryside. Once the home of a branch of the O'Donel family, descended from the famous fighting Earls of Tir Connell and cousins to 'Red Hugh' of Irish history, it is now a superb example of a lovingly maintained Georgian Mansion House.

Encircled by mountains, lakes and streams, Newport is within easy reach of some of Ireland's most beautiful rivers. Renowned as an angling centre, it holds private salmon and sea-trout fishing rights to 8 miles of the Newport River; and the prolific waters of the stunning Lough Beltra West are close by. Less than twenty minutes drive from the hotel are Lakes Mask and Corrib, while the nearby Loughs Feeagh and Furnace are the site of the Salmon Research Trust of Ireland.

The discerning golfer has the pleasure of the 18-hole championship course at Westport as well as the more relaxed 9-hole course near Mulrany.

Outdoor activities are numerous amidst the breath-taking scenery of County Mayo. Riding is easily arranged or try swimming and diving on wide and often empty beaches, while hang-gliding is a relatively new sport gaining popularity from the local Achill Cliffs. One of the best recreations though is simply walking across the ever changing panorama of mountain, forest and sea.

Warmth and friendliness fill this beautiful hotel in a country already famed for its hospitality. The house is furnished with a tasteful collection of fine antiques and paintings and the elegant bedrooms are individually decorated. Food is taken seriously, with much of the produce collected fresh from the fishery, gardens and farm. Home-smoked salmon and fresh sea-food are specialites, and all the dishes are complemented by a carefully chosen and extensive wine list.

Many of the staff have been long in the service of the estate, up to forty years in one case. Combine this with the solid background of the house and there is a rare feeling of continuity and maturity so rare in modern hotels today.

Newport House
Co. Mayo
Ireland
Tel: (010 353 98) 41222
Fax: (010 353 98) 41613

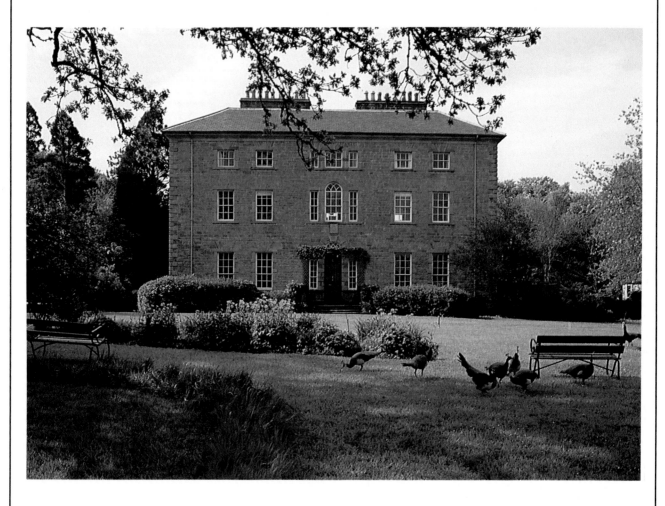

Coopershill is a fine example of a Georgian family mansion. Home to seven generations of the O'Hara family since it was built in 1774, it combines the spaciousness and elegance of an earlier age with the comfort and amenities of today. Five of the seven bedrooms have four-poster or canopy beds and all have their own private bathrooms. The rooms retain their original regal dimensions and much of the furniture dates from the time that the house was built.

Guests can relax in front of a log fire in the large and comfortable drawing room. Dinner by candle light with family silverware and crystal glass, a wide choice of wines and the personal attention of the hosts all add to the special Coopershill atmosphere.

Standing in the centre of a 500 acre estate of farm and woodland, separation from the outside world seems complete. There are many delightful walks and wildlife is abundant and undisturbed.

One of Ireland's finest limestone lakes, Lough Arrow, is five miles away. Best known for the Mayfly hatch, the lough fishes almost as well at other times of the year. Large indigenous brown trout are caught during the late evenings of summer and autumn. Boats and ghillies are available.

The river from the lake flows through the property. It contains large brown trout which are mainly bottom feeders and a real challenge to the fly fisherman.

Long uncrowded beaches, spectacular mountains and hills for walking, lakes and megalithic monuments all add to make Sligo, which is Yeats' country, an ideal place to visit.

Coopershill is two miles from the village of Riverstown and 13 miles from Sligo town, signposted clearly from the Sligo to Dublin route N4.

We are served by two airports; Sligo Airport is 15 miles away with daily flights to Dublin; Knock Airport is 30 miles away with daily flights to Luton, North of London. Car hire is available at both Sligo and Knock.

Coopershill
Riverstown
Co. Sligo
Ireland
Tel: (010 353 71) 65108
Fax: (010 353 71) 65466

It is not just catching fish that matters to the Irish, it is the sport combined with the company, the stories and the hospitality enjoyed in the many riverside pubs. A wicked sense of humour blends with informality and a welcome that is renowned throughout the world.

Fermanagh and Donegal reveal some wild and rugged land, almost beyond compare. Trout fishermen will be in their element. The Kilyreagh Hotel (036587) 221 is a good spot from which to explore the many local waters and the Kilyhevlin Hotel (03656) 323481 has a superb setting on the shores of Lough Erne, amidst the lakeland scenery of Fermanagh. The Lough Erne Hotel (03656) 31275 is similarly welcoming. The Hilton Park (047) 56007 in Scotshouse, near Clones, is a first class hotel. The many visitors wishing to fish Lough Melvin should contact Gillaroo Angles (0232) 862419, who have excellent local contacts. Once again, bed and breakfast accommodation is available throughout the area but one particular recommendation is Lake House (072) 41808 in Cloghan, or Mountain View (072) 41525 in Gurteendarragh. Both are well situated for the fishing.

If you are looking to fish the vast waters of the Foyle System, then you should find some excellent sport in this northerly corner of the country. Rathmullan House (074) 58188 has a glorious setting above Lough Swilly in the wilds of Donegal. The cuisine which is based on local game is also first class. In Kilmacrennan, the Anglers Haven (074) 39015 should also be noted. The Haw Lodge (074) 41397 near Lifford is well positioned, close to the border.

In Northern Ireland itself, an excellent hotel is Blackheath House—a former rectory and an ideal place from which to tour the area. All types of fishing—salmon, trout and sea fishing—are possible in the vicinity.

County Down offers yet more sensational scenery and a golf course to delight followers of the fairways. Lovers of fishing will also find some good opportunities here and the Tourist Board for Northern Ireland (0232) 231221 is very helpful. If you are fishing the River Bann then the Downhill Inn in Castlerock (0265) 848090 offers good value accommodation. The Bann System produces some outstanding fishing and the River Bush is also well worth trying, especially in the early autumn. Last, but certainly not least, the Bushmills Inn (02657) 32339 is a friendly and informal inn with a charming atmosphere.

People who are visiting County Galway will once again be rewarded with some superb countryside and a variety of inns, hotels and manor houses. A fine place to start one's trip is the splendid Moycullen House (091) 85566, which overlooks Lough Corrib. The proprietors can organise fishing for guests and for those who love traditional Irish hospitality, this is a must. Incidentally, it is worth noting a really outstanding restaurant nearby, Drimcong House (091) 85115, which enjoys a similarly stunning setting. Further round the lake we find a country house hotel of distinction at Oughterard, Currarevagh

House (091) 82312. The house dates back to the mid nineteenth century and is a mere 100 yards from Lough Corrib. It is a delightful hotel in which to stay and is thoroughly recommended, especially if you enjoy fishing. Surely an hotel with one of the world's most stunning settings must be Ashford Castle (092) 46003, overlooking Lough Corrib. The hotel is part thirteenth century castle, part French-style chateau and is one of the most delightful places to stay.

North of Lough Corrib, we find Lough Mask. Hotels are not so prolific in this area but the scenery of the Partry Mountains is quite majestic. The Park View House Hotel (092) 41263 is an hotel with pleasant rooms and Cushlough House (092) 41180 offers an intimate and friendly atmosphere. Another modest, but equally comfortable establishment in the area is Alder House (092) 41148.

Lough Carra is another delightful water to fish and is quite remote. Good value bed and breakfast accommodation can be enjoyed at Loughbawn (092) 43046 in Partry. This idyllic and unspoiled countryside offers many opportunities for the fisherman and just driving through this beautiful part of the country is quite an experience. Those anglers who are seeking to fish in the south west of County Mayo on Western Galway will surely find some good sport. One hotel to note here is Cashel House (095) 310001, standing at the head of Cashel Bay and an idyllic house with a superb restaurant. The Ballynahinch Castle Hotel (095) 310006 is a superb hotel in which to stay with some good shooting and fishing. There is a delightful atmosphere here and it is a fine base from which to explore the surrounding countryside. The Rosleague Manor Hotel (095) 41101 overlooks Bertraghboy Bay to the Connemara National Park and is one to recommend for all lovers of good hotels. Our final thought for the area is the Delphi Lodge (095) 42213 which stands within the Delphi Estate, making it one of the finest sporting lodges in Ireland.

The North West of Ireland is scattered with numerous loughs and rivers and encompasses some of the most renowned fishing in Ireland. Although some of the waters are well known in fishing circles, others remain relatively undiscovered. While every enthusiast will seek to explore the best known waters, large rewards lie in store in the less celebrated waters and a beat off the better trodden tracks will often offer up some exciting fishing. However, we start our journey at one famous fishing hotel: The Newport House Hotel (098) 41222. The hotel lawns reach down to the estuary and this Georgian mansion boasts a civilised and friendly atmosphere—the ideal base for a fishing foray. The hotel offers a number of fishing opportunities, while home smoked salmon and fresh seafood feature heavily in the splendid restaurant. In short, Newport House Hotel provides a perfect place to holiday, surrounded as it is by breathtaking scenery and excellent fishing.

Crossmolina also offers some first class fishing opportunities and a superb hotel here is Enniscoe House, Castlehill (096) 31112. This is another splendid Georgian house with a grand but welcoming atmosphere. Fine food and lovely views add to its charms. Lough Conn offers brown trout and spring salmon fishing in season. River salmon are also available, as well as a whole range of other leisure pursuits. If you are feeling somewhat exhausted, then fear not. This a place to relax and unwind.

Alternatively, those who are journeying to the wilds of Bangor Erris should consider The Hillcrest (097) 83494, a good value and out of the way establishment with much appeal. If you are staying in Ballina then there are a number of hotels to choose from. The Downhill Hotel (096) 21033 has another fine setting with gardens overlooking the River Brosna. Open fires combine with a lively cosmopolitan atmosphere in this friendly establishment. There is an extensive range of leisure facilities which will keep even the most sports mad family occupied. Another outstanding hotel keen to organise game fishing for you is the Mount Falcon Castle (096) 21172. This is a place to catch salmon, to explore deserted beaches and generally relax and enjoy yourself in luxurious surroundings. Mount Falcon Castle has fishing on the River Moy and salmon and trout fishing in Lough Conn is free to guests. The hotel is efficiently run by Constance Aldridge and she ensures that all guests are completely pampered during their stay. Other pursuits on offer include horse riding and shooting. The Alpine Hotel (096) 36144 also offers a warm welcome and offers some good value fishing.

Someway south of here we come to Pontoon. The Pontoon Bridge Hotel (094) 56120 has a school of fishing running from April to October. Also available are permits, licences and tackle hire. The restaurant boasts one of the best fish menus in the area. Healys Hotel (094) 56443 is another friendly hotel of note in the area. Visitors should also remember that there are numerous bed and breakfasts in places such as Foxford and Swinford which are excellent value. Equally abundant are the many smaller loughs in the surrounding countryside which offer some compelling fishing.

Those of you who enjoy brown trout fishing will no doubt head for Lough Arrow. Here, you find the splendid Coopershill (071) 65108 in Riverstown. The hotel has been in the O'Hara family since 1974 and stands proudly, surrounded by a five hundred acre estate providing the ideal base from which to explore the surrounding countryside, commonly referred to as 'Yeats Country'. This is a country house hotel of distinction and a perfect place for a short stay. The Cromleach Lodge (071) 65153 is another first class hotel in the region which offers good fishing and another excellent restaurant. The Rock View (079) 66073 on Lough Arrow is smaller and less expensive but still has much charm and is ideal for the fisherman.

Although it might seem some distance away when on the map, we should not overlook Rosses Point. There are a number of delightful loughs here and some superb golf too. A restaurant of character is Reveries (071) 77371. Magnificent views of Sligo Bay are complemented by some first class Irish cooking and this is well worth a special trip. A fine hotel nearby is the Ballincar House (071) 45361, an extremely elegant hotel.

River Brosan (Downhill Hotel)

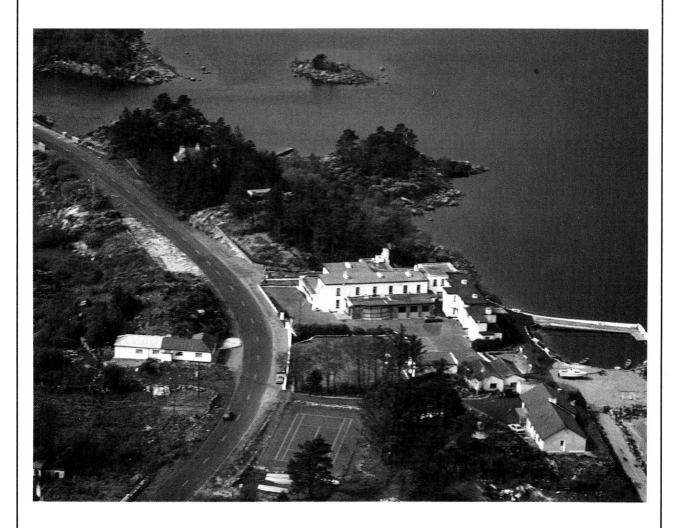

Set between Lake Conn and Lake Cullin and the mountain ranges of Nephin and Ox, the Pontoon Bridge Hotel was built towards the end of the 19th-century to cater for fishermen and their families from both Ireland and abroad; it still retains some of the ancient guest registers of the time. Little seems to have changed in the surrounding area; there is no industrialisation, no housing schemes, no intensive farming, instead, nearby is an old oak wood, where, still growing, are the oldest oak trees in the country.

Inside the hotel though are all the amenities that the modern guest has come to expect; direct-dial telephones, colour T.V. tennis court as well as In-house movies and nightly entertainment.

For the fisherman, Pontoon Bridge must surely be one of the most attractive hotels in the world. Its own School of Fly Fishing was launched in May 1987 and is now directed by Alan Pearsen from Buckinghamshire, a well-known author of many angling books and journalist. The School is most careful to cater for the experienced angler, male or female, as well as the complete novice; individual tuition can even be arranged outside of normal school schedules, both on the River Moy and surrounding lakes. The School offers both two and four day courses from April to October and full details are available on request.

The hotel also houses a School of Landscape Painting. The courses under the professional tuition of Mr Pat Gough are designed to cater for both the experienced and the beginner. Teaching is provided on both a group and an individual basis and is particularly directed towards the special needs or artistic aims of the participants as they draw their inspiration from this setting of unparalleled beauty.

Besides these specialised concerns the Pontoon Bridge Hotel is ideally situated for a number of activities; there are five excellent golf courses within easy distance, as well as pony trekking, water sports, beaches, a wildlife sanctuary and endless walks amidst the splendour of the Irish countryside.

Pontoon Bridge Hotel
Co. Mayo
Ireland
Tel: (010 353 94) 56120 / 56688 / 56699
Fax: (010 353 94) 56120

Far away from polluted air and water is the Downhill Hotel adjacent to the River Moy which is famous for its salmon fishing, attached to Lough Conn and flowing into Killala Bay provides an area rich in fresh and sea water fishing, coarse angling also available. We are in a position to organise a boat for your day trip be it on the lake, estuary or river (advance booking necessary). For that perfect game angling holiday come to the Moy and stay at the Downhill Hotel in the West of Ireland.

This Grade A hotel offers excellent cuisine, personal and friendly service and fine facilities. Bedrooms are luxurious with TV/video, satellite TV, radio, telephone, tea/coffee making facilities and trouser press. The Downhill is situated in beautiful grounds and offers Frogs Pavilion Piano Bar, split level restaurant with extensive menu, swimming pool, sauna, jacuzzi, gymnasium, squash, snooker room, sunbed and craft shop. If you are unable to escape from work the Downhill offers excellent conference facilities and is equipped to meet the most exact requirements.

The Downhill Hotel is conveniently located from Knock Airport and Sligo Airport both 35 miles away. In addition to excellent game angling guests may enjoy golf on one of the three championship courses close by, Enniscrone, Rossespoint and Westport. For those in search of a more peaceful break, a walk on one of the many beautiful sandy beaches or perhaps a scenic tour.

Downhill Hotel Limited
Ballina, Co Mayo
Ireland
Tel: (010 353 96) 21033
Fax: (010 353 96) 21338

One of the most exclusive hotels in the country, the Innishannon effortlessly lives up to its reputation as 'the most romantic hotel in Ireland'. Dating back to 1720 when it began its varied life as a substantial farmer's residence, it grew up beside an ancient ford, the first point at which the Bandon River could be crossed, and an important commercial centre in medieval times.

Conal and Vera O' Sullivan, the owners/managers like to see their hotel as 'a restaurant with rooms', and have gone to enormous efforts to ensure that the food is of a superlative quality. The hotel has been awarded an AA rosette for gastronomic excellence. Only fresh herbs and vegetables from surrounding farms are used, along with local meat and game. Seafood such as brill, turbot, salmon and Dublin Bay prawns, live lobsters and crayfish are served on the same day as they are landed in nearby Kinsale. An excellent selection of carefully chosen wines complements superb cuisine, served in a dining room as elegant as the food itself.

The hotel also boasts a lounge bar, cosy snug and ballroom catering for special occasions such as weddings, thoughtfully self-contained for privacy.

All of the bedrooms offer the modern amenities of colour television, direct-dial telephone cum clock/radio with extension in the bathroom. All bedrooms are, of course, en suite and have been individually decorated and furnished with traditional woods, chintzes and a selection from the O' Sullivans' extensive collection of original paintings and prints, which also brighten the walls of the public rooms.

Boating and yachting are available in the Innishannon's grounds. The boat is also available for fishing. Indeed the avid angler will find tremendous opportunites here. There is salmon and sea-trout fishing from the hotel lawns on both banks of the Bandon, or on the quarter-mile stretch of the Brinny River where the hotel holds exclusive rights. Permits can also be obtained for fishing other stretches. Deep sea angling can be arranged by the hotel for those with an interest in those waters.

It would be presumptious of me to try to describe the beauty of the surrounding countryside, when poets such as Edmund Spencer have already done so, but perhaps a small poem by local girl Alice Taylor, 'Return to Innishannon', best captures visitors' sentiments:

> **I have lived my life
> Far from here
> But I have taken
> This little place
> This little walled garden
> Of my heart
> To rekindle
> My tranquillity.**

Innishannon House Hotel
Innishannon
Eire
Tel: (010 353 21) 775121
Fax: (010 353 21) 775609

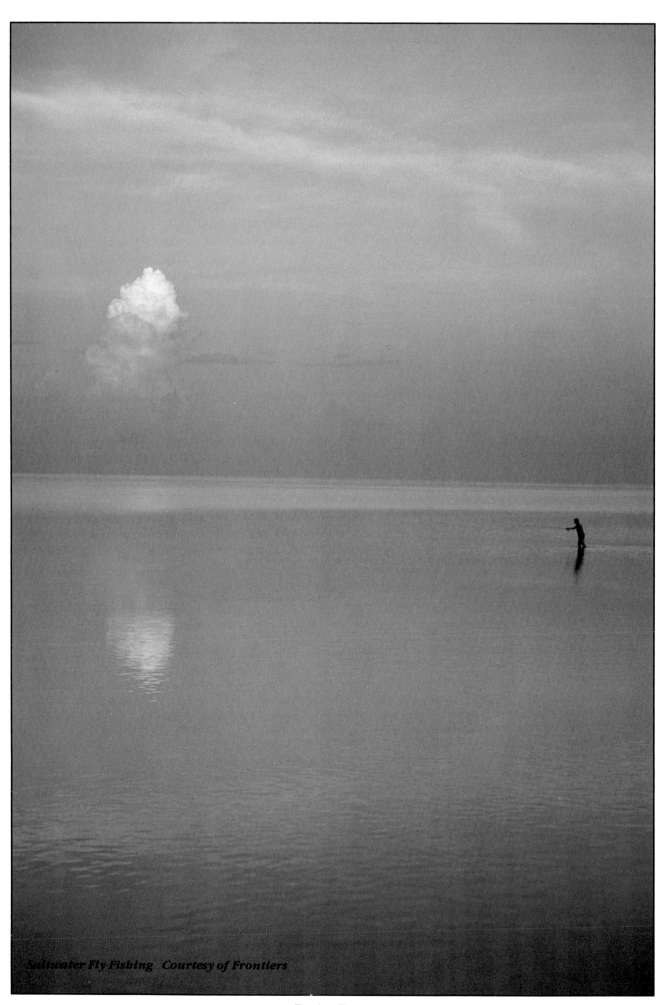

Saltwater Fly-Fishing Courtesy of Frontiers

Fishing in Great Britain and Ireland remains amongst the most competitive in the world, despite the various well-documented problems of recent years. Nevertheless, a fishing holiday abroad holds enormous—often exotic—appeal for every fisherman, whether it be for sport or simply pure adventure. Such a holiday of a lifetime is not within the means of everybody, and so for both arm-chair and intrepid explorers alike, we offer a tantalising glimpse of some of the most spectacular fishing imaginable.

This final section is not designed to go into great detail about the fishing available worldwide, but to give you a taste and to whet your appetite for the delights that can be discovered, ranging from the vast expanses of Canada to some fine sea trout fishing in Chile or fishing in the spectacular surroundings of New Zealand, Russia and even Nepal.

Fishing trips worldwide are not inexpensive but for the fishing experience of a lifetime, some of *the* fishing contained within these pages cannot be surpassed, either for the quality or quantity of the catch, or for the magnificent locations in which the fisherman will find himself. As you can probably imagine, if we tried to give a detailed account of the fishing just in Canada, for example you would now be the proud owner of a 600 page book. So what we have tried to do here is to describe some of the best fishing along with giving some useful numbers so that you can either arrange your own package or use one of the experienced fishing tour operators who offer a number of very tempting tours, each with different itineraries.

Fishing in Russia with Usser Tours

Today keen anglers are looking farther afield for new sport fishing, not only to more remote and unspoilt rivers, but also for different and less well known fish to catch.

Russia

Russia has to be one of the most exciting new destinations to have emerged for fishermen in recent years. Of the republics that make up the former Soviet Union, Russia is by far the greatest in area, stretching from the Baltic Sea to the Pacific. In this vast area there are literally thousands of rivers to explore and of course thousands of fish!

Ussher Tours Ltd is a small, Yorkshire-based tour operator, headed by former Gurkha officer, Christopher Ussher. The company specialises in fishing and wildlife expeditions to the Russian Far East, and trekking, rafting, fishing and wildlife safaris to Nepal. In 1991 the company took the first exploratory fishing expeditions to Russia and found the most fantastic fishing for Pacific Salmon, Arctic and East Siberian Char, Grayling and the mysterious Taimen. The two principal areas in the Russian Far East are the stunningly beautiful Kamchatka Peninsula with its snow-capped volcanic peaks, and the mountainous wilderness of Khabarovsk Province on the Western shores of the Sea of Okhotsk.

In Kamchatka the crystal clear Asacha River provides excellent fishing for the Coho, or Silver, Salmon, (averaging 7lb-20lb) in late August and September. Earlier in the season there is also good fishing for the King Salmon.

Khabarovsk (Ussher Tours)

In Kamchatka we have good tented camp accommodation, fully staffed with cooks, guides, interpreters and boatmen. You are dropped at the camp by Aeroflot helicopter after a spectacular flight from Petropavlovsk-Kamchatsky over the volcanic scenery of the peninsula.

There is a greater variety of fish to be caught in Khabarovsk Province where all six species of Pacific Salmon can be caught between June and September. In particular, the Coho, Chum (or Dog), Cherry (or Masu) and the Pink (or Humpback) Salmon can all be caught in large numbers on rivers such as the Ul'baya, Khutu, Koppi and Uda Rivers, where both log cabin and tented camps are available. In addition to this there is excellent fishing for East Siberian and Arctic Char, Lenok and Arctic Grayling.

However one of the most exciting fish to be found in the Khabarovsk region is the mighty Taimen (Hucho taimen); this massive fresh water fish is the world's largest salmon species and can be found in several rivers throughout the season. The average size for Taimen in the area is 50lb but they have been known to reach much greater weights. Most types of spoons and spinners are good for Taimen fishing but the local people like to use an artificial mouse fished across the surface, this is particularly exciting at night when you suddenly feel a great tug on the end of the line!

In Khabarovsk we have both tented and log cabin accommodation, Located on the river banks, these have a mess hut, and sauna huts for washing, and are fully staffed as in Kamchatka. Again we use Aeroflot heli-copters to transfer you from Khabarovsk city to the river.

One of the joys of fishing in the Far East of Russia, apart from the fantastic fishing, where you have the whole river to yourselves, is the adventure of travelling to some of the most remote and isolated places on earth where few people have ever fished on a fly. This unspoilt area is rich in also wildlife such as bear, wolves, snow sheep, caribou, and even the elusive Siberian tiger, which you may be lucky enough to see in the surrounding taiga! This is undoubtedly one of the most wonderfully untouched and unique places to fish in the world. All trips include a stopover in Moscow where we will give you a guided tour of the main sights, such as Red Square and the Kremlin. Extensions to your holiday to include more time in Moscow and some time in St.Petersburg can also be arranged.

Nepal

When the British first went to the Indian sub-continent they found in the many rivers flowing out of the Himalayas a family of predatory fish, the Mahseer; a fish worthy to be classed amongst the great game fish of the world. The handsome Mahseer, with its strong take and fighting qualities continues to attract sportsmen from all over the world. Several species are found in the river systems of Nepal, including the Golden Mahseer, (Tor puti-tora) and the Silver Mahseer, (Tor tor).The Mahseer, known as Sahar in Nepal, are migratory. In Winter they live and feed in the lowland rivers of the Terai, but in March and April, as the snow melts, they move into the lower gorges of the Himalayan foothills. Here they feed

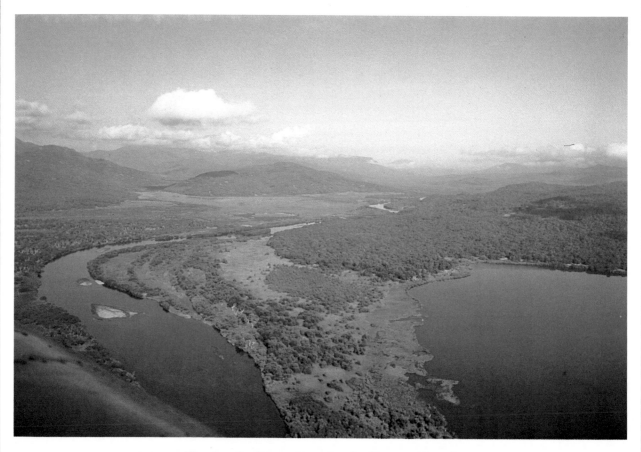

The Asacha River, Kamchatka (Ussher Tours)

greedily before travelling into the fast, rocky, snow-fed headwaters to spawn during the monsoon. In October, as the rivers begin to drop and clear, the Mahseer migrate down-river again. It is during these migratory journeys that the Mahseer provide the best fishing, with November into early December and mid- February to April being the optimum time when the rivers are running clear. Fine Mahseer, up to 60lb, can still be caught in Nepal, but any fish over 20lb will give you a most memorable fight before it is finally beached. The Kosi River in the east and the Karnali River in the far west remain the best fishing rivers for Mahseer and especially the lower reaches of the Karnali where it leaves the Himalayas and runs for some twenty miles through the beautiful Royal Bardia National Park.

Given the size of these rivers, spinning with a Toby, or similar salmon lures, is the most productive means of fishing, but a fly rod can be effective on the smaller tributaries, such as the Babai in October and November. Here the Indian Trout, (Barilius bola) can also be taken, whilst the deep pools hold the Giant Catfish, or Goonch, (Bagarius bagarius). Fishing for Mahseer, like the salmon, can be unpredictable and good catches can never be taken for granted. The fishing should not therefore be regarded as the sole object of any holiday in Nepal. It is a unique country in terms of its culture, wildlife and the stunning scenery of the Himalayas, and there are wonderful opportunities for trekking, game-viewing, and river-rafting, all of which can be organised as part of a Mahseer fishing holiday. As a small, specialised company, Ussher Tours are able to offer an extremely personalised service to our clients and are happy to organise tailor-made holidays to suit your exact requirements, both in Russia and Nepal. For further information on fishing expeditions to Russia and to Nepal please contact Christopher Ussher, Mike Allen, Sarah Petrie or Angus Fraser at the following address: Ussher Tours Ltd, The Estate Office, Harewood, Leeds LS17 9LQ Tel: (0532) 886573 Fax: (0532) 886045

Canada

What can be said about Canada? There are literally thousands and thousands of rivers and lakes, some of which have probably never seen a hand crafted fly before; each Province has a speciality, whether it be fishing for salmon (Atlantic and Pacific), 30lb lake trout or Arctic grayling. This is only to be expected from a country which has probably a third of the freshwater available worldwide. We will not attempt here to classify the fishing or draw up a table of merit, but allow the readers to judge for themselves, from the descriptions and from the words of those who have had the privilege of fishing these waters.

It is hard to choose which province to start with. For ease of reading we will start in the east and head west.So we begin the journey in Newfoundland and Labrador. Fishing in Labrador, it is impossible to practically define the difference between good and great fishing, for it has world class salmon and trout fishing. You will be fishing in surroundings where the day's activities will often be interrupted by the sighting of moose, black bear, caribou and countless other species of wildlife. You can fish for Atlantic salmon averaging 15lb-20lb, though fish over 20lb are regularly hooked (the Eagle River is world famous) and if you are unfortunate enough to fail to bag one of these beauties then there are plentiful grilse of up to 8lb. Another marvellous test of your fishing skill is the hard fighting brook (speckled) trout with trophy size fish of

Labrador (Go Fishing Canada)

5lb-6lb being caught. Labrador holds four world records (IGFA) for brook trout in different categories but all were taken using fly rods, and were caught on Minipi lake and Minipi river. Don't let their size fool you into a false sense of security, they'll fight you all the way in.

If Labrador sounds like the place for you, it is probably best to know that, like a lot of fishing in Canada, it is not for the weak willed or faint hearted. A lot of the best fishing is off the beaten track, so the accommodation is comfortable but basic, but by the time you're hooked into one of the many fish to be had, your few worries about comfort will have evaporated. The salmon season runs from 1st July to 15th September, while brook trout can be fished between 2nd June to 15th September, with a few local differences.

To get there, a number of UK based opeators have several packages available. Choose between Nimroo Safaris Ltd (0285) 810132, Ker & Downey (071)-629-2044, Go Fishing-Canada (0371) 876785, Sport Elite Ltd. (093589) 477, Newfoundland and Labrador Tourism (0101-709) 576 2830. In Nova Scotia, which is renowned for its wildlife, such as numerous species of birds including a vast colony of puffins which act as a superb backdrop to the fishing, you will be drawn again by the prospect of some excellent Atlantic Salmon fishing. One of the beauties of Canada is that unlike a lot of the great fishing in Europe, nearly all the waters are accessible, meaning that you can enjoy salmon and trout fishing on nearly all of the rivers and lakes of Nova Scotia.

Traditional methods of fly fishing work perfectly here, in fact, probably better than you're used to. The catches here can be so prolific that limits on the numbers of fish you are allowed to keep are strictly enforced and, indeed, as elsewhere in Canada, the use of barbless hooks is enthusiastically encouraged. When you buy your licence each fisherman is issued with ten tags. Each which will have the number of your permit on them, which must remain on the fish you keep up until the moment you cook them; this in no way will ruin your enjoyment of the sport. As long as you return the fish immediately, you can catch as many fish as you want, so the main enjoyment—the thrill of the chase—is still there.

Although the season varies throughout the province, most of June through to September is open season, but remember Nova Scotia is a strict fly fishing only province. If any of this apparent red tape has dampened any of your enthusiasm then think again. Nova Scotia has some of the best, and most prolific Atlantic Salmon fishing, dare we say, in the world. The most bountiful rivers are Medway and Lehave in the south, Stewiacke and St Marys in mid-province and Margeree in the north. Having said that, there are a number of rivers with substantial but smaller salmon runs throughout the province, so keep your ears open for any titbits imparted by the locals. We don't want to give the impression that Nova Scotia has nothing but Atlantic salmon—if that wasn't enough it has some marvellous fishing, whatever your particular favourite happens to be. It might be fishing for landlocked salmon, slightly smaller than its saltwater

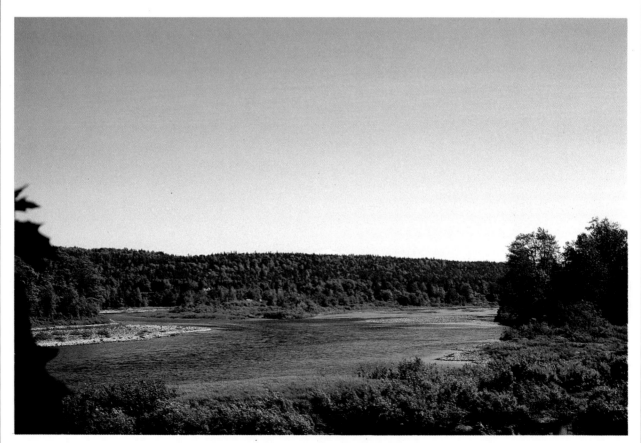

Miramichi (Go Fishing Canada)

brethren, known locally as Sebago salmon, found primarily in Shubenacadie Grand Lake, although smaller numbers can be fished in countless other lakes.

If you get bored with landing salmon after salmon, or you feel you want to give your arms a rest, brook trout offer a challenge but need slightly lighter tackle. As the sport of landing one of these fighting beauties is much sought after, the best fishing can be had off the beaten track. Take yourself off to the following counties: Cape Breton, Cumberland, Halifax, Guysborough and Lunenburg. The brook trout that manage to avoid the unwelcome attention of the fisherman migrate to the open sea and after a couple of years return as sea-trout. These provide truly exceptional sport on many of the rivers more famous for their salmon catches. If you think travelling to Nova Scotia to fish for rainbow trout is odd, don't worry. The rainbows you will encounter in North America bear little relation to their European counterparts. They are ferocious fighters and their added benefit is that they make delicious eating.

The best lakes are Levers, Umsey and Clearwater. The brown trout introduced from Europe in 1923 can be found in numerous lakes, although if you want to fish for large trout, the lake trout growing upwards of 20lb can be fished in Sherbrooke lake although it must be said in lesser numbers.

Go Fishing-Canada (0371) 876785, Fresh Adventures Ltd. (0462) 816424 and Sport Elite Ltd. (093589) 477 have a number of packages including trips to the Margeree river, one of the most famous salmon rivers in Canada. If you feel you would prefer to organise your own trip then the Nova Scotia Tourist Office (071)-930-664 will be more than happy to help. Off the coast of Nova Scotia can be found Prince Edward Island which although it cannot boast the vast array of fishing that other provinces can, the fishing is good enough to make a trip well worth while with Atlantic salmon on the Morel River and rainbow and brook trout on most of the rivers and lakes. The best people to speak to before you arrange your trip here are the Department of Tourism on (0101-902) 892-3420. New Brunswick again shares the jewels that its sister provinces boast both in terms of the fishing and the scenery. Eighy-eight per cent of New Brunswick is covered in forest so wherever you find yourself fishing it is guaranteed to be in splendid surroundings. The country is dissected by three major river systems, and not surprisingly for Canada they are very good salmon rivers, the Estigouche, the Saint John and the mighty Miramichi. The Miramichi, with its many tributaries, literally drains the entire centre of the province by itself, providing salmon in huge numbers—so much so that the Miramichi is responsible for half the Atlantic salmon caught in North America. Again, the true sports fisherman is rewarded as only fly fishing is allowed for sea run salmon. They are quite strict on the size of fish that can be retained, which, in the interest of keeping a good stock of trophy fish, has to be applauded. Any fish under sixty-three centimetres must be released; salmon steal the show again with salmon caught on the Miramichi weighing up to 40lb (10lb-12lb being the average). With your thoughts being on catching salmon after salmon, many being trophy size, your departure date will come all too soon, but less of these depressing thoughts. New Brunswick can also boast an alternative if you should so desire in the form of brook trout and landlocked salmon, known locally as ovananiche.

Go Fishing-Canada (0371) 876785 have introduced New Brunswick into their programme this year; Fresh Adventures Ltd. (0462) 816424 and Escape Activities (0754) 23812 also operate to New Brunswick. For those who prefer the Do-it-Yourself trip, New Brunswick Tourist office (0101-506) 453-2444 will be happy to assist.

If someone asked you if a land the size of Texas, covered by forest with thousands of lakes and rivers whose neighbours boasted marvellous fishing, had anything to offer the serious game fisherman, then you would probably hazard the guess—yes. Well, you'd be right: Quebec is twice the size of Texas, with just over half its area an ideal location for game fishing of all varieties, including what many consider to be the ultimate game fish, the Arctic char.

With over a million lakes, rivers and streams you will not have difficulty in fishing for one or two if not all of your favourites. In the west of Quebec are the renowned Moisie and Chaloupe rivers which are famed for the abundance, and the fighting spirit, of the Atlantic salmon. The rivers here are not large, so for those of you who enjoy your fishing in waders, Quebec offers a reasonable alternative to the Miramichi. There are other fine but less prolific rivers to accompany the Chaloupe and the Moisie. The problem of overcrowding does not exist in Canada, with only ten rods per sixty miles of river in many cases. In the North there are two rivers which offer excellent sport, the Delay and Melezes, which both flow into the Koksoak. There are over one hundred and twenty miles of fishing here on these two rivers, where trophy salmon of over 30lb can be caught although the average is more around the 12lb mark. The Moisie holds

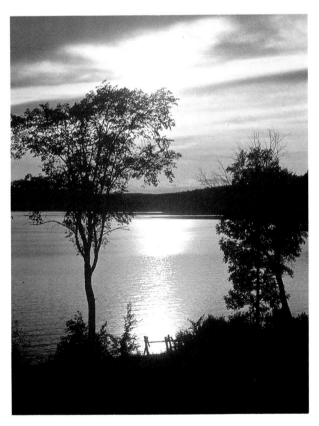

Quebec (Quebec Tourist Board)

one of the world records (IGFA) for an Atlantic salmon caught in freshwater by fly with a fish weighing 44lb 12oz.

The Gaspe Peninsula has two very good rivers, the Bonaventure and the Cascapedia but, unfortunately, a lot of the fishing is private. This is not surprising as the Cascapedia holds the all time world record (IGFA) for a salmon caught in freshwater using a fly, weighing in at 47lb. Another premier salmon river is the George which runs through the Ungava territory in the north into Ungava Bay. One of the reasons for the superb fishing is quite simply the inaccessibility of the locations.

As I mentioned earlier, one reason for travelling to Quebec is to fish for Arctic char, found in large numbers in the estuary of the Tuksukatuk River. These fish, which can be caught up to weights of 25lb, are greatly admired for the formidable fight they put up, worthy of a salmon of one and a half times their weight; once fished you will understand why they are so highly regarded by the serious sports fisherman. The lake from which this river flows, the Tuksukatuk, is the venue for some excellent lake trout fishing. They can be caught up to weights of 30lb and as the waters are so cold they do at least swim relatively close to the surface.

For some light relief, but still wishing to enjoy a spirited scrap, the brook trout (some weigh up to 8lb), will prove to be an admirable opponent and can be found in the rivers or in many of the coves and inlets of the lakes, one of the best being the Assinica Broadback River. Bag limits have been imposed, but most of you will be happy to release them, satisfied completely with the combination of the idyllic surroundings and the thrill of combat. The Quebec experience is heightened by the different culture, the majority of Quebec enjoying a French influence. Look out also for the largest caribou herd in the world.

Two companies who have already recognised the potential of Quebec are Fresh Adventures (0462) 816424 and Go Fishing-Canada (0371) 876785. Quebec's Tourist Office (071)-930-8314 can (if you should so desire) give you full details on all the rivers and lakes but I would imagine that the details here, although brief, will satisfy the appetite of the most voracious fisherman.

We move sedately onto Ontario. It has both the capital Ottawa and the commercial centre Toronto. If you've come to Ontario to fish for salmon, then, unfortunately, you've come to the wrong place, apart from a little titbit that we will impart slightly later. There is fishing and it is good fishing. It is all in the North and the majority of the best sport is to be had at the fly-in fishing camps—you really are fishing out in the wilderness. In fact it boasts some of the best conditions in the world for brook trout and the all time world record (IGFA) of 14lb 8oz so if these glorious fighting fish are your particular cup of tea, then you will find little better. The price you pay for fishing two of the best rivers, the Nettogami and the Sutton is that you have to pay for it in sweat and toil. You will have some exhilarating sport but you will feel as though you've earned it.

Now, as promised, that little titbit. There is salmon fishing in Ontario; well there's one salmon to be precise, and it will be in lake Ontario from May 1st onwards. The Toronto Star, the local newspaper, organises what is known surprisingly enough as the Toronto Star Salmon Hunt. Now this may not appeal to the purists of you out there, because traditional fly techniques are unlikely to

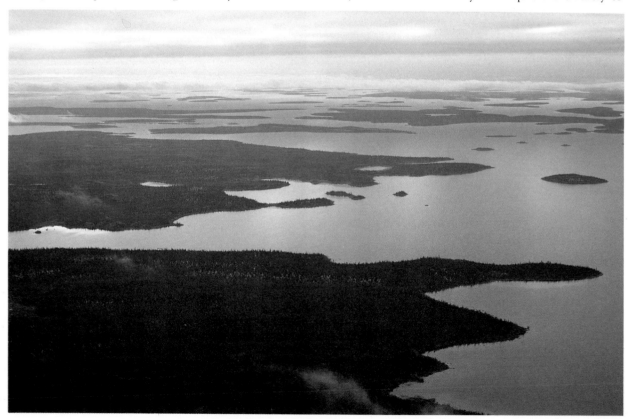

Manitoba (Anglers World Today)

prove successful, although you may well be tempted to push your morals to one side for the day, for the lucky fisherman who bags this tagged salmon will receive $1,000,000. Go Fishing-Canada (0371) 876785 specialise here or alternatively contact the Ontario Tourist Board on (071)-245-1222 if you are tempted by either the brook trout or early retirement.

If you're looking for somewhere in the world to fish, matching the thrill of salmon fishing, but fishing for what can only be described as monster trout, then you are unlikely to be disappointed by Manitoba where the lake trout, the native of North American waters, can reach upwards of 50lb, although they average out between 15 and 25lb. The official record is 62lb and if you can't imagine a trout that size, then you'll just have to go out there and experience one for yourself.

These fish can match and probably beat the Atlantic salmon pound for pound for the length and toughness of the battle. They only inhabit lakes that are clear, cold and highly oxygenated. In the spring when the surface water is cold, they can be caught using light tackle or spinning gear. During the summer months, as they prefer the cold, you will find them in the deeper parts of the lake, although fly fishing techniques can be used all season in the northern parts of the lakes due to the surface water remaining cold.

The big two, where the majority of the big catches have been taken, are Nueltin and Nejanilini lakes. Big catches have been recorded in numerous others but not in such prolific numbers. The trout family continues to entertain in Manitoba with brook trout and the rainbow. For the purist who is primarily interested in quality rather than quantity, then again, fly fishing for Brookies with their zesty fighting qualities is hard to match. The best places

to find the Brook are the South Knife River, Gods River and East Blue; Bower Deep and Barbe lakes for the rainbow, although, as usual, there are plenty of marvellous alternatives, producing good catches but again, not in the same quantities. You may also come across the European brownie when fishing for rainbow on East Blue lake or on Williams lake.

Finally we come to the Arctic grayling: I say finally, but purely because it is the last fish to be mentioned and not a true game fish by right, but it is a superb fish for the traditional fly fisherman. It has few rivals for its beauty, being known as the Sailfish of the North because of its high sail-like dorsal fin. It is a small fish by comparison but it more than makes up for it with its spectacular show, often leaping clear out of the water; it is found only in extreme northern streams, preferring cold clear flowing waters. The best of Manitoba's Arctic grayling fishing is to be found around and on Munroe and Kanapakaksis lakes as well as Nueltin and Nejanilini.

Again, you can leave all the worries of organisation to the experienced Anglers World Holidays (0246) 221717 who offer a package with a nice extra, that you can extend your holiday if you haven't had enough fishing after seven days, which is very unlikely. There is a rumour that one gentleman is still there after two and a half years! Manitoba's Tourist Office can be reached on (0101-204) 945-3777.

Northwest Territories' name in itself gives you a fairly good idea of what to expect. Although it takes up almost a third of all Canada, it is home to only 55,000 people, the population of a small English town like Warwick. It has ocean coastline, countless fresh water lakes, mountains, glaciers, Precambrian Shield, Tundra and Polar desert, all on an unbelievable scale; it includes two of the world's

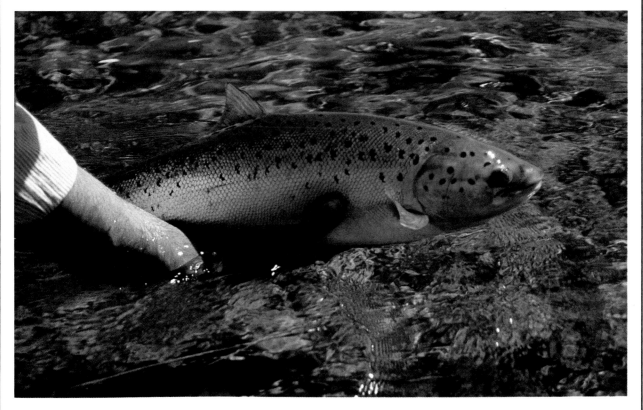

Courtesy of Nimrod Safaris

largest lakes, the Great Bear and Great Slave, the enormous Mackenzie River and Virginia falls, (twice the height of Niagara). The sport here tends to be exceptional, due primarily to the shortness of the season. It lasts only eight to twelve weeks, the rest of the time it is frozen over. Like Manitoba you are here to fish for lake trout and Arctic grayling. They encourage a catch and release policy, a practise which would greatly improve the fishing everywhere if more fishermen were sympathetic to it. This means that there is a good chance that some of the fish or maybe even all the fish that you will catch will be of a good size.

Northwest Territories hold the world record (IGFA) for a lake trout at 65lb, but also the freshwater fly record (IGFA) of 21lb, both being taken on the Great Bear and the world records (IGFA) for Arctic grayling, freshwater fly as well as the all time world record (IGFA) of 5lb 15oz. There are countless lakes in Northwest Territories. Three of the best for quality and accessibility are Fergeson, Drum and the Great Bear itself. Although you can never guarantee catching a big fish on whatever water you fish, Northwest Territories is one place where you get pretty close. Anglers World Holidays (0246) 221717 who specialise in fishing for trophy size lake trout will be happy to advise you what is on offer. Go Fishing-Canada (0371) 876 785 have also introduced this area. The tourist office of Northwest Territories can be reached on (0101-403) 873-7200.

We've told you about two locations for trophy size lake trout and Arctic grayling. Due to the sheer size of Canada, there are three more: Saskatchewan, the Yukon and Alberta. Anglers World Holidays (0246) 221717 were planning to include Alberta this year, to continue their itinerary of lake trout fishing and also the marvellous fishing offered on the Bow river. The tourist offices to be contacted are, Saskatchewan (0101-306) 787-2300, Yukon (0101-403) 667-5340 and Alberta (071)-491-3430. With a choice like this it may be easier to toss a coin; they all have exceptional fishing in unsurpassed settings.

British Columbia

British Columbia is further to fly to from Britain, but the one thing that will get you on that plane without a second thought is that this quite simply is the Pacific Salmon capital of the world. Nowhere else can you fish for five types of salmon, each one possessing a different characteristic, making catching each type a unique experience. If that doesn't stir the emotions, then how about the prospect of catching a 70lb plus salmon, the Chinook as it is known by the Indians, or simply as the King salmon. However you refer to it, there can be no experience like it. With reports of four to five hour battles, the thrill of landing one of these beautiful specimens will cap even the most travelled and experienced of fisherman's careers. It should be said that a lot of the fishing in British Columbia for salmon is run on a highly commercial basis—you go out on trawler-like boats, and almost dredge the waters for salmon using three rigs of many lures. The salmon hang themselves on these, rather like hanging coats on a coatstand—this operation is known as 'trolling'. If all you want to do is to say, 'I've caught a 70lb salmon,' then that's fine, the Campbell River will suit your requirements perfectly. If you don't, then don't despair, the sports fisherman is still offered an abundance of fishing, the whole enjoyment and just as important the pride of catching a fish using the more traditional methods. The five species of salmon to be found in British Columbia are the Chinook, the Chum, the Coho, the Pink and the Sockeye. Each one offers a different and exciting challenge. The Chinook after taking the line will dive to the depths of the river or lake in an effort to shake you off. It can be a long and tiring struggle, but I'm sure you'll agree it is well worth it for the chance of landing a seventy-pounder. The Coho will put up a fight, no less ferocious, but certainly more spectacular with many often leaping and dancing clear of the water, a spectacle to behold.

British Columbia also offers some 22,000 lakes, with rainbow trout predominating, boasting the freshwater fly world record (IGFA) of 28lb, taken on the Skeena River, these waters also have Brook trout and wild cut-throat trout, which, if caught, you are particularly asked to release unharmed. You can also find some marvellous Steelhead fishing rainbows who have migrated to the sea and returned, so as you can imagine, a rainbow with two years, ocean experience on top of its natural fighting instincts is a formidable foe. In the north you can fish for Arctic grayling in the colder clearer waters; look out also for the Dolly Varden trout, a local good quality fish.

It does sound like a fishing paradise and it comes very close to being one. There are few, if any, places that can offer sport of this stature anywhere in the world and if you wish to fish here, you have a good choice of specialist tour operators who will try and make your day-

British Columbia (Go Fishing Canada)

dreams become reality—Nimrod Safaris Ltd (0285) 810132; Ker & Downey (071)-629-2044; Anglers World Holidays (0246) 221717; Go Fishing-Canada (0371) 876785; Fresh Adventures Ltd (0462) 816424; British Columbia House (071)-930-6857.

Canada, as you have read, has an abundance of fishing to suit every enthusiast, from the relative beginner up to the veteran of many waters. It's hard to put into words exactly what the whole experience is like, so to really appreciate its waters, you will have to travel there yourself.

If after reading about Canada you have the impression that it has all the world's best fishing, you'd be mistaken for although it does have a wealth of marvellous fishing, it certainly doesn't have a monopoly. Chile, the next country we take a look at, has every reason to stake its claim as having some of the worlds best fishing, as do all of the countries to which the remainder of the section is devoted.

> Manitoba—Northwest Territories—quite simply it is the most exciting, underfished trout fishing in the world, fishing for the worlds biggest trout.
> John Wilson, Go Fishing Television programme

Sport fishing visitors to the Yukon will not only remember the exceptional fishing for native Lake trout, Dolly Varden trout, rainbow trout, Arctic grayling, pike and four salmon species. They will marvel at the natural beauty of the midnight sun. They will also experience the legends of the Klondike gold rush days nearly a century ago and take with them some of the friendly independent spirit which lives on in Yukon's 25,000 residents.
> Don Toews, Fisheries Department—Yukon Government.

The Bow River (Alberta) provides the finest dry fly fishing for rising rainbow that I have experienced anywhere in the world.
> Leigh Perkins, CEP of Orvis, Fishing Tackle Manufacturer.

Anglers agree the Bow River in Alberta offers the finest fly-fishing in North America. Fly-in fishing in remote northern Alberta fishing lodges provides the ultimate in trophy fishing.
> L. Dowling, Director of Tourism.

Quebec, with eighteen per cent of the world's fresh water supply and over a million lakes, is a land of fishing thrills second to none. Almost all of the most sought after species—trout, salmon and Arctic char—can be found in abundance there.
> Michel Leblanc, Official of Marcel Gignac, the Government of Quebec.

Saskatchewan has some of the finest fresh water fishing in North America. Here you can catch trophy size Lake trout, Northern pike, pickerel and Arctic grayling.

With its many fishing lodges and wilderness campgrounds Saskatchewan allows you to return to nature in its grandest setting, without giving up the comforts of civilization.
> Ted Hornung, Official of the Government of Saskatchewan.

A life-time experience—grandeur, challenge, limitless excitement-primeval wilderness, soaring eagles, massive whales, towering forests—and the marvellous harvest of the North Pacific is yours to seek. There's nothing like it!
> Garde B. Gardom Q.C., Agent General of British Columbia.

The world records mentioned here are recorded by the IGFA (The International Game Fish Association) using their methods of verification; and the records are either for fly fishing only with the occasional record being for the all time weight which does not specify technique used. The Association was formed in 1939 and only records catches that they could personally verify are mentioned, so it explains why Mrs Ballantine's salmon is not included in their records. We can only hope that one day your name and catch will be included in their number.

Chile
The trout you will fish for in Chile were introduced at the turn of the century. They took to the clean unpolluted waters that Chile has to offer, and now rainbow and brown trout thrive in these lakes and rivers. If this, in itself, does not tempt, many of the fish are now migratory and return as Steelhead and sea-trout and it is more for these fish that Chile is famed. Those of you who have fished for either will appreciate the magnificent sport that they both offer. The best rivers in the Lake District are the San Pedro, the Pretrohue and the Golgol. The beauty of fishing in Chile is that not only is the sport superb, the scenery unforgettable, but the summers in Chile are perfect for enjoying your favourite pastime. Patagonia, the fjord country of Chile, also offers some marvellous fishing. The lake district is heavily fished, although in no way am I suggesting that it is fished-out. The rivers to head for in Patagonia for Steelhead and sea-trout are the Simpson, the Cisnes, the Plaena, the Baker and its tributary, the Cocherin, whilst the Nirehuao is famous for brown trout. You may be surprised to learn that you can also fish for King and Coho salmon. They were first introduced in the late seventies to early eighties and there have been a few reported sightings of the salmon returning to their spawning grounds, with the experiment repeated three years ago—only time will tell whether they will have taken to these waters. You may, of course, raise a few eyebrows when you return home purporting to have fished for salmon in Chile, but at the moment it is a little known secret. Who knows, it may become the warm alternative to British Columbia. It seems odd that, with the rivers teeming with some exceptional sport already, the locals would bother trying to introduce new species, although financially salmon have always been a lucrative lure to fishermen. There are two specialist tour operators who offer great packages to Chile, Nimrod Safaris Ltd (0285) 810132 and Sport Elite Ltd. (0935) 891477.

The Falklands
The Falkland Islands will, of course, be known to all of you as a place of conflict in 1982, but perhaps what you are less aware of, is that it is a marvellous venue for the serious game fisherman. If you're a bit concerned about your fishing break being marred by the military presence, although there are still 2000 active troops on the Islands and you will see the occasional military vehicle on the roads, the vast majority of the Falklands carries on

its daily routine as though nothing ever happened.

The brown trout were introduced to the Falkland Islands almost forty years ago, as the only trout nature endowed the Islands with was the Falkland trout, which isn't technically a trout or even a char. The brown trout quickly adapted and a fast growing migratory strain soon established itself and very soon populated most of the Islands rivers. These give us today some of the world's best sea trout fishing, the record to date taken on a fly was caught on the Malo and weighed in at over 20lb. A larger fish was taken of 23lb but it was caught using a spinner.

The rivers to look out for are the Chartres (subject to availability of accommodation), the Warrah on West Falkland, and the San Carlos on East Falkland. Most of the rivers are fishable for brown trout, but they tend to be small, a symptom of the acidity of the rivers. You may be thinking that although the fishing sounds very tempting its a long way to go to what many think to be a barren, cold and inhospitable place to fish for large sea trout. Well, you will be surprised to learn that the summers are remarkably temperate with weather very similar to that of eastern England, and is still warmer during winter, as the Falklands lie on the same latitude south as London is north. On top of this, you will be surrounded by what is literally a conservation park, full of elephant seals, dolphins and numerous species of birds.

The lodges you'll be staying in operate honesty bars, where you settle up at the end of your stay, but drink is remarkably cheap due to the different taxation laws. Port Stanley does have five pubs, so its worth popping in to meet the locals.

The only way to get to the Falklands at the moment is by AF Tristar, but if that panics you Nimrod Safaris Ltd (0285) 810132 and Sport Elite Tours (093589) 477 have complete packages for fishing the Falklands.

River Warrrah (Falkland Islands Tourism)

Finland

Like Canada, Finland offers the fisherman the complete choice of game fishing. Being so long the landscape changes gradually along its entire length from gently rolling hills in the south to the mountainous regions of the north with elevation of over at thousand feet. It is known as the land of 10,000 lakes, but after an exhaustive study the true count is just a little under 188,000. Finland also offers a wide selection of wild animals, with 65 species, bears, wolves, 120,000 elk and the Finnish equivalent of the cow, the reindeer!

Back to the form of wildlife you are primarily interested in, the fish. Atlantic salmon can be found in good numbers in the Teno, Tornio Naatamo, Simo and Kiiminkl rivers, in fact, Finlands record salmon caught in the Tornio was just over 94lb. Information on how it was landed is not available, but may I suggest—with a little help from his friends! The restrictions they impose is that the salmon must be over sixty centimetres to be retained, and, thankfully, due to an active stocking programme, the numbers of salmon are increasing.

Sea-trout, which have improved once again due to heavy stocking, thrive even in the waters around Helsinki, with the record being 41lb but the average being more around the 6lb-10lb mark. Again the named salmon rivers are where you'll find the sea trout.

In the big lakes, primarily of southern Finland, and the rivers and lakes of Lapland, you'll find a good number of brown trout. Lapland boasts the record, with a brown trout weighing close to 34lb being caught from Lake Inari. Father Christmas was not involved in the catch!

Success (Falkland Islands Tourism)

Goose Green (Falkland Islands Tourism)

Norway (Courtesy of Frontiers)

In many of the areas where you'll find brown trout you will also find the brook trout, especially in the north of Finland, and because of this you are asked to return all trout under the length of thirty-two centimetres, as the brook trout is almost indistinguishable from the young brown trout. In this way the brown trout will be allowed, hopefully, to grow to spawning size and help continue its presence in these waters.

You may be lucky to catch an Arctic char—although they are quite rare—if you're fishing on the lakes in Lapland or very occasionally in Lake Saimaa, Finland's largest water system.

Grayling are again found in suitably large numbers, primarily in the north and east of Finland, and they are a favourite of a number of fly fisherman because of their intense fighting spirit. A grayling of 15lb which is rare, was caught at Lake Konnevesi in central Finland. They are also a very tasty fish when grilled.

When fishing in Finland the best people to contact are Lapland Travel (010 358) 6016052.

Norway

Many a keen fisherman will know of Norway's reputation. For many this is the mecca for salmon and sea—trout fishing in Europe and possibly the world. Norway is the home of the fjord, where a superb vista of mountains and trees awaits you. Anglers are fortunate that in all the places we have featured, and Norway is no exception, they can enjoy some of the world's best fishing in some of the world's most memorable scenery.

Although we are not awarding marks for different rivers, it is important that you are aware that the Vosso ranks in the top five salmon rivers in the world, although most of the fishing is done by spinning. It isn't as good as it used to be but the average catch, since records began 100 years ago, is still a remarkable 25lb. Unlike the great Icelandic rivers, it is not horrendously expensive to fish the Vosso but the waiting list can be long.

Other beats in Norway are much sought after, particularly on such renowned waters as the Tana and the Alta which boasts a number of world records (IGFA) using fly fishing techniques—a fish of 38lb 8oz was caught in 1983. Laerdal, the Driva (once a very good river, it has suffered recently due to a virus gyro-dactilus which unfortunately kills the smolts) Eira, Orkla, Gaula, Aaro, Aa and Surna are also good, but they do command some high prices.

Some relatively inexpensive fishing can be had by staying at the hotels who own private stretches, this is especially true in the north. The best salmon fishing is in June and July but the season extends from May to September 5th, with the best sea-trout fishing being in August—the perfect way of finishing off the season. If the cost of salmon fishing proves prohibitive there are some marvellous alternatives, in the shape of brown trout and char fishing. Around Oslo there are numerous well stocked lakes and streams, if you don't mind travelling further afield, twenty-five pound trout have been caught on the Andselvern, the Drammen and on Norway's largest lake, the Mjosa.

In the deep cold mountain lakes Arctic chars prefer, you will be rewarded with the thrilling sport the char are famed for, although as many will know, it is a difficult art, many years in the learning. To fish in Norway may we suggest Nimrod Safaris Ltd (0285) 810132, Ker and Downey (071)-629-2044 and Fresh Adventures (0462) 8164224.

Iceland

There are some countries in this world where you could be forgiven for thinking that they were specifically designed with the fisherman in mind. Iceland is one of them. It is a land of cold, fast flowing rivers, enormous glaciers and countless lakes. It is also volcanic, the zone as its referred to is approximately 25,000 square kilometres, with ten per cent of the country being glacier while fifty per cent is covered with trees like birch and willows together with alpine sub-arctic Flora.

So once again you can enjoy your favourite sport in some splendid surroundings. There are numerous species of birds, puffins, guillemots, gannets a large colony of seals, with over seven species of whales in the territorial waters. Although the climate of Iceland is milder than you might expect due to the Gulf Stream, it is still affected by quick changes in the weather and high winds.

Another feature of Iceland is twenty-four hours of daylight during the summer months (21st June through to August) so, if you are into long stints, then Iceland will accommodate you.

Due to the esteem in which Iceland's salmon rivers are held worldwide, there are sixty salmon rivers, over half being classified as first class. They are difficult to get on and obviously are quite expensive but if you can afford it they offer some of the best Atlantic salmon fishing in the world. Iceland is very keen to promote alternative fishing as the salmon fishing is always booked well in advance of the season opening. There are 1500 trout rivers and lakes so you can keep the expense of a fishing trip to Iceland reasonable by mixing two or three days salmon fishing with some very good trout fishing, with the occasional surprise of a salmon in most of the lakes.

The best areas for brown trout, char and sea-trout include Lake Medalfellsvatn near Mount Esja and three lakes north of Hvalfjorour, Geitabergsvatn, Porisstaoavatn and Eyrarvatn. Some other superb sport can be found on six small lakes on Snaefellsnes peninsula, the Vatnsholtsa lakes. If you prefer river fishing, the Bruara east of Ejykjavik and Varma and Thorleifslaekur near Eykjavik offer some good char fishing.

The best people to contact for fishing in Iceland are Icelandair (071)-388-5599 and Arctic Experience Limited (0737) 362321.

There is one point that fisherman should be aware of. To prevent the spreading of infectious diseases of freshwater fish to Iceland from other countries, the wearing of waders, rubbers boots and other equipment that has been used in other waters is prohibited unless it has been disinfected for ten minutes in a solution of two per cent formaldehyde. A valid certificate from an authorised veterinary officer is acceptable if presented on entering Iceland.

New Zealand

Having travelled to one side of the earth visiting Canada we now travel to the other side, New Zealand. It is renowned for some of the finest trout fishing in some of the most spectacular scenery you will find anywhere in the world—a formidable partnership.

There are dozens of rivers that run from the mountains into the sea, where you will find good fishing for rainbows and brownies and their migratory cousins, steelhead and sea-trout. Although the fishing here can often be excellent, it is not this fishing that New Zealand is famed for. The best and most prolific fishing is enjoyed in the lake systems where most of the fishing is reserved for fly only; so it is again the venue for the purist. It is

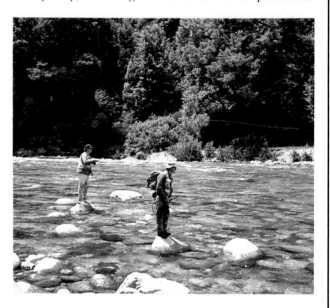

New Zealand (Courtesy of Frontiers)

fair to say that two distinct categories describe New Zealand's fishing: Otorua and Taupo for rainbow and steelhead fishing. This is primarily winter fishing, the best lakes being Taupo and Tarawera, with the Tongariro River offering some rugged sport. The winter season runs April to September/October, the summer fishing runs from October to April.

Travelling to the South Island, you will find some good salmon fishing in the Akaia, Wainmakariri, Angitata, Ashburton and Waitaki rivers, the season in the south is from October to April with the months of January, February and March being the prime months, but be prepared to get up early as that's when you'll experience the best that's on offer. Although spinning is the primary method of fishing, slowly but surely the pursuits are educating the locals and fly fishing is becoming more and more popular. Take the time to explore the culture of New Zealand, the Maoris are well known for their friendliness. Don't be frightened off by the Haka; I am assured that it is kept now only for ceremonial and public events, and of course for the All Blacks.

To organise your fishing trip to New Zealand, Nimrod Safaris Ltd (0285) 810132 will be happy to advise and organise tailor made packages.

Argentina

Alongside New Zealand, Argentina ranks as the greatest trout fishing destination in the world. Due to the nature of the lakes and rivers in southern Argentina, which benefit from the snowfall of the Andes to the west, Argentina has the densest population of wild trout to be found anywhere. The difference between New Zealand and Argentina is that New Zealand has fewer larger fish, whilst Argentina holds a huge volume of wild fish including some large ones.

The snow melts off the Chilean Andes running into lakes in the foothills, which act as both giant filters and nurseries for young trout. From these lakes run crystal clear rivers where wild trout abound. Their staple diet is not only insect life but, more particularly, the panchora or freshwater crayfish. These rivers continue through the desert lowlands like linear oases—often lined with willow trees. In many cases they will flow into another lake or fjord, which not only acts as a nursery but also holds very large trout which only run the rivers to spawn, hence March and April can often be very productive. The size of the rainbows, browns, and brook trout can range from tiny all the way up to 20lb-30lb—though these are rare. The average size is more likely to be in the 2lb-2½lb range with fish up to 6lb-7lb common.

It is a myth that the British can take credit for bringing trout to Argentina. It was actually the Argentines themselves with some aid from the Americans who took initial action. The idea that it was the British who stocked Argentina comes frm the fact that the fish, which came from the United States, arrived via the United Kingdom because the British ships were faster and better equipped to carry the fish and eggs.

The best areas for trout fishing in Argentina are in the region of Patagonia with the fishing centering around towns such as Bariloche, San Martin and Esquel. From these towns, rivers such as the Chimehuin, Collon Cura, Alumine and Malleo can be fished. One of Argentina's greatest assets is that it offers fishing for everybody, from the skilled fisherman wishing to stalk large fish to the novice cutting their teeth on their first wild trout. In terms of techniques used, the variation continues with rivers such as the Malleo offering the finest in dry-fly-fishing, whilst rivers such as the Collon Cura and Alumine can be floated in rafts fishing lures downstream or dry flies upstream. Nymph fishing up or downstream are also well-used techniques. Perhaps the highlight is to skate a grasshopper dry fly across a run and watch the trout trying to attack it. All this in rivers so clear that one can see every stone on the bottom.

One particular British expatriate has had a dramatic effect on some particular Argentine rivers to the far south in the archipelago of Tierra del Fuego. When John Goodall first stocked rivers such as the Rio Grande with brown trout, little did he realise what a phenomenon he was creating. Many of the rivers of Tierra del Fuego, particularly the Rio Grande, have developed a strain of sea-going brown trout (sea-trout) that have grown to astonishing sizes. In 1993, for example, the famous Kau-Tapen Lodge took over 600 sea-trout averaging 10lb-11lb during the short two month season. The largest fish over the last three years was a shade under 30lb. The Rio Grande is a kind river with easy wading, yet it is mystical and hides the lies of its large fish. It is a challenging river to a fisherman though not physically demanding. The wind, which is almost better known than the river itself, blows very hard but the prevailing direction is always down the river. Many fishermen will have achieved their longest roll-cast on the Rio Grande!

Argentina's charm, particularly Tierra del Fuego's, is not just in the fishing. The wildlife is both abundant and innocent, quite unafraid of man. It includes a myriad of raptors, guanaco, armadillo, silver or Arctic foxes, beavers, mink, otters, plus many species of wildfowl including Magellan geese, ashy-headed geese, yellow-billed teal, black-necked swan and the torrent duck. A trip to Argentina will certainly be a fulfilling one not only for the fishing but also for the wildlife and the Argentine people.

Argentina (Courtesy of Frontiers)

Russia (Courtesy of Frontiers)

As catches of Atlantic salmon almost reached rock bottom worldwide, Russia's Kola Peninsula provided a breath of fresh air and a second opportunity for the Atlantic salmon world.

Though there is also great fishing in other parts of Russia, the most practical region seems to be the Kola Peninsula which lies east of northern Norway. The main city in the area is Murmansk. To the south, on the mainland, there are highly productive rivers as far east as the Ural mountains, but these have short seasons and it would not be particularly easy to the resource. From east of the Ural mountains the rivers provide Taimen, Lenox and Pacific salmon, with prime fishing on the Kamchatka Peninsula and in the Khabarovsk region across the Bering Sea from Alaska.

The wildlife in these areas is awesome but again the practicalities of establishing an economic operation are such that a western-style programme is difficult. Fuel supplies, for example, are a major problem.

The Kola Peninsula is already famous for its productivity with numerous fishermen catching in excess of a hundred fish for their week. However, with time it is likely that the techniques used, along with the productivity, will make the Kola Peninsula perhaps the greatest of Atlantic salmon destinations. The Russian fish are probably the most aggressive of the Atlantic salmon strain. The action is so extraordinarily visible that one can find oneself fishing just to see the spectacular explosive takes rather than the fight of a fish.

Dare I say it, there is no other Atlantic salmon nation which provides such explosive visible takes. Canada is probably the nearest for it is the home of the dry and skated fly for Atlantic salmon. These techniques work so well in Russia that the fishing experience is ten-fold. because the action is all so visible. This is why Russia will become the great destination for Atlantic salmon. The fact that there are prolific numbers of fish on which to use these techniques is the icing on the cake. But we should be wary of becoming too numbers-conscious.

There are various operators on the Kola Peninsula, each working on what they believe to be the best rivers with the biggest fish. Rivers such as Strelna, Ponoi, Varzuga and Umba are perhaps the best known, along with others packaged as the 'Northern' and 'Outlying' rivers. If one puts these rivers into perspective they are all outstanding compared to the majority in other countries. It is the operators who run the transport and camps on these rivers who need examining and careful consideration. Typically, it seems that the Americans are doing the best job at present.

In terms of tackle for the Kola Peninsula, double-handed rods work well and are the preferred tool, but if ever threre was an opportunity to catch big fish on a single-handed rod this is it. Bear in mind that the fishing is catch and release and therefore single barbless hooks are favoured. Patterns such as theAlly, Shrimp, Baldrick, Garry Dog and Thunder and Lightening are highly effective. Low-water hooks are much better especially when using the riffled-hitch. Bombers for skating across the glassy pools are also a must.

Our last destination is not one particular place but a series of Central American areas as well as one or two islands in the Pacific, such as Christmas Island. Saltwater fly-fishing is relatively young in fly-fishing terms, yet the sport has become vastly popular in the United States and is beginning to take off in Europe with the better tackle shops starting to equip themselves with the right tackle and flies.

There are three major aspects to saltwater fly-fishing. First, it has released pressure on many trout fisheries around the world with the added bonus of a year-round season.

Saltwater fishing (Courtesy of Frontiers)

Secondly, it offers very exciting fishing because of the enormous strength of the fish. Also the nature of the sport, which is practically all sight fishing, demands great stealth and accuracy.

Thirdly, it all takes place in an excellent climate often with either other watersports or cultural interests nearby. The added bonus is the the cost is not that expensive compared to many of the prices that are paid for salmon fishing these days. Price per person is rarely over £2,000, including flights, unless one is seeking particularly luxurious accommodation. Of course some lodges are better than others in terms of the service and food they provide as well as the amount and sizes of fish. However, each lodge has its own merits and it often pays to start with places that are sympathetic to early mistakes before taking on greater challenges.

The main quarry is the bonefish which is not large averaging around 2lb in weight going up to record fish over 10lb. But do not be misled. These fish are extraordinarily powerful and require special tackle to control them. Many fishermen do not believe in the power of these fish until they have felt them for themselves.

Perhaps the most exciting quarry is the tarpon which can go from anything between 10lb-200lb. The tarpon is famous for not only its size but also its athletic ability to jump high into the air whilst running great distances from the fisherman often pulling the hook at the same time.

The permit is maybe the most challenging of the three main species because it is so difficult to hook on the fly and so spooky. A large disc-shaped fish, the permit is also capable of long and powerful runs with larger fish in the 30lb-60lb range taking a long while to land. The average size of a permit is perhaps 7lb-10lb.

Other species that one will come across when out bone-fishing might include shark, trevelly, snook, barracuda, jacks, snapper and grouper. All will willingly take a fly if presented in the right way.

The best destinations for saltwater fly-fishing might include Belize, Mexico, Venezuela, Costa Rica, Bahamas, Florida Keys and Christmas Island. Each destination has its merits in terms of numbers and size of fish, and each in turn is worth a visit. Some specialise in certain species, others are capable of producing all species but perhaps not as big as those in an area which specialises.

In terms of saltwater fly-fishing tackle one enters a new world where rods are specially designed, reels need drag systems and knots have to be merciless in their efficiency. The American rod manufacturers all produce a saltwater fly-fishing series of rods which include an extra fighting butt for resting on the tummy when playing fish. These fly rods will be specifically protected from potential damage from saltwater and may even be matt finish in order to minimise the flash from the rod. Specific fly lines have been designed to maximise casting efficiency and presentation, whilst shock-proof leaders have also been designed to reduce the risk of losing fish when they run or jump.

The world of saltwater fly-fishing offers the keen travelling fisherman an entirely new angle of fly-fishing in which to become absorbed. It is a demanding skill yet highly rewarding in terms of sport, whilst happily not heavy on the pocket.

We've hopefully stirred your emotions in looking outside of the confines of the British Isles for your next fishing foray or the trip of a lifetime—the culmination, if you like, of all those days that went unrewarded. I think that most of you will agree that if you have spent twenty years fishing or more, contenting yourself with the occasional 12lb fish, you deserve to fish for the big fish, at least once. Much of the fishing described cannot be bettered anywhere so choosing which country will be difficult, but I am sure most will warm to the prospect of knowing that the only decision you really face is in selecting which particular surroundings you want to propel yourselves.

As a final note; to allow all fisherman, now and in the future, the chance of enjoying fishing for trophy sized fish everywhere in the world, if you are not going to eat it, release it. They are beautiful creatures to watch when they are left in their natural surroundings, they lose all their beauty when surrounded by wood and glass, so enjoy the sport for now and for the future. The thought of great rivers like the Miramichi or the Margaree being fishless is one of the saddest things I can think of.

As from the 1st April 1993 Frontiers International opened a small office in London. This major step allows Frontiers to offer their European clients the same high standard of programmes serviced with the added bonus of the back-up and experience from their head office near Pittsburgh, Pennsylvania, in the United States.

Patagonia (Courtesy of Frontiers)

Frontiers International Travel was founded by Michael and Susan Fitzgerald in 1969 organising activity travel in over twenty-five countries. They have built up the family business from just the two of them to a total of forty-five employees, including their children who have grown up with the business. Through their excellent reputation for attention to detail, first-hand knowledge enabling the ability to compare destinations and efficient service, Frontiers has reached a position whereby they are qualified to give advice in order to enhance standards. Frontiers International was among the first organisations of its kind anywhere in the world. No other organisation has a similar base of experience and product knowledge. With Frontiers there is no need to shop around; it has been done for you and they are able to offer a wealth of comparative information to assist you.

The majority of Frontiers programmes are priced in US dollars, which is generally the currency used by operators. Frontiers pass on the exact price from the operator in US dollars to their clients. No mark-ups or currency speculations have been built into the prices. Their knowledge of products enables them to offer programmes to suit everybody's taste and pocket. They have organised payment facilities to maximise client convenience. Frontiers produce a Destination Directory which gives a brief account of the myriad of destinations which have been thoroughly researched by Frontiers staff. The destination directory includes the following:

Freshwater Fishing

Argentina

San Martin
Junin de los Andes
Classic fly fishing for big trout amid spectacular scenery with the fine guides of Patagonia Outfitters (Nov-April).

Esquel
Patagonia trout fishing at its best on remote waters of the Argentine frontier with veteran guides (Nov-April).

Tierra del Fuego
Best stream fishing for trophy brown trout in the world on the legendary Rio Grande River, holding big browns up to 25lb. Great accommodations at Kau-Tapen Lodge (Jan-Mar).

Chile

Mike Konak–Isla Monita
A proven alternative in Chile, with dry-fly fishing on remote lakes and rivers in the Southern Andes (Nov-April).

Heart of Patagonia Lodge
John Jenkin's new operation near Coyhaique promises to provide great trout fishing in coming seasons (Nov-April).

Venezuela

Manaka Lodge
The best peacock bass fishing in South America, plus other hard-fighting exotic species in the Orinoco River basin (Dec-mid April).

Brazil
Virgin peacock bass fishing in remote areas of Amazon (Jan-Feb/Sept-Nov).

New Zealand

North Island
Remarkable trophy trout fishing with the best guides and lodges. With tailor-made itineraries to fit your objectives (year-round).

South Island
Stalk trophy trout in remote wilderness areas with emphasis on sight fishing. Great guides and fine accommodations (mid Nov-mid April).

Alaska

Frontiers offers the foremost fly-out lodges, fixed camps and float trips for the most productive fishing in North America for five species of salmon, trophy rainbow trout and other species. Ask for their comprehensive Alaska guide (June-Sept)

Canada

Sutter Lodge, New Brunswick
Atlantic salmon fishing from a fine lodge on the famous Miramichi (June-Sept).

Botswana

Spectacular tiger fishing combined with extraordinary game viewing from full safari camps at a special introductory price (Sept-Nov).

South Africa

Beautiful trout streams in scenic surroundings with selective wild trout to challenge the serious fly fisherman (Nov-Apr)

England

Chalk Streams
Dry-fly and nymph fishing for brown trout on the storied Test and Itchen Rivers from seven excellent estates (May-Sept).

Iceland

Laxa I Adaldal
Iceland's most famous Atlantic salmon river and a Frontiers favourite for twenty plus years. (June-Aug).

Norway

Alta
Incomparable for reliable numbers of the largest Atlantic salmon in the world. A storied river of great tradition and beauty (June-Aug).

Russia

Ponoi River
American hosted and managed Atlantic salmon fishing. This wonderful wilderness river, accessed from Helsinki, is recognised as one of the best in the world (June-Sept).

The American West

Craig Fellin's Big Hole River Outfitters in Montana, Three Rivers Ranch in Idaho, Elk Creek Lodge in Colorado and the Bighorn River in Montana prvide Western trout fishing at its finest. Ask for their comprehensive guide (June-Oct).

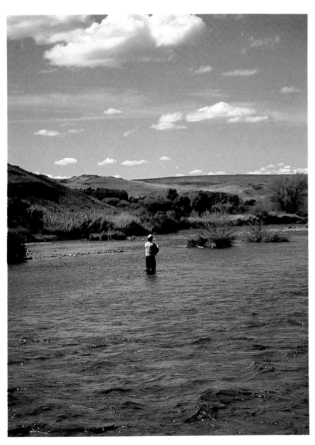

Patagonia (Courtesy of Frontiers)

—————Saltwater Light-tackle Fishing—————

Christmas Island
You can celebrate Christmas year-round at this bonefishing paradise. Weekly departures from Honolulu at reasonable costs (year-round).

Mexico

Casa Blanca Lodge
Great bonefish, permit and tarpon fishing at wonderful Ascension Bay. Fine lodge with all amenities (Oct-June).

Casa Redonda
Your own private flats, fishing lodge on Ascension Bay, accommodating four anglers for bonefish, tarpon, permi-tand snook (Jan-July).

Boca Paila Lodge
Excellent flats, fishing for permit and bonefish in a beautiful setting with special hospitality and ambience on the Mexican Yucatan (year-round).

Belize

El Pescador
Turneffe Flats Lodge
Belize River Lodge
Turneffe Island Lodge
Offering the best in Belize for tarpon on the flats, bonefish and reef fishing at costs reflecting great value (year-round).

Venezuela

Los Roques
Productive bonefishing with accommodations at Macabi Lodge (April-Sept).

Costa Rica

Casa Mar Fishing Club
Bill Barne's venerable lodge remains a standard for great tarpon fishing and seasonal snook (Jan-Apr/Sept-Oct).

Rio Parismina Lodge
New attractive facility on Parismina River with fleet of twenty-one foot boats to access ocean tarpon (year-round).

Saltwater flies by Mike Sugg

Bahamas

Deep Water Cay
Beautiful accommodations and classic Bahamas bonefishing (Jan-July/Oct-Dec).

Andros Island Bonefish Club
Known for its big bonefish and knowledgeable guides (year-round).

Dunmore Beach Club, Harbour Island
Timeless Bahamian retreat, according to Harper's Hideaway Report. Charming accommodations and exquisite meals combine with great bonefishing, tennis, beautiful white sand beach.

Peace and Plenty, Exuma
Two lodges located in Georgetown and a new fishing lodge scheduled for completion late 1993 on productive bonefish flats. Great for the angler with non-fishing companions.

Walker's Clay, Abaco
Total resort offering all water sports, white sandy beach and secial bonefishing packages utilizing Dolphin skiffs and expert Florida Keys guides.

Australia

Barra Base Lodge
Rustic fishing camp on remote Bathurst Island offers exciting fishing for barramundi and other saltwater species (May-June/Sept-Nov).

Seven Spirit Bay
Deluxe accommodations in the pristine wilderness of the Cobourg Peninsula. Enjoy exciting sportfishing for barramundi and numerous species in remote, virtually untouched waters (May-June/Sept-Nov).

Canada

Banksland Marine Group
Live aboard the 180-foot M.V. Banksland while fishing the rich waters of the Queen Charlotte Islands for trophy king salmon and other species. (May-Oct).

─────── *Saltwater Offshore Fishing* ───────

Australia

Great Barrier Reef
Fish with award-winning Capt Calvin Tilley in pursuit of the 'Granders'—black marlin in the 1000lb class (Sept-Dec)

Cape Bowling Green
Pioneered by Capt. Calvin Tilley and considered by many the best light-tackle billfishing grounds in the world. There's no better place to take a black marlin on the fly (May-Sept).

Venezuela

La Guaira
Billfishing for marlin, sailfish and other species (year-round).

Panama

Tropic Star Lodge
Still maintaining its fine reputation for excellent accommodation, billfishing and reef-fishing (Dec-Aug).

Costa Rica

Pesca Bahia Garza
Located on Guanacaste Peninsula, Garza offers quality offshore fishing with experienced captains who are fly fishing experts. Great accommodations (year-round).

Bahia Pez Vela
More world records than any other billfishing lodge in Costa Rica! (Jan 20-Oct 20).

El Ocotal
The ideal combination of resort living and quality billfishing (year-round).

Villas Pacifica
Productive billfishing operation with accommodations in private villas and fine dining (year-round).

Flamingo Bay Pacific Charters
A premier fishing operation in the Flamingo area (year-round).

Guanamar
Superb offshore bill and light-tackle fishing in areas protected from winter trade winds.

Quepos
The Quepos region offers outstanding sport for marlin and sailfish (Dec-Aug).

Phoenix
Deluxe mothership concept along Pacific coast with two Sportfishermen available for charter to follow billfish migrations (year-round).

If you wish to receive a Destination Directory or full colour brochre on any of the above please contact Frontiers at:

14 Old Bond Street
London W1X 3DB
Telephone: 071 493 07978
Fax: 071 491 9177

Tierra del Fuego (Courtesy of Frontiers)

Foreign Forays fishermen are usually adventurers seeking something that little bit different. So an opportunity to fish for the world's largest freshwater species in virgin waters as yet untouched by rod and line is an unusual proposition with fairly immediate appeal. Add to that the bonus of fishing in an unfamiliar environment—new and unusual fauna, flora and birds—in climatic conditions that require no forward planning to catch fish and it all adds up to an inexpensive fishing opportunity of a lifetime.

The High Dam on the river Nile at Aswan was commissioned by President Nasser of Egypt in the sixties and he created the largest man-made lake in Africa. Lake Nasser is 310 miles long, covers 2400 square miles and has a shoreline of more than 5000 miles. The lake is massive and it quite possibly contains a record example of the world's largest freshwater fish, the Nile perch. But until now it has, for largely security reasons, been off-limits to tourism.

Tim Baily, an African born specialist in adventure travel in his homeland, is to conduct a protracted reconnaissance of the lake, its lakeside environment and its fish stocks and their distribution on behalf of the Egyptian Ministry for Tourism. He has recruited the support of Britain's Salmon & Trout Association with the help of whose members he plans to compile a detailed study to help ensure that the resource is not over-exploited.

The fishing is very varied in terms of species and style. Nile perch run from 2lb-200lb plus and can be caught on the fly or light spinning tackle from the shore at the smaller end of the scale or from boars using large, deep-diving lures depending on the size of quarry you are after. Those who prefer to fish the fly are in for a rare treat.

Travelling light with a nine-foot trout rod and 3lb tippets and a selection of suitable lures can bring outstanding sport. And one is talking not just about Nile perch but also of the bream-like tilapia and the ferocious and hard fighting tiger fish which, with its piranha-like dentistry, deeply forked tail and torpedo lines, is built for strength and speed.

The Lake Nasser experience includes a first and last night stay at a luxury hotel in Aswan but the lake foray itself is camping on desert islands, many with sandy beaches and all with cool, refreshing swimming—vital during the summer months. A lakeside barbeque does not disappoint either. Nile perch and tilapia are both delicious eating . . . but tiger fish, with flesh like cotton wool full of pins, is best savoured for its sporting qualities!

Salmon & Trout Association Press Officer, Pat Mackreth, has been to Lake Nasser and can help with advice on tackle, clothing, equipment and travel. He can be reached at PO Box 17, Tiverton, Devon EX16 7YW; telephone: (0823) 673051 or fax: (0823) 673052. If you visit Lake Nasser with the S&TA you can help with the survey and, by doing so, will be supporting Britain's guardians of our own game fishing environment.

By Penny Mackreth

Finland is one of the least known trout and salmon fishing territories in Europe—except, of course, to the Finns, who are fishing fanatics!

The possibilities for fly fishing in Finland are excellent and also very special. It is a huge country, stretching from the more developed region of Southern Finland through the 'Land of Lakes' of Middle Finland right up to and beyond the Arctic Circle to Lapland, the 'Land of the Midnight Sun'.

Fly fishing for salmon, trout and grayling has been practised in Finland for a long time. English and Scottish businessmen visiting in the mid-nineteenth century took their favourite pastime with them and were the major influence in the development of the sport in Finland.

Numerous rivers start their journey to the Baltic Sea from the lakes of Middle Finland. Many of these lakes are connected to each other by a short series of fast-flowing rapids known as kosket, where large brown trout stay and feed. The minimum sized fish you can keep is forty centimetres (fifteen inches). Fish run up to 8lb and larger, and landing them once hooked is an experience to remember. Fly fishing dry, nymph or streamer is available, while spinning is also permitted for those who wish. The scenery of Middle Finland is breathtaking, and the rivers run large and wild. Trout fishing at its best!

One of the greatest salmon rivers in Europe, found in northernmost Lapland, is the mighty River Teno, where commercial and sport fishing lands over 300,000lb of salmon every year if the Norwegian stretch of the river—the Tana—is taken into consideration. In August, the big fish are running up to 50lb, and at least two hundred metres of backing will be needed on your reel. The Teno is most often fished by boat though wading is also successful as the fish run quite close to the shore. The river is very accessible with roads running along both banks.

Travelling to and around Finland can be easily arranged. Helsinki is well served by international airlines and domestic flights are regular and safe. Railways and buses do exist but if travelling independently a hire car might be your best bet.

Farmhouse or log cabin accommodation is usual for a fishing holiday and although summers are reasonably warm rain-gear should be remembered along with chest waders. For further information on fishing in Finland, the best people to contact are Finfish Holidays (071) 490 1840.

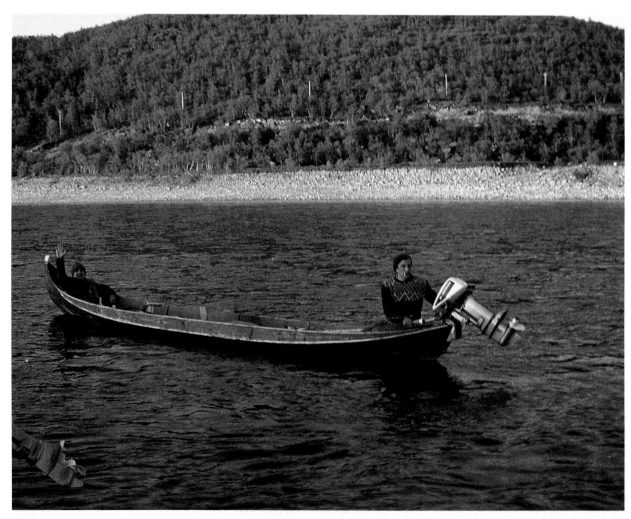

Courtesy of Finfish

Nimrod Safaris specialise in organising safaris in some of the world's more remote and beautiful locations. They invite you to expand your sporting horizons to encompass places and quarries that you may have only read or dreamed about.

Freshwater Fly-fishing

Russia

Lying on the Arctic Circle in north western Russia, the Kola Peninsula has a reputation for large runs of fresh salmon and sea trout. Great advances have been made in the comfort and service provided in such a remote area.

Siberia

Kamchatka Peninsula is emerging as a region with excellent fishing in remote and beautiful wilderness amidst spectacular volcanic scenery of Eastern Siberia's 'Rim of Fire'. Its many rivers support large runs of Pacific salmon and char as well as hard fighting, resident rainbow trout.

Alaska

The name Alaska is synonymous with fishing and conjures up images of cold, swift rivers filled with running salmon and large resident trout. Alaska is not just about fishing but is also a land teeming with wildlife to watch and photograph.

Argentina

Argentina's top quality, guided trout fishing amidst spectacular and unspoilt Andean scenery, has earned it a high reputation amongst fishermen. Tailor-made holidays capitalise on all that this wonderful country has to offer, taking advantage of the best of Argentinian food and hospitality.

Chile

A contrast to the well established fishing of the Argentine, Chile offers remote, wild scenery and water that has rarely been fished.

Montana

Known as the Big Sky Country and home of catch and release fishing, Montana offers some of the world's finest and most accessible wild trout fishing.

New Zealand

Fishing for truly wild trout in clear running water is a reality in New Zealand, which offers a huge amount of fishing on both the North and South Islands.

South Africa

South Africa's wonderful trout fishing comes as a surprise to many fishermen. This vast land has an extraordinary variety of fishing on both river and lake.

The Falkland Islands

Brown trout were introduced to the Falklands in the 1950s and have thrived in their waters. The Islands offer some of the most exciting sea trout fishing in the world.

Saltwater Fly-fishing

Christmas Island

Over the last fifteen years fishermen have returned again and again establishing the Island as the world's finest bonefishing destination. An added bonus is the mile upon mile of remote and untouched white sand.

Bahamas

Experienced guides will take you out to fish from comfortable, well maintained, flat bottomed skiffs. The size of the bonefish is one of the area's attractions with fish of up to 10lb being caught.

Mexico

It is variety which makes this area one of the most interesting places to fish in the Caribbean where it is possible to achieve a sort of saltwater 'Macnab' by catching a bonefish, tarpon and permit on a fly.

Costa Rica

This small, beautiful country with its rain forests and Pacific and Caribbean coastlines is fast gaining a reputation for exotic fishing of a very high quality.

Courtesy of Nimrod Safaris

Big Game Fishing

Kenya

There are some places which feature prominently in big game fishing and Kenya is one of them. Opportunities abound for fishing for sailfish, marlin, wahoo, kingfish, runner, tuna, dorado, broadbill swordfish and shark.

Bom Bom Island

Bom Bom is a small jungle covered island situated on the northern tip of Principe, some fifty miles off the West Coast of Gabon. It must rate as the newest, most remote and one of the most beautiful and exclusive big game fishing destinations in the world.

Madeira

There is superb sailfish and marlin fishing from this semi-tropical island, renowned for its lush vegetation and warm climate.

Costa Rica

The fishing in the Pacific, off the west coast of this small but beautiful country, arguably offers some of the finest sailfish fishing in the world, caught on both big game tackle or fly.

Flexibility, one of the bywords of Nimrod Safaris and although they cannot, due to the nature of sport, guarantee you success they will do all they can to ensure that your chances are maximised with the criteria set. Wherever possible they will accommodate all your requirements so that your holiday will be of the desired length and in the location of your choice, incorporating business trip or family holiday as necessary.

For further information please telephone (0285) 810132.

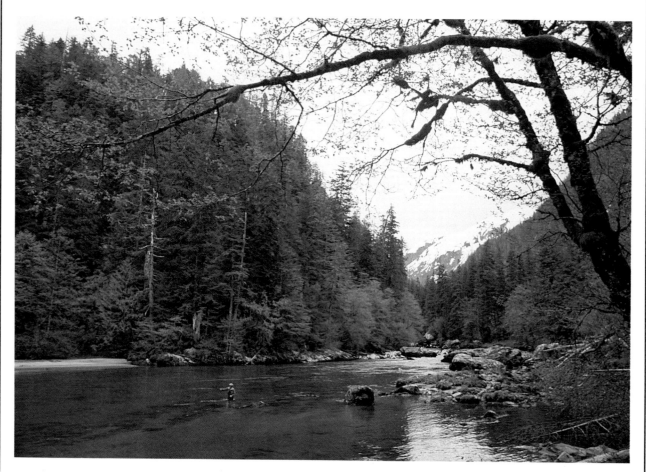

Go Fishing - Canada specialises in fly-fishing holidays to Canada as the name indicates. The company offers a wide range of fishing packages. There are fishing holidays that will appeal to the fly fishing experts as well as the less experienced angler, fishing families and fishermen accompanied by non fishing companions.

Canada has been described as a fishing paradise. Those visiting the eastern Canada venues of Labrador, Newfoundland, Nova Scotia and New Brunswick can expect to enjoy large runs of Atlantic Salmon and Sea Trout. In Labrador there are also huge Arctic Char and Northern Pike to catch. If you choose the superb fishing in the wilderness of Northern Labrador you have to fly in by float-plane to your fishing lodge, an experience in itself.

Alternatively, there are the more gentle and enticing attractions of the other two eastern seaboard provinces. Here one will find the world famous rivers of Nova Scotia; the Margaree and the Stewiacke and the superb Miramichi river in New Brunswick. All offer equally exciting prospects for the salmon and trout fisherman: south eastern Canada provides a leisure experience that can be enjoyed by those who fly-fish and their non-fishing companions.

Fishermen visiting British Columbia on the western seaboard of Canada will enjoy lifetime-lasting memories of fishing some of the most prolific Pacific Salmon rivers in the world. In addition, Go Fishing-Canada features holidays to the Babine River where Trophy Steelhead have the reputation of being the world's best fighting game fish.

Some splendidly exciting, specimen trout fishing is also to be found in the beautiful rivers of Alberta (the Bow) and Ontario.

For the truly dedicated fly-fishing expert the Moisie river in Quebec, the home of the famous Seize-Vingt Club where 20lbs salmon are fished for with flies tied on size 16 hooks, will be an inescapable challenge together with superb salmon fishing on the St.Jean and Godbout rivers.

Go Fishing-Canada will be happy to tailor a fishing package designed to fit your individual requirements. In the first instance, please contact one of our staff on the telephone number given below.

Go Fishing - Canada
Swan Centre
Fishers Lane
London W4 1RX
Tel: 081 742 3700
Fax: 081 994 7388

The Game Angling Code

A guide to good practice prepared by the Salmon & Trout Association, in conjunction with leading conservation and angling bodies with support from Laphroaig.

The Principles of the Code

Environment
All anglers should be actively concerned in protecting the environment.

Conservation
Fishing and the management of fisheries, should be conducted so that healthy fish populations are maintained.

Behaviour
Moderation, courtesy and consideration for others are the marks of a sporting angler.

The Sport
There is more to fishing than catching fish.

Introduction

Rod fishing is a traditional and pleasurable pastime. As more people take up the sport of game fishing there is increasing pressure on wild fish stocks and more demand is put on the limited space on rivers, lakes and lochs; at the same time there is an increasing public concern for the environment and for wildlife.

The purpose of this Code is to encourage proper standards of sportsmanship among game anglers and those who manage and regulate game fishing and help them show regard for the environment, the sport, their quarry and for each other. All involved with game angling are expected to obey the relevant laws and fishery regulations and to avoid any behaviour which might bring the sport into disrepute. In this Code, Game Angling covers fishing for salmon, sea-trout, grayling and char.

Fishery Owners and Managers

Standards
The Code expects that all owners, managers, associations and clubs will set and maintain high standards of sportsmanship and encourage mutual courtesy among rods fishing their own and adjacent waters.

Conservation
Wherever there are wild fish, angling pressure should be regulated to ensure that the natural stock can regenerate and be preserved. Where there is any danger of over-fishing, owners and managers of fisheries should control catches by adopting some of the following measures;

• By limiting the use of certain baits or methods of fishing

• By voluntary alteration of the number of days fished

• By introducing catch limits daily, weekly or annually

• By discouraging the sale of rod caught fish by anglers

• By limiting the number of rods or fishing effort.

Artist: D F Dane WAITING Courtesy of Rosenstiel's

Fishing Methods

This general Code cannot attempt to define the proper use of all legal fishing methods in every locality and in varying water and weather conditions. Appropriate fishing methods are established by regulation and often by tradition. Where particular baits or methods of fishing are reasonably damaging to fishing stocks or to the interest of other anglers, or are seen locally to be unsporting, they should be prohibited.

Stocked Fisheries

Many fisheries, both stillwater and river, depend on regular stocking. Stocking should take account of the ability of the water to support, in a healthy condition, the number of fish introduced. Natural populations of wild fish need to be preserved. Stocking policies should take account of the risk involved by the introduction of conflicting species. To avoid genetic change through interbreeding, local broodstock should be used wherever possible.

Fishery Managers should set catch limits (in size and numbers) and have a clearly understandable policy on fish to be returned. They should keep, and are encouraged to publish, accurate records of numbers and weights of fish stocked and caught.

Competitive Game Fishing

Rules for fishing competitions should comply with the principles of this code.

Responsibilities

Owners and managers are encouraged to:

• Draw up and publish fishery rules based on this Code
• Provide adequate supervision to ensure compliance
• Co-operate with adjacent fisheries
• Make provision for local anglers

Owners and fishery managers should call for the introduction of bye-laws or regulations by the relevant authority wherever this is necessary to ensure that the principles of this Code are applied.

The Game Angler
The Environment

Good anglers are the watch-dogs of the water and its environment. Any sign of deterioration must be reported immediately to the fishery manager and the appropriate authority in the area. The report should include:

• What has been noted
• Where the occurrence was spotted
• When the event was noticed
• The extent of any pollution

Anglers should take great care to avoid damage to the waterside or disturbance to wildlife. No tackle or litter must be discarded and particular regard should be paid to the hazards to wild life from monofilament nylon.

The Fish

Fish retained for food should be promptly and efficiently despatched. All other fish should be released as quickly as possible. Fish should only be handled with wetted hands; they should never be thrown back into the water, but held facing upstream in running water until they swim free. Where Catch and release is practised, barbless hooks are recommended.

Fishing Conduct

Angling as a sport and recreation is a fragile and personal experience which can so easily be disrupted by external interference. However, water space is in great demand both from anglers and other activities and therefore its enjoyment has to be shared. The following points should be observed by every angler:

• Ensure you have permission to fish and a rod licence where appropriate

• Observe the bounds of any beat to which you have been assigned.

• Be prepared to give way after you have fished a drift or pool and never fish too long in one place

• Never crowd or obstruct an angler near to you on the bank or in a boat

• Do not walk into or cut across another person's fishing and avoid unnecessary wading

• Give consideration to anglers on the opposite bank

• Make sure you can distinguish between takeable and non-takeable fish

• Where there are no bag limits, exercise restraint in the number of fish taken, particularly when fish are easily caught

• Accept that the blank days are part of the experience of fishing

• Acknowledge considerate behaviour by other legitimate water users

• Follow the Country Code, particularly in relation to the control of dogs, the risk of fires and fastening gates

• Wear unobtrusive clothing and respect the peace of the countryside

• Do not park vehicles so that they obstruct gateways or.cause a hazard on the road

• Support the organisations which safeguard your sport

Safety

All anglers should be aware of the inherent dangers of fishing, not only to themselves but to others. They should:

• Wear head and eye protection, particularly when casting in windy conditions

• Look behind before casting

• Keep rods and lines away from overhead electric power lines

• In an electric storm cease fishing put the rod down and move well away from it

• When wading in difficult conditions, use a wading stick and always have one foot firmly on the river bed before moving the other

• Wear personal buoyancy aids wherever appropriate and be familiar with the location and use of any other buoyancy or life saving equipment provided by fishery owners

• Be prepared to help anyone in difficulty.

The following index lists the major lochs, rivers, lakes and stillwaters emphasised in *Fishing Forays*—a number of smaller tributaries or waters located near to these are not included in the index, but should of course be considered when planning a fishing foray.

Highland River - Wendy Reeves 24ins x 36ins

The Waterfall - Elizabeth Halstead
30ins x 20ins

An Early Start - Wendy Reeves 43ins x 53ins

Peaceful Moments - Don Vaughan
24ins x 36ins

Fishing in Calm Waters - George Cammidge 40ins x 16ins

Valley of the Stags - Elizabeth Halstead 20ins x 30ins

Fishing from the Bank - Spencer Coleman

10 x 12ins 25 x 30cms

Hoping for a Bite - Spencer Coleman

10 x 12ins 25 x 30cms

Trout Fishing, County Mayo - Clive Madwgick

24 x 32ins 60 x 80cms

Fishing Scene, Loch Earn - Clive Madgwick

24 x 36ins 60 x 80cms

The Fisherman - Frank Wright - 20 x 24ins 50 x 60cms

Loch Tummel - Clive Madgwick 22 x 28ins 56 x 70cms

Order Form

Crofters Cottage -David Dane 10 x 13ins

Highland Cattle -David Dane 10 x 13ins

Prints	Artist	Size	price not includingVAT	Qty.	Cost
Crofters Cottage	David Dane	10 x 13ins	£23		
Highland Cattle	David Dane	10 x 13ins	£23		
Highland River	Wendy Reeves	24 x 36ins	£13		
The Waterfall	Elizabeth Halstead	30 x 20ins	£13		
An Early Start	Wendy Reeves	43 x 53 ins	£23		
Peaceful Moments	Don Vaughan	24 x 36ins	£13		
Fishing in Calm Waters	George Cammidge	40 x 16ins	£13		
Valley of the Stags	Elizabeth Halstead	20 x 30ins	£13		
Fishing From the Bank	Spencer Coleman	10 x 12ins	£2.40		
Hoping for a Bite	Spencer Coleman	10 x 12ins	£2.40		
Trout Fishing County Mayo	Clive Madgwick	24 x 32ins	£18		
Fishing Scene Loch Earn	Clive Madgwick	24 x 36ins	£18		
The Fisherman	Frank Wright	20 x 24ins	£13		
Loch Tummel	Clive Madgwick	22 x 28ins	£18		

I enclose a cheque for the sum of £_____ Payable to Kensington West Productions.

Please debit my: Access / Visa / Amex / Diners Card by the sum of £ _____

No. ☐☐☐☐☐☐☐☐☐☐☐☐☐

Address _____

Tel. No _____ Signature _____

All orders should be sent to Kensington West Productions Ltd,
5 Cattle Market, Hexham, Northumberland NE46 1NJ Telephone your order on 0434 609933

The Kensington West Collection

The Kensington Collection (second edition)

As people continue to demand more for their money, so hoteliers have created all manner of short breaks to catch the imagination. The Kensington Collection has been produced to reflect this demand. It earmarks all manner of information from prices to what activities each hotel has to offer. Whether you enjoy a stroll in the country or a ride in a hot air balloon, you'll find something to enjoy, with an interesting foreword written by the Duke of Roxburghe.

Travelling the Turf (ninth edition)

The complete guide to racecourses of Great Britain and Ireland. Travelling The Turf incorporates colour maps, extensive illustrations, many previously unpublished racing scenes with illuminating and witty analysis of every aspect of the racing scene. Comprehensive features on hotels, restaurants, pubs and bed and breakfasts are backed up with points and places of interest for the non-racegoer. A powerful resume of the worlds most stylish sport. Foreword by Lord Zetland.

Following the Fairways (seventh edition)

The complete guide to the golf courses of Great Britain and Ireland. Following The Fairways contains a comprehensive directory of over 2,000 golf courses and in-depth features on one hundred of the nation's most celebrated golfing tests. An authoritative guide to the world's fastest growing leisure pursuit with a foreword by one of sports most respected personalities, Bobby Charlton.

Fishing Forays (third edition)

Fishing Forays embraces in-depth appraisals of famous beats, maps of lochs, lakes and rivers with helpful tips for beginners to the sport on where to fish. Contacts on particular waters make the book a first class investment and provide a short cut to finding how, when and where to fish the celebrated rivers of Britain and Ireland. An engaging summary of one of the world most exclusive sports. Includes a foreword by Chris Poupard, Director of the Trout and Salmon Association

Ping Womens Golf Year 1992-1993

The Ping Women's Golf Year—perhaps the first ever 'coffee table' type book covering the women's golfing season. And what a season it was. From Mission Hills to Dalmahoy and beyond, with special emphasis on the history making Solheim and Curtis Cup wins, the world's major tournaments and tour statistics are reported and charted. With more than 120 superb photographs, this is an attractive pleasurable read for every golfer. Foreword by Mickey Walker.

Visions of Sport

A celebration of the worlds leading photographic agency, **Allsport**. This unique collection of 160 sporting photographs covers a range of sports to delight the enthusiast as well as interest the amateur photographer. Articles by a select group of sporting celebrities include; David Gower, Rory Underwood, Daley Thompson and Alain Prost, coupled with a lively commentary, ensures a first class read. The book has been printed on the highest quality paper to ensure the outstanding photography appears in all its glory.

Highland Spring

Produced for Highland Spring, world famous purveyor of Natural Mineral Water, The Watering Holes of Scotland is a comprehensive and picturesque guide to the heritage, hotels and restaurants of Scotland. Offering the best in cuisine, leisure facilities and spectacular scenery, along with world famous golfcourses, this guide helps you to select your break at leisure. Enjoy too, the humour and art found within the covers, together with a foreword from one of Scotland's most famous sons, Jackie Stewart.

Travelling the Turf, Following the Fairways, and Fishing Forays are also available in b/w Pocket Guide Form, see prices below.

Order Form

	Softback	Hardback	Quantity	Value
The Kensington Collection	1871349966 £12.95	1871349028 £14.95		
Travelling the Turf 1994	1871349664 £14.95	1871349710 £15.95		
Following the Fairways 1994	1871349761 £14.95	1871349818 £15.95		
Fishing Forays 1994	1871349915 £14.95	1871349869 £15.95		
Travelling theTurf in Your Pocket	1871349079 £4.95			
Following the Fairways in Your Pocket	1871349079 £4.95			
Fishing Forays in Your Pocket	1871349176 £4.95			
Canon's Visions of Sport	187134932X £14.95			
The Watering Holes of Scotland	1871349567 £14.95	1871349613 £20.00		
Ping Women's Golf Year		1871349516 £12.95		

Please send your order to Kensington West Productions Ltd, 5 Cattle Market, Hexham, Northumberland NE46 INJ, Tel: 0434 609933, Fax: 0434 600066 Cheques (payable to Kensington West Productions Ltd) /Access/Visa/AMEX/Diners

Card no _____ Address _____

Expiry Date _____ _____

The Kensington West Collection

A range of fine sporting and leisure publications

Following the Fairways
1994

Travelling the Turf
1994

Fishing Forays
1994

The Kensington Collection

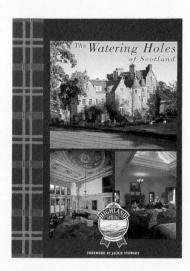

The Watering Holes of Scotland

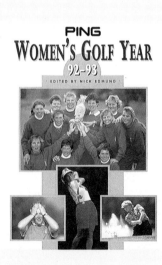

PING WOMEN'S GOLF YEAR 92-93

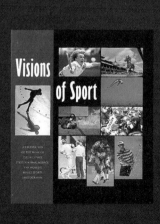

Visions of Sport

Kensington West Productions publish a range of fine sporting and leisure publications, designed to suit the interest and pocket of one and all. We are renowned for producing books in full colour, superbly illustrated with art and photography of the highest quality, to grace the shelves of any library. Our sporting annuals also provide an infinite source of reading pleasure with their informed commentary and travel guidelines. From this wealth of experience comes our new pocket series, ideal reference works for both beginners and experts which make up in price what they lack in colour. No such problem with Visions of Sport, in our opinion quite simply the best value collection of sporting photographs ever assembled.